D1562903

THE ARCHAIC COMMUNITY
OF THE ROMANS

THE ARCHAIC COMMUNITY
OF THE ROMANS

BY

ROBERT E. A. PALMER

Department of Classical Studies
University of Pennsylvania

CAMBRIDGE
AT THE UNIVERSITY PRESS
1970

Published by the Syndics of the Cambridge University Press
Bentley House, 200 Euston Road, London N.W.1
American Branch: 32 East 57th Street, New York, N.Y. 10022

Library of Congress Catalogue Card Number: 77-92252
I.S.B.N.: 0 521 07702 8

Printed in Great Britain
by Alden & Mowbray Ltd at the Alden Press, Oxford

PARENTIBVS OPTIMIS

ROBERT E. A. PALMER

JOSEPHINE SCHREIBER PALMER

CONTENTS

APPENDICES

MAPS

PREFACE

During the academic year 1963–4 I gave a graduate course on the archaic history of Rome while I continued research into the history of Roman *vici*. Since the latter organization supplied a means of integrating non-Romans into the life of the City, I asked myself how the Romans had absorbed the outsider before the development of its urban *vici*. I suspected that the word *vicus* implied the 'pre-urban' communities which later came to be known as Rome. However, the urban *vici* have yielded no certain evidence of an organization that might have served as a vehicle for the formation of historical Rome. Nevertheless before the year was passed I believed that the answer to my question lay in the nature of the obscure Roman curias and their assembly. With a grant from the University of Pennsylvania I spent a summer of research in Rome and began writing what I thought would be an article or two on the curias which could serve to clarify my own ideas on integration in early Rome and to break a path for my thesis on the nature and origin of urban *vici*. Four years later the work in hand was a finished book.

In the help of my friends I have been singularly fortunate. Some parts of the book have been read by T. R. S. Broughton, H. M. Hoenigswald, A. D. Momigliano, J. H. Oliver and J. W. Poultney. All of them made contributions to its improvement. In personal conversation I have learned from L. W. Daly, R. M. Ogilvie, M. Ostwald and L. R. Taylor. None who shared his knowledge with me is responsible for the conclusions reached in the following essay.

In attempting to elucidate the earliest history of Rome I have not mastered all that has been written before me. No doubt I have even overlooked acknowledgement to my predecessors on some points. On the other hand, I hope that I have omitted no piece of ancient evidence having importance for my work. I have tried to take into consideration contemporary essays on the history and structure of early Rome. In such work as ours theory easily supplants the missing facts. I have not wished to gainsay or argue with those who are or have recently been engaged in this common pursuit. Thus I have not put before the reader every recent theory on early Rome only to deny its validity. With other students I feel strongly about the integrity of the Romans' traditional early chronology. Hence, I have not felt the need to discuss E. Gjerstad's theories. A. Alföldi's *Early Rome and the Latins* contains much of value, but little of use to me in the present book. As its reviewers have remarked, it is a work that cannot expect easy assent. Finally, I have all but ignored the many years of work by G. Dumézil, for it seems founded on no Roman evidence whatsoever where it touches on subjects treated here.

My special debts are many. Thanks are owed to Professors E. Gabba, A. Magdelain and A. D. Momigliano for offprints of their articles pertinent to my topic; to the University of Pennsylvania's Committee on Research for a grant so that I might spend the summer of 1964 in Rome; to the Library of the University of Pennsylvania and its staff, particularly Dr Joan Gotwals; to the American Academy in Rome that offered me hospitality and its splendid library facilities, particularly to its executive secretary Principessa Rospigliosi and its library director Signora Longobardi; to their translator, J. W. Poultney, and to the directors of the American Philological Association, their publisher, for permission to quote from the English translation of the Iguvine Tables with my own modifications; to Wesleyan University for inviting me to address an audience on the curias and members of its faculty for hospitality; and, lastly, to those of my colleagues who have patiently humored me when my enthusiasm, frustration or distress over this and allied works has turned many a conversation on things Hellenic, tragic and poetic to a disquisition on early Rome and the Romans.

After this work left my hands, I read A. Magdelain, 'Recherches sur l'"Imperium": La loi curiate et les auspices d'investiture', *Travaux et Recherches de la Faculté de Droit et des Sciences Economiques de Paris*, ser. 'Sciences Historiques', 12 (1968). While I regret not having had the benefit of Professor Magdelain's latest contribution, I have not altered my conclusions where they differ from his, especially on the date and nature of the *lex curiata*. Indeed some of his new arguments had already been sketched in the two previous works on the subject.

In the preparation of the typescript I have enjoyed the expert services of Lydia De Marco and Robert White. In the book's edition I have been fortunate in the cooperation of the Press' editorial staff. The University of Pennsylvania made a generous contribution towards publication.

LIST OF ABBREVIATIONS

Bremer   F. P. Bremer ed., *Iurisprudentiae Antehadrianae quae Supersunt.*
             2 vols in 3. Leipzig, 1896–1901.
CIL   Th. Mommsen ed. *et al., Corpus Inscriptionum Latinarum.* Berlin,
             1863 to present.
Diz. Epigr. E. De Ruggiero ed. *et al., Dizionario Epigrafico de antichità
             romane.* Rome, 1895 to present.
FGH   F. Jacoby ed., *Die Fragmente der griechischen Historiker.* Berlin
             and Leiden, 1923 to present.
FIRA   S. Riccobono ed. *et al., Fontes Iuris Romani Antejustiniani.* Vol. 1,
             2nd ed., Florence, 1941. Vol. 2, Florence, 1940.
Fontes[7]   C. G. Bruns and Th. Mommsen ed., *Fontes Iuris Romani
             Antiqui.* 7th ed. by O. Gradenwitz. Tübingen, 1909.
FTVVRP   G. Lugli ed., *Fontes ad Topographiam Veteris Vrbis Romae
             Pertinentes.* Rome, 1952 to present.
HRR   H. Peter ed., *Historicorum Romanorum Reliquiae.* Vol. 1, 2nd ed.,
             Leipzig, 1914. Vol. 2, 1906.
ILLRP   A. Degrassi ed., *Inscriptiones Latinae Liberae Rei Publicae.* Vol. 1,
             Florence, 1957, reprinted with corrections 1965. Vol. 2,
             1963.
ILS   H. Dessau ed., *Inscriptiones Latinae Selectae.* 3 vols in 5, re-
             printed Berlin, 1954.
MRR   T. R. S. Broughton, *The Magistrates of the Roman Republic.*
             Usually cited herein by the year(s) *B.C.*, *s.a.* or *s.aa.*
RE   *Paulys Realencyclopädie der classischen Altertumswissenschaft.*
             Stuttgart, 1893 to present.
TLL   *Thesaurus Linguae Latinae.* Leipzig and Munich, 1900 to
             present.

CHAPTER I

THE PROBLEM

Roman writers unashamedly admit the ethnic mixture of the Roman people. Centuries before the emperor Claudius astutely affirmed the political advantage of admitting foreigners to citizenship and of opening the ranks of the privileged to newcomers, the Romans had shown greater readiness to weave the outsider into the political fabric than other ancient peoples. This continuing political attitude partially illustrates the peaceful success of the Roman empire. The fruits of archaeology appear to confirm Roman tradition which proclaims the growth of the Roman state from diverse communities on and around the famous seven hills. Even if we except the pretensions of Trojan families, we may still respect the claims asserted for the Latin, Sabine and Etruscan ancestors of the Roman people.[1]

Ancient research into Roman prehistory attributes the oldest religious and political institutions to kings. According to the method then followed in writing prehistory each king followed his own inclinations and excelled in certain branches of government: Romulus, the founder and warrior; Numa, archpriest; Servius, lawgiver and reformer; the Tarquins, builders and imperialists. Except in the case of Romulus, an element of historicity may be attached to the name and acts of the kings. Ancient writers understood an historical process of the birth and growth of a city sired and educated by experts. Since first things come first, the oldest communal institutions were the creation of Romulus, namesake of the city and the citizens.

The Romulean constitution rested upon a primary ethnic division of the people into three tribes and a secondary military division of thirty curias.[2] At the time when the curias had ceased to be either an

---

[1] Claudius' speech is *CIL* xiii, 1668 = *ILS* 212. Besides the ancient material on a mixed origin of the Italians discussed below in chapter 2, see G. Devoto, 'Le origini tripartite di Roma', *Athenaeum* 31 (1953), 335–43; A. Bernardi, 'Periodo sabino e periodo etrusco nella monarchia romana', *Riv. St. Ital.* 66 (1954), 5–20; P. G. Scardigli, 'Le origini linguistiche di Roma', *Par. Pass.* 16 (1961), 181–9; and A. Bernardi, 'Dai *Populi Albenses* ai *Prisci Latini* nel Lazio arcaico', *Athenaeum* 42 (1964), 223–60. On Trojan families see Appendix iii.
[2] E.g., Cic. *Rep.* 2. 8. 14; Livy 1. 13. 6–8; D. H. 2. 7; Festus 42 L. Cicero's *Republic*

important or living Republican institution they did indeed number thirty. They exercised the vestiges of their communal power through the thirty assistants (*lictores*) of their officers (*curiones*). To the thirty lictors who had once summoned the curias to vote the curias consigned the function of casting ballots no longer polled among the members of the curias.[1] However, it remains to be proven that the curias had always numbered thirty. Perhaps this final number was reckoned the creation of the non-existent Romulus in the same manner as one author thought all the later thirty-five tribes had been formed on a single occasion whereas the ancient evidence points to the successive creation of tribes until they numbered thirty-five in all.[2]

Laelius Felix, commenting on the jurist Q. Mucius, distinguishes the Roman political assemblies by contrasting the centuries which are organized by age and census, the tribes which are organized by place and region and the curias which are organized *ex generibus hominum* (in A. Gellius 15. 27). Some have argued a *genus* in this context is a clan (*gens*) which a curia comprised; others have proposed that a curia held more than one clan and that this aggregate is called a *genus* because it is a larger family group.[3] When a Greek wrote about curias he equated them to the Hellenic phratries which

and Livy's Book 1 illustrate as well as any work Roman attitudes towards their kings as political specialists. Dionysius' *Roman Antiquities* 2. 7, 2. 13–14 and 2. 21–3 contains the most complete ancient discussion of the curias. It is reliable insofar as it depends on his autopsy of the cult practices.

[1] On lictors, see Cic. *L. Agr.* 2. 12. 31; Antistius Labeo in A. Gellius 15. 27. 2; *CIL* VI, 1885–92. On curions Varro, *LL* 5. 83, 6. 46; Dion. 2. 7, 2. 21; Festus 42 L. Curio Maximus: Livy 27. 8. 1–3; Festus 113 L.

[2] D. H. 4. 15. 1 retails three conflicting Roman opinions on the number of Servian tribes. See L. R. Taylor, 'The Voting Districts of the Roman Republic', *Amer. Acad. in Rome: Papers and Monographs* 20 (1960), 3–7. Cf. Festus 42 L., quoted below, p. 71, n. 2.

[3] Two recent works on the Roman constitution contain the pertinent bibliography: Francesco De Martino, *Storia della costituzione romana*, 1² (Naples, 1958), 120–31; Pietro De Francisci, 'Primordia Civitatis', *Pont. Inst. Utr. Iur. St. et Doc.* 2 (1959), 483–91, 572–83 and *passim*, to be supplemented by his 'La comunità sociale e politica romana primitiva', *SDHI* 22 (1956), 1–86. E. S. Stavely, 'Forschungsbericht: The Constitution of the Roman Republic 1940–1954', *Historia* 5 (1956), 84–90, touches on the *lex curiata* and has a bibliography (pp. 120–2). Arnaldo Momigliano, 'An Interim Report on the Origins of Rome', *JRS* 53 (1963), 109–12, treats certain points in ancient evidence and modern discussion which have gone unquestioned in spite of their improbability and raises questions to which this work may provide some answers. On the nature of a curia Momigliano (p. 111) denies a basis of kinship. De Francisci, 'Primordia', pp. 483–91 and 572–7, tries to reconcile fact and fiction by positing two kinds of curia, the older of which are family corporations (*consorterie gentilizie*) and the later of which are military units (*quadra di leva*). Needless to say, a curia was from beginning to end a curia although its functions might change. I do not believe that there could have been what I would call natural and artificial curias.

they resemble in their actual religious functions during the late Republic and in their supposed military functions in the kingdom. But even a phratry marshalled at Troy (*Iliad* 2. 362) presupposes by its name a kinship which the word 'curia' does not. Furthermore the Roman curias have left no recorded military history comparable to that of the archaic and classical Greek phratry. The ancient equation of curias and centuries is supported by no evidence other than its statement as fact and the arithmetic of 3 tribes times 10 curias of 100 men equals a legion of 3,000.[1] Curial observance of certain festivals, the control of certain family matters and a comitial act concerning the magistrates elect are the later traces of the curias' one-time prominence in public affairs.

Besides the conflict of the ancient testimony there remains the chief difficulty in any study of the problem. The Romans maintained three kinds of civil assemblies. Only the curiate assembly had an even number of voting units. In the centuriate and tribal assemblies the number of voting units was odd in order to anticipate an evenly divided ballot. The even number of curias points to an origin and basis different from those of the other assemblies. Corollary to this problem are the questions why the Romans always voted by units and why an entire assembly is designated by the plural *comitia* 'meetings'.

The greatest blight upon the story of the curias to my mind has been the comparative method which does not truly rely upon historical material from other places and other times, but upon neat and tidy learned accounts of phenomena which at first blush appear so similar. Yet the authors of these accounts had no better historical data than the Romanist dealing with curias. Valuable as they are, the testimonies of the archaic Hebrew, Greek, German and Iguvine systems do not speak with the authority of history because we are bereft of an historical account of nearly all their early development.

In Rome itself we can easily discern change in the centuriate and tribal organizations even though we cannot easily understand the change. The marvelous Roman adaptability to real political change without changing names stands out on the pages of Roman history. A nation among which a century does not contain a hundred men and

---

[1] D. H. 2. 7 spells out the Romulean system and offers the Greek counterparts. His probable authority was Varro's *Antiquities*; see Varro, *LL* 5. 35 (*tribus*, a 'third'), 5. 89 (*miles*, 'one one-thousandth of a tribal levy') and 5. 91 (*turma*, 'three times ten horsemen from three tribes'), and below, chapter 3.

3

a Latin is anyone but a resident of Latium does not make history an easy exercise. In this regard, I have tried to analyze the value of political technical terminology. My results give us no date for the various acceptations of words.

In the following chapters the data on the curias and the character of their evidence are examined. After a demonstration of how untenable are the ancient theories of curias as phratries and military units, I offer a new interpretation of the one ancient legal definition of the curias and of their role in the government of both the Roman kingdom and early Republic.

It would be unkind and untrue for me to assert the incontrovertible historicity and validity of what I have chosen to publish concerning the curias. This study stands as nothing more than a provisional statement and is provisional because any work on the curias is provisional if and until the earth restores to man's vision their archaic public documents.

CHAPTER 2

THREE, THIRTY AND THREE HUNDRED

The three numbers, three, thirty and three hundred figure prominently in archaic Latian history and legend. Historically there were three Roman tribes, thirty Roman curias, thirty soldiers in a Roman cavalry squadron (*turma*) and three hundred horsemen in the primitive Roman cavalry.

The word *tribus* suggested to the Romans themselves an etymology from three (*tres*).[1] The Roman tripartition would seem to have a parallel at Mantua which is said to have had three tribes with four curias each, but the Mantuan arrangement has probably come straight from Greek political theory.[2] Otherwise, a *tribus* stands alone at Umbrian Iguvium[3] and in the Umbrian territory called Tribus Sapinia.[4] These two examples and the later thirty-five Roman tribes, named after places, families and perhaps a people,[5] constituted either a territorial whole or territorial division. They were not 'thirds' or 'one part of three'. Thus, to defend the notion of three tribes, we are left with the tripartition of archaic Roman territory and the etymology of *tribus* from *tres*. In common usage *tribus* retained no sense of threeness or thirdness nor did its derivative *tribuere* mean to triple or to divide into thirds. As we shall see in chapter 3, the common artificial division of territory was based upon the square and not on three. It is impossible to put three into four evenly. Evidence for the loss of one or two tribes is totally lacking, whereas the growth of the number of later 'Servian' tribes is well documented at Rome from the year 495 B.C. Therefore the tripartition of the

---

[1] Varro, *LL* 5. 35, 5. 55; cf. D.H. 2. 7.

[2] Serv. on *Aen.* 10. 202; cf. on *Aen.* 2. 278, 8. 475, 11. 9, discussed in chapter 4. On the Greek theory, see below, pp. 14–16.

[3] See chapter 4.

[4] Livy 31. 2. 6, 33. 37. 1. It was another name for the Ager Boiorum. It is quite likely that this *tribus* was one of 112 *tribus*. Pliny, *NH* 3. 116 reports Cato (= *Orig.* fr. 44 P.): 'in hoc tractu interierunt Boi quorum tribus CXII fuisse auctor est Cato, item Senones, qui ceperunt Romam'.

[5] The Tribus Romilia, lay on the edge of Etruscan territory across the Tiber (Taylor, 'Voting Districts', p. 38) and may have received its name from Etruscans calling it 'Roman', for *Romilius* comes from the ethnic *Romulus* as *Rutilius* from *Rutulus* and *Sicilia* from *Siculus*. The clan Romilia may have taken its name either from the tribe or from Romulus independently. See below, p. 40.

land into three parts called *tribus* seems unfounded from two sides, although the ancients assert the etymology, since Rome is the only place where we encounter three tribes and Rome could have been the only community to have three tribes at one time. Varro remains our chief source on the three archaic *tribus*:

> The Roman territory was first divided into three parts which were called the tribe of the Titienses, the tribe of the Ramnes and the tribe of the Luceres. According to Ennius the Titienses were named after Tatius, Ramnenses after Romulus and, according to Junius, the Luceres after Lucumo. All these words are Etruscan according to the playwright of Etruscan tragedies, Volnius.

> The military tribunes are so called because at one time one was sent to the army from each of the three tribes of the Ramnes, Luceres and Tities.

> Soldiers are called *milites* because the first legion comprised three thousand (*tria milia*) men and each of the tribes of the Titienses, Ramnes, and Luceres sent one thousand soldiers (*milia militum*).

> The squadron is called *turma* from *terima* (*e* changes into *u*) because there was a threefold draft of ten horsemen from each of the three tribes of the Titienses, Ramnes and Luceres. Accordingly the early decurions of each decuria were so called who are still assigned three to each squadron.[1]

Varro's word *terima* is unique and unparalleled by other numbers. His etymology of *miles* is likewise unsupportable in the face of such terms as *satelles*, *velites*, etc. which share the same construction and are designations of armed men, although it is based upon the fact that the archaic military unit, called a tribe and commanded by a tribune, consisted of 1,000 men as the Greek translation of *tribunus* into *chiliarchos* proves.

Livy tells us that Romulus enlisted three centuries of horsemen who were called the Ramnenses after Romulus and the Titienses after Titus Tatius and the Luceres whose name and origin were uncertain.[2] Cicero also records the names of the cavalrymen, the Titienses, Rhamnenses and Luceres.[3] Commenting on Vergil's *tres equitum numero turmae* involved in the Ludus Troiae Servius informs us that

---

[1] *LL* 5. 55, 5. 81, 5. 89, 5. 91. Cf. D.H. 2. 7, 2. 13, Festus 484 L. The evidence and interpretations of king T. Tatius, the tribules Titienses, the Curia Titia (see below, chapter 5), and the Sodales Titii (see below, chapter 6) are canvassed and discussed by J. Poucet, 'Recherches sur la légende sabine des origines de Rome', *Univ. de Louvain Recueil Trav. Hist. Philol.* ser. 4, fasc. 37 (1967), pp. 265–410. His literary analyses are excellent; his historical views want support. For instance, he denies the existence of three archaic tribes which he considers merely three centuries of horsemen. The title of the three *tribuni* and the lack of evidence for naming Roman military centuries argue against this interpretation.

[2] Livy 1. 13. 8. [3] *Rep.* 2. 20. 36; cf. 2. 8. 14.

men were the Titienses, Ramnetes and Luceres.[1] Festus offers
Titienses, Ramnes, Luceres.[2] Plutarch reduces the names to one
form: Ramnenses, Tatienses and Lucerenses.[3] Paulus' rendition of
Festus yields the *tribus Titiensis* and the Luceres or Lucere(n)ses
(alias Lucomedi).[4]

A summary of the order and form of the three names are:

Ennius:	Titienses, Ramnenses, Luceres
Varro:	Titienses, Ramnes, Luceres
	Ramnes, Luceres, Tities
	Titienses, Ramnes, Luceres
Cicero:	Titienses, Rhamnenses, Luceres
Livy:	Ramnenses, Titienses, Luceres
Propertius:	Tities, Ramnes, Luceres
Plutarch:	Ramnenses, Tatienses, Lucerenses
Festus:	Titienses, Ramnes, Luceres (Lucere(n)ses)
Servius:	Titienses, Ramnetes, Luceres

The order T–R–L is met seven times, R–L–T once, and R–T–L
twice. The first order, however, may have descended from Ennius'
hexameter line,[5] so that an official order cannot be known for certain. As to form, Lucerenses seems quite inauthentic. Varro avoids
Ennius' Ramnenses in favor of Ramnes while he also attests Tities
against his usage of Titienses twice. It is worth emphasis that only in
the case of Paulus' Titiensis does the name of the tribe itself survive.
All other surviving examples are the names (masc. pl.) of tribules.
Both ancient etymologies and modern interpretations[6] of the names
rest upon the supposition that they derive from eponymous heroes.
R(h)amnes surely has an Etruscan look about it. Yet Ramnenses and
Ramnetes[7] are ethnic or toponymous formations as is the almost
certain Titienses. Elsewhere the writer has offered reinforcement of

---

[1] On *Aen.* 5. 560, where Varro is cited.

[2] Festus 468 L.; cf. p. 484 where the lexicon cites Curiatius, an authority known to us
only from Festus, who gives the same etymology as Varro in *LL* 5.91. His vital dates,
nature of his work and relation to Varro (if any) are quite unknown; see M. Schanz and
C. Hosius, *Geschichte der römischen Literatur bis zum Gesetzgebungswerk des Kaisers Justinian* I
(Munich, 1927–35), 175 and 586. The same order noted above is to be found in [Asconius]
p. 227 St.

[3] *Rom.* 20. 2.   [4] Pp. 106–7, 503 L.

[5] Cf. Prop. 4. 1. 31: 'hinc Tities Ramnesque viri Luceresque Soloni'.

[6] W. Schulze, 'Zur Geschichte der lateinischen Eigennamen', *Abhandlungen der Königlichen Gesellschaft der Wissenschaften zu Göttingen*, Philol.-hist. Kl. 5. 1 (1904), 182–3, 218,
297, 581, claims Etruscan origins for all three. The methodological warrant comes from
folk etymology and an unknown Etruscan playwright.

[7] Servius doubtless mistook *Ramnes* (nom. pl.) for *Ramnes* (nom. sg.), *-etis*, whom Vergil
makes a Rutulian augur and adviser of Turnus. See on *Aen.* 9. 358, 10. 655.

the derivation of Luceres from *lucus* ('grove').[1] Those who would rely on the Hellenistic myth-mongering of eponymous Romulus, Titus Tatius and Lucumo (alias Lucerus) run the risk of entering the land of R(h)ome (alias Valentia), Doros, Ion, Aiolos, and Hellen.

In sum, the names of the tribules of the three archaic tribes survived into historical times. Romans and Etruscans made of them what they would. The origin of the names cannot be ascertained. They do not belong to any known compound of personal names. The survival of the names after the demise of the tribes is accounted for in two ways: first, the probable retention of the three units in drawing up the list of senators (see chapter 9) and, secondly, the number of cavalrymen assigned to the Roman legion. Since the number 300 figures here, we excuse ourselves for passing from the number three to the number 300. Roman tradition maintained Romulus' cavalry contained 300 Celeres.[2] According to Polybius the cavalry unit assigned to each legion consisted of 300 men.[3] The Livian accounts always record 300 or a multiple of 300 horsemen.[4] Once Livy records a unit of 300 Campanian horsemen, but the allies, who fielded a proportionately larger cavalry, did not maintain this numerical system.[5] After the Second Punic War when our evidence grows more detailed two Latin colonies had 300 cavalry colonists but their foot-soldiers numbered 3,000 and 3,700.[6] Similar and incidental evidence confirms the enlistment of 300 cavalrymen who fought in ten squadrons of thirty men divided into three detachments of ten men. These minor detachments of ten were the decurias commanded by decurions.[7] Such were the facts. Of other facts and some fictions in this regard we shall have more to say later.

There were three major units of the archaic cavalry. We know their names, the tribes of Titienses, Ramnes (alias Ramnenses) and Luceres. Was there an archaic squadron called *turma*? If there was, each

---

[1] See R. E. A. Palmer, 'The King and the Comitium', *Historia* Einzelschriften Heft 11 (1969), and below, pp. 250–3.

[2] E.g. Livy 1. 13. 8, D.H. 2. 13, Fest. *Epit.* 48 L.

[3] Pol. 1. 16. 2, 6. 20. 9.

[4] E.g. Livy 8. 8. 14, 9. 5. 5, 10. 25. 2, 21. 17. 3, 21. 17. 5, 21. 17. 9, 22. 36. 3, 35. 2. 4.

[5] Livy 23. 4. 8, 23. 31. 10: 300 Campani. In Livy 21. 17. 3: Romans, 24,000 foot-soldiers, 1,800 horsemen (i.e. six legions); allies, 40,000 foot-soldiers, 4,400 horsemen. Cf. Pol. 6. 26 and F. W. Walbank thereon, *A Historical Commentary on Polybius*, vol. 1 (Oxford, 1957).

[6] Livy 35. 9. 7 (Castrum Frentinum) and 35. 40. 5 (Vibo). On the colonies which had only 300 colonists see below, p. 28, n. 5.

[7] Pol. 6. 25, Varro, *LL* 5. 91, Festus 484 L.; cf. D.H. 2. 7, 2. 13.

tribe contributed ten men (*decuria*) towards its complement and the three tribes were broken into ten squadrons which in turn were broken into three components of ten men. In Polybius' time there was no tactical unit called the tribe, but there were squadrons and their three decurias. Indeed, the enrollment and assignment of the cavalry did not differ from that of the infantry.[1] Hence, I conclude that there was no relation of *turmae* to *tribus* of 100 men and that the *turmae* and perhaps their *decuriae* were introduced in relation to a grand number of 300 which was the residue of three defunct cavalry tribes of 100 cavalrymen each. The 300 men had once been divided into three units of 100 men called tribes. Such a unit could not be equally divided into squadrons of thirty men. At any rate, by the second century the 300 men were divided into ten units of thirty men.

Now the number thirty requires attention. All ancient authorities agree that there were thirty curias. This number was an historical fact. What origin and purpose the number thirty possessed could be interpreted any way the simple fact allowed. Thirty was a military number. Besides the thirty men of the three decurias in a squadron (*turma*), the legion had sixty centuries, thirty maniples and ten cohorts.[2] Thirty is reckoned as a ritual number among the Latins.[3] Evidence of this number's ritual quality is taken from the least impeccable sources and is couched in the least historical terms. Lycophron states that Aeneas founded thirty stations (*pyrgoi*) in the land of the Boreigonoi.[4] Alba Longa founded thirty colonies.[5] There were thirty people of the Latin Name.[6] And, of course, there was the prodigious sow who littered thirty piglets so that Aeneas might console himself with thirty of something. Usually, the thirty was thought to foretell a thirty-year reign for Ascanius at Lavinium.[7] Cassius Hemina (fr. 11 P.) tells the story differently from others. The thirty piglets appear to Romulus and Remus for dividing the rule of Rome. They build a shrine (*fanum*) to the Lares Grundiles or

---

[1] See Walbank on Pol. 6. 20. 9; cf. Pol. 6. 25. Polybius states that an old system has been supplanted by what he describes.
[2] Cincius, *Res Mil.* in Gellius, *NA* 16. 4. 6. Cf. Serv. on *Aen.* 11. 463, Isid. *Etym.* 9. 3. 47.
[3] Bernardi, '*Populi Albenses*', pp. 227 f.
[4] *Alex.* 1251 ff.   [5] D.H. 3. 31, 3. 34.
[6] Livy 2. 18. 3, D.H. 6. 63, 6. 74–5.
[7] Cato, *Orig.* in *Origo Gent. Rom.* 12. 5, cf. 17. 1; Varro, *RR* 2. 4. 18, *LL* 5. 144; Verg. *Aen.* 1. 269, 8. 43 ff. on which see Servius; D.H. 1. 56, 1. 66.

Grunting Heroes.[1] The height of absurdity is reached in reckoning a ritual value for the thirty Latin colonies existing during the Second Punic War.[2] A liberal dose of scattered notices in Livy or two chapters of Velleius Paterculus (1. 14–15) might retard myth-mongers, for the number of Latin colonies grew from one onward without the slightest scruple for a ritual number thirty.

As for the number of adherents to the Alban League, there is not a shred of supporting evidence for the asserted thirty communities. No doubt some lists of Alban League constituents lie to us, but that is immaterial. The following summary yields no less than seventy possible Alban peoples without analyzing possible duplications. Cato's list contains the names of eight peoples who participated in the dedication of Diana's Arician grove.[3] The names of twenty-nine peoples who subscribed to a Latin treaty struck at the Caput Aquae Ferentinae comes from Dionysius.[4] However, Dionysius elsewhere tells us forty-seven joined in the Latin Festival.[5] The least understood evidence is found in Pliny who in fact supplies two lists, the first of towns in no order and the second of peoples in alphabetical order. Dionysius' list was also alphabetized but it does not coincide with Pliny's. Pliny begins his first, analphabetical list with the words 'in the first region there were in Latium the famous towns...' and closes 'with them (these) peoples used to take the meat on the Alban Mount'. After he ends the alphabetical list he says, 'thus fifty-three peoples disappeared from archaic Latium without a trace'.[6] The second, alphabetized list of peoples contains either thirty or thirty-one names according to whether one counts both Albenses and Albani. The first, analphabetical, list of towns has twenty names. Thus two

---

[1] See Tac. *Ann.* 12. 24 for the *sacellum Larum*, one of the four points in the Romulean pomerium. For 'grunting' Lares see also Nonius, p. 164 L., Arnobius, *Adv. Nat.* 1. 28. For pig sacrifice to Lares, Prop. 4. 1. 23: 'parva saginati lustrabant compita porci'.

[2] See Alföldi, *Early Rome and the Latins* (Ann Arbor, n.d. [1965]), pp. 16–17 and *passim*. The text is Livy 27. 9. 7.

[3] *Orig.* fr. 58 P. from Priscian.

[4] D.H. 5. 61; he calls the place Ferentinum (i.e. *ad caput (aquae) Ferentinae*) where the Latin Festival was held. His list distinguishes between the Laurentes and Lavinians, a single historical community. One editor, Stephanus, has a thirtieth item, *Trikinōn*, which has no MS warrant, although its existence has prompted some later editors to emend and include it. There never was a thirtieth name on the treaty because it was a compact against the Romans, the thirtieth people. Dionysius (6. 63. 4) acknowledges the existence of thirty people of the Latin name; but see below.

[5] D.H. 4. 49. 2–3.

[6] *NH* 3. 68–70: 'in prima regione praeterea fuere in Latio clara oppida....et cum iis carnem in monte Albano soliti accipere populi....ita ex antiquo Latio LIII populi interiere sine vestigiis'.

or three names have been lost to make up the total of fifty-three. Dazzled by the alphabetized thirty or thirty-one, students have overlooked Pliny's express statement that the peoples took meat with towns(men) he had just cited. Manifestly Pliny had one artificially compiled list to which he added the names of twenty towns omitted in the alphabetized compilation. The duplication of Politorium of the first list and the Poletaurini of the second list bears out our interpretation. Finally in the following lists are found towns participating in the Latin Festival which are attested by Livy and Cicero. None of these seven communities is found in Pliny's lists which alone represent members of the so-called Alban League which celebrated the Feriae Latinae.[1] Less fervent disciples of political numerology will see that no solace can be taken from these lists. Pliny's and Dionysius' alphabetized compilations which approximate thirty names agree on Bube(n)tani, Coriolani, Pedani, Querquetulani, Tolerini and perhaps on Bovillani/Bolani, Fortineii/Foreti, Nomentani/Numinienses. Furthermore, Dionysius' list agrees with Pliny's analphabetized first list on the Norbani, Scapteni and Telenii. Eight of Pliny's fifty or fifty-one names certainly coincide with eight of Dionysius' twenty-nine. Even the addition of the three doubtful identifications hardly supports the opinion that the ancients knew the names of the one and only ritually numbered thirty.

Then what can be said for the historicity of the ritual number of thirty piglets, thirty years, thirty stations, thirty Alban peoples, thirty Latin colonies and thirty curias? Nothing can be said for their historicity. All the thirty things come from a single factual, real, historical thirty, the thirty curias of the archaic Roman state. Nevertheless, if we wish, we can learn an historical lesson from the thirty colonies and thirty peoples. Such numbers were not constant. The entities grew in number and decreased in number.

Whoever first saw the efficacy of the thirty knew the number of Roman curias and also knew about the fixed decimal military units of centuries and decurias and the standard but by no means fixed number of colonial settlers. The earliest writer who mentions an

---

[1] See Bernardi, 'Populi Albenses' and Alföldi, Early Rome. Typical of the latter's use of sources is his acceptance of the emendation Sanates for Manates so that one reads Longani Sanates Macnales Munienses, etc. (p. 13, n. 2). The state of the MS tradition is not good but hardly warrants forgetting the ABCs. Forgeries also exist in Pliny's list of towns, viz. Saturnia which was Old Rome and Antipolis which was the Janiculum on which I say more later. All lists are given on pp. 12–13.

Cato	Dionysius (alphabetized)	Pliny 3. 68	Pliny 3. 69 (alphabetized)	Other
			1 Abolani	
			2 Accienses	
			3 Aesolani	
			4 Albani	
			5 Albenses	
		6 Ameriola		
		7 Amitinum		
		8 Antemnae		
		9 Antipolis (Ianiculum)		
10 Ardeatis Rutulus	Ardeates			Ardeates (Livy 32. 1. 9)
11 Aricinus	Ariceni			
			12 Bolani	
	13 Bovillani			Bovillae (Cic. *Planc.* 23)
	14 Bubentani		Bubetani	
	15 Cabani			
		16 Caenina		
		17 Cameria		
	18 Carventani			
	19 Circeiates			
		20 Collatia		
21 Coranus	Corani			
	22 Corbinti			
	23 Coriolani		Coriolani	
		24 Corniculum		
		25 Crustumeria		
			26 Cusuetani	
		27 Ficana		
			28 Fidenates	
			29 Foreti	
	30 Fortineii			
	31 Gabini			Gabii (Cic. *Planc.* 23)
			32 Hortenses	
	33 Labicani			Labici (Cic. *Planc.* 23)
34 Lanuvinus	Lanuvini			Lanuvium (Livy 41. 16. 1)
			35 Latinienses	
36 Laurens	Laurentini and			Laurentes (Livy 37. 3. 4)
	36a Laviniates			

12

8 peoples	29 peoples	20 towns	31 peoples	7 towns and peoples
			37 Longani	
			38 Macrales	
			39 Manates	
		40 Medullum		
			41 Munienses	
	42 Nomentani			
	43 Norbani	Norbe		
			44 Numinienses	
			45 Octulani	
			46 Olliculani	
			Pedani	
			Poletaurini	
	47 Pedani	48 Politorium		
		Pometia		
49 Pometinus				
	50 Praenestini			
	51 Querquetulani		Querquetulani	
				52 Roma (*passim*)
	53 Satricani	Satricum		
		54 Saturnia (Roma)		
		Scaptia		
	55 Scapteni			
	56 Setini			
			57 Sicani	
			58 Sisolenses	
		59 Sulmo		
		Tellena		
	60 Tellenii			
	Tiburtini			
61 Tiburtis		62 Tifata		
	63 Tolerini		Tolerienses	
	Tusculani			
64 Tusculanus			65 Tutienses	
			66 Velienses	
	67 Velitrani			
			68 Venetulani	
			69 Vimitellani	
			70 Vitellenses	
8 peoples	29 peoples	20 towns	31 peoples	7 towns and peoples

Italian 'triacad' was the Greek Lykophron. The Greeks, to whom the Romans went time and time again for theoretical explanation, bear the responsibility for the political numerology of the thirty curias.

The retrospective pursuit of the number thirty tied Rome's origins to the history of Troy through Aeneas and his putative descendants. This was no less an accomplishment than a genealogy traced to Adam and Eve. Its historical value lies in its capacity to undermine the numerological edifice which goes by the name of the Romulean constitution after a member of the Aenead house.

By far the most famous thirty were the Thirty of the Athenian tyranny who are said to represent the 3,000 of the ancestral constitution.[1] The Athenians also regularly employed thirty judges or dikasts. Each of the ten Kleisthenic tribes supplied three men for this panel.[2] A triacad at Athens contained thirty families.[3] Along with the public messes the Spartan triacads were created for warfare by Lycurgus.[4] Any theoretical discussion of the lawgiver Romulus had to adduce the exemplary Lycurgus.[5] Such stuff takes us from the realm of fact to the land of fancy. Plato's twelve tribes have thirty representatives on the council so that the latter numbers 360. His number thirty reflects the numbers of days in a month. But the basis of the Platonic speculation is duodecimal as can be seen from his discussion of the total number of citizens, 5,040.[6] The numbers of phratries, demes and *komai* should be commensurable with 5,040 and agree with one another.[7] Plato's phratry, like an actual Athenian phratry, mediated citizenship.[8] Plato's numbers belong entirely to theory.[9]

Because Athenian practice did not conform to numerological rules, Lycurgus' creation of the Spartan state could stand as model. Her Lycurgan military system was said to include three units of cavalry whose hipparchs chose 100 men. There were six *morai* of cavalry and infantry.[10] Religiously, the nine Spartan tribes (*phylai*) and twenty-seven phratries shared in the *skiades* of the festival

---

[1] See, e.g., Arist. *Ath. Pol.* 34–6.   [2] *Ibid.* 53.
[3] *IG* ii², 1214 (= Ditt. *SIG*⁴ 3. 912), Pollux 8. 111 (cf. Arist., below p. 15).
[4] Herod. 1. 65. 5, Polyaenus 2. 3. 11.   [5] Cic. *Rep.* 2. 15, 2. 42–3, 2. 50, for example.
[6] *Leg.* 6. 756, 6. 758, 6. 771.   [7] *Ibid.* 5. 746–7.
[8] *Ibid.* 6. 785; cf. Arist. *Ath. Pol.* 21. 6.
[9] See G. R. Morrow, *Plato's Cretan City* (Princeton, 1960) pp. 113 ff. on the citizens' 5,040 lots, pp. 121–8 on tribes and phratries, pp. 419–20, 496–9 on the three groups of four tribes for selection of *exegetes*, pp. 389–98 on the common meals and military organizations and especially pp. 343–50 on the role of mathematics and astronomy in an ideal education.   [10] Xen. *Resp. Lac.* 4, 11. 6.

Karneia. Then nine *skiades* were set up so that nine men or three phratries might participate under one *skias*.[1] Of course, this report runs against the evidence of the three tribes universal to Dorian Greeks and the five *obai* at Sparta.

Aristotle states that the land of Sparta could support 1,500 horsemen and 30,000 hoplites.[2] Is it not strange that it could not support 1,613 horsemen and 31,251 hoplites? However the lawgiver in Aristotle takes charge of civil division into messes, phratries, tribes.[3] Aristotle counsels reformers to destroy old bonds by creating new tribes and phratries just as had been done at Athens by Kleisthenes and at Cyrene.[4] The Aristotelian state rests upon a partnership of clans and villages whereby the phratries and clubs provided the needed religious and social means of public responsibility and recreation.[5] Aristotle reflects Plato's view of the Spartan and Cretan communal messes which were a part of the latter's division into *syssitiai*, phratries and tribes.[6] As political organs the phratries, *lochoi* and tribes should preserve copies of fiscal transactions to anticipate embezzlement.[7] Besides voting assemblies in the tribe, the deme or of the whole citizen-body, the citizens could participate in their phratries by exercising the suffrage.[8]

Aristotle's more sober and less paradigmatic treatment of the phratry's place in the state has its imaginative side. In a fragment attributed to his *Constitution of the Athenians* Aristotle commences from the fact of four tribes (*phylai*) known in most Ionian Greek states. There are four tribes because there are four annual seasons. Each tribe has three phratries or *trittyes* ('thirds'). There are these twelve parts (*moirai*) because there are twelve months of the year and three belong to each of the four seasons. Every phratry has thirty clans (*genē*) and every *genos* has thirty members (*gennētai*) because each of the twelve months has thirty days.[9] It is debatable whether Aristotle's construction marks an improvement over Plato's twelve tribes which gave thirty councillors. At least, it demands more intricacy. Whereas Plato's sexagesimal system wrought 360 councillors, Aristotle's twelve phratries yielded 360 clans and 10,800

---

[1] Demetrius of Skepsis in Athenaeus 4. 141 E, F.
[2] *Pol.* 2. 1270 a.   [3] *Ibid.* 2. 1264 a.   [4] *Ibid.* 6. 1319 b.
[5] *Ibid.* 3. 1280 b–1281 a, *Eth. Eud.* 7. 1241 b.
[6] *Pol.* 2. 1264 a.   [7] *Ibid.* 5. 1309 a.   [8] *Ibid.* 4. 1300 a.
[9] Arist. in *Lex. Demosth. Patm.* p. 152 S. *s.v. gennētai* = fr. 5 Opp., fr. 385 R.; Schol. on Plat. *Axoch.* 371 D; Harp. *s.v. trittys.*

clansmen. It would be a useless exercise to combat Greek political numerology. Suffice it to say that, whereas it did not reflect realities,[1] it entered the mainstream of political literature.

These Greek theories provide the background for any sensible discussion of a constitution imputed to a single lawgiver. The Romans believed that they had once lived under a constitution which was granted them by their eponymous lawgiver, Romulus and was based upon an arithmetical scheme. Its composition demanded comparison with archaic Greek constitutions such as were known to the Romans mostly from theorists. The Greek historian of Rome's founding, Dionysius of Halicarnassus, laid down the Greek equivalents of the Roman constitutional components. From Dionysius students of Roman history have taken the equations and pursued the study of the curias, equivalent of the Greek phratries, using the comparative method. This method presupposes that the Romans of one city-state in Italy had at one time enjoyed a political system which showed close similarity or identity with the system of the Greeks who, in fact, constituted hundreds of city-states. To ascertain the curias' history for a period when no history had been written Romanists looked to their Greek predecessors in historiography. With some facts at their disposal the Romans created a history of the founding of Rome. The facts which they adduced were applied to the story of a formal foundation of a city-state.

Before and after the publication of Marcus Terentius Varro's *Roman Antiquities of Human and Divine Matters* the Romans believed that their lawgiver Romulus had excogitated a political and military system based upon three tribes and thirty curias. The former were named after three men, the latter after thirty Sabine women. Varro's work does not survive but Dionysius of Halicarnassus made use of it in writing his Roman 'archaeology' in which, in fact, he weds antiquarian research to a rhetorical and tedious history of Rome down to the eve of the First Punic War. Before any examination of Dionysius' Varronian statements on curias the student who places a

---

[1] On phratries in general see the recent work of H. T. Wade-Gery, 'Demotionidae', *CQ* 25 (1931), 129–43 (= *Essays*, pp. 116–34); K. Latte, *RE* 20. 1 (1941), cols 745–58; C. Hignett, *A History of the Athenian Constitution* (Oxford, 1952), pp. 55–74; A. Andrewes, 'Phratries in Homer', *Hermes* 89 (1961), 129–40 and 'Philochoros on Phratries', *JHS* 81 (1961), pp. 1–15. On trittyes see F. R. Wüst, *Historia* 6 (1957), 176–91 and 8 (1959), 1–11. On the phratries in the above fragment of Aristotle see Latte, col. 748; F. Jacoby, *Atthis: The Local Chronicles of Ancient Athens* (Oxford, 1949), pp. 316 ff., n. 140; and Hignett, pp. 59 ff.

high value on history will want to assess Varro's opinions and methods in treating his own antiquity in order to estimate the worth of his neat description of the system of tribes and curias. After an assessment of Varro's work the historical value of Dionysius' account can be evaluated on its own merits and not on the merits of its rationalism in comparison with the eponymous Sabine virgins.

Varro saw clearly the simplified absurdity of popular accounts and replaced it with what passed for scientific research into the past. His acumen basked in the sunlight of admiration until the famous Christian bishop of Hippo picked out detailed rationalizations from the books on divine matters and held them up for the readers of his own Divine State to mock and deride. Varro came from the Sabine town of Reate, knew the Sabine language, and found Sabinisms in every nook and cranny of Roman life. Patriotism and knowledge of geography moved him to set the navel of Italy in the Reatine territory.[1] In his *Origins* Cato had traced the Sabines through one Sabus, 'The Pious', back to Lacedaemon.[2] Thus folk-legend and history could trace Roman ancestry through the tribe named after Titus Tatius all the way back to Laconia and Spartans. After all Heraclides of Pontus and Aristotle of Stagira had called Rome a city of Hellenes.[3] Without sorting the strands of his sources, we summarize Dionysius' views on the origins of the Italians. The early Romans were Hellenes (1. 4–5). Among the peoples of central Italy were found the Sicels, Aborigines, Pelasgians, Latins who were formerly the Aborigines, the Leleges who were the Aberrigines (*sic!*), the Achaeans, the Arcadians who were the Oenotrians who included the Sicels, Morgetes and Italici (1. 9–13). The Pelasgians had come from Thessaly to Umbria and also settled Caere (= Agylla) and Pisae (1. 17–20). Hence we learn of the defunct city of Larisa, Fescennium and Falerii which first held Sicels and then Pelasgians (1. 21). The Sicels migrated to Sicily where they lived as the Sicani after the arrival of the Sabines (1. 22). After discussing the origins of the Etruscans, Dionysius turned to primitive Rome which he considered Arcadian or Peloponnesian because the Palatine hill was named after Pallanteus (1. 31–4). These Arcadians gave the Romans the alphabet. Then came the Trojans who were also Hellenes. With the Latins

---

[1] See Pliny, *NH* 3. 109 and Solin. 2. 23. 'Sabinism' is found in *LL* 5. 73, 74, 107, 159; 6. 13; 7. 29, 77 (cf. 5. 123, 6. 5 and Serv. on *Aen.* 7. 657). Poucet's work is of great importance in studying the putative Sabine ancestry of Rome.

[2] *Orig.* fr. 51 P.; cf. D.H. 2. 49.   [3] In Plut. *Cam.* 22. 3–4.

they founded Lavinium, Alba and the two colonies of Pallantium and Saturnia which Rome later comprised (1. 45–69). About fifty Alban families joined Romulus in the foundation of Rome (1. 85–9). Romulus' Rome embraced Aborigines who were also Oenotrians and Arcadians, Pelasgians who were also Argives, Arcadians of the Palatium, Peloponnesians of Mt Saturnius and Trojans (1. 89, cf. 2. 2–3). The new Romans spoke Aeolic Greek (1. 90), probably because no one indigenous language could please such a motley majority. The curias took the custom of corporate dinners from the Lacedemonians (2. 23) perhaps because the Sabines whose deity Juno Curitis sponsored the dinners (2. 54) were of Lacedaemonian extraction (2. 49).

Dionysius honestly inherited this hodgepodge. Unique in the annals of ancient historiography, I believe, is his roster of sources for Books One and Two; for archaic Rome (1. 6–8) Hieronymus of Cardia, Timaeus (cf. 1. 67, 74), Antigonus, Polybius (cf. 1. 32, 74), Silenus, Fabius Pictor (cf. 1. 74, 79, 80, 2. 38–40), Cincius Alimentus (cf. 1. 74, 79, 2. 38–9), Porcius Cato (cf. 1. 74, 79, 2. 49), Fabius Maximus, Valerius Antias (cf. 2. 13), Licinius Macer (cf. 2. 52), the Aelii (cf. 1. 80), Gellii (cf. 2. 31, 76), and Calpurnii (cf. 1. 79, 2. 38–40); on Italian origins (1. 11–12) Porcius Cato, Gaius Sempronius, and Antiochus of Syracuse (cf. 1. 22, 35, 73); 1. 13 Pherecydes of Athens; on the towns of the Aborigines near Reate (1. 14–15), Varro's *Antiquities* (cf. 2. 21, 47–8); on the Sicels (1. 22) Philistus of Syracuse, Thucydides (cf. 1. 25) and Hellanicus of Lesbos' *Troika* (cf. 1. 28, 35, 48); on the Etruscans (1. 27–9) Herodotus, Xanthus of Lydia, and Myrsilus; on Aeneas (1. 48–9) Menecrates of Xanthus, Kephalon of Gergis (cf. 1. 72), Hegesippus, Ariaethus' *Arcadia*, Agathyllus of Arcadia (cf. 1. 72); (1. 61) Phanodemus' *On Attica*; on the Penates (1. 68) Callistratus' *On Samothrace*, Satyrus and Arctinus; on the founding of Rome (1. 72) Demagoras, Damastes of Sigeum, Aristotle, Callias' *Deeds of Agathocles*, Xenagoras, and Dionysius of Chalcis; and on the Umbrians (2. 49) Zenodotus of Troezen. Aristotle's statement in 1. 72 that Rome was an Achaean and Trojan foundation is usually assigned to his *Barbarian Customs*.[1] With such warrants Dionysius surely felt secure. Even if he had not read all these authors, he could invoke their authority. Needless to say, he

---

[1] Fr. 609 R. = *FGH* 840 F 13a. Fr. 610 R. = *FGH* 840 F 23 of the *Nom. Barb.* is *Cam.* 22 (p. 17, n. 3).

has illuminated *obscurum per obscurius* in regard to primitive Rome.

Dionysius explicitly cites Varro's *Antiquities* on Reatine topography (1. 14. 1), curial priests and the curias' names (2. 21. 2, 2. 47. 4) and the purchase of the Sibylline Books (4. 62). Presumably Varro on the Sabine town of Cures, the Sabine word for spear (*curis*) and Quirinus also comes from the same work (2. 48). When quoting L. Mallius or Manlius on an inscribed tripod at the temple of Zeus at Dodona, Dionysius (1. 19. 3) was actually using Varro[1] and particularly his *Antiquities*.

Varro himself was not immune to the opinion that the Romans descended from Greeks. His *De gente populi Romani* is a tract on that very theme. For instance, the Romans at first ate in a sitting position, a custom borrowed from Lacedemonians and Cretans.[2] Varro considered it quite appropriate to deal with the earliest Romans not only in a Greek frame of reference but also as if they were the Greeks' close relatives and imitators. When Varro came to treat Roman beginnings he followed a methodology at least as old as Cato's *Origins* which was tempered by his own linguistic inventiveness and conception of numbers with non-numerical values. The very principles of numbers drew nine rolls from Varro (*De principiis numerorum*, now lost but mentioned in the Catalogue). As we shall see, numbers played a part in Varro's treatment of political institutions.

We have already remarked on Varronian etymologies of *miles* and *turma* based upon numbers. Varro may fairly be described as obsessed with numbers. On the number three (besides the three tribes), Varro held that there were only three Muses;[3] with the Pythagoreans that a series generated from an odd number is finite, a series generated from an even number is infinite and that a ternary number is perfect;[4] there was some significance to three gates and three roads;[5] with the Etruscans that there were twelve kinds of lightning of which four gods had three bolts each;[6] that there were 300 Jupiters.[7] In his

---

[1] See Varro in Macr. *Sat.* 1. 7. 28. For Dionysius' sources see the important study of E. Gabba, 'Studi su Dionigi di Alicarnasso', *Athenaeum* 38 (1960), 175–225.

[2] From Serv. on *Aen.* 7. 176. This is Fraccaro's fr. 37, p. 285. P. Fraccaro, *Studi Varroniani: De gente populi Romani Libri IV* (Padova, 1907) is a fine introduction to Varronian method and matter.

[3] Serv. on *Ecl.* 7. 21.   [4] *Ibid.* on 8. 75.

[5] Serv. Dan. on *Georg.* 1. 34; cf. *LL* 5. 164–5, Pliny, *NH* 3. 66, Serv. Dan. on *Aen.* 1. 422 (from the Etruscans).

[6] Serv. on *Aen.* 1. 42, *ARD*; cf. 1. 47 on the physical trinity.   [7] See p. 68, n. 5.

Antiquities of Divine Matters he asserted three kinds of theology and three kinds of Roman gods while invoking the authority of Pythagoras for his numerology.[1] Septenary numbers prompted Varro to write his *Hebdomades* in which seven exclusively figured alone or in multiples. He could find significance in the seven laps at the circus.[2] Varro's interest in seven seems to come from his knowledge of the hebdomadary week which the Etruscans propagated through their *Libri Rituales*.[3] In his linguistics Varro examined the properties of octonary and novenary numbers.[4] Varro's ancestors had surveyed with a duodenary number so that one land measure comprised twelve decurias.[5] A centurion commanded a century of men because a centenary number is a *iustus numerus*.[6]

Besides *The Principles of Numbers* Varro wrote a treatise entitled *Atticus de numeris*.[7] His geometry was based upon the divisions of the year and the months.[8] Even in a discourse on names he could write that the Romans had 1,000 family names and about thirty praenomens.[9]

Calendar numbers had a special appeal for Varro. Censorinus' treatise on the birthday contains some of Varro's choicest numerology. By fifteens he apportions the human life span into climacteric years (*DN* 14): *puer* 1–15, *adolescens* 15–30, *iuvenis* 30–45, *senior* 45–60, *senex* 60 onwards. Varro dwelt on the birthdays of cities. The twelve vultures which appeared at Rome's birth foretold spans of 120 or 1,200 years of life (*DN* 17. 15 from Book 18 of the *Antiquities*). In fact, Varro had an Etruscan expert cast the horoscope of both Romulus and Rome. Tarutius, philosopher and mathematician, told him that Romulus had been conceived in the first year of the second Olympiad in the Egyptian month of Choiak, twenty-third day, at the third hour after sunset at the time of eclipse and had been

---

[1] Tert. *Apol.* 47; Aug. *CD* 6. 5 etc. See Agahd, 'M. Terenti Varronis Antiquitatum Rerum Divinarum libri I XIV XV XVI', *Jahrbücher für classische Philologie*, Supplbd. 24 (1898), 144 ff. and above, p. 19, nn. 4, 6, and W. Theiler, *Die Vorbereitung des Neuplatonismus*[2] (Berlin/Zurich, 1964), pp. 18–19, *Forschungen zum Neuplatonismus* (Berlin, 1966), p. 109.

[2] Gellius, *NA* 3. 10.   [3] Cens. *DN* 12. 6, 14. 6.

[4] *LL* 9. 86–8, 10. 43 and in Arn. *Adv. Nat.* 3. 38.

[5] *LL* 5. 34.   [6] *LL* 5. 88.   [7] Cens. *DN* 2. 2.

[8] [Boethius] in *Röm. Feldmesser*, p. 393 L. See also Mart. Cap. 6. 578, 6. 639, 6. 662 and Varro, *LL* 6. 13. The work used by Capella for geometry may have been the *Disciplinarum Libri, De mensuris* or *De ora maritima* (cf. Solin. 11. 6). See Dahlmann, *RE* Supplbd. 6 (1935), col. 1253. For instance, in his geography Varro insists that there were but three major rivers in Europe; Gellius, 10. 7.

[9] [Val. Max.] *Praen.* 3.

born in the month of Thouth, the twenty-first day about daybreak and that Rome had been founded on the ninth day of Pharmouthi between the second and third hour.[1] The day of foundation in the Roman calendar was the eleventh before the kalends of May when Jupiter was in Pisces and Saturn, Venus, Mars and Mercury were in Scorpio, and the sun was in Taurus and the moon in Libra. The day was the festival of Parilia.[2] Thus Varro might have known to what year Rome remained safe after 120 years of life and to what year Rome lived after 1,200 years. This scientific datum gives pause to reflect on the canonical year of the founding of the city for which Varro is partly responsible.

Before baring the Varronian interpretation of the nature of the city founded by Romulus, we state the extent of our knowledge on Varro's use of the two philosophers on whom he based his political numerology. First of all, he cites Pythagoras on the *quadripertitio* but the knowledge seems to come from Aristotle.[3] Likewise, the perfection of the number three apparently was mediated by Aristotle.[4] Varro retailed Pythagorean doctrine in his *Tubero de origine humana* (*DN* 9. 1). However, this reference to Pythagoreanism probably also came from Aristotle because Varro's discussion of mankind's climacteric years and the twelve hebdomades of human life in the Etruscan books of destiny introduced an Aristotelian term (*DN* 14). Varro elsewhere invokes Aristotle on language (*LL* 8. 11) and his *History of Animals* (in Gellius *NA* 3. 16. 6). Finally and of greatest importance, Varro knew Aristotle's *Barbarian Customs* (*LL* 7. 70) to which is usually attributed the Aristotelian view of Rome's origin found in Dionysius.[5] Varro perhaps passed on this Aristotelian reference to Dionysius.[6] Varro (*LL* 5. 113) also knew Polybius. However, his debt to Polybian history and political theory cannot be assessed.

Varro's *Antiquities* contained a discussion of the numerological

---

[1] Thus far from Plut. *Rom.* 12. 3–6.
[2] From Solin. 1. 18–19.
[3] Varro, *LL* 5. 11–13 (cf. Varro in Servius on *Georg.* pr.); Arist. *Meta.* 1. 985b–986b.
[4] E.g. Arist. *Caelo* 1. 268a.
[5] See above, p. 18, n. 1. Plut. *QR* 6 has a fragment of Aristotle on Trojans in Italy assigned to the *Barb. Customs* (fr. 609 R.). F. Jacoby, *FGH* 840, F 13 and 23 accepts the possibility of an Aristotelian *Nomima Romaiōn*. See also Gabba, pp. 195–6.
[6] For instance, Varro shared Timaeos' etymology of *Italia* from *vitulus* (in Gellius, *NA* 11. 1. 1 from the *Antiquities*) which Dionysius cites from Hellanikos and rejects (1. 35). Varro very likely brought together both views but Dionysius just cites the one.

C   21

significance of the twelve vultures which appeared at Rome's inauguration. From this fact and from Plutarch's and Solinus' treatment of the horoscope cast by Tarutius for Varro's use, we assume the horoscope was intended to amplify the prediction. Now Solinus' (1. 16–19) account of Tarutius' horoscope and the inauguration of Rome accompanies Varro's (*auctor diligentissimus*) assertion that Rome was first called *Roma Quadrata* ('squared Rome') because it was laid out *ad aequilibrium*. Plutarch also knew of *Roma Quadrata* but does not immediately connect the term with Tarutius' horoscope (*Rom.* 9. 4) and Dionysius (2. 65) bases a topographical argument upon the concept of a *Roma Quadrata* which embraced only the Palatium set out in Solinus. Hence, the foundation of *Roma Quadrata*, we deduce, was also treated in the *Antiquities* of Varro. The concept of the squared Rome is integrally related to the Varronian concept of the curias which also were handled in the *Antiquities*. Thus it is time to test the method Varro followed in writing his antiquarian work.

Although the *Antiquities* perished with Augustine, Cicero has left us an illuminating statement on Varro's antiquarian research. Around 45 B.C. Cicero published his *Academics,* a dialogue between the orator, Atticus and M. Terentius Varro. At the outset Cicero praises Varro for his contributions to Latin letters. Varro responds with a statement on his debt to and connection with Greek philosophers, and he closes in saying how he tried to write in a philosophical way in the very prefaces of his *Antiquities*. The author of the dialogue pays Varro a high compliment in his own person:

Your books found us wayfaring strangers in our own city as if sojourners and led us homeward so that we could somehow learn who and where we were. You unlocked to us the secrets of our country's age, the divisions of time, sacral and priestly law, the learning of war and peace, and the names, classes, functions and causes of sites, regions, places and indeed of all divine and human matters. You have shed much light upon our poets and upon wholly Latin letters and words [Varro's linguistics] and by yourself you wrought a poem rich and polished in almost every meter [Varro's Menippean satires]. In many passages you have established a Latin philosophy which was quite enough for stimulation but too little for education. Moreover, you adduce a probable reason. For either the learned prefer to read the Greeks or the ignorant to read not even them. ...Why do those steeped in Greek literature read Latin poets and not read philosophers? Because Ennius, Pacuvius, Accius and many others give pleasure by expressing the force of Greek poets and not their words. How much greater pleasure will philosophers give if they would follow in the tracks of Plato, Aristotle and Theophrastus just as the poets after Aeschylus, Sophocles and Euripides.[1]

What survives of Cicero's book is devoted to an exposition of Varro's debt to the Greek philosophers. Cicero's letters are very enlightening on the subject of his composition of the dialogue and his method of assigning discussions to Varro, who could represent the teaching of his master Antiochus.[2] Nevertheless, Cicero's composition can be said fairly to reflect Varro's education, learning and literary aims, which were pervaded with antiquarian lore.

So fine was Cicero's tribute and so widespread was the reliance on Varro that Augustine could take no better literary work than Varro's for his historical and philosophical criticism of the pagans. Augustine preserves from Varro's *Liber de philosophia* an analysis of the 'tripartite distribution of philosophical sects' whereby Varro arrived at the conclusion that there were no less than 288 sects. There is no need to repeat the intricacies of Augustine's summary here, provided that we emphasize Varro's doubling and trebling of the duodenary number to attain his sum.[3] Augustine admired Varro's *Antiquities* and supplies us with a summary besides incidental allusions and quotations.[4] This summary makes clear that Varro himself followed his numerological penchant in arranging the books of the *Antiquities* as well as in writing the *Hebdomades*. Varro divided the whole work of forty-one books into two parts: twenty-five books of human matters and sixteen books of divine matters. Human matters were so apportioned as to give six times four according to subjects: 'In the first six he treated men, in the second six places, in the third six times, and in the fourth six things. Four times six gives twenty-four. But he prefaced them with a single book on all human matters together.' I will not repeat Augustine's report of the analyses of the division of

---

[1] *Acad.* 1. 2. 8–3. 10. Cf. Cic. *Brut.* 15. 60, 56. 205. Cicero's superlatives were picked up by almost all later authors who referred to Varro. Varro's *Antiquities* was published too late for Cicero's use in writing the *Republic* and the *Laws*. Besides his acknowledgement of Plato by his titles and to others, Cicero may have used some 'constitutions' of Dicearchus (*Ad Att.* 2. 2). In a letter to Varro written in 46 Cicero certainly expects Varro's sympathy on the subject of his *politeiai* (*Fam.* 9. 2. 5). The extent of Antiochus' teaching on the origins of states and lawgivers which his pupils, Cicero and Varro, acquired cannot be assessed: compare Cic. *Luc.* 136–7 (= Antiochus fr. 84 Luck) with *Leg.* 1. 21. 54, 1. 22. 57, 2. 6. 14–15.

[2] See O. Plasberg's preface to the Teubner edition of the *Academica* (Leipzig, 1922) where he has collected the pertinent epistolary passages and treats them in some detail, and G. Luck, *Der Akademiker Antiochos* (Diss. Bern, 1953).

[3] *CD* 19. 1.   [4] E.g. *CD* 4. 1.

the sixteen books of divine matters. The report affirms that Varro had confused his readers when he proclaimed his faith in the numerology of book publishing. Augustine believes that the division was five groups of threes making fifteen plus the one introductory book, giving a total of sixteen books on divine matters.[1] How Varro could have felt at ease with a work whose books totaled forty-one is hard to figure. Before turning to Varro's analysis of the beginning of Romulean Rome, we can but repeat Augustine (*CD* 6. 6): 'O Marce Varro, cum sis homo omnium acutissimus et sine ulla dubitatione doctissimus, sed tamen homo, non Deus, nec spiritu Dei...subvectus, cernis....'

The foregoing discussion has centered on the importance of numbers in political philosophy. Some of these numbers were theoretical inventions intended to provide a basis for an ideal state. Other numbers were drawn from the political realities of certain Hellenic city-states. From the Roman and Latin past were received the numbers three, thirty and 3,000. The Romulean state appeared to have been based upon the conception of a tripartite political and military organization: three tribes, thirty curias, and 3,000 soldiers in a full archaic levy. The Romans believed that their word *tribus* meant one-third, an etymology which enjoys linguistic warrants. However, three tribes, and three tribes only, are known to have existed only at Rome. Furthermore, we know nothing of the development of these tribes. If we examine the history of the development of the tribes that replaced the archaic three, we find that the later tribes grew in number from at least four (but probably more than four initially) to a total of thirty-five. Thirty were the historical curias, but other Latian groups of thirty, which are considered analogous, prove to be spurious on close inspection. The legion of 3,000 foot, divided into regiments of 1,000, seem to have served as the Romans' primitive army. However, this likely military organization does not lend credence to Varro's analysis of *miles* as 'thousand-man'. Both Varro and Dionysius, who are our most explicit witnesses of the archaic constitution, have left us a scheme of a primitive state which has been propounded after the manner of political theorists. What is even more

---

[1] *CD* 6. 3; cf. 6. 4–7. The fragments of the *ARH* are collected and commented on by P. Mirsch, 'De M. Terenti Varronis Antiquitatum Rerum Humanarum Libri XXV', *Leipziger Studien zur Classischen Philologie* 5 (1882), 1–144; the fragments of only a part of the *ARD* by R. Agahd. Especially the latter can be supplemented with R. Merkel, *P. Ovidii Nasonis Fastorum libri sex* (Berlin, 1841), pp. xcix–ccxlvii.

damaging to any trust in the received opinion remains the lack of any ancient feeling for a process of change in the history of the primitive state. In this respect the myth of Rome's formal foundation usurped the place of a history.

CHAPTER 3

VARRO'S SQUARED COLONY

Along with many others Varro held Rome to have been a colony of settlers duly sent out from Alba Longa to the site of the new city which Romulus ritually laid out with his plow marking its sacral boundary, or pomerium.[1] In the preceding chapter we remarked how Varro in his *Antiquities* called this archaic Palatine Rome 'Squared Rome'. Whatever Varro's interest in political numerology, here he was expounding the manual of practices carried on by Roman colonial surveyors, the *agrimensores* or *gromatici*. In 59 B.C. Varro was one of a twenty-man commission sent to lay out a colony for veterans on the land of Capua which perhaps had been without a proper civil government since the surrender and dismantlement in 211 B.C.[2] Varro had an insatiable curiosity and he could engage himself enthusiastically in whatever he pursued. No doubt both knowledge and new questions were the result of his experience with the land commission. Just the simple act and terminology of surveying titillated his linguistic skills: 'Many things our ancestors measured by duodenary number as the *actus* which comprises 12 decurias. The *iugerum* is called that because two squared *actus* are joined together. A century was called from the fact it contained 100 *iugera* at first, later the century was doubled but kept its name.' Thus Varro wrote in his *Latin Language* (5. 34–5), and doubtless erred on the last point. A century of 200 *iugera* took its name from the number of settlers and not the number of *iugera* as we shall see in a moment.

At one place Varro devoted his research to the study of land survey:

The very beginnings of boundaries come from the Etruscan lore because the haruspices divided the earth into two parts and called the northern

---

[1] *LL* 5. 143–4. The *ktisis* is found in the two oldest Roman historians Fabius Pictor (D.H. 1. 74, Plut. *Rom.* 14 = frr. 6, 7 P.) and Cincius Alimentus (D.H. 1. 74 = fr. 4 P.). For a discussion of the Greek literary predecessors of the first two Roman historians see Jacoby, pp. 284–5, nn. 73, 75 and 397–8, n. 56, who rightly stresses Pictor's and Alimentus' substantial reliance upon Greek sources, literary modes, etc.

[2] *RR* 1. 2. 10: Pliny, *NH* 7. 176; see Broughton, *The Magistrates of the Roman Republic* (vol. i, New York, 1951; vol. ii, 1952: Supplement, 1960) *s.a.* 59. An intervening colony was planned but its life was in doubt.

part the right and the southern part the left from east to west because the sun and moon face in that direction just as certain architects wrote that shrines rightly face the west. The haruspices divided the earth with another line from south to north and named the other side of this line the back and this side of the line the front. From this groundwork our ancestors seem to have established a fixed order in land measure. First, they drew two boundaries: one from east to west which they called the tenth and another from north to south which they called the hinge. Moreover the tenth used to divide the field on the right and left, the hinge on this and that side. Why a tenth from ten rather than from two since every field is divided by this boundary into two parts? Just as the ancients used to say *duopondium* and *duoviginti* for what we call *dipondium* and *viginti*, so too the *duodecumanus* ('twelfth') became the *decumanus* the 'tenth'. The hinge takes its name from the straight line of the sky according to the hinge. For the sky indubitably turns in the northern hemisphere. Later on some men followed another method because they had forgotten this.... And certain men look to the east but they are so turned around that they are going contrary to the right order. For example, in the Ager Campanus which surrounds Capua, the hinge runs eastward and the tenth southward.... At first they made a measure of land enclosed by four boundaries, often one hundred feet in both directions (this the Greeks call a *plethron*, Oscans and Umbrians a *versum*), but our ancestors wished that there be 12 ten-foot measures (*decempedae*) and marked out 120 feet in both directions so that one of the four sides was like a day of 12 hours, and a year of twelve months....Thereafter these two *iugera* when joined make one squared field because there are two *actus* in all directions etc.[1]

In his treatise on farming (1. 10) Varro naturally introduces the subject of land surveying but also interjects an historical and anti-quarian tidbit:

In Further Spain they measure (the countryside) by yokes, in Campania by *versa*, among us in Roman and Latin territory by *iugera*. They call a yoke what yoked oxen can plow in one day. They call a *versum* a hundred feet squared wheresoever one turns; a *iugerum*, what has two squared *actus*. An *actus* is squared which is 120 feet wide and long: in Latin this measure is called an *acnua*. The smallest section of a *iugerum* is called a *scripulum*, that is ten square feet.... They called an inheritance (*heredium*) the two *iugera* that were said to have been allotted by Romulus to each man because they could be inherited. Later on this was the century of one

---

[1] Varro, from Frontinus, *De limitibus* in *Röm. Feldmesser*, pp. 27–30 L. (condensed). I take all translated here to be Varronian. Some of it echoes the passage from *RR*, dis-cussed below. The Capuan information is such that Varro could have known it first-hand. The explanation of *decumanus* is purely Varronian as is the relation with temporal divisions. Cf. Hyginus, *Lim. Const.* in *Röm. Feldmesser*, p. 166 L. for more on the *disciplina haruspicum*. Frontinus, *Agr. Qual.*, pp. 5–6 L. quotes a splendid Varronian etymology of *ager arcifinius ab hostibus arcendis* (cf. *LL* 5. 151 *arx ab arcendo*). See also p. 20, n. 8.

hundred. A century is squared on all four sides so that its sides are 2400 feet long. Furthermore, the four centuries so joined that there are two on both sides are called the *saltus* in fields publicly allotted to individuals.[1]

Squaring one or another measure belongs to the surveyors' skill in plotting land for colonies.[2] In a rare political joke Varro even refers to the *septem iugera forensia*, by which he perhaps meant some colonial standard.[3] The regularly laid out Roman camp also formed a square.[4]

Now Varro's reports of the measurement in land survey and colonial allotments surely are factual even if his etymologies sometimes miss the mark. When Varro expressed the view that Romulus' foundation was *Roma Quadrata* ('Squared Rome'), he had in mind a formal, proper colony. Such colonies did exist. They were not the 'Latin' colonies but the Roman colonies, set on the coast like a camp, with 300 settlers who each received two *iugera*.[5]

Our concern for *Roma Quadrata* need go no further. Varro's preoccupation with numbers had a factual basis. But in his *Antiquities* he carried numerology beyond the bounds of actual practice into horoscopes and birthdays. Indeed, Varro doubtless knew of reckoning the years of colonies whose foundation dates were secure, unlike Rome's.[6] In one African town the *natale civitatis* was celebrated at a curial festival with a flamen in attendance.[7] According to Solinus (1. 17) Varro believed Rome was squared because it had been laid out *ad aequilibrium*. The balance was apparently maintained by assigning each colonist two *iugera*. A squared town and two measures of land calls for a colony comprising a fixed number of settlers, say for example, of 300 families. On to this stage of Roman history entered Varro's curias.

Dionysius of Halicarnassus invokes the authority of M. Terentius Varro five times: (1) *Antiquities* on the dwelling places of Aborigines

[1] Cf. Pliny, *NH* 18. 7 (who may have used Varro here; see below, p. 93, n. 2); Fest. *Epit.* 47 L.; and *RR* 1. 18. 5.
[2] E.g. *Röm. Feldmesser*, pp. 115, 122, 136, 152, 189–90, 195–6, 209–10, 215, 219, 228 245–6 L.
[3] *RR* 1. 2. 9; cf. Taylor, *Roman Voting Assemblies from the Hannibalic War to the Dictatorship of Caesar* (Ann Arbor, 1966), p. 25 and n. 28.
[4] Polyb. 6. 27–31 on which see Walbank.
[5] Livy 8. 21. 11, 32. 29. 3–5, 34. 45. 1–5. See above, p. 8, nn. 2–6, for 300 horsemen in some Latin colonies. On this interpretation of Roma Quadrata see P. Mingazzini, 'L'origine del nome di Roma ed alcune questioni topografiche attinenti ad essa: La Roma Quadrata, il sacello di Volupia, il sepolcro di Acca Larenzia', *BC* 78 (1961–2), 7–15.
[6] *ILS* 157, 5317 (= *ILLRP* 518), 9279.
[7] *ILS* 6824.

in the Ager Reatinus (1. 14), (2) *Antiquities* on the curial priesthoods (2. 21 ff.), (3) on the proper names of curias (2. 47. 3-4), (4) on the name of the Sabine town Cures, the god Quirinus and the Sabine word for spear (*curis*) (2. 48), (5) *Antiquities of Divine Matters* on Tarquinius' purchase of the Sibyl's books (4. 62). Besides these five citations I also attribute to Varro's *Antiquities* Dionysius' report of: (1) the Romulean organization of the people into three tribes and thirty curias and of the land into thirty equal parts (2. 7), (2) the Romulean cavalry of 300 Celeres (2. 13), (3) the number of settlers with Romulus at the time the colony was founded (2. 2; 2. 16), (4) the first Romulean senate of 100 elders and the second Romulean senate of 200 elders divided into decurias of ten men (2. 12; 2. 47; 2. 57).

First let us recall that Varro interpreted the *tribus* as a third, the cavalry *turma* as three times a decuria from each of the thirds, and a soldier, the *miles*, as one one-thousandth of an infantry *tribus*.[1] Varro's Squared Colony had equal lots for each man.[2] Such a division of land implies the thirty equal assignments to the thirty curias only if the number of settlers who accompanied Romulus was equal in each curia. Finally, Varro believed that Romulus' calendar year comprised only ten months.[3]

It is the thesis of Gabba and his predecessors that chapters 7-29 of the second book of Dionysius' *Roman Antiquities* go back to a tendentious political pamphlet which, Gabba argues, ought to be dated to the Sullan era. However, chapter 16 repeats the datum of chapter 2 that Romulus had 3,000 infantry and 300 cavalry settlers with him at the foundation of Rome. Chapter 2 does not come from the pamphlet. Secondly, Gabba cannot deny the possibility that Varro inspired chapter 13 since a connection with Lacedaemonian custom is made by Dionysius.[4] Thirdly, within the given limits of composition Dionysius explicitly cites Varro's *Antiquities* on curial religion described in chapters 21-2. Finally, in chapter 7 Dionysius gives a

---

[1] Above, pp. 5-6. Varro had already written his *Antiquities* when working on the *LL* (see 6. 13 and 6. 18). Although Ambrosch, *De Sacerdotibus Curialibus*. (Bratislava, 1840), pp. 1 ff., remarks on discrepancies in Dionysius' accounts of the curias in the chapters noted above, it is not a discrepancy of sources. For Varro is responsible for the etymologies and the notion of a Romulean division of equal lots to the curias of the colony in 2. 7, which chapter contradicts parts of 2. 21-3. Dionysius knew the concept of Roma Quadrata which he adduces in a context not connected with the foundation of the city although he recognized its pertinence to Romulus' wall (D.H. 2. 65. 3). See below, p. 34, n. 1.

[2] See above, pp. 27-8.   [3] *LL* 6. 33-4.   [4] Gabba, especially pp. 185-6.

29

variant linguistic analysis of the title *celeres* which he attributes to the annalist Valerius Antias. Now Peter emphasized that in three cases later authorities apparently cite Valerius Antias from Terentius Varro.[1] Moreover, in chapter 47 Dionysius reports that, since the number of Sabine women was 527, the thirty curias could not have been named after all of them and that Varro knew the proper names of the curias came from the names of persons and places. This number of Sabine women is Valerius Antias' number given by Plutarch (*Rom.* 14). Therefore, this fourth Sabine item (see last note) must have been taken by Dionysius from Varro who quoted Valerius Antias' research. If, then, chapter 7 contains a citation of Antias' opinion on the name of the *celeres* varying from that of another, the other opinion has every likelihood of being Varro's especially because Varro can be shown to have cited Antias on other occasions.

Even if this evidence on Dionysius' further use of Varro is circumstantial, we have further proof of Dionysius' debt to Varro in the chapters mentioned above. Over 120 years ago Merkel demonstrated Ovid's indebtedness to Varro's *Antiquities* in the composition of his poem on the *Fasti*.[2] Ovid's description of Romulus' ten-month year comes from Varro. According to Ovid the five-year *lustrum* lacks ten months and the year has ten months, for man has ten fingers, women carry their babies for ten months and mourn for their dead husbands ten months. Furthermore, Romulus divided 100 Fathers into ten units (*orbes*), created ten units (*orbes* or *corpora*) of *hastati, principes, pilani* and knights, and divided the Titienses, Ramnes and Luceres into ten parts. He ordained the beginnings of the year on 1 March when the houses of the priest–king and flamens and the meeting-houses of the curias were to be festooned with fresh bay leaves.[3]

Macrobius supplies the proof that this Ovidian treatment goes back to Varro who, we know from the *Latin Language* (6. 33–4), held that the original civil year had ten months whose names can be linguistically analyzed in one manner reported by Macrobius. Also, Macrobius notices the change of the bay leaves on 1 March.[4] Elsewhere in the same discussion Macrobius cites Varro's *Antiquities*

---

[1] Peter *HRR* I[2], ccxxi. The passages are: the Sabine origin of the name Ancus (*Praen.* 4); Valerius Poplicola's relation to the Sabines (Asc. on Cic. *Pis.*, p. 13 Clark); and the institution of the Ludi Saeculares by a Valerius (Cens. *DN* 17. 8).

[2] See p. 24, n. 1.   [3] *Fasti* 3. 119 ff., cf. 1. 27 ff.

[4] *Sat.* 1. 12; Varro cited at 1. 12. 13, 27.

of Divine Matters, Book 5, on Janus Quirinus whose epithet comes from the Sabine word for spear, *curis*. This etymology of Quirinus and of the town Cures is also met in Ovid and Dionysius.[1]

Let us return to Dionysius' account of the Romulean constitution. First of all, the number of settlers, 3,000 foot and 300 horse, is necessary to the equal political and agricultural divisions (2. 2. 4; 2. 16. 2). Dionysius' three tribes have ten curias which contain ten decurias of men, who live on the thirty greater lots of land (2. 7). These three tribes are thirds, in Greek *trittyes*. Varro's *tribus* is also a third. The 300 *celeres* were constituted of ten men from each curia. Valerius Antias' analysis of the word *celeres* is given as the minority opinion. Their style of fighting was a Lacedaemonian tradition (2. 13). The etymology of *celeres*, the citation of Valerius Antias and the reference to Lacedaemonian usage are certainly redolent of Varro. Are the military divisions of chapter 7 which are implicit here in the curial contingents of ten men also Varronian? Ovid reports that the cavalrymen had ten *corpora*, like the *hastati*, *principes* and *pilani*. Ten *corpora* must be Varro's *turmae* of three decurias of horsemen whereby each one of the three tribes assigns one decuria to the *turma*.[2] Ovid's Titienses, Ramnes and Luceres are divided by Romulus into ten parts each. Dionysius' three tribes are divided into ten curias. Ovid's account of the tribes' parts follows upon his mention of the ten divisions of knights and warriors. Presumably Ovid's tribes and their parts were military and certainly Dionysius' tribes and curias were military.

Ovid's Romulean senate contained 100 Fathers divided into ten decurias (*orbes*, for the sake of the meter). Dionysius' earlier Romulean senate has 100 men (2. 12) to which another 100 were added after T. Tatius brought his Sabines into the Roman state (2. 47) and this later Romulean senate was divided into decurias of ten men for the sake of the interregnum (2. 57). Not only are both the latter chapters outside the influence of Dionysius' pamphleteering source, but in chapter 47 Dionysius cites Varro on the origin of curial names and Valerius Antias' number of Sabine women without giving the latter's name just as in chapter 7 he mentions Valerius Antias without the names of those holding an opposite view on the origin of the title *celeres*. Dionysius mentions the decurias of the Fathers in relation to the senate at the time of Romulus' death when the interregnum took

---

[1] *Fasti* 2. 475 ff.; D.H. 2. 48, also citing Varro; *Sat.* 1. 9. 16.   [2] *LL* 5. 91.

on importance while Ovid simply adduces the ten decurias of the senate of 100 Fathers to demonstrate the esteem in which the number 10 was held when the ten-month year was created by Romulus.

The analysis demonstrates that the numbers of men and divisions supposed for the Romulean constitution are owed to Varro's *Antiquities of Divine Matters* which Dionysius explicitly cites even when following the tendentious pamphlet and which Ovid and Macrobius also used. Although all three authorities cite or draw on others than Varro, there is no other source attributable to the material under discussion which is common to all three authors. Of this we can be sure because Dionysius and Macrobius frequently do mention their authorities throughout the relevant passages.

To summarize Dionysius' description of the colony of Rome. At the outset Romulus had 3,300 subjects, 3,000 infantrymen and 300 horsemen. He divided the colonists into three larger groups called tribes which equal the Greek *phylai* or *trittyes*. Their commanders were tribunes whom Greeks would call phylarchs or trittyarchs. The tribes were divided by Romulus into ten parts called curias which are the equals of the Greek phratries or *lochoi* ('companies'). Their captains were curions whom the Greeks would call phratriarchs or *lochagoi*. Each of these thirty divisions were in turn subdivided into ten parts commanded by decurions. Thus we have three infantry units; three tribes of 1,000 men each; thirty curias of 100 men each; and 300 decurias of ten men each. Dionysius' translation of Latin *tribus* by Greek *trittys* is an etymological equation based upon some linguist's speculation. We can attribute the analysis *tribus* < *tres* either to Varro or to Curiatius whose work is cited by Festus (see p. 7, n. 2), but to no other known author. In any event Dionysius does not cite Curiatius whereas he cites Varro. On the other hand, the regular and normal Greek translation of *tribus* is *phyle* and of *tribunus, chiliarchos*. Varro (*LL* 5. 81) derived *tribunus* directly from three (*terni tribus tribubus*).

Romulus' cavalry of Celeres numbered 300 men. Each of the thirty curias supplied a decuria of horsemen. The whole force had a leader under whom served three centurions, commanders of 100. This system Romulus took from the Lacedaemonians.[1]

He apportioned equal lots (*klēroi isoi*) to the thirty curias which supplied the horse and foot so that the division both of men and

[1] Cf. Serv. Dan. on *Aen.* 11. 602.

territory evinced the greatest communal *isotēs*. The 'equality' of which Dionysius speaks was doubtless based upon Romulus' initial foundation of *Roma Quadrata* which, Solinus' report of Varro states, was set out *ad aequilibrium*. The equal curial lots imply the allotment of two *iugera* for each colonist which Varro attributes to Romulus (see above, p. 27). Also they presuppose knowledge of the curial lands whose boundary markers are remarked by a single author who perhaps followed Varro (see below, p. 93, n. 2).

Romulus arranged that each of the thirty curias were to elect two men to administer curial religion. Qualifications for the office required the priests to be 50 years old, of good family and without physical impairment. In return for their religious administration these sixty priests enjoyed a life term and exemption from military and political offices.[1] The thirty curions comprised one-half of these sixty curial priests.[2]

At once, the two flaws in Varronian political numerology destroy the Romulean system insofar as the curias are involved. First, curions who were exempt from military service and have assumed office at the age of 50 years could not have commanded a curial century of troops. This is clear from the internal evidence. Secondly, from the external evidence, as we shall see later, the curias which were simply military centuries of adult males could have been multiplied by Servius Tullius who, universal tradition implicitly records, exercised his royal authority to supplant the curial centuries of soldiers with mere centuries of soldiers. If curias had been no more than military centuries, there was no need to create centuries. If curions were no more than military centurions, then they could not have been exempt from military service.

Roma Quadrata, a colony of regular territorial size and population, was an invention of Varro's. The putative founder assigned two measures of land to each colonist, divided the colonists and the land into thirty equal parts. The thirty sections handled conscription for their units of infantry and cavalry and provided the curial citizen with appropriate religious rites. Indeed, Varro based himself on certain factual data such as on the century of 100 infantry and of 200 *iugera* of land, on the decuria of ten horsemen (there is no evi-

---

[1] Varro in D.H. 2. 21. Below we devote an entire chapter to curial religion. See Gabba, pp. 189–90.

[2] Cf. D.H. 2. 64. 1, 2. 65. 4. See below, pp. 80–1.

dence of infantry decurias), and perhaps on the *tribus* which may or may not have been originally a 'third' of the land and of the infantry force.

Varro's analysis bears a resemblance to the primitive Athenian system described by Aristotle and cited in the previous chapter:

Athens		*Rome*
4	phylai/tribes	3
12	phratries/curias	30
360	clans	(300?)
10,800	adult males	3,300

Of course the two descriptions differ. Aristotle started from a given of four Ionian *phylai*, Varro from a given of three tribes. Thence, Aristotle followed a regular solar–lunar calendar whereas Varro proceeded to the next given of thirty curias and to his notion of a Roman colony of 300 families from which came Romulus' army of 3,000 foot and 300 horse. His divergence did not trouble Varro because Romulus' calendar year notoriously comprised ten months which could also be related to the army. Also Varro transferred the temporal divisions to the division of land since he could not attribute them to the divisions of the people.

Because we may learn from other systems, in the next chapter we examine certain other ancient organizations dated to comparable stages in the development of their primitive societies. Suffice it to emphasize the incorrigible fact that the squared or quadrangular Palatine settlement of Romulus with its number and organization of settlers was excogitated from certain practices in colonial foundations and did not historically set a precedent for such foundations.[1]

---

[1] Thus D. H. (1. 88, cf. 2. 65) has accepted squared Rome as the precedent for historical colonial foundations rather than the product of those foundations.

CHAPTER 4

OTHER SYSTEMS

Students of a state's primitive history rightly ask themselves what happened in other states at roughly the same stage of political development. It seems necessary to put before the reader materials which have at least a superficial bearing upon the Romans' archaic tribes and curias. It is equally necessary to emphasize that the very comparative method which inheres in any presentation of this kind has its roots in the antiquity discussed in this book. It is a valuable exercise and its results illumine but they do not offer proof.

A state which intends to defend itself from an external enemy must arrange for an armed force. If a state does not exist, no regular, permanent military system exists. Primitive societies lack chroniclers to transmit to posterity a description of their organizations. In many cases, the scanty gleanings in ancient authors leave the impression that uncoordinated bands under a local leader assumed the defense of his and theirs. A state which may or may not have emerged from a union of such elements may function for the sole purpose of co-ordinating the adult males in concerted ventures of defense and aggression.

THE ISRAELITE SYSTEM

A kingdom of Israel became the aspiration of the Hebrews of the Twelve Tribes at the time of Saul. This writer has no particular competence to evaluate the Old Testament's record. Samuel, in the tradition opposed to the kingship, foretold that one disadvantage of a king would be his appointment of captains of the thousands and of the fifties (1 Sam. 8:12). Needless to say, such a military system is put back into prehistoric times. In a representation having folklore similarities with Homer's account of Nestor's advice to Agamemnon on the army marshalled by tribes and phratries, the author of Exodus 18:19 f. (cf. Dt. 1:15) has Moses' father-in-law Jethro counsel a political division into thousands, hundreds, fifties and tens over which their several rulers will dispense justice. According to Josephus' *Jewish Antiquities* (3. 70–2), a work in the tradition of Varro and Dionysius, the father-in-law, now named only Raguel (one of his Old Testament names), advises Moses to impose the same division. But Josephus not only adds thirties and twenties to the other numerical units but also makes these divisions military units, a notion absent from Ex. 18 where they are units for administering justice. Despite these references to the system in the pre-Palestinian period, I believe that the institution was regal and was inspired by the Philistinian system of the so-called Pentapolis. Samuel's prophecy came true and Saul had a census taken which indicated 300,000 Israelites and 30,000 Judaites. Whereupon the new king arrayed them all into three regiments (1 Sam. 11:8–11). In an actual campaign against the Philistines Saul enlisted 3,000 men of which 1,000 served under Jonathan and 2,000 under himself. The Philistines who met him were arrayed by 30,000 chariots, 6,000 horsemen and a host like the sand on the seashore. In flight Saul found a mere 600 men had accompanied him to face three regiments of Philistines (1 Sam. 13). Saul took another head count and found 200,000 infantrymen and 10,000 Judaites (1 Sam. 15:4). In flight from Saul David first commanded a band of 400 irregulars. Saul taunted his men by asking whether David would put them in charge of thousands and hundreds (1 Sam. 22:2, 7). With about 600 men David turned against the Philistines (1 Sam. 23:13). These he divided into two companies: one of 400 to fight and one of 200 to guard the camp (1 Sam. 25:13, 30:10, cf. 27:2). Saul, who commanded regular forces, had 3,000 (1 Sam. 24:2, 26:2). The army of Philistines which David joined arrayed itself against Saul by thousands and hundreds (1 Sam. 29:2).

When David was king, 600 men of Gath fled with him from Absalom (2 Sam. 15:18). David's army, in this writer's opinion, represents a system developed by the son of Jesse after years of fighting with and against the Philistines. Against Absalom David divided his army into three parts under three generals and yet the king's army marched by thousands and hundreds (2 Sam. 18:1–4). The 23rd chapter of 2 Samuel is entirely devoted to the subject of the three mighty men with David and the thirty chieftains, and includes their names; the greatest man of the three earned his priority because he had slain 300 men. When David ordered his census it took a month (twenty-nine days) and yielded 800,000 Israelites and 500,000 Judaites (2 Sam. 24:8–9).

Solomon had twelve overseers each serving one month of the year. Every day Solomon's household received thirty measures of fine flour and sixty measures of coarse flour. Solomon's proverbs numbered 3,000, his songs 1,005. (1 Kings 4.) Solomon in his wisdom levied 30,000 men. Of these 10,000 worked every month in Lebanon, 20,000 in Israel. Another 30,000 served him as carriers and 40,000 as hewers. In charge of his levy Solomon put 3,300 overseers (1 Kings 5). His harem embraced 700 wives and 300 concubines (1 Kings 11:3).

The author of Chronicles, of course, has a greater amount of detail to relate. For instance, the 7th chapter of 1 Chronicles contains the genealogies, names, and numbers of household chieftains and the total number of family warriors. All of the numbers are rounded at hundreds and all too large. The division into troops of 1,000 and 100 is interpreted by the Chronicler to have been co-ordinated by David into monthly service so that the total was 24,000 (1 Chron. 27:1–15, 28:1; cf. 1 Chron. 11–13).

No clear picture emerges from these Old Testament figures. Many numbers are exaggerated. Except for the military forces and perhaps more modest sums of the labor forces, the totals given in round numbers demand no credence. The military organization in Palestine seems to have been based upon decimal units of 1,000, 100, and 50. The three regiments perhaps had no more than 1,000 men each. Hence, the three commanders of the thousands probably directed ten captains of the hundreds who would have been David's thirty mighty men. What relation, if any, the thousands, hundreds and fifties bore to the twelve tribes is hard to imagine. The tribes varied much in size and strength, and could hardly have been expected to supply the same number of soldiers. Finally, the Israelite organization cannot be translated into classical terms because we are not dealing with the communities of city-states or their forebears.

HELLENIC SYSTEMS

The variety of constitutional developments in Greek states and the paucity of our evidence of themselves hardly warrant the little space we can devote to the tribes (*phylai*) and brotherhoods (*phratrai*). The Dorian states usually had three tribes and Ionian states four. Below the tribe were ranged the phratries. Homer has Nestor counsel

D

Agamemnon to array the troops by tribes and phratries (*Il.* 2. 362–3) which advice Agamemnon praises and ignores. A recent suggestion by Andrewes makes the phratry as a military unit an aristocratic device of the ninth and eighth centuries but interpolated into the heroic age.[1] Later we shall remark on some western Greek phratries.[2] Despite the evidence adduced in an earlier chapter from the philosophers[3] there is no reliable historical evidence for the numerical regularity or relation to the tribes. Varro and Dionysius viewed the curias as relics of the archaic age which primarily served a religious function. The phratries served a like function although they had once been the basis of conscription and yielded military companies. The latter function of Greek phratries could have suggested a similar role for the Roman curias after an identification was made on the criterion of the religious similarity.

Elsewhere in the *Iliad* (16. 168–210) Homer describes the Myrmidon force. On each of fifty ships were fifty men. Under Achilles' command were five captains of the units called *stichoi*. The *stichos*, however, does not belong to any known political system. Like the Israelite decimal units, it may well have been a military unit at one time.

THE ETRUSCAN SYSTEMS

Festus (358 L.) describes the content of the Etruscans' *Libri Rituales* as directions on: with what rite cities are founded, altars and temples consecrated, how to sanctify walls and gates lawfully, how tribes, curias and centuries are arranged, armies founded and arrayed and all else of such character pertaining to war and peace. Insofar as such a manual might have made a practical contribution to political organization the *municipia* which Rome sponsored in non-Italic cities had voting units of curias that doubtless were artificially organized.[4]

[1] A. Andrewes, 'Phratries in Homer' and 'Philochoros', *JHS* 81 (1961), 1–15 in which he also discusses clans, clansmen, and the loose application of kinship terms. See also p. 16, n. 1, and W. G. Forrest, *The Emergence of Greek Democracy* (New York, 1966), chapter 2.
[2] See below, pp. 155–6. [3] Above, pp. 14–16.
[4] *Lex Municipii Tarentini*, line 15 (*CIL* I², 590 = *ILS* 6086 = *FIRA* I², no. 18); *Lex Municipii Malacitani* sects. 52, 53, 55–7, 59 (*CIL* II, 1964 = *ILS* 6089 = *FIRA* I², no. 24); and twenty-three curias at Turris Libisonis on Sardinia (*CIL* x, 7953 = *ILS* 6766 quoted below, p. 59). Cf. Pliny, *NH* 3. 85: 'colonia Turris Libisonis'. Curias are frequently attested by inscriptions from Roman Africa.

According to Vergil his native Mantua was a *gens illi triplex, populi sub gente quaterni*.[1] Servius comments that Mantua had three tribes with four curias, each of which was commanded by a *lucumo* and then that all Etruria was divided into twelve peoples like prefectures commanded by *lucumones*.[2] Elsewhere, he translates the second kind of *lucumo* with Latin *rex*.[3] This interpretation rests upon the Twelve Etruscan Peoples who annually sacrificed together.[4]

Servius' first interpretation hardly fits the Vergilian passage (*Aen.* 10. 201–3):

> Mantua, dives avis, sed non genus omnibus unum:
> gens illi triplex, populi sub gente quaterni,
> ipsa caput populis, Tusco de sanguine vires.

Although I should like to believe that Servius and his predecessors knew curias were *populi*, I cannot agree with Servius. Mantua was blessed with many ancestors but all of them did not belong to one race (*genus*). She has three distinct stocks which lord it over four states. Mantua, herself the head of the league of states, takes her strength from her Etruscan blood. The three stocks which composed Mantua are not far to seek. Servius himself tells us that Mantua was blessed with many ancestors because it was first founded by Thebans, then Etruscans and finally by Gauls or, as some claim, by the Sarsinates who settled Perugia. The ancestors share no one origin because they stem from the Etruscans who ruled Mantua, and the Veneti in whose territory it was situated but is now called Cisalpine Gaul.[5] Vergil certainly considered *sanguis Tuscus* the most important of the three stocks and presumably also had in mind the Veneti and Galli. Aside from the nonsense about tribes and curias, Servius' analysis of line 202 conforms to what Vergil wrote and he had written on lines 200 and 201: 'omnium populorum principatum Mantua possidebat: unde est "ipsa caput populi" '. Servius' analysis of three tribes and twelve curias must be referred to an overactive imagination. What Vergil meant was this: Mantua ruled over a league of twelve cities like the more famous league in South Etruria. There were four cities of each of the three nations which also comprised Mantua herself.

---

[1] *Aen.* 10. 202.   [2] On *Ibid.* 10. 202.
[3] On *Ibid.* 2. 278; cf. on *Ibid.* 8. 475, 11. 9.
[4] See J. Heurgon, 'L'état étrusque', *Historia* 6 (1957), 86–93. Later there were fifteen peoples; cf. *ILS* 1429, 5013, 6576, 6615.
[5] On *Aen.* 10. 201; cf. on 200. According to Pliny, *NH* 3. 130, Mantua was the only Etruscan city remaining across the Po River in Venetian territory. Cf. Serv. pr. to *Aen.*: 'civis Mantuanus, quae civitas est Venetiae'.

One curia from one Etruscan town is known and will be discussed at the end of the chapter.

Although its name does not illustrate the kind of civic or military organization we have just examined, the name of the community Septem Pagi which lay across the River Tiber opposite Rome demonstrates how fragile are theories based on numbers and how a single community might be formed out of several. According to the tradition Septem Pagi ('Seven Districts') at first belonged to the state of Veii, became Roman, was recovered by Veii and finally incorporated in the Ager Romanus.[1] It is thought to have belonged to the Roman tribe Romilia.[2] The name Romilia would have certified the Roman character of the land across the Tiber.[3] Septem Pagi, as a name, shows archaic synoecism as does the Etruscan town Novem Pagi.[4] A similar union on a lower level is evidenced by an altar bearing this inscription: T. Quinctius Q. f., L. Tulli[us – – f. – –] Caltili(us) Calt(iliae) l., mag(istri) de duobus pageis et vicei Sulpicei.[5]

The report of the Etruscan *Handbooks of Rites and Ceremonies* does not truly represent evidence of Etruscan political systems. The Servian commentary on Vergil hardly conforms to the poet's intention and bears the marks of political theory. But for the solitary curia from one Etruscan town we would not know that any Etruscan community had an organizational unit that could be rendered by the Latin *curia*. Our knowledge of the communal organization of the towns according to constituencies can be extrapolated from the names 'Seven Districts' and 'Nine Districts'. These, however, tell us little about any or all primitive Etruscan states.

THE IGUVINE SYSTEM

Although the evidence of the Iguvine Tables does not bear directly on the problem of sources and tradition of the Roman curias, their

---

[1] D.H. 2. 55. 5, 5. 31. 4, 5. 36. 4, 5. 65. 3 (cf. Livy 2. 13–14): Plut. *Rom.* 25. 5. The Greek authors render Latin *pagus* 'district' by Greek *pagoi* 'hills'.

[2] De Sanctis, *Storia dei Romani*, II[2] (Florence, 1960), 118–19; Taylor, 'Voting Districts', p. 5, n. 9. The *pagi* Succusanus and Lemonius became Roman tribes; Taylor, 'Voting Districts', pp. 5–6.

[3] Above, p. 5, n. 5.

[4] Pliny, *NH* 3. 52 in an alphabetical list which assures the name. Cf. *ILLRP* 1271c wherein a single college of four mayors sets up a dedication to the one Jupiter Victor of Decem Pagi and *ILLRP* 719 wherein a dedication to Jupiter Compages.

[5] *CIL* VI, 2221 = 32452 = I[2], 1002 = *ILS* 6078 = *ILLRP* 702.

priestly records from Umbrian Iguvium contribute much to our knowledge of Italic civil and religious structure. The archives of the Atiedian Brotherhood survive to us in part. Understanding of their text has been improved within the past generation. Frequently in our examination of curial religion among the early Romans we shall have occasion to demonstrate Iguvine analogues. For now it suffices to detail the structure of the Iguvine state in general and to set forth the limitations of the inscribed testimony on any estimation of archaic Roman affairs.

The entirety of Iguvium finds mention in the Tables from four aspects: *totas, trifu, puplum* and *numem*. Except for the first word all are used by the Romans in the same or a similar way: *trifu* corresponds to *tribum, puplum* to *populum*, and *numem* to *nomen*. The state as a community of all the citizens is designated by *totas* which Latin *civitas* exactly renders without doubt.[1] The use of Umbrian *numem* is exactly paralleled in the Latin use of *nomen* as in *nomen Latinum*. However, the Umbrian correspondence with the Roman *populus* and *tribus* was perhaps lost because of semantic shifts in Latin. But despite these shifts we shall see that the archaic Latin usage approximates that of Iguvium.

One passage from the Iguvine Tables, which is by no means unique in the archives, amply illustrates the Iguvine distinctions:

Prestota Šerfia Šerfer Martier, tiom esir vesclir adrir popluper totar iiouinar, totaper iiouina, erer nomneper, erar nomneper. Prestota Šerfia Šerfer Martier, preuendu uia ecla atero tote tarsinate, trifo tarsinate, tursce, naharce, iabusce nomne, totar tarsinater, trifor tarsinater, tuscer, naharcer, iabuscer nomner, nerus šitir anšihitir, iouies hostatir anostatir, ero nomne. Prestota Šerfia Šerfer Martier, futu fons pacer pase tua pople totar iiouinar, tote iiouine, erom nomne, erar nomne, erar nerus šihitir anšihitir, iouies hostatir anostatir. Prestota Šerfia Šerfer Martier, saluom seritu poplom totar iiouinar, salua serituu totam iiouinam. Prestota Šerfia Šerfer Martier, saluo seritu popler totar iiouinar, totar iiouinar nome, nerf, arsmo, viro pequo castruo, frif. salua seritu futu fons pacer pase tua pople totar iiouinar, tote iiouine, erer nomne, erar nomne. Prestota Šerfia Šerfer Martier, tiom esir vesclir adrer popluper totar iiouinar, totaper iouina, erer nomneper, erar nomneper.

Prestota Serfia of Serfus Martius, thee (I invoke) with these black vessels for the *populus* of the state of Iuguvium, for the state of Iguvium, for the name of the *populus*, for the name of the state. Prestota Serfia of Serfus

[1] These words, with full references, may be found in Poultney's index, *The Bronze Tables of Iguvium* (1959), pp. 313, 318, 328, 329; their form in our text is that of this index.

Martius, in every way turn thou evil against the Tadinate state, the
Tadinate tribe, the Tuscan, Narcan and Iapudic name, against the senior
warriors with swords and without swords, against the young men under
arms and not under arms, of the Tadinate state, of the Tadinate tribe, of
the Tuscan, Narcan and Iapudic name, and against their name. Prestota
Serfia of Serfus Martius, be favorable and propitious with thy peace
to the *populus* of the state of Iguvium, to the state of Iguvium, to their name,
to the name of the state, to its senior warriors with swords and without
swords, to its young men under arms and not under arms. Prestota
Serfia of Serfus Martius, keep safe the *populus* of the state of Iguvium, keep
safe the state of Iguvium, Prestota Serfia of Serfus Martius, keep safe the
name of the *populus* of the state of Iguvium, (the name) of the state of
Iguvium, keep safe the warriors, the priesthoods, the lives of men and
beasts, the fruits. Be favorable and propitious with thy peace to the
populus of the state of Iguvium, to the state of Iguvium, to the name of
the *populus*, to the name of the state. Prestota Serfia of Serfus Martius,
thee (I invoke) with these black vessels for the *populus* of the state of
Iguvium, for the state of Iguvium, for the name of the *populus*, for the
name of the state.[1]

The Iguvine state and the Iguvine *populus* here are not identical.
The 'young men under arms and not under arms' (*iouies hostatir
anostatir*, i.e. Latin *iuvenibus hastatis inhastatis*) represent the citizens
eligible for, and active in, military service. As we shall see, Latin
populus originally meant the 'army' and most probably the centuriate
army.[2] Mention of the elder warriors and young men can be related
to mention of the *populus*. The priority of the *populus* in these prayers
is explained by the prominence of the young men and the elder
warriors and by the Martial deity to whom the prayers are addressed.
But, most important of all, these ceremonies belong to the lustration
of only the *populus* (vib, 48) during which the men of Iguvium are
ordered to arrange themselves in priestly and military ranks (vib,
56, on which see Poultney). The Iguvine *populus* is a part of the state,
it is not the state itself, as the formula *popluper totar iiovinar totaper
iiovina* (i.e. Latin *populo civitatis Iguvinae, civitati Iguvinae*[3]) demonstrates.
Nor is it the entire citizen-body. If it were, emphasis would not fall
on the elder warriors, the young men and the military ranks. In
Roman terms these two age groups are the *seniores* and *iuniores*. The
order to array themselves in priestly ranks as well as military ranks

[1] viia, 9–19. Cf. ib, 2, 5, 10, 40; vib, 58–62; viia, 3, 6, and *passim*. The translation is
Poultney's except for minor changes and the rendering of *populus* and *nerus šitir anšihitur*.
[2] Below, pp. 157–60. Latin *iuvenes* (cf. *iuniores*) frequently has the special sense of soldier.
[3] The Romans expressed a similar idea differently: *populus Romanus Quiritium*.

seems to arise from two causes. At Rome certain priests such as the Dial flamen could not serve in or with the army. If a similar situation were to be found at Iguvium, then some priests remained outside military ranks. Secondly, lustrations required at least the attendance of priests who may have been passively involved in the purificatory rites. On the other hand, if the Iguvine *populus* was the entire citizen-body as the Latin word signifies in later times, we must assume either the same semantic development as occurred among the Romans or a direct borrowing from the Latin. Iguvine and Latin share the same peculiar sense of *nomen*. However, the Iguvine *trifo* must differ from the Latin *tribus* at the time of the Tables' inscription. Also, Latin does not know the Oscan–Umbrian sense of *totas*. On the contrary, if *totas* is cognate with Latin *totus* ('all'), the Iguvine *totas* signifies the entire citizen body. Therefore, the possibility of a semantic development of *puplum* parallel to the Latin remains, but is remote.

In this passage the *trifor* is not Iguvine. Both here and in the similar prescriptions of Table ib, 10 ff. the Tadinate state and Tadinate *trifor* are to be cursed. Since both curses stand in a lustration of the *populus*, they offer an analogue to the Romans' *Poplifugia* (below, chapter 9).

Iguvium's *trifu*, however, is attested twice in prayers for sacrifices to Jupiter and Pomonus Poplicus on behalf of the Atiedian Brothers, the fire-carriers(?), the Iguvine state and the Iguvine *trifu* (III, 19–31). These prayers are quoted below in full. We are sure that Iguvium had only one *trifu*[1] and was unlike archaic Rome for which three are attested. Hence, it is improbable that the words *trifu* and *tribus* ought to be linguistically related to the Indo-European word for three. At Rome and elsewhere *tribus* designates a territory. At Iguvium it is not a territorial division of the state, but the whole territory. Therefore, it would correspond to the Ager Romanus which was divided into *tribus*.[2] The sacrifice to Pomonus, a deity of vegetation, agrees with the sense of *trifu* as land. Lastly, 'the young men

---

[1] See Poultney on vib, 53–4; Momigliano, 'An Interim Report on the Origins of Rome', *JRS* 53 (1963), 116, and above, p. 5, n. 4.

[2] Latin *tribus* was also a military unit (see pp. 152 ff.). Hereafter Umbrian *trifu* and Latin *tribus* are rendered by English 'tribe' even though we colloquially no longer use the word in the ancient sense. A reader suggests to me that contamination of the root *treb-> Latin *trabs*, Germanic *daurp* with *tribhu-> Latin *tribus*, Umbrian *trifo* may have taken place. In Oscan *triibum* means 'house' and a derivative verb means 'to build', whereas the related Umbrian verb, *trebeit* (via, 8), means 'to stay in'.

43

under arms and not under arms of the Tadinate tribe' in the Iguvine curses may be the full Tadinate military levy since the pre-hoplite Roman army evidently consisted of three tribes of soldiers levied from three tribes of land and commanded by three tribunes. Otherwise the bane is asked for the territory of the Tadinate state.

The generic name of the communal units at Iguvium presents a more complicated problem than the generic names for the state as a whole. Two sections of the Iguvine Tables require close scrutiny together. The older section has been adduced in demonstration of decimal organization in the three archaic Roman tribes.[1] The older section cannot be understood without the later section.

Semenies tekuries sim kaprum upetu⟨ta⟩ tekvias fameřias pumperias XII. 'Atiieřiate, etre Atiieřiate, Klaverniie, etre Klaverniie, Kureiate, etre Kureiate, Satanes, etre Satane, Peieřiate, etre Peieřiate, Talenate, etre Talenate, Museiate, etre Museiate, Iuieskane, etre Iuieskanes, Kaselate, etre Kaselate, tertie Kaselate, Peraznanie,' teitu. Ařmune Iuve Patre fetu.

At the decurial festival of Semo the decurias (and) the twelve troops of five slaves shall choose a pig and a he-goat. Say: 'For the Atiedias and for the Second Atiedias, for the Clavernii and for the Second Clavernii, for the Cureias and for the Second Cureias, for the Satani and for the Second Satani, for the Peiersias and for the Second Peiersias, for the Talenas and for the Second Talenas, for the Museias and for the Second Museias, for the Juvescani and for the Second Juvescani, for the Casilas, for the Second Casilas, and for the Third Casilas, and for the Peraznanii.' Sacrifice to Jupiter Arsmo.[2]

The adjective *tekuries* may be a borrowing from Latin; the difficulties in *tekvias* are monumental[3] What is certain about *tekvias* is the lack of secure connection with the ten names and twenty communal units which editors variously call *tekvias*, *decuviae* or *decuriae*. The

[1] iib, 1–7, vb, 8–18. The former is quite old, the latter a later addition which conforms with the early evidence. See Poultney, pp. 22–4.

[2] iib, 1–7. The translation of lines 1–2 is Palmer's 'The Censors of 312 B.C. and the State Religion', *Historia* 14 (1965), 300 where the sense of *fameřias pumpeřias* is discussed, pp. 298–300. My views are modified only to the extent of the present discussion of *tekvias*. The textual emendation upetu⟨ta⟩ is suggested by Palmer, *loc. cit.* The rest of the translation (lines 3–7) is Poultney's without his interpolation of *decuvia*; his commentary should be consulted. A. J. Pfiffig, 'Religio Iguvina', *Oesterreich. Akad. d. Wissensch. Philos.-hist. Kl.* 84 (1964), 65 offers more or less the same interpretation as Devoto and Poultney.

[3] See Poultney, pp. 190–3; E. Vetter, *Handbuch der italischen Dialekte*, 1 (Heidelberg, 1953) translates it *munificae*; A. Ernout, *Le Dialecte ombrien* (Paris, 1961) considers *tekuries* a possible borrowing from Latin (p. 63) and *tekvias* a word of uncertain meaning (p. 133). In his lexicon on pp. 65–7 Ernout discusses the proper names of iib, 2–7. In Buck, *A Grammar of Oscan and Umbrian* (Boston, n.d. [1928]), no. 3, an inscription of Pompeian public works is met, the *via Dekkviarim* ('Decurial Street'), which Buck, p. 240 (cf. p. 139), thinks was named after a building called the Decuria.

attribution of the generic word to the ten proper names and their divisions is purely inferential. Of these ten proper names six are toponymous and singular (in Latinized form, Atiedias, Cureias, Peiersias, Talenas, Museias and Casilas), two are gentilicial and plural (Clavernii and Peraznanii), and two are plural and are either toponymous or gentilicial (Satani and Juvescani). Their forms will take on importance in an analysis of the names of Roman curias. Eight communal units have been divided once, the ninth has been divided twice (Casilas) and the tenth has remained untouched (Peraznanii). The first eight then display the same pattern. The last two are exceptional. The facts that no generic name at all is applied to the proper nouns and that the last two units of the supposed ten are in a sense exceptions already undermine the putative decimal organization.

The later passage from the Tables which must be compared with this contains a contract between the Atiedian Brothers and two of these communal units to insure a supply of sacral grain:

Clauerniur dirsas herti fratrus Atiersir posti acnu farer opeter p. IIII agre Tlatie Piquier Martier, et śesna homonus duir puri far eiscurent, ote a. VI. Claverni dirsans herti frater Atiersiur Sehmenier dequrier pelmner sorser posti acnu vef. X cabriner uef. V pretra toco postra fahe, et śesna, ote a. VI. Casilos dirsa herti fratrus Atiersir posti acnu farer opeter p. VI. agre Casiler Piquier Martier, et śesna homonus duir puri far eiscurent, ote a. VI. Casilate dirsans herti frateer Atiersiur Sehmenier dequrier pelmner sorser posti acnu uef. XV cabriner uef. VIIS, et śesna, ote a. VI.

The Clavernii are required to give to the Atiedian Brothers each year four pounds of choice spelt from the Ager Tlatius of Picus Martius, and dinner for the two men who come to fetch the spelt, or else (to give) six *asses*. The Atiedian Brothers are required to give to the Clavernii at the decurial festival of Semo each year ten portions of pork and five portions of goat-meat, the former pickled, the latter roasted, and dinner, or six *asses*. The Casilas is required to give to the Atiedian Brothers each year six pounds of choice spelt from the Ager Casilas of Picus Martius, and dinner for the two men who come to fetch the spelt, or else (to give) six *asses*. The Atiedian Brothers are required to give to the Casilas at the decurial festival of Semo each year fifteen portions of pork and seven and a half portions of goat-meat, and dinner, or six *asses*.[1]

---

[1] vb, 8–18. The translation is Poultney's except that the interpolation of *decuvia* is omitted and the last dinner is restored to the translation according to the Umbrian text. For our purposes the word *vef.* (which here is treated as an abbreviation), rendered 'portion', needs further study.

At once the relation between the numbers of pounds of grain and of portions of meat and the number of divisions of the two communal units attracts attention. From what was certainly commonly owned land each division provides two pounds of spelt. The Clavernii (masc. nom. pl.), constituting two divisions, give four pounds and receive in return ten portions of pork and five of goat meat; the Casilas (fem. nom. sg.), constituting three divisions, gives six pounds of grain and receives fifteen portions of pork and seven and a half portions of goat meat. If we were to forget the necessity of sacral grain, the price would seem high. Probably these portions of meat, even if whole animals, did not suffice all the citizens in the five divisions of Clavernii and Casilas. If *vef.* equals whole animal the price is exorbitant. The possibility of a *vef.* greater than standard weight of a whole animal is precluded.

Semo's festival was decurial. The word can and does mean only 'group of ten', usually ten men. The meat is enough for ten or fifteen men, particularly if the *vef.* was but a serving or any standard weight less than a standard weight of a whole beast. Herds of pigs and goats are implied in IIb, 1. But a herd of twenty-six pigs and a herd of fourteen goats appear enormous expenditures for Semo and the units which were remunerated for ten pounds of grain, no matter how choice and sacred.[1] Only the decurias, one from Clavernii and one from Casilas, must have received (and eaten) the meat on behalf of Casilas I, II, and III and Clavernii I and II. Each man received one *vef.* of pork and one-half *vef.* of goat meat. We can further say that Casilas I, II and III were each represented by five men. The Atiedian Brotherhood itself was divided into two *puntes*, 'groups of five men', when they elected the *uhtur* (Latin *auctor*) and when they inspected the victims before sacrifice.[2] These *puntes* can represent Atiedias I and II. The five representatives from each division of the unit tell us more. First, the festival of Semo became decurial only after each unit was divided into a second so that each division had five representatives and the whole unit had ten representatives who constituted a decuria. This means that only Casilas I and II may have existed at that time and that the tenth unit, Peraznanii, either did not exist at that time or existed as Peraznanii I and II, the second

---

[1] Compare VIIb where the brother superior must supply twelve heifer victims or pay a fine of 300 *asses*.
[2] III, 4, 9, 10. See below for two additional members.

of which later died out, or that the arrangement of eight (or nine) units into two divisions imposed the name decurial on the festival although Peraznanii (and perhaps Casilas) was exceptional. When we study the history of the Roman curias we will see reason to suppose the Peraznanii were a later addition. Secondly, if the Atiedian Brothers constituted two groups of five men making a decuria, all eight (or nine) units at one time had priestly decurias, five from each of two divisions, which participated in the Semonian festival. This appears to be the sense of IIb, 1–2 and vb, 8–18. Thirdly, if the decurial festival refers to priestly representatives of their peculiar political divisions, the *tekvias* should refer to the decurias of ten men and not to 'ten tenths' of the Iguvine state. Finally, the division of the units into I, II or III was made perhaps on the basis of population because the commonly owned land of Ager Tlatius of Picus Martius and Ager Casilas of Picus Martius seems not to have been divided or expanded into five *agri* for Clavernii I and II and for Casilas I, II and III. Presumably all divisions of a given unit shared equally what had belonged to the original, single and undivided unit. In this respect it is noteworthy that the Atiedian Brothers, representing in quintuplets Atiedias I and II, had no land sacred to Picus Martius. This means the units, however named and whatever the number of their divisions, did not necessarily reflect an equal, artificial (decimal) apportionment of the whole Iguvine territory. By inference, however, we may assume there was a field under the Brothers' special care (III 11, 13), but we cannot be sure it belonged to Atiedias I and II.

In sum, the list of units and their division in Table IIb cannot be decurias of the type we have just described because if they were Atiedias I and II would be represented by two decurias, but they are in fact represented by *puntes*, probably two in number, combined into a single decuria. According to the agreement of vb the supply of grain and the recompense of meat are in proportion to the divisions of Clavernii and Casilas, but the meat was not sufficient to feed the entireties of these units nor was it appropriate for their sacrifices because it was not on the hoof. The portions were apparently made on the basis of the quintuplet of each division of the unit. The quintuplets had probably tended the cultivation of the two fields. The quintuplet was drawn from the division of the unit; in at least eight cases two quintuplets were reunited into a single decuria.

Our discussion comes to the word *tekvias*. The word is said to be derived *tekvias*<**dekuwias*<**dekw-*. This derivation is beset with difficulties. In order to make it a tenth of ten, an ordinal analogically formed after something like *octavus/octavius*, itself a unique formation, must be assumed.[1] One has to stretch the imagination to bring this analysis into line with the Roman notion of a *centuria* of land which comprised a hundred plots for the same number of smallholders.[2] In consideration of its unique attestation and the frailty of its etymology, we conclude that *tekvias* must be understood only in relation to the decurial Semonia, that *tekvias* were the religious groups of ten men, and that the proximity of the word to a list of twenty divisions does not warrant application of the generic word *tekvia* to the twenty divisions.[3]

The generic word for the constituents of these twenty divisions may lurk unnoticed in the Iguvine Tables.

The Atiedian Brotherhood comprised a brother superior (*fratreks*, Latin **fratricus*). Also an official called the *arsfertur* (Latin **adfertor*) oversaw or performed many of the Brotherhood's religious observances. Only by inference is the full number of the Brotherhood brought to twelve. The *fratreks* and *arsfertur* have been recently introduced into the Brotherhood to make the college one of twelve members. The inference is based upon a passage where the brother superior is responsible for supplying twelve heifer victims or payment of a fine of 300 *asses* (VIIb).[4] The liturgy of a brother superior was heavy and may well have been imposed on an outsider since a regular liturgy of twelve large victims might well have impoverished the perpetual brothers. In addition to these officers were the quaestor and the *uhtur* (Latin *auctor*). The latter was certainly elected by the *puntes* of the Brotherhood (III 4–6, below, p. 50, n. 2) and was an eponymous officer of the Brotherhood (Va, 1–3, 14–15, below). The *uhtur* probably came from among the Brothers since his duties would have required a certain expertise. The quaestor, whose title represents a borrowing from Rome,[5] appears to be a later eponymous official (Ib,

[1] Poultney, pp. 106–7, 63, following Devoto. See above, p. 44, n. 3.
[2] Varro, *LL* 5.35 (on which see Collart), *RR* 1. 10, 18; Col. 5. 1. 7; Festus 47 L.; *Röm. Feldmesser*, pp. 153, 159 L. (= Thulin, *Agrim.* pp. 117 ff.) See in the *TLL* s.v. *centuria* col. 834, *centuriatio*, 1. *centurio* col. 837.
[3] Momigliano, 'Interim Report', pp. 114 ff., follows the major editors and understands the *tekvias* as tenths and tries to fit the scheme into the reported curiate system.
[4] See Poultney, pp. 20–1. There is no evidence to connect the number of twelve heifers with the unexpressed number of Brothers.
[5] *Ibid.* p. 23 and on Va, 14–vb, 7 (pp. 223–4).

45, IIa, 44) supplanting the *uhtur* in this capacity. He shares certain functions with the brother superior, for either of them may call for a vote of the Brothers (va, 22–vb, 7, below). Since the quaestor and brother superior were probably wealthy men, both of them could have been members *ex officio* of the college. However, there is no certainty any officer was elected from outside the Brotherhood of (two) *puntes*. The *uhtur* is the least likely to have come from outside.

The problem of the Atiedian place of assembly or assembly (*kumnakle*) next demands our attention:

Frater Atiieřiur esu eitipes plenasier urnasier uhtretie K. T. Kluviier. Kumnahkle Atiieřie ukre eikvasese Atiieřier, ape apelust muneklu habia numer prever pusti kastruvuf, et ape purtitu fust muneklu habia numer tupler pusti kastruvu, et ape subra spafu fust muneklu habia numer tripler pusti kastruvu, et ape frater çersnatur furent ehvelklu feia fratreks ute kvestur sve rehte kuratu si sve mestru karu. Fratru Atiieřiu pure ulu ben-urent prusikurent rehte kuratu eru eřek prufe. Si sve mestru karu fratru Atiieřiu pure ulu benurent prusikurent kuratu rehte neip eru enuk fratru ehvelklu feia fratreks ute kvestur panta muta ařferture. Si panta muta fratru Atiieřiu mestru karu pure ulu benurent ařferture eru pepurkurent herifi etantu mutu ařferture si.

(va, 14–vb, 7.)

The Atiedian Brothers resolved as follows at the regular annual festival during the *auctorship* of C. Cluvius, son of Titus. At the Atiedian assembly on the Mount, among the Atiedian *eikvases*, when (the *adfertor*) has slain (the victims) he shall receive a donation of a single *nummus* per head, and when the presentation has been made he shall receive a donation of two *nummi* per head, and when the distribution has been made he shall receive a donation of three *nummi* per head, and when the Brothers have dined the brother-superior or the quaestor shall call for a vote whether (the dinner) has been provided in a satisfactory manner. If a majority of the Atiedian Brothers who have come there declare it has been provided in a satisfactory manner, it shall be well. If a majority of the Atiedian Brothers who have come there declare it has not been provided in a satisfactory manner, then the brother-superior or the quaestor shall call for an expres-sion of opinion on the part of the Brothers as to how great a fine shall be (imposed) on the *adfertor*. Whatever fine a majority of the Atiedian Brothers who have come there demand so great a fine shall be (imposed) on the *adfertor*.

(Poultney's translation, modified.)

The word *eikvasese* is crucial to our understanding. It is in the ablative case with the locative suffix *-e*, modified by *Atiierier*. Poultney renders the phrase 'among the members of the Atiedian college'

49

and Devoto 'nelle communità Atiedie'. Poultney begins the sentence with *kumnahkle*, Devoto with *eikvasese*.[1]

The *arsfertur* was paid for his services either by the Brotherhood or another body. That other body may be the Atiedian 'communities'. The *eikvases Atiierier* are the constituents of the Atiedian assembly (*kumnahkle Atiierie*) which met on the hill (*ukre*). The Tables observe carefully specific references to the Brothers as in the passage under discussion. The *eikvases* are not to be identified with the Brothers. The Brothers are prescribing a procedure for the *eikvases*, over whom they have some control. The one assembly is the meeting of both Atiedias I and II. Either the *eikvases* are the two divisions of Atiedias or of all the individual constituents of Atiedias I and II. In archaic Rome this would be the meeting (*comitium*) of the curia or of the *curiales* of the curia.[2]

A second passage clarifies the situation:

Esuk frater Atiieřiur eitipes plenasier urnasier uhtretie T. T. Kastruçiie. Ařfertur pisi pumpe fust eikvasese Atiieřier, ere ri esune kuraia, prehabia piře uraku ri esuna si herte et pure esune sis. Sakreu perakneu upetu revestu, puře teřte eru emantur herte, et pihaklu pune tribřiçu fuiest akrutu revestu emantu herte. Ařfertur pisi pumpe fust erek esunesku vepurus felsva ařputrati fratru Atiieřiu prehubia, et nuřpener prever pusti kastruvuf.

(va, 1–13.)

[1] G. Devoto, *Le tavole di Gubbio* (Florence, 1948), p. 69 (cf. p. 104); Poultney, p. 223.
[2] See below, pp. 80–1, 202 ff. The word *kumnahkle* may mean either assembly or place of assembly. Vetter renders it *in curia* and Ernout *in conventu*. Table III 1–8 contains the only other mention of the assembly: Esunu fuia herter sume ustite sestentasiaru urnasiaru. Huntak vuke prumu pehatu. Inuk uhturu urtes puntis frater ustentuta puře fratru mersus fust kumnakle. Iinuk uhtur vapeře kumnakle sistu. Poultney translates: 'Sacrifice is required to be performed in the final period of the regular bi-monthly festival. First purify the jar in the Grove. Then the Brothers, rising in groups of five, shall elect an *auctor* who shall be in accord with the customs of the Brothers in assembly. Then the *auctor* shall sit on the stone seat in the meeting-place.' Poultney's rendition of the relative clause 'who shall be in accord with the customs of the Brothers in assembly' seems to violate the Umbrian syntax. The last word *kumnakle* belongs to the predicate of the future copulative *fust*. Ernout, who believes *puře* is a relative adverb, also understands the *kumnakle* to be predicative: 'quomodo fratrum ex legibus erit in conventu'. He defends his *quomodo* on pp. 58–9; but see Poultney on IIa, 26 and pp. 111–13. Pfiffig, p. 16, follows Vetter and renders *kumnakle* 'in der Kurie' but considers this locative with the verb of 'election' (*ustentuta*); *puře* he translates 'was (wie es)'. I would render the clause, 'who according to the Brothers' customs shall be (present) at the assembly', because the potential *uhtur* belongs to one of the (two) Atiedian quintuplets and, secondly, because he will preside over the selection of the victims after his appointment. In this passage the *eikvas-* are not cited so that we do not know whether this was a full assembly of Atiedias I and II or merely an assembly of the Brothers. In the lustration of the *populus* the *kumne* (Comitium) of Iguvium is cited in reference to the heifer chase.

The Atiedian Brothers resolved as follows at the regular annual festival during the *auctorship* of Titus Castrucius, son of Titus. Whoever shall be *adfertor* among the Atiedian *eikvases*, he shall look after the religious ceremony, and provide what is necessary for the ceremony, and decide what persons shall be present at the ceremony. He shall select the sacred articles and those brought from elsewhere. Whatever are offered, he shall examine whether any of them should be accepted, and when there is to be a triad of propitiatory offerings, he shall make an inspection in the field, whether they should be accepted. Whoever shall be *adfertor*, he shall provide vegetables in connection with the unburned sacrifices, at the discretion of the Atiedian Brothers, and at the rate of one new *dupondius* per head.

(Poultney's translation, modified.)

The *arsfertur* is clearly the officer of the *eikvases*. Since the Atiedian Brothers in this case, too, pass on the conduct of the *arsfertur* who again is reimbursed, the *arsfertur* apparently was not a member of the Brotherhood.

Finally, there are two sacrificial prayers wherein a derivative of *eikvas-*, the adjective *eikvasatis* (abl. pl.), is mentioned:

Inenek vukumen esunumen etu. Ap vuku kukehes iepi persklumař kařitu. Vuke pir ase antentu. Sakre sevakne upetu Iuvepatre prumu ampentu testru sese asa fratrusper Atiieřies, ahtisper eikvasatis, tutape iiuvina, trefiper iiuvina. Tiçlu sevakni teitu. Inumek uvem sevakni upetu Puemune Pupřike apentu. Tiçlu sevakni naratu. Iuka mersuva uvikum habetu fratuspe Atiieřie, ahtisper eikvasatis, tutaper iiuvina, trefiper iiuvina.

(III, 20–30.)

Then go into the grove for the sacrifice. When you reach the grove, call (them) there to the ceremony. In the grove place fire upon the altar. The young pig without blemish, which has been selected, slay first in honor of Jupiter, at the right of the altar, for the Atiedian Brothers, for the fire-carriers of the *eikvas-*, for the state of Iguvium, for the tribe of Iguvium. Pronounce the day solemn. Then slay the unblemished sheep, which has been chosen, in honor of Pomonus Poplicus. Announce that the day is solemn. Use the accustomed words in connection with the sheep, for the Atiedian Brothers, for the fire-carriers of the *eikvas-*, for the state of Iguvium, for the tribe of Iguvium.

(Poultney's translation, modified.)

The prayer's beneficiaries are named in ascending order: (1) the Atiedian Brothers, (2) the fire-carriers(?) of the *eikvas-*, (3) the Iguvine state, and (4) the Iguvine tribe. Between the Brotherhood and the state as a whole ought to stand the Atiedian community as

51

a part of the whole state. The precise character of the *ahtis* ('fire-carriers') is far from certain.[1] The adjectival *eikvasatis*, modifying *ahtis*, is likened to those toponymous adjectives of the type *Arpinas*, *-atis*, attested in some of the proper names of the twenty communal divisions.[2] Since *eikvasatis* answers the question *cuias?*, it may very well have an analogue in Latin *quirites* which is discussed later (chapter 6). A Roman curia's Juno was surnamed *quiritis*. If *eikvasatis* is the adjective analogous to *quiritis*, the phrase *eikvases-e Atiieřier* contains the generic name of the entirety of the two divisions Atiedias I and II and *eikvas-* would correspond to the Latin *curia*.

The etymology of *eikvas-* presents considerable difficulty which in no way detracts from our interpretation resting upon understanding of the contexts of the three passage just quoted and examined. The word is usually related to the Latin *aequus* and the orthography of *eikv-* is explained as archaistic.[3] The absence of rhotacism may be accounted for by assuming an archaic form or assuming that the *s* represents a geminated or otherwise protected *s*.[4] The whole suffix remains without satisfactory explanation.[5] Nevertheless, the etymology from the root of the Latin *aequus* is attractive because both the Spartan 'peers' (*homoioi*) and the notions of *isopoliteia* and *isonomia* offer us semantic parallels. Furthermore, the etymology of *curia* and *Quirites* which we accept and discuss below (chapter 6) exhibits a similar sense, for 'fellowship of men' and 'fellow men' approximates an *eikvas-*, 'community of equals'. The cluster *-kv-* may indicate that the Iguvine word was borrowed from the Latins.

Lastly, the office of *arsfertur* seems to require re-evaluation. The word itself need not indicate a religious functionary. Rather he may be either priest or magistrate of the (two) *eikvas-* which according to our interpretation are Atiedias I and II. He may have served as a priest just as the Roman magistrates and curions performed religious duties. His religious services were reimbursed, probably from the treasury of Atiedias I and II, and were subject to the stringent approval of the Atiedian Brothers. The nature of the title, *arsfertur*,

[1] See Poultney on III, 24 and Ernout, p. 107. Vetter, p. 208, renders the phrase *pro vitis – – -ibus*.
[2] Poultney, p. 207.
[3] Buck, *A Grammar of Oscan and Umbrian*[2], pp. 26–7, Poultney, pp. 39, 219. Ernout, p. 117, says a relation with *aequus* is 'peu vraisemblable'.
[4] Poultney, pp. 73–4.
[5] Buck, p. 301; Poultney, pp. 303–4 and this page, nn. 3–4. From Hispellum, situated in Umbria south of Iguvium, we have record of a man named Aequasius (*CIL* XI,

can support an interpretation of a political magistracy.[1] It has its parallel in the Latin *lator* (*legis* or *rogationis*) and the idiom *legem* or *rogationem ferre*, a function only of Roman magistrates.[2] The supposed praenomen *Fertor* given to Resius, king of the Aequiculi, may be no more than his true official title. It is applied to no one else.[3] The Etruscan praenomen *Lars*, *-tis* may also have originally been a title. The coincidence of Fertor Resius, leader of the Aequi (Aequi-coli is composed through a folk etymology)[4] and the Iguvine *arsfertur* of the *eikvas-* is most striking. Varro for no good reason says that Latin has no word *fertor* (= *lator*) as if he knew of the meaning of the dialect word.[5] The parallel between the Aequi and the *eikvas-* (= Aequates?) suggests some kind of unification or synoecism of peoples who insisted upon their mutual equality. Under these circumstances the Iguvine *arsfertur* becomes an unlikely candidate for *ex officio* membership in the Brotherhood.[6]

Before examining some details of the Brothers' functions, let us sum up our tentative observation on the structure of the Iguvine state. The Iguvines distinguish between their state (*totas*), their army (*puplum*) and their territory (*trifu*). The citizen-body was divided into twenty units to which the generic word *decuria* or *decuvia* has been attributed heretofore. The *tekvias*, however, stand in relation to the *decuriae* which participated in the decurial festival of Semo. In at least eight, and at one time very probably in a ninth, doubled units,

---

5276 = *ILS* 5377). The goddess Aecetia, attested on a cup found in Etruscan Volci, may be related to the political sense of the root *aequ-* (*CIL* I[2], 439 = xi, 6708 = *ILS* 2957 = *ILLRP* 32). The name Aequasius may be likened to Pontificius, Flaminius, etc. which are derived from official titles. Aecetia, on the other hand, may be compared with the epithet of the curial Juno, Quiritis/Curitis (Dion. 2. 50. 3; Festus 43 L.) and perhaps also with Lucetius, an epithet of Jupiter (Festus 102 L.). Most apposite of all parallels is the name of the Italic people, Aequi; see below.

[1] However, the dialectical Latin *arferia* (Festus 10 L.) is a religious term. See Ernout–Meillet, *Dictionaire étymologique de la langue latine*, 4th ed. (Paris, 1959), *s.v.*

[2] Latin *adferre* may or may not be a technical term; see *TLL*, cols 1197–8, 1203. The phrase *nuntium adferre* may be related to augural language; see below, p. 149.

[3] See the archaic or archaistic inscription *CIL* I[2], p. 202 = vi, 1302 = *II* xiii, fasc.3, no.66 = *ILS* 61 = *ILLRP* 447. In [Val. Max.] *Praen.* 1 the name is given as *sertor* or *fertor* Resius by the MSS; it comes from Varro. *Sertor* in Festus 460 L. is not connected with Resius.

[4] I cannot follow the interpretation of the name Aequi put forth by S. Ferri, 'Aequi—Aequiculi—Aequus: La fortuna lessicale di un etnico', *Acc. Naz. Lincei*, Rendic. 20 (1965), 388–91.

[5] *LL* 8. 57. See p. 53, n. 3 for Varro. Livy 34. 2. 5 has a good and simple example of *fero* in the language of the Roman assembly: 'id quod ad vos [*sc.* Quirites] fertur'.

[6] Momigliano, 'Interim Report', pp. 114–15 following Coli, 'Regnum', *Studia et Documenta Historiae et Iuris* 17.1 (1951), holds that the *auctor*, quaestor, *adfertur* and *fratricus* are all officers of the 'corporation'.

two quintuplets (*puntes*) constituted the *decuria*. The members of the decuria were called brothers. The two communities of Atiedias I and II were called *eikvas*-, which may mean 'peership' or 'fellowship'. Two communal units of double and triple division severally owned common land. No distinction of the division is noticed in the ownership and size of the land, but the division is observed in requisitioning sacral grain. The same distinction of a double and triple division prevails in awarding compensation in viands to the decurias of Clavernii and Casilas. The decuria of Casilas numbered fifteen men of three *puntes*, but at an earlier stage of Iguvine history Casilas III may not have been formed and the subsequent incorporation of Casilas III did not alter the description of the Semonia as decurial. The communal division (*eikvas*-) apparently had a combined religious decuria and a single *arsfertur*. At least this is the case with Atiedias I and II. Since two divisions of Clavernii and three divisions of Casilas supply grain from land held in common by both Clavernii and all three Casilas, the divisions of all Iguvine units reflect an increase of manpower, not of territory. Otherwise, we assume, only Clavernii I and Casilas I would supply grain from land they alone held and worked.

The decimal partition of either the territory or army of Iguvium cannot be substantiated. Nothing indicates only the ten named communities existed at one given moment. If the twenty communal units did not bear the generic, technical name *tekvias*, there is even slighter basis for credence in a decimal partition. Nothing indicates whether the twenty units are political units of an assembly or military units of a full levy. The prayers offered up at the decurial Semonia do not include the *populus* or the *iuvenes hastati inhastati;* the rites are agricultural by implication of the name Semonia. The entirety of Atiedias I and II voted together on religious questions and elected only one *arsfertur*. If eight communities could be divided once and a ninth could be divided twice, the extent of potential division is not determined by decimal numbers.

The constituents of the Brotherhood were the Brothers, grouped into sections of five participants, who elected the *uhtur* presumably from their own decuria. In addition to these the brother superior belonged to the Brotherhood and shared certain responsibilities with a quaestor. The *uhtur* does not appear to have financial obligations; his title implies a religious competence (see below). This competence would have been best found in a regular, perpetual member of the *puntes*. Despite his broad and demanding religious functions, the *arsfertur* was by virtue of his office neither a brother nor an officer of the Brotherhood. The eponyms of the Brotherhood were either the *uhtur* or the quaestor. Presumably they and the brother superior presided over meetings of the Brotherhood.

Of Iguvine political structure we have no more to say. More can be said at this point about the functions of the Atiedian Brotherhood to supplement our later discussions of curial priesthoods and religious observances at Rome.

The Brotherhood derived its religious authority from Atiedias I and II. The use of words related to the Latin *frater* in Italic and Greek need not point to real family connections, although ancient and modern commentators on such organizations might infer from a title like *frater* a consanguineous relationship. However, the use of *frater* and its cognates certainly did not allow unlimited participation by any family in the social fabric of the brotherhood in its wide Hellenic sense or narrow Iguvine sense. No clan of Atiedii is known at Iguvium, but this silence proves nothing.[1] On the other hand, we do know the family names of three officials of the Brotherhood and two clans (*natine*) for whom the Brothers prayed. Lucius Tetteius son of Titus was quaestor (ib, 45; iia, 44); Titus Castrucius son of Titus and Gaius Cluvius son of Titus served as *uhtur* (va, 3; va, 15). To the god Hondus Jovius the Brothers sacrificed on behalf of the clan Petronia of the Atiedian Brothers (iia, 21, 35) and to Jupiter (Sancius?) they sacrificed on behalf of the clan Lucia of the Atiedian Brothers (iib, 26). A clearer statement of the relation of these two clans to the Brotherhood cannot be stated. In fact we do not know whether the Brothers sacrificed for the sake of the clans or instead of the clans.

Religious responsibilities for the state, the *populus* and the territory of Iguvium fell to the Brothers. Whether these obligations devolved upon the Atiedian Brothers alone is a question that cannot be answered, since the other communities had similar decurias which

---

[1] At Attiggio, whose ancient name is presumed to be Attidium, a gentilicial name Attidius is attested; see *CIL* xi, 824–5, nos. 5676, 5677. Pliny *NH* 3. 113 notes the existence of Attidiates in Umbria who are distinct from the Iguvines. However, modern Attigio lies some distance from Gubbio. Pliny's *Curiates*, resembling another Iguvine unit the *Kureiate*, are also distinct from the Iguvines. The Roman family name Curiatius may have a similar origin.

could have performed the same services. The Brothers' lustration of the *populus* and the attendant auspices[1] find striking parallels among the Roman curias which we shall suggest later. The banishment and cursing of certain foreigners may have taken place at Rome, but there is no proven connection with the curias.[2]

The *arsfertur* took the auspices with an augur who is only cited by circumlocution.[3] At Rome an *uhtur* would have been an *auctor*. The Roman *patres auctores* show similarities. The Iguvine *uhtur* was elected by the Brothers and served the Brotherhood; he is not a magistrate of the Iguvine state.[4] Both the *arsfertur* and *uhtur* may also be analogous to a Roman curion, especially if the *uhtur* is the official, cited periphrastically, who joins the *arsfertur* in taking the auspices.[5]

At the end of this discussion of the Iguvine evidence the student of comparative institutions should be warned of the very serious defect in applying any Iguvine institution to the interpretation of Roman curial institutions. Roman curias were very old indeed and retained relatively little political or religious influence and force after *c*. 300 B.C. Without doubt they continued to exist. Yet their existence reflected customs of high antiquity. The Iguvine Tables on the other hand display a continuing growth of a priesthood down to the day of Roman influence and domination. The quaestorship, for example, is borrowed from the city on the Tiber. The date of the Tables' inscription and the chronology of the several Tables cannot be fixed with certainty. However, the usual view puts the inscription of the earlier tablets in the native alphabet no earlier than 300 and the later tablets after the Social War. Tablet IIb is one of the oldest. Because it contains the list of the twenty communities, we can see considerable

---

[1] Ia, 1–2, Ib, 13–14, VIa, 1–7, 15–21, VIb, 46–52; the *speturie* of IIa, 1–3 was an 'augural section' of the Brotherhood.

[2] Ib, 16–19, VIb, 52–62. On the Roman Poplifugia see below, chapter 9 and Palmer, *Juno in Archaic Italy* (Philadelphia, forthcoming).

[3] IIa, 16, VIa, 1–7.

[4] III, 4–6, va, 2–3, va, 14–15. Catalano, 'Contributi allo studio del diritto augurale I', *Università di Torino, Memoria del Istituto Giuridico*, serie 2, mem. 107 (1960), 28–9, n. 7, 129, 209–10 and 531, follows the suggestion of some of his predecessors and considers the *uhtur* the supreme religious and civil magistrate of all Iguvium. How did ten men from the priesthood of two out of twenty divisions gain the right to elect the town's chief magistrate? The evidence only permits assigning him to the eponymous office of the Brotherhood. The *uhtur* selects sacrificial victims but his choice is approved by the quintuplets of the Brotherhood (III, 4–10). Momigliano 'Interim Report', p. 115, believes all four officers belong to the 'corporation' and not to the state. To refine this attribution we argue the *uhtur, fratreks* and quaestor are officers of the Brotherhood whereas the *arsfertur* is the priest or magistrate of Atiedias I and II.

[5] VIa, 1–7, 15–18 (cf. Ib, 12–14).

development of the Iguvine politico-religious structure had preceded its inscription.[1]

Clearly we must exercise caution in comparing the Roman and Iguvine evidence, widely disparate as it is in time and language. Further, we are dealing with two different states. One of them was an Italian backwater, the other mistress of Italy. The Romans discarded their primitive political system in the course of dominating central Italy. The Iguvines lived in the shadow of the Etruscans and other neighbors who were important enough to be cursed or banished, and they lived subject to the Romans whose name is not found in the Iguvine curse. The Romans called the tunes to which people like the Iguvines danced. The former's military demands on the latter could well have reshaped the entire political structure of Iguvium.[2]

GERMAN SYSTEMS

With some hesitation we turn finally to the ancient classical evidence of German organization which is far older than any German evidence.[3] Tacitus' implicit and explicit contrasts of Romans and Germans, his awareness that the ancient Romans had once been what the contemporary Germans were, and his use of ethnographical commonplaces, leave open to question whether he idealizes his Germans as primitive Romans, the view of whom was also an idealization:[4] 'The number of elite footsoldiers is fixed: one hundred come from each district (*pagi*) and they are called the Hundred in their own language because that was the original number. But today it is but a title and rank.'[5] With this statement we must compare: 'They carry into battle certain emblems and standards which they have taken from groves. Neither chance nor accidental massing causes their squadron and wedge formation. Rather they mass according to families and kinship. This arrangement is an especial inducement to

[1] See Poultney, pp. 22–4 on the dates of inscription and chronology.
[2] Iguvium was a *civitas foederata* until the Social War which meant it might supply support troops to Rome (Cic. *Balb.* 46–7). The date of the treaty between Rome and Iguvium is unknown; see De Sanctis, 2. 348 ff. After Iguvium's enfranchisement, it lost whatever prominence it had once enjoyed; see I. Rosenzweig, 'Ritual and Cults of Pre-Roman Iguvium', *Studies and Documents*, 9 (1937), 3–4. The borrowed quaestorship is attested in Tables I and II, both of which are among the earlier inscriptions; an overlord's paymaster is always an important official.
[3] On the whole subject see J. G. C. Anderson's edition of Tacitus, *De origine et situ Germanorum* (Oxford, 1938), pp. lvii–lxii and commentary to the passages cited below.
[4] *Ibid.* Introduction.   [5] *Germ.* 6. 5.

valor.'[1] The Hundred elite foot-soldiers may reflect the primitive Roman century. The deployment by family and kinship may echo the legendary Fabii who fell at the Cremera: 'In the same meetings the chiefs are elected to render justice in the assizes of the districts (*pagi*) and hamlets (*vici*). One hundred men from the commoners attend these chiefs and offer advice and support.'[2] This judicial system bears a marked resemblance to Rome's centumviral court. Compare this garbled condensation of Festus (47 L.): 'Centumviral judgements are named after the Hundred. For when Rome had the 35 tribes which are also called curias, three men from each tribe were elected to serve as judges and were called the Hundred. Even though they numbered 105, they were called the Hundred because it was an easier name.'[3]

After his generalizations about all Germans Tacitus attributes the Semnones' prestige among the Suebic Germans to the fact that they occupied 100 districts (*pagi*).[4] However, Caesar speaks of the hundred districts (*pagi*) of the Suebi and of the 1,000 men each district could field every year.[5] The last statement is incredible. Both Tacitus and Caesar seem to have been taken in by an oral report stressing the size of the Suebi or Semnones in a round number.

The Roman statesman who sought ethnological information would have taken a special interest in the extent of a levy in the several districts of a nation. He was bound to use the language at his disposal to explain outlandish customs and practices. Nevertheless, it is remarkable that in all five passages where they mention 'hundreds' the 'districts' *pagi* are also cited: 100 elite foot-soldiers from the *pagi*; the 100 commoners assigned to judges in *pagi* and *vici*; the 100 *pagi* of the Semnones; the Suebic 100 *pagi* and their levies of 1,000. The word *pagus* is frequently used by authors describing the Gaulish and German countryside and community. It is clear from an idealizing treatment of *pagi*, *pagani* and *Paganalia* that these Roman country districts had at one time before Augustus served a function, subordinate to the tribe's, in the collection of taxes and conscription of troops. Since the institution is assigned to Servius Tullius, an author would look to both the institution and its antiquity for ethnographical comparisons.[6]

---

[1] *Germ.* 7. 3. With Tacitus' account of the Germans may be compared Ammianus (31. 2. 1–11) on the Huns.   [2] *Germ.* 12. 3.
[3] On the institution see Mommsen, *Römisches Staatsrecht* II[3] (Leipzig, 1887), 231–2.
[4] *Germ.* 39. 4.   [5] *BG* 1. 37. 3, 4. 1. 4.   [6] D.H. 4. 15; see above, p. 40, nn. 1–2.

In conclusion I consider the Roman treatment of these German organizations too slight for any profound comparison because the treatment is couched in Roman terms and looks rather to the Roman past than to the German present. The greatest difference, of course, remains the fact that any comparison of Germans and Romans is exposed to serious objection that the latter enjoyed settled, civil government whereas the former lived for many years after the classical reports in a manner far dissimilar from a primitive Mediterranean city-state. Comparison of archaic Rome with Germanic nations is as hazardous as the contrast of Romans and Hebrews, for only the Romans developed a city-state.

NON-ROMAN CURIAS

As divisions of the city-state and not as a senate or its building, curias are known to have existed at Tibur, Lanuvium, Caere and perhaps at Falerii and Velitrae.

The Caeretane curia is attested by a single inscription (*CIL* xi, 3593):

Deos Curiales, Genium Ti. Claudi Caesaris Augusti p(atris) p(atriae) Curiae Aserniae A. Avellius Acanthus, M. Junius Eutychus dictatores de suo posuer(unt).

The editors of the *Corpus* remarked the similarity between *dei curiales* and the *theoi phretrioi* from Naples.[1] The cognomens of the Caeretane dictators, the town magistrates, ought not to lead us into believing the Caeretane curia was inspired by Greeks, for its name Asernia looks quite Etruscan. Its gods were coupled with the emperor Claudius' Genius. This connection with the ruler-cult may not have been a violent break with tradition inasmuch as the thirty curias of Rome had their Genii (*daimones*).[2] Although the curias at Sardinian Turris Libisonis can not claim great age, their one dedication serves to reinforce the connection with ruler-cult and to explain another Caeretane document:

Q. Allio Q. f. C[o]l(lina) Pudentillo auguri, curiae XXIII et ministr[i] Larum Aug(ustorum) ex [a]ere collato (*CIL* x, 7953 = *ILS* 6766)

The freeborn citizens must be represented by the curias and the town's freedmen by the Ministers of the August Lares.

[1] Cf. *IG* 14. 759 (721–3) and see Latte, *RE* 20 (1941), cols 756–8.
[2] See below, chapter 6.

In A.D. 113 one Ulpius Vesbinus, an imperial freedman, sought permission of the Caeretane *municipium* to build a *phetrium* at his own expense if the town gave him a place. The local senate took delight in the prospect and gave a site so that the Augustales would have their *phetrium*.[1] The Caeretane curias of the *municipium* doubtless resembled those at Turris Libisonis but were much older.[2] However, the curias may not have admitted the freedmen who, in any case, wanted something like a curia of their own. This the *phetrium* supplied. There is no doubt that the name is originally *phretrion*, for the word *phatr(ia)* and the place *phratrion* are attested.[3] A strong Greek influence at Caere is to be noticed in another inscription which records some freedmen's Latin and Greek plays, or games (*ludi*), in A.D. 25.[4] From the foregoing discussion it appears that curias and phratries were related in the popular mind as much as in the literature. However, at Caere a *phetrium* for the Augustales was not on a par with a curia: the decurions assured the *curator* that the site given for it was neither useful nor profitable.

The curias of a Lanuvium are attested by three inscriptions. One is a dedication of an equestrian statue to the municipality's patron who in return: 'viritim divisit decurionibus et Augustalib(us) et curi(i)s n(ummos) XXIIII et curi(a)e mulierum epulum duplum dedit'.[5] The Lanuvinian curias obviously comprised the citizens and are treated the same way as senators and Augustales. The town ladies who had formed their own curia received second prize.

The second inscription is a dedication to the municipal aedile by *municipes curiales* [*e*]*t curia* [– – –]*amonal(is)*.[6] Editors place a comma after *municipes* but that is not good Latin; cf. *municipes et incol(ae)*.[7] Rather the curial citizens and the specific curia were the dedicants. As at Caere and Turris Libisonis, the freedmen were apparently excluded or separate. In the first Lanuvinian inscription just the Augustales received the money gift along with decurions and the curias. The name of the one curia, to which the aedile perhaps belonged, has been restored [*Fl*]*amonal(is)* or emended to [*Fl*]*amonae*, but neither of these readings is necessary.

---

[1] *CIL* x, 3614 = *ILS* 5918 a., a very interesting document containing the dedication and a passage of the daily proceedings of the municipality which has the deliberations and two letters. The word *phetrium* is so spelled four times. When the decurions wrote to the town's *curator*, they did not need to explain what a *phetrium* was.
[2] Cf. p. 38, n. 4, above.   [3] *GEL s.vv. phratra, phratrios.*   [4] *ILS* 5052.
[5] *CIL* xiv, 2120 = *ILS* 6199.   [6] *CIL* xiv, 2114 = *ILS* 6201.
[7] *Ibid.* 6209; cf. 5671, 6562.

The last inscription merely reads: Curia Clodia Firma.[1] The name resembles the names of legions such as VII Claudia, XI Claudia or XVI Flavia Firma.[2] Indeed at African Lambaesis we meet *Curia Hadriana Felix veteranorum leg(ionis) III Aug(ustae)*.[3] Since we know there was a plurality of curias in Lanuvium and other municipalities (one bearing the name Asernia) and at Lanuvium itself a *curia* [– – –]*amonal(is)*, I do not believe that Curia Clodia Firma was made up of veterans. It looks very much as if the Curia Clodia had received an honorific after some meritorious act. Such an occasion was offered when Octavian borrowed money from a Lanuvinian sacred treasury to support himself against Lucius Antonius.[4]

In a comment on *Aeneid* 1.17 we learn of the existence of curias at Tibur:

habere enim Iunonem currus certum est. sic autem esse etiam in sacris Tiburtibus constat ubi sic precantur 'Iuno Curitis, tuo curru clipeoque tuere meos curiae vernulas.'[5]

The cult of the thirty Iunones Curites is well founded at Rome. Varro took pains to assert—wrongly—that the epithet was derived from the Sabine word *curis* ('spear'). Accordingly, the Servian datum very likely goes back to Varro.[6] The cult does not concern us for the moment.

The crux of the prayer is the word *vernulae*, the members of the curia whom Juno is asked to protect with shield and car by the priest speaking the words. In Republican Latin a *verna* commonly meant the slave born to a slave woman whereas its adjective in the same period means simply 'native-born' without respect to status. *Vernaculus* is synonymous with *domesticus* or antonymous to *peregrinus*. In the Tiburtine prayer the *vernulae* can hardly have been the slaves of a curia who could hope to enjoy the protection by a civic warrior patron. The cult of Juno is not servile.

One author defines *vernae* as follows:

---

[1] *CIL* XIV, 2126 = *ILS* 6202.

[2] For the last see *ILS* III, pp. 458–9. There are many other appellations like *firma*: constans, fidelis, certa, pia, ferrata, fulminata, victrix, adiutrix, vindex, triumphalis.

[3] *ILS* 6847. I do not intend to examine the many curias attested by African inscriptions.

[4] Appian *BC* 5.24.

[5] Serv. Dan. on *Aen.* 1.17.

[6] See below, pp. 167–8: Varro's *Antiquities of Divine Matters* is quoted by Servius, e.g. on *Aen.* 1.42, 378, 382, 415(?), 532, 740; also, *De ora maritima*, *De lingua Latina ad Ciceronem*, *De vita populi Romani*.

Vernae are those born in country houses in the spring (*ver*) because that season is naturally productive and then Numa Pompilius instituted cult for Mars towards the reconciliation of Sabines and Romans so that the *vernae* might live and not conquer. They called Romans *vernae*, i.e. born at Rome, because the Sabines who had united with the Romans thought it criminal to conquer them.[1]

The thinker responsible for this definition has garbled a folk-etymology from *ver*, cults for Mars at the onset of spring, and the well-known *ver sacrum* especially practiced by Sabine folk. However, none of these elements explains the statement that *vernae* are those born at Rome. The scholiast on Persius 4. 22 satisfies by his brevity: '*Vernae* are those either born at Rome or slaves born at home'. Since a Roman meant 'native to us' when he wrote *vernaculus*, the inescapable conclusion is that *verna*, meaning a 'slave born at home', is a specialization of what was not the original Latin word for 'native', viz. *ingenuus*.[2] Indeed, the Tiburtine evidence leads us to conclude that *vernulae* meant at least 'native' member of the curias, if not 'free-born' or 'citizen'.

Just one tantalizing item of Tiburtine history may add to our knowledge of the curias there. Dionysius (1. 16. 5) reports that even in his own day a section of the Tiburtine *polis* was named *meros Sikelikon*. He is following an old tradition that Sicilians had once inhabited central Italy. Cato had researched into the history of Tibur and decided that the town was founded by the 'Old Sicani' from a town in Sicily.[3] The Latian Siculi or Sicani, usually related to the islanders, are well attested.[4] The fact of Sicani in the old Alban League surely generated 'Sicilians' of Latium.[5] Nor ought we to reject an ethnic Siculus for this same Latian people, for there is no tangible denotative difference between Romulus/Romanus and Siculus/Sicanus. Furthermore, the name of the archaic consul Sicinius probably betrays the same ethnic root.[6] Cloelius Siculus, priest-king at Rome in 180, may also have borne an ethnic cognomen

---

[1] Festus 510 L.

[2] The word has an Etruscan look. However, the supposed Etruscan cognomen 'Verna' has proved to be a misreading of *veru*; see Rix, *Das etruskische Cognomen* (Wiesbaden, 1963), p. 186, n. 94.

[3] *Orig.* fr. 56 P. from Solinus 2. 8; cf. Verg. *Aen.* 7. 670–2.

[4] Varro, *LL* 5. 101, Pliny, *NH* 3. 56, Hyginus in Serv. Dan. on *Aen.* 8. 638 (cf. on 7. 795, 11. 317).

[5] Pliny, *NH* 3. 69.

[6] Sicinius Sabinus was consul in 487; on both names see Broughton, *MRR s.a.* Hyginus (above, p. 62, n. 4) says the Sabines replaced the Siculi.

related to the same Latian people; he belonged to a patrician clan of supposed Alban provenience.[1]

The precise name of the Sicans' community cannot be known. However, either the Sicans died off, were massacred, or joined other communities such as Tibur. What does Dionysius intend by the noun *meros*? For the Latin *regio* he uses *moira*; for *vicus, stenopos* or *oikēsis*.[2] Yet one might expect a Vicus Sicanus or Siculus like Vicus Tuscus. For Dionysius the divisions (*moirai*) of the people are the curias and tribes.[3] No Latin identification of *meros* can be demonstrated. The Faliscans also had a cult of Juno Quiritis/Curitis which the Romans respectfully preserved.[4] However, we know of no curias there and of only one Juno bearing the cognomen.

The last documented curia outside Rome is attested by a Volscan inscription from Velitrae which linguistically leaves many questions open. Its word *covehriu* is of great importance in the study of curias:

deve declune statom sepis atahus pis velestrom façia esaristrom se bim asif vesclis vinu arpatitu sepis toticu covehriu sepu ferom pihom estu ec se cosuties ma ca tafanies medix sistiatiens.[5]

Vetter's version into Latin is:

divae *Declonae statutum. siquis attigerit, qui arbitrarium faciat, piaculum sit: bovem, asses (cum) vasculis, vino conferto. siquis publico conventu sciente asportare pium esto. Eg(natius) Cossutius Se. (filius), Ma(raeus) Tafanius C. (filius) meddices statuerunt.

It would be rash to believe our knowledge of the curias can be much advanced by this document. Nevertheless, we agree with Untermann that the *covehriu* need not be the town's senate.[6] The adjective *toticu* does mean 'of the state'[7] but there were many curias at Rome whose *sacra* were *publica*.[8] Nor is there the slightest hint that Roman

---

[1] See below, pp. 133–7, 290–1. [2] D.H. 3.22.8, 4.14.1, 4.39.5, 5.36.4. [3] *Ibid.* 2.7.

[4] There are a few points of similarity in the cult of Faliscan Juno and the thirty Junos of the Roman curias; see Palmer, *Juno*. Cf. D.H. 1.21, 2.22. Tert. *Apol.* 24.8, following Varro (cf. *Ad Nat.* 2.8.6), has the curious statement: 'Faliscorum in honorem patris Curr⟨it⟩is et accepit cognomen Iuno.' He is speaking of the gods peculiar to certain Italian towns. We are left in the dark as to who the *pater* was.

[5] Von Pl. no. 240 = Conway no. 252 = Vetter no. 222. Treated in the last place by Ruth Stiehl in Altheim and Felber, *Untersuchungen zur röm. Geschichte* 1 (Frankfurt/Main, 1961) 79–87.

[6] J. Untermann, 'Die Bronzetafel von Velletri', *Indog. Forsch.* 62 (1955–6), 123–36, Stiehl (last note) to the contrary notwithstanding. Any assumption of *covehriu* as *curia decurionum* must imply that the Volscan word underwent the same semantic development as its Latin equivalent.

[7] Cf. Iguvine *totas*, above, p. 41. The *meddix tuticus* was the chief magistrate of Capua.

[8] See chapter 5, p. 71, n. 2.

curions and curial flamens were not officially priests. The word *sepu* which stands by *toticu covehriu* is yet to be explained to this writer's satisfaction. Why not a 'curia Sepa'? Or is it an abbreviated proper name? We do not know that the *meddices* were magistrates of the whole town. Semantically *meddix* equals the Latin *iudex*! The goddess Declune (latinized: Declona or Deculona or Decolona or Decelona) arouses sympathy by her very insignificance. Recall the Lanuvinian curia with the mutilated name *-amonal(is)*. The Roman curias had their peculiar deities and all worshipped Juno, whom one Tiburtine curia also venerated.

The circumstances in which the Italian curias discussed above are met suggest a few general remarks before closing the chapter. The Curia Asernia belongs to the once powerful Etruscan city of Caere whose citizens obtained Roman citizenship without the vote sometime in the fourth century.[1] In 338 the Lanuvinians received Roman citizenship and exchanged cults with Rome.[2] Tibur lost some land but retained its independence of Rome until *c.* 90 B.C.[3] Velitrae, however, suffered greatly in 338 and received Roman settlers.[4] Although Falerii was basically a community using a Latin-related language, it regularly allied itself with Etruscans, who much influenced the Faliscans. On the morrow of Rome's first success against Carthage she destroyed Falerii except for the shrine of Juno Quiritis and relocated her people.[5] The privileged position under Rome enjoyed by Lanuvium and Caere and the independence from Rome exercised by Tibur may account for their retention of their own internal systems. The evidence for the curias in these three cities all survived into the era of the principate. Whoever first researched into the prayer of the Tiburtine curial priest found it comprehensible and perhaps modernized. Lastly, the Caeretane and Tiburtine evidence seems to evince some conservative socio-political element in its exclusion of freedmen from curial participation. This inference is drawn partly on the basis of the inscription from Sardinian Turris Libisonis, where curias cannot have been very old but numbered only twenty-three which does not conform with any number of elementary

[1] See M. Sordi, *I rapporti romano-ceriti e l'origine della civitas sine suffragio* (Rome, 1960) for a collection of all pertinent testimony.
[2] Livy 8. 14. 2.
[3] *Ibid.* 8. 14. 9, Appian *BC* 1. 65; cf. Livy 9. 30. 5-10, *ILS* 19.
[4] Livy 8. 14. 5-7 who reports that Velitrae had comprised Roman citizens before the Latin War.
[5] Palmer, *Juno.*

political units known elsewhere. This odd number was surely inspired by the ordinary necessity of avoiding tie votes in the local public assembly.

Before summarizing the results of our examination it is worthwhile mentioning the peculiar social and civil arrangement in Locri of South Italy although particulars are lacking. The Locrians of South Italy counted 100 *oikiai* as an aristocracy designated in the metropolis before the colony was sent to Italy.[1] This information would carry little weight were it not for the fact that in certain cases a Locrian might be tried before the court of the Thousand according to Zaleukos' constitution.[2] The Hundred Houses and Thousand Judges may have had some influence in the development of political theory because Zaleukos enjoyed a widespread reputation as a law-giver among the Western Greeks.[3] In the two philosophers, his constitution drew praise.[4] Hence Cicero can easily speak of Zaleukos in the same breath with Lycurgus, Solon and the Romans' Twelve Tables[5] and claim that Plato followed Zaleukos.[6]

CONCLUSION

In the foregoing chapter we have gathered together data which may cast light upon the obscure Roman curiate system. The Israelite system which I believe is no older than the kingship and was inspired by a Philistine model represents to us mainly a military organization of decimal units of fifties, hundreds and thousands. Their relation to the twelve tribes of Israel is not known, but cannot have been equal—if it existed—because, for all we know of the tribes, their size and resources were most unequal.

As for Hellenic systems, the phratries' contribution to the pre-hoplite and early hoplite armies is likewise unknown. Military contingents from phratries and tribes were fielded as late as the second century in Sicily.[7] However, we ought to point out that there is no explicit and reliable evidence of the thirty Roman curias or curias in other Italian cities fielding their own companies in a concerted force.

---

[1] Pol. 12. 5 who is here waging his polemic against Timaeus. See J. Bérard, *La colonisation grecque de l'Italie méridionale*[2] (Paris, 1957), pp. 199–207.
[2] Pol. 12. 16.　　　　　[3] Cf. Diod. 12. 20–1.
[4] Plat. *Tim.* 20a, *Leg.* 1. 638; Arist. *Pol.* 2. 1294a.　　　[5] *Leg.* 1. 22. 57.
[6] *Ibid.* 2. 6. 14–15; cf. Plat. *Leg.* 4. 722, Cic. *Ad Att.* 6. 1. 18.　[7] See below, pp. 155–6.

Among Etruscans curias or what were called curias in Latin did exist. The one statement on their organization turns out to have been an egregious misunderstanding of a Vergilian passage and to have been inspired by some political numerology comparable to Aristotle's neat rendition of four seasons, twelve months and thirty days.

The Iguvine Tables, often mistaken for the Umbrian system, display the priestly organization of twenty units. The decurias of Iguvium contained two groups of five priests from these units. The testimony has great value for appreciation of Roman curial priesthoods and religion but no value for assessing an Iguvine military organization.

Caution must be applied to classical interpretation of the Germanic organization. Units of Hundreds bearing the name only out of respect for the past—just as a Roman military and comitial century had long ago ceased to contain 100 citizen soldiers—stand in contrast with tactical masses of kinship groups. A body of 100 assessors resembles Rome's centumviral court. And, finally, the division of a people or a primitive nation into 100 districts has no bearing on the curias of a small Latin town. All German data rest upon a decimal system.

Lastly, a few scraps of information on curias in central Italian towns do not corroborate the contention of a military system and give no help in ascertaining the number of curias in Italian towns.

The Italian evidence does directly and indirectly point to vestiges of amalgamation and synoecism. Three disparate nations contributed to the formation of Mantua's league. So, too, Rome's three archaic tribes were said to represent Latin, Sabine and Etruscan elements. A community of South Etruria called Septem Pagi was absorbed by the early Romans. Another Etruscan community named Novem Pagi existed in the first century A.D. The Iguvine state has twenty political units: eight divided once, one twice divided and the tenth intact. Their generic name, recovered in this chapter, *eikvas-*, apparently reflects the assertion of civic equality. For instance, the men of Casilas I are peers with the men of Casilas II and III, and so on. At Tibur the members of the curia are locally styled 'indigenous'. A sector of this *polis* takes its name from the Latian Sicani or Siculi who had once participated in the Latin Festival on the Alban Mount.

Now we turn to examining the problem of what a curia was.

CHAPTER 5

WHAT WAS A CURIA?

DEFINITIONS OF A CURIA

Upon the basis of the Volscan word *covehriu* Kretschmer argues that the Latin *curia<co-viria*, 'fellowship of men'. We accept this etymology and the connection of the word to Quirites, the usual appellation of Roman citizens in the assemblies.[1] The compound expresses equality of the units and of the units' members. If our comparison and interpretation of the Iguvine *eikvas-* and their *arsfertur* and of the Aequi and their *fertor* are roughly analogous, other Italic peoples had developed similar groupings whose history lies beyond our grasp.

The curias are first mentioned in a Latin context by Plautus who attempts to render the Greek institution with which his Greek original confronted him. In the *Aulularia* Plautus' miser Euclio conceives a plan of making himself seem poor by asking for a handout from a local politician. 'Our mayor of our curia (*magister curiae*) has said he will hand out some money to each man. If I don't go after it, everyone will suspect that I have money at home.' Hence he goes off to collect his donation. But he was disappointed: 'Not a single member of the curia (*curialis*) nor the mayor who ought to have divided the money came.'[2] Later in the same play Plautus makes an elaborate pun on *curiosus, cura* and a sacrificial lamb so thin that is was an *agnus curio*.[3] The word *curio*, of course, was the title of the chief of each curia.

A *magister curiae* did not exist in the Roman curias. However, it will be clear in a moment that Plautus did not translate Greek *phratriarchos* into Latin *magister curiae*.[4] The Greek institution he renders as *curia* is the Attic *dēmos*, 'village', the *magister*, the Attic *dēmarchos* and the *curiales, dēmotes*.[5] The Greek title *dēmarchos* rendered the Latin *tribunus plebis*.[6] At a later date someone considered the

---

[1] See below, pp. 156–60, 221, n. 1.   [2] *Aul.* 109–10, 179–80.
[3] *Ibid.* 561–6.   [4] Cf. Ambrosch, pp. 28–30.
[5] Cf. Arist. *Ath. Pol.* 21. 4–6.   [6] Cf. Pol. 6. 12. 2.

Attic *dēmoi* the equivalent of Roman *pagi*.[1] The chiefs of *pagi* were titled *magistri*.[2]

This Plautine play evidently influenced Varro who researched the authenticity of all plays passing for Plautus' own.[3] In two different works he derives *curia<cura*.[4] Furthermore, Varro's researches into the curias doubtless led him to examine the great annual festival of the Greek phratries, the *Apatouria*.[5] One of its sacrifices was called *koureion* and one of the days of the festival was the *koureōtis* (*hēmera*) that is the day of cutting boys' hair before they enter their phratry.[6] Did Varro know the name of this day and add it to his etymological baggage? He read his Plautus and found a sacrificial *agnus curio*, a pun which he turned to his advantage. One Roman scholar thought the Plautine *magistri curiarum* were the *divisores* of the thirty-five Roman tribes.[7] But Plautus intended his *curia* and *curiales* to represent a *dēmos* and its *dēmotes*.

According to Cicero Theophrastus wrote that Cimon had offered his *curiales Laciadai* the generous use of his property.[8] Fortunately this story is also told by Aristotle and Plutarch who certify for us that Cicero is rendering *dēmotes* into the Latin *curiales*.[9] Until Varro the Roman *curia* etc. could be used to render the Greek *dēmos* etc. although no surviving political theorist argues an equivalence.

Citizenship in an Attic deme was a notorious qualification for Athenian citizenship after Kleisthenes. Nevertheless, the new citizen was enrolled in both deme and phratry as well as in a *phyle*.[10] The Hellenic practice helps to explain the supposed royal assignment of new peoples into Roman tribes and curias.[11] Certain citizens might

---

[1] Fest. *Epit.* 63 L. On curias and *pagi* see chapter 6, p. 124, n. 1.
[2] For an example, see above, p. 40, n. 3.   [3] Gellius, *NA* 3. 3.
[4] *LL* 5. 155, 6. 46 (see below, p. 71, n. 2), *De Vita Populi Romani* in Nonius, p. 79 L.
[5] Tertullian (*Apol.* 39. 15) writes: 'tot tribubus et curiis et decuriis ructuantibus acescit aer.... Apaturiis, Dionysiis, mysteriis Atticis cocorum dilectus indicitur'. This is a patent distortion of Varro's *Antiquities*; on the curial dinners, see below, pp. 97 ff. Tertullian used Varro (see above, chapter 4, p. 63, n. 4) and cites his *Antiquities of Divine Matters* (*Ad Nat.* 2. 1. 8). Varro told him there were 300 Jupiters (*Apol.* 14. 9, *Ad Nat.* 1. 10. 43) and a threefold division of Roman deities (*Ad Nat.* 3. 9. 3; cf. *Ad Nat.* 1. 10. 17, 2. 2. 19, 2. 3. 7, 2. 5. 2, 2. 12. 5). For the *Apatouria* see Her. 1. 147, Xen. *HG* 1. 7. 8, *IG* ii², 1237 = *SIG*³ 921.
[6] Pl. *Tim.* 21b; *IG* (last note) line 28. See H. T. Wade-Gery 'Demotionidae', 116–34, especially translation on pp. 120–2; K. Latte, *RE* 20 (1941), cols 752, 754.
[7] [Asconius] pp. 212–13 Stangl. See pp. 124–5.   [8] *Off.* 2. 18. 64.
[9] Arist. *Ath. Pol.* 27. 3, Plut. *Cim.* 10 (cf. *Pericles* 9).
[10] *IG* i², 110 = Tod *GHI* no. 86; ii², 103 = *GHI* no. 133; ii², 237 = *SIG*³ 259 = *GHI* no. 178.
[11] Below, pp. 132, 137.

be designated by their Roman curias. According to a very late Ciceronian commentator a Roman citizen was pointed out by his praenomen or name or cognomen or his kinship or the tribe in which he was rated or his curia or his census rating, as if he were senator or Roman knight.[1]

Plautus and Cicero thought of curias as demes; Varro and Dionysius thought of curias as phratries. The older acceptation implies a discrete community attached to the major divisions of the larger community; the Varronian acceptation explicitly rests upon the identity of a lesser archaic unit of the major division which had formerly supplied troops and in the present observed quaint, outmoded religious customs. The only common link between the two views is the criterion for Athenian citizenship. From an historian's standpoint both views are of limited usefulness by their very premise of translation and ethnological comparison. Why should the Roman curia be the identical equivalent of any Greek institution? A unique and priceless clue to the nature of the curias comes from an obscure Laelius Felix who after A.D. 100 wrote a commentary on the systematic Jus Civile of Q. Mucius Scaevola, the third member of a great legal family in the last years of the Republic. The fragment of Laelius Felix's work arises from its attention to republican legal procedure and, we may suppose, to the actual Roman constitution rather than some antiquarian's scheme.[2]

The entire passage containing Laelius' major fragment is worth rendering:

In his first book on Q. Mucius, Laelius Felix writes that Labeo wrote an assembly is called (*calata*) which is held before the pontifical college for inaugurating the priest king or the flamens. And, Felix continues, Labeo also wrote some of them are curiate and others are centuriate assemblies; the former is called (*calari*), i.e. convoked, by a curiate lictor, the latter by a hornblower. In the same assembly [Gellius continues], which we said is named the called assembly the forswearing of religious rites and wills used to take place. We have inherited three kinds of wills: the first takes place in a called assembly at the meeting of the people (*contio populi*), the second in battle order when men used to be summoned to the line of battle for

[1] [Asconius] p. 213; see above, p. 68. Val. Probus, *De iuris notis* 2 (in *FIRA* II², 454 ff.) remarks the existence of abbreviated names of curias, tribes, assemblies, etc. The commentator is explaining *Q. Verrem Romilia* (sc. *tribu*). To my knowledge, no abbreviated curial name survives.
[2] See Berger *RE* 12. 1 (1926), col. 416. Paulus twice cites Laelius on matters of inheritance. (On the curias and testaments see chapter 9.) Laelius was alive under Hadrian. See *Dig.* 5. 3. 43, 5. 4. 3.

F   69

fighting, and the third took place through emancipation of the household at which the bronze and balance are applied. In Laelius Felix's book he wrote: 'Whosoever summons some part of the people and not the whole people should announce a meeting (*concilium*), not an assembly (*comitia*). Furthermore tribunes neither summon patricians to them nor can they consult them on any business. Accordingly the plebiscites accepted at the proposal of plebeian tribunes are not even properly called laws. At one time tribunicial bills did not bind the patricians until the dictator Q. Hortensius proposed the law that all Roman citizens (*Quirites*) were bound by that injunction (*ius*) which the plebs had set.' Likewise in the same book he wrote: 'When a vote is taken according to kinds of men (*genera hominum*), the assembly is curiate; when according to census rating and age, centuriate; when according to regions and places, tribal. It is contrary to proper usage to hold a centuriate assembly within the pomerium because the army must be commanded outside the city and because it is not right to command it within the city. Therefore, the centuriate assembly was usually held and the army usually commanded for the sake of a garrison in the Campus Martius on the assumption that the people might have been overcome in the act of balloting.'[1]

The rule on holding the centuriate assembly to which Laelius Felix refers was never violated. The prohibition against an armed force in the city is amply attested by other practices. Unless the rule was imposed long after the organization of the curias, the curias as purported military units should never have met within the pomerium. Since the curiate assembly was regularly held in the city, it should never have been considered a military organization. The curiate assembly 'according to kinds of men' (*genera hominum*) is a vexing definition. At once it can be said that *genus* does not support the opinion of a curial military division. But there are all kinds of kinds. Some scholars hold that *genus*, like its cognate *gens*, is a clan or kinship group or, more precisely and less informatively, a super clan.[2] The word can mean 'family'. However, nothing supports this view. Why did not Laelius Felix write *gens* or *familia*? Both words belong to legal terminology. If *genus* means 'clan', then the *hominum* is otiose. The Varronian interpretation of the curias says nothing about kinship. Of course, *phrator* equals *frater* but Dionysius makes nothing of it. And well he might have told his Greek audience, supposedly

---

[1] Gellius, *NA* 15. 27. The last clause renders *quoniam populus esset in suffragiis ferendis occupatus*. If we render it 'the people were engaged in balloting', it makes no sense in context. Laelius has reference to the flag on the Janiculan Hill which warned of an enemy's nearness (Livy 39. 15. 11; Dio Cass. 37. 28).

[2] See p. 2, n. 3.

innocent of Roman history, that the Romans' linguistic equivalent of *phrator* meant *adelphos*. Varro rightly corrected the folk legend of curias named after Sabine girls; he recognized gentilicial names and toponymous names.[1] This proves nothing about families. Surely far from all citizens belonging to those later tribes bearing gentilicial names belonged to that *gens*. And we can equally well suppose that Fabia Tribus named the clan and not the clan the *tribus*. Where is the gentilicial name in *Manios med fhefhaked Numasioi*? All truly Latin gentilicial names are originally adjectives and never lost that quality.

The Romans distinguished between *sacra privata* for the clans and *sacra publica* or *popularia* for the state and its political parts.[2] On this account alone we are justified in suspecting the validity of any equation of *genus* with *gens* ('clan'). One definition runs as follows:

A house (*domus*) of one family is a dwelling such as the city of one people or the world as domicile of the whole human race (*genus*). Moreover, there is a kind (*genus*) of household called the family or the wedding of man and wife. It starts from two and is a Greek word. For a family (*familia*) is made up of children (*liberi*) conceived in accordance with free laws (*ex liberis legibus*) from the femur. A *genus* is called either after the act of generation of after the definition of the other descendants, such as 'nations' which are called races (*gentes*) demarcated by the appropriate blood relationship. A people (*populus*) is made up of a human host allied by the agreement and harmonious communication of law....A people is a whole citizen body. ...Tribes are called as if curias and discrete communities of peoples, and take their name from the fact that in the beginning Romulus divided the Romans into three parts.[3]

The word *genus*, frequently with adjective, e.g. *genus Punicum*, commonly denotes a stock or race. Whereas in the historical period

---

[1] See below, pp. 76 f., 124–5.
[2] Varro, *LL* 6. 46: 'curiae, ubi senatus rem publicam curat, et illa ubi cura sacrorum publica, ab his curiones'. Festus, *Epit.* 42 L.: 'curia locus est, ubi publicas curas gerebant. calabra curia dicebatur ubi tantum ratio sacrorum gerebatur. curiae nominantur in quibus uniuscuiusque partis populi Romani quid geritur, quales sunt hae, in quas Romulus populum distribuit, numero triginta, quibus postea additae sunt quinque, ita ut in sua quisque curia sacra publica faceret feriasque observaret, hisque curiis singulis nomina curiarum virginum imposita esse dicuntur quas virgines quondam Romani de Sabinis rapuerunt.' Festus 284 L.: 'publica sacra, quae publico sumptu pro populo fiunt, quaeque pro montibus, pagis, curis, sacellis, at privata, quae pro singulis hominibus, familiis, gentibus fiunt'. Of course there were curial festivals which were not public; Festus 54 L.: 'curionia sacra quae in curiis fiebant'. With this compare Festus 146 L.: 'municipalia sacra vocantur, quae ab initio habuerunt ante civitatem Romanam acceptam; quae observare eos voluerunt pontifices, et eo more facere quo adsuessent antiquitus'.
[3] Isid. *Etym.* 9. 4. 3–7; cf. 11. 1. 2 = Festus, *Epit.* 88 L.

the Romans might meet by curias (*curiatim*), formerly they could be said to have met by race or stock (*generatim*). When Caesar says the Gauls and Germans were divided into what we today call tribes he uses the word *generatim*. The Gaulish and German *genera* had enough in common to be called Gauls and Germans and yet differences divided them into *genera*. Caesar also uses *generatim* of more disparate ethnic groups: Romans, Hispani and Gaditanes. Common bonds bring *genera* together.[1]

Cicero, too, uses *genus* to distinguish groups and sub-groups of people: the Greeks as a whole, Asiatics or the Ionians, Aeolians and Dorians (*tria Graecorum genera*).[2]

Next in chronological order of authority is Livian usage. Livy supplies what I consider the oldest official sense of *genus*. Therefore we shall examine his usage more closely. Alone *genus* means 'race'.[3] It may be modified by an ethnic, e.g. *genus Italicum* or *Hispanum*.[4] Or Livy could write after the pattern of *genus hominum*: *genus Rutulorum, Libyphoenicum* (cf. *equites Libyphoenices, mixtum Punicum Afris genus*), *Aetolorum*, and *Illyriorum*.[5] According to Livy (34. 9. 1–3) Emporiae in Spain was in fact two towns made up of Phocaean Greeks from Massilia and Spaniards to which Caesar added a third *genus* of *Romani coloni*. This brings us to a *genus* as a part of a community.

In 199 B.C. envoys from Umbrian Narnia protested to the Romans as follows: 'ad numerum sibi colonos non esse et immixtos quosdam non sui generis pro colonis se gerere'.[6]

---

[1] *BG* 1. 51. 2; 7. 19. 2; *BC* 2. 21. 1. See *TLL, s.v. genus* 1A4.

[2] *Ad Q. Fr.* 1. 1. 28; *Flacco* 27. 66, 27. 64. Varro, too, could use *genus Etruscum* (Festus 340 = Mirsch fr. 8. 12). Cf. Pliny, *NH* 3. 104: *Apulorum genera tria*. (viz. Teani, Lucani, Daunii).

[3] Livy 4. 3. 13, 4. 4. 7, 34. 17. 6; see below, p. 74, n. 4.

[4] Livy 21. 21. 2, 22. 13. 2, 22. 43. 3, 29. 1. 16, 30. 20. 5, 33. 17. 11. In this sense I would take the *genus Cilnium* of Arezzo which fell out with the rest of the Arretini and was reconciled to them by the Romans; Livy 10. 3. 2, 10. 5. 13. The incident is far from free of suspicion as a late addition to the annalistic; see De Sanctis II², p. 324, n. 146 and p. 332. However, Livy's use of *genus* as *gens* is unique in such a context. Furthermore, it seems unlikely an army would have been considered a necessity to impose peace on the Arretini on account of one 'clan'. Augustus wrote a letter to C. Cilnius Maecenas (in Macr. *Sat.* 2. 4. 12) calling him 'ebony of the town Medullia, Etruscan ivory, Arretine assafetida, an Adriatic diamond, a pearl from the Tiber, an emerald of the Cilnii, jaspar of the Iguvines, a beryl of Porsenna [bought at auction; cf. Livy 2. 14. 1–4, Plut. *Popl.* 19. 10], a ruby from Hadria'. See Malcovati on Aug. *Ep.* fr. 32. Whatever Augustus' joke, he seems to class the Cilnii with towns and peoples. Perhaps, the Cilnii were at one time the ruling *ethnos* in the Ager Arretinus. No wonder then that Horace wrote *Maecenas atavis edite regibus*.

[5] Livy 21. 7. 2, 21. 22. 3, 27. 32. 1, 27. 32. 4.   [6] Livy 32. 2. 6.

An apposite notice on the censorship of 179 B.C. casts light on this use and sense of *genus* (Livy 40. 51. 9): 'mutarunt [sc. censores] suffragia regionatimque generibus hominum causisque et quaestibus tribus discripserunt'. Accepting the interpretation of Lange and Botsford, Miss Taylor considers these *genera* as a distinction between the freeborn and freedmen, and supposes that a notice of the censorship of 169 which does concern freedmen refers to 179. However, in the notice of the latter year Livy (45. 15) states that the arrangement was made in the most recent census (*proxumo lustro*, i.e. in 174) and Livy has one of the censors of 169 refer to the freedmen as an *ordo*, not a *genus*. Less explicable is the plural *genera* if the entire business refers to freedmen. Why distinguish between them and freeborn and why not mention freedmen outright? What the censors did in 179 concerned arrangements made in the period from 188 to 181. In 188 a tribunician law prescribed the tribes into which the new Roman citizens of Formiae, Fundi and Arpinum should be enrolled (Livy 38. 36. 7–9). I propose that these former non-Roman *genera* would have been enrolled upon presentation before the censors in 184 and 179. Secondly, in 184 the citizen colonies of Pisaurum and Potentia were sent out; in 183 Parma, Mutina and Saturnia, and in 181 Graviscae were founded. The already Roman citizens of these colonies were enrolled in specified tribes according to colony and regardless of the colonists' former tribes. Hence the censors adjusted the voters from one tribe to another (*mutarunt suffragia*). We know for fact that non-Romans were enrolled in new tribes at their inception and in 184 a censor enrolled the Sallentine poet Ennius, at least, in a citizen colony (Cic. *Brut.* 79). Therefore, *genera hominum* may have also been considered in the enrolment of colonists into tribes as well as of towns. Censorial enrolment would have followed both colonial enrolment and settlement so that the censors could rate the citizen and his property. The occasion or nature of the grant of citizenship are the *causae* to be noted by the censors for the sake of drawing up tribal rosters. The phrase *genera hominum* has the ring of a formula. In the case of the censors of 179 the *genera* cannot be considered *gentes*, which censors did not acknowledge (Cic. *Leg.* 3. 3. 7), because it makes nonsense to examine family lines at the same time that they investigate *causae* region by region. What the censors wanted to know were how the applicant had become a Roman citizen (*causa*) and whence he originated (*genus*). The transfer of voters was an entirely different matter (as the syntax indicates) because it concerned those who had been Roman citizens before the census.[1]

Unequivocal official usage of *genus* as a stock, race or people is witnessed by a document of the emperor Claudius. It is most important because it is nearer the era of Laelius Felix who would have wanted his readers to benefit from his commentary by modern explication. In A.D. 46 Claudius issued an edict on the citizenship of the Anauni. The controversy went back to Tiberius. Claudius seems to have his and Caligula's file on the matter. The following is Claudius' decision:

quod ad condicionem Anaunorum et Tulliassium et Sindunorum pertinet, quorum partem delator adtributam Tridentinis, partem ne adtributam quidem arguisse dicitur, tametsi animadverto non nimium firmam id genus hominum habere civitatis Romanae originem, tamen cum longa usurpatione in possessione eius fuisse dicatur et ita permixtum cum Tridentinis, ut diduci ab eis sine gravi splendidi municipi iniuria non possit, patior eos in eo iure, in quo esse se existimaverunt, permanere beneficio meo, eo quidem libentius, quod plerique ex eo genere hominum etiam militare in praetorio meo dicuntur, quidam vero ordines quoque duxisse, nonnulli allecti in decurias Romae res iudicare.[2]

No better example could be required. The *genus hominum* is the people called Anauni. They were a discrete people. Yet they provided praetorian guards, legionaries (*ordines*) and jurors (*decuriae*). Every and any group might contribute to the armed forces but that fact does not explain their origins! Furthermore, it is most noteworthy that this *genus hominum* is *permixtum cum Tridentinis* since such phraseology echoes Livy's description of the Libyphoenicians and his report of the Narnienses' complaint.

Two years later Claudius delivered his eloquent address to the senate on honoring certain Gauls.[3] The oration echoes Livy[4] and is itself echoed by Tacitus.[5] Although Claudius gave the speech in the

[1] See Taylor, 'Voting Districts', pp. 139–40, 18–20, 67, 115 and chapter 7, E. T. Salmon, 'Roman Colonisation from the Second Punic War to the Gracchi', *JRS* 26 (1936), 47–67 and 'Roman Expansion and Roman Colonization in Italy', *Phoenix* 9 (1955), 63–75. For a *genus ingenuorum hominum* in legal phraseology see Lex Municipii Malacitani (*CIL* II, 1964 = *ILS* 6089 = *FIRA* I², no. 24), sect. 54; the *genus* was evidently defined in a lost clause which preceded.
[2] *CIL* v, 5050 = *ILS* 206 = *FIRA* I², no. 71, lines 21–33.
[3] *CIL* XIII, 1668 = *ILS* 212 = *FIRA* I², no. 43.
[4] Livy's speech of Canuleius: 4. 3. 13 and 4. 4. 7 ('oriundi ex Albanis et Sabinis non genere nec sanguine').
[5] *Ann.* 11. 23–4: 'indigenos consanguineis populis; coetus alienigenarum; Clausus

senate and had it published, what actually survives contains mention of no *genus* where we might expect it. This piece of Claudius is rhetorical whereas his edict was formal, official and probably based on chancery precedents.

We conclude that Laelius Felix meant a curiate assembly was distinguished by balloting according to stocks or former communal groups. None of these would have been great communities or greatly disparate in language or in culture. Rather, his evidence pointed to the vestiges of villages and hamlets in the vicinity of archaic Rome. By a closer examination of the curial testimony we can appreciate what the *genera* were and how they come to comprise Rome.

The word *curia* < *co-viria* suggests to us a band of men who claim equality among themselves and with other bands of men. Their need of equality arises not so much for want of internal equality but from political and social hazards inherent from a united, amalgamated state which grew into one state by an orderly process. This process had to take into account different backgrounds and to pave the way for synoecism. The ancient tradition acknowledges the fact of synoecism. The vocables of the Latin language both confirm the fact of synoecism and destroy the fiction of a Roman people constituted of but a minor third speaking the Latin language. For us the question is not whether there was synoecism. Our problem is what was its orderly process?

Sometimes the synoecism is obvious. For instance, the community of Septem Pagi, already obviously unified from seven districts, was absorbed by the Tribus Romilia. This act belongs to the early history of Rome. What of the growth itself of this early, tiny Rome?

CURIAS' PROPER NAMES

In this section I shall review the value of the proper names of seven surely known curias and two very likely curias.

Until Valerius Antias, folklore belief held the curias took their names from thirty Sabine girls carried off by Romulus and his Romans. Antias trivialized the legend by adducing a much larger number of Sabine girls. Varro, however, knew his Sabine onomastics

origine Sabina; conditor nostri Romulus tantum sapientia valuit ut plerosque populos eodem die hostis, dein civis habuerit'; etc. For the emperor's debt to his literary predecessors and his legacy see the comment and bibliography of R. M. Ogilvie, *A Commentary on Livy Books 1–5* (Oxford, 1965), pp. 533 ff.

and in his *Antiquities* declared that Romulus bestowed names upon his divisions of the people after their leaders (*hēgemones*) and after their districts (so we understand *pagoi*).[1] Thus we are justified in assuming that from Varro's standpoint curial names differed in kind not at all from tribal names: some names were derived from gentilicial names and others from place names. Varro's statement does not contradict the evidence. For the names of seven certain curias are Acculeia, Faucia, Veliensis, Velitia, Foriensis, Rapta and Titia. The two very likely curias bore the names Tifata and Hersilia.

Rapta has a place of honor not only because it was one of four 'Old Curias' but also because its name manifestly generated the legend that all curias took their names from the stolen (*raptae*) Sabine girls and perhaps even generated the legend of the rape itself. The word surely is not gentilicial and an unlikely adjective (or participle). In form it resembles the name of the city Scaptia, one of the lost towns of Latium (Pliny, *NH* 3. 68) which later gave its name to the Roman Tribus Scaptia (Festus 464, 465 L.). If Tifata, which in any event was a place name, may be adduced as evidence, Rapta may be neuter plural.

Veliensis, another 'Old Curia', is doubtless related to the hill called Velia or Veliae, near the Palatine. The compound indicates either a toponymous name, an ethnic, or both.

With Rapta and Veliensis is recorded Foriensis (Festus 180/2). A *forum* would not have constituted a *pagos* ('district') according to Varro's statement. At any rate, like Veliensis the name Foriensis is toponymous, ethnic, or both.

The last of the four recorded 'Old Curias' is Velitia. The name has all the appearances of a gentilicial formation.[2] Velitia may have a toponymous origin. Tarquitius, for example, seems to be derived from *Tarquitis, -is*, the ethnic of the town Tarquinii. Many such formations are discernible in Etruscan onomastics.[3]

Acculeia represents a not uncommon form of gentilicial name (cf. its possible dialect doublet Appuleius) but the Gens Acculeia or Accoleia was not prominent at Rome.[4]

---

[1] See above, chapter 3.

[2] See Schulze, pp. 91, 259–60, 428 and 436 on Velitius, Veletius and Veledius. In his epoch-making study Schulze notoriously derives Latin names of all sorts from putative Etruscan origins. A sober counterweight to his method can be had by reading Rix, pp. 1–10, and observing the latter's scrupulous methods. For Schulze both the Curias Velitia and Faucia had latinized Etruscan names. See below, p. 77, n. 1.

[3] Cf. Rix, pp. 232–6. [4] See Schulze, pp. 427, 453

Faucia is also an attested gentilicial name of a clan equally obscure.[1]

Titia, the last certain proper name of a curia, presents complications. Titia is a gentilicial name and seems derived from the praenomen Titus just as, *inter alia*, Marcius from Marcus, Quin(c)tus/ Quinctius, Sextus/Sextius, Tullus/Tullius and Hostus/Hostius. The name perhaps bears a relation with the archaic Tribus Titiensis and its tribules Tities or Titienses.[2] However, no one who discusses the old tribe introduces Curia Titia which is known from only one notice wherein it, too, takes its name from king Titus Tatius (Festus *Epit.* 503 L.). Whereas the tribe bears a toponymous or ethnic name, Titia is simply an adjective from *tit-*. If the Curia Titia takes its name from a clan, it is to be classed with Curias Acculeia and Faucia, names shared with obscure families.

Hersilia can be dealt with in short order. The only named Sabine lady is Hersilia, sometimes wife of Romulus and sometimes wife of his henchman Hostus Hostilius.[3] Presumably the Romans would never have accepted the folk-tale of thirty curias named after Sabine girls unless Hersilia had been made a curia. Indeed, the lady is fictional and took her name from a curia. The form is common enough as a gentilicial name, built with the suffix *-li-* to an *i*-stem (e.g. Manius/Manilius, Servius/Servilius, Hostius/Hostilius, Quinctius/Quin(c)tilius, Sextius/Sextilius). However, we know little of a Gens Hersilia nor personal names *Hersus and *Hersius in Latin. Varro said the curias took their names from leaders and districts. If Hersilia were classed with the latter, the name patterns with Romulus/Romilius, Siculus/Sicilia, Rutulus/Rutilius. But no notice of a district or a people with this name survives.

The evidence for a Curia Tifata is not so much inferential as equivocal. Pliny (*NH* 3. 68) claims that there had once been a Latian town of Tifata. *Tifata*, which is a neuter noun, also named a mountain range near Capua in Campania. In fact, the intervocalic *-f-* of the word would have been more appropriate to an Oscan than a Latin tongue (cf. Tiber and Tifernum). The dialectal character

---

[1] Schulze, pp. 150–1, 365 and 555, relates the name to Etruscan *pauca* etc. But see Rix, p. 365, n. 153 who looked at *CIE* 1170 and does not read or accept a possible reading *pauca*.

[2] See above, pp. 5–9.

[3] She had two children by Hostilius, Prima and Avillius; for a fuller account than most see Plut. *Rom.* 14, 18. (The kindest of Romulus' acts was to die without issue.) For the gentilicial evidence see Schulze, pp. 174, 455 and Ogilvie on Livy 1. 11. 1–4.

does not alter the facts that there was a Latian town Tifata and at least two *tifata* in or near Rome. Unfortunately all three notices come from Paulus' epitome of Festus:

> Curia tifata a Curio dicta est qui eo loco domum habuerat. (43 L.)
> Tifata iliceta. Romae autem Tifata curia. Tifata etiam locus iuxta Capuam. (503 L.)
> Mancina tifata appellabantur, quod Mancinus habuit insignem domum quae publicata est eo interfecto. (117 L.)

From one passage it is clear that *tifata* means 'oak groves'. The same passage betrays the carelessness of the epitomator. For, even if Festus had not remarked the Campanian mountains were so called because oak groves grew on them, he would not have called the mountains a *locus*. Both of the other notices contain what appears to be a commonplace on houses whose owners named the groves in which they were erected. Of Mancinus we know nothing. However, a man named Mancinus should have given the name Mancinianus, even though Mancinus is also adjectival. Whatever lurks behind this notice on *Mancina Tifata* seems to be based on a popular aetiology. Some particulars of Curius Dentatus' story are examined later.[1] However, the only other account which comes from the *De viris illustribus* (33. 10) inspires no confidence: 'ob haec merita domus ei apud Tiphatam et agri iugera quingenta publica data'. This anonymous authority has reduced *tifata, -orum* to *Tifata, -ae*. Clearly Festus believed that the three entries were required in his lexicon. Two of them as viewed by Paulus appear aetiological. The third is straightforward lexicography. However, his notice of *Tifata Curia* (on p. 503) is no more informative than that of *Tifata locus iuxta Capuam* which is misleading. A gentilicial Tifatius and some similar names are found.[2] Perhaps the curia was called variously Tifata and Tifatia.

In sum, three of the seven certain curias bear names which they share with undistinguished families: Acculeia, Faucia, Titia. A fourth name can be gentilicial or ethnic: Velitia. The other three are named after places or peoples as their formation indicates and one of them can be related to a Roman hill: Veliensis, Foriensis and Rapta. The two names of doubtful curias are doubtful names. Tifata

---

[1] See below, pp. 94, 165.
[2] Schulze, pp. 374, 531. On *tifata* see E. T. Salmon, *Samnium and the Samnites* (Cambridge, 1967), p. 149, n. 7.

is a place name beyond doubt. But after that is said, doubts arise. Hersilia can be interpreted as a gentilicial or ethnic name.

In chapter 4 we discussed the names of the Curia Asernia from Caere and the Curias Clodia Firma and -amonal(is) at Lanuvium.[1] The Etruscan curia has a latinized Etruscan proper name that can be toponymous or gentilicial.[2] Lanuvinian Curia Clodia Firma bears a gentilicial and an honorific name. Although the pronunciation Clodia was plebeian in Rome, we have no reason to hold that the same was true at Lanuvium. The secondary, honorific 'cognomen' can be compared with those given to legions[3] or to towns.[4] The other Lanuvinian Curia -amonal(is) is unique despite its mutilation. The name resembles adjectives formed from gods' names. Furthermore, the suffix type -on- is also commonly met in place names of Etruria, Umbria and Latium but its ethnic suffix is regularly -ensis. Finally, in light of the Roman curias Veliensis and Foriensis the identification of the Tiburtine mēros Sikelikon[5] with a Curia Sicana, or the like, becomes possible.

Since the word curia has feminine gender, all Latin curias probably had feminine names which could be and were interpreted as the names of women. Varro's statement on the names of curias is borne out by an analysis of the Roman names which are either toponymous or gentilicial, or susceptible to both derivations. Except for -amonal(is) of Lanuvium, the names of non-Roman curias also follow Varro's interpretation of the Roman names of curias and the Sicilian part of Tibur.

---

[1] See above, pp. 59–61.

[2] Schulze, pp. 129, 163, relates it to As-inius. The stem is *aser-*. An analogous latinized toponym is Tifernum < *Tifer- = Tiber and gentilicial Perperna. Compare also the Clavernii at Iguvium (chapter 4) and Arezzo's Cilnii (chapter 5, p. 72, n. 4).

[3] See above, p. 61, n. 2.

[4] Cf. Pliny, *NH* 3. 52: Arretini Veteres, A. Fidentiores, A. Iulienses.

[5] See pp. 62–3, 174.

CHAPTER 6

CURIAL ORIGINS AND RELIGION

Any treatment of curial religion must begin with Dionysius' three chapters in the second book of his *Roman Antiquities*. He expressly states two sources for the account, M. Terentius Varro and his own experience.[1] Most of his data are treated in a detailed manner in this chapter. In order to make the picture complete and to represent his method and entire account, the gist of these chapters is here given.

Romulus as lawgiver created sixty priesthoods to carry on religious worship in curias on behalf of the entire city-state (*ta koina peri tēs poleōs*). He enjoined each curia to elect two wealthy men, 50 years of age, of outstanding family and sound body. The tenure of their office was unlimited and carried with it exemption from all military and civil offices. Their wives and children, when both parents lived, were to assist the priests. The wives (*flaminicae*) were to attend to purely female rites. Childless priests had to choose the children of other families (*oikoi*) of the curia to assist them. The boys would serve until puberty, the girls until marriage. (Two inferences must be drawn here from Dionysius: first, the priests (or, at least, the thirty flamens) had to have wives; secondly, the children never had to be the priests' offspring because a man at 50 years of age is not likely to have qualifying children.) Dionysius believed these young persons, *tutulatae* and *camilli*, had Greek counterparts which proved the Romans had borrowed the practice from Greeks. The curias were also designated the electors of all Roman priests and *leitourgoi*. Next, Romulus appointed the rites, gods and *daimones* peculiar to each curia and fixed the sacrificial expenses which the curias received from the public treasury. With their priests the *curiales* kept their own sacrifices and dined in common at the curial hearth. Every curia had a dining-hall of its own with its own hearth. The dining-halls and the curias have the same name still in Dionysius' time. He likens the halls to the Greeks' *prytanea* and more especially to the Spartan

[1] D.H. 2. 21–3.

phiditia ('public messes') which Romulus borrowed from the Spartan lawgiver Lycurgus. With the addition of details of the dinners treated later, Dionysius' description ends.

To his description of Romulus' contributions to curial religion must be added T. Tatius' installation of a Juno Quiritis in every curia. Dionysius based this attribution upon a Varronian derivation of the epithet from a Sabine word. Evidently this was the only deity worshipped by every curia. Otherwise the several curias had their own *sacra* and *ritus*, gods and *daimones*.[1] The latter word means *genius* in Latin. The Roman people, city-states, colonies, municipalities, districts, neighborhoods, camps, corporations, legions, centuries, squadrons, mountains, fountains, provinces, places, roads and emperors all had *genii* of their own. The Lares, who are connected indirectly with the thirty curias, could also be classed as a species of *daimones*,[2] for they were almost inseparable in the Italian ruler-cult. In any case, a curia's *daimon* would have been its peculiar tutelary divinity. Varro obviously dealt with curial ceremonies and deities at greater length than Dionysius cares to repeat. Its distorted reflection can be seen in Tertullian who recalls the Varronian comparison of curias and phratries.[3] Such passages in Tertullian as those on strange local deities which he took from Varro[4] illustrate to some extent the method Varro may have followed in writing on the curias. Unfortunately, whatever Varro wrote about the peculiar divinities and rites of the several curias has not survived in a manner attributable to his discussion. Festivals observed by all the curias

---

[1] *Ibid.* 2. 50. 3, following Varro (cf. 2. 48). D.H. 2. 23. 1; 'ταῦτα περὶ τῶν θρησκευόντων τοὺς θεοὺς καταστησάμενος διῄρει πάλιν . . . κατ' ἐπιτηδειότητα ταῖς φράτραις τὰ ἱερά, θεοὺς ἀποδεικνὺς ἑκάστοις καὶ δαίμονας οὓς ἔμελλον ἀεὶ σέβειν . . .'

[2] *Ibid.* 4. 14 uses 'heroes' for Lares; cf. D.H. 1. 32. 2. It was the official version; see *Mon. Ancyr.* 19, 32. 2. See Varro in Arn. 3. 41 = Agahd, p. 189. For the epigraphic and other evidence see Cesano in De Ruggiero's *Diz. Epigr. s.v. genius*, especially pp. 450–3 and Vitucci, *ibid. s.v. Lares*. The thirty pigs and the Lares Grunduli, seen by Romulus and Remus, imply a connection between curias and cult of the Lares; see above, chapter 2, pp. 9–10. In the 14th Region is recorded a *vicus Larum Ruralium* but the reading had already been challenged before the discovery of *CIL* vi, 36811, one of three altar dedications found outside the Porta Portuensis: *Lares semitales, Lares [C]uriales, Lares Viales*. This inscription raises the possibility of Lares Curiales. See *CIL* vi, 975 = *ILS* 6073 with Dessau's n. 21, Huelsen in Platner–Ashby, *A Topographical Dictionary of Ancient Rome* (Oxford, 1929), p. 608, and Vitucci, *loc. cit.* p. 405.

[3] *Apol.* 39. 15 where he mentions the phratries' Apaturia; see above, p. 68, n. 5. It is distorted because the simplicity of curial banquets described by Dionysius can hardly be squared with Tertullian's 'The air is rancid among so many puking tribes, curias and decurias.'

[4] *Ad Nat.* 2. 8. 1–7, *Apol.* 24. 7–10; = Agahd, pp. 161–2.

severally or together are known. The particular festivals are subject to conjecture. In any event, Varro discerned variety rather than uniformity in the actual religion of the thirty curias. By itself this conclusion of Varro's attests the curias' diverse origins. The equation of curias with phratries was appropriate in this respect. However, the equation was carried beyond the religious element into the military organization where the direct evidence ran counter to the interpretation. Furthermore, the indirect evidence ran against a curial military system. Whereas the oldest kind of tribune did indeed perform at the head of an armed force, the curion and curia took their names, thought Varro, from *cura sacrorum publica*.

Even the primary source of our reconstruction of the curias' expansion has been told with the simple mind unused to dealing intelligently with any pre-historical material.

OLD AND NEW CURIAS

The beginning of the curias does not lie in any military organization. They left no mark upon any military system in Roman history. Curial officers (*curiones*) had to be 50 years of age, were exempted (or excluded) from civil and military duties and *curiones* enjoyed life-tenure which no military officer possessed except for the king,[1] while the officers of three Romulean tribes (*tribuni*) had a prominent place in Roman military history.

According to Festus the curias found their first headquarters too small and Romulus built new headquarters to which seven curias refused to move on religious grounds. Four curias, Foriensis, Rapta, Veliensis and Velitia, observe their rites in the Old Curias (*veteres curiae*). From other evidence we know Old Curias were situated within the Palatine boundary and this knowledge is supported by the situation of the Velia, a hillock of the Palatine Region.[2] On the basis of the four named curias editors have changed the number of curias given by Festus from seven to four. However, the verb tenses uphold the MS reading of seven: seven could not move (*potuerunt*)

---

[1] D.H. 2. 21. 3 '. . . ἀλλ' ἐξ ἑκάστης φράτρας ἐνομοθέτησεν [ὁ Ρομύλος] ἀποδείκνυσθαι δύο τοὺς ὑπὲρ πεντήκοντα ἔτη γεγονόντας γένει τε προὔχοντας τῶν ἄλλων καὶ ἀρετῇ διαφόρους καὶ χρημάτων περιουσίαν, ἔχοντας ἀρχοῦσαν καὶ μηδὲν ἠλαττωμένους τῶν περὶ τὸ σῶμα· τούτους δὲ οὐκ εἰς ὡρισμένον τινὰ χρόνον τὰς τιμὰς ἔταξεν ἔχειν, ἀλλὰ διὰ παντὸς τοῦ βίου, στρατειῶν μὲν ἀπολελυμένους διὰ τὴν ἡλικίαν, τῶν δὲ κατὰ τὴν πόλιν ὀχληρῶν διὰ τὸν νόμον'. See Momigliano, 'Interim Report' p. 110 and below, p. 146, n. 2.
[2] For these and other sites consult the maps, below, pp. 307–9.

and four still observe (*fiunt*) their religious duties at Old Curias at
the time of Festus or his authority. The new meeting-place (*novae
curiae*) stood near the crossroads of Fabricius which we locate inferentially on the Caelian Hill.[1] Heretofore it has been held that
twenty-three or twenty-six curias had religious reunions at New
Curias. Probably they did not. Insofar as we are informed, all the
curias met on the Capitoline for religious purposes (*comitia calata*) or
at the Comitium off the Forum for political purposes (*comitia curiata*).[2]
Furthermore, Dionysius 2. 23. 1–2 speaks of religious meetings in
each curia and not among united curias and makes no mention of
either Old or New Curias or curiate assemblies. The silence of
Dionysius and our other sources suggests that Old and New Curias
held united meetings when neither the Forum nor Capitol was a
civic center. Confirmation of Festus' vaguely worded statement that
thirty curias were supposed to meet at New Curias is not supported
by other evidence.

Old Curias must have been the earliest place of assembly at least
for the settlers of the Palatium, Velia and, no doubt, the Cermalus.
The proximity of New Curias to a crossroads suggests that the crossroads was originally a natural meeting-place for the inhabitants of
the Caelian with dwellers from other hills after a merger. If this
merger included the Palatine, subsequent religious meetings at New
Curias were not of the older curias. After the meetings of all the
curias were moved to the central districts of Rome, the Capitol and
Forum, Old and New Curias were preserved for religious purposes.
The formation of more new curias blurred the distinction between
Old and New Curias until an antiquarian found a reason for the two
buildings in two places: the creatures of the founding father Romulus
had outgrown their first house and he made them a new one. In fact,

---

[1] Festus 180/2 L.: 'Novae curiae proximae compitum Fabricium aedificatae sunt,
quod parum amplae erant veteres a Romulo factae, ubi is populum et sacra in partis
triginta distribuerat, ut in is ea sacra curarent, quae cum ex veteribus in novas evocarentur, septem curiarum per religiones evocari non potuerunt. itaque Foriensis, Raptae,
Veliensis, Velitiae res divinae fiunt in veteribus curis.' Cf. Varro, *LL* 5. 155. For the situation of Old Curias see Tac. *Ann.* 12. 24 and *CIL* vi, 975, col. 2. 1; for the situation of the
Vicus Fabrici in Augustan Region I see *CIL* vi, 975, col. 1. 46 (the Capitoline Base). For
a discussion of its location see A. M. Colini, 'Storia e topografia del Celio nell'antichità',
Atti d. Pont. Accad. ser. 3, *mem.* 7, pp. 72 and 440; Colini believes New Curias faced Old
Curias. On New Curias see De Francisci, 'Primordia Civitatis', pp. 572–7.

[2] *Curia Calabra* and *comitia calata* on the Capitol: Varro, *LL* 6. 27; Festus 42 L.; Serv.
Dan. on *Aen.* 8. 654; Macr. *Sat.* 1. 15. 10; Gellius, 15. 27. 1–3; Gaius, *Inst.* 1. 109. On the
comitia curiata in the Comitium of the Forum, Varro, *LL* 5. 155: 'comitium ab eo quod
coibant eo comitiis curiatis et litium causa'.

Old and New Curias are the oldest witnesses to the expansion of the community through the formation and addition of curias.

THE TWENTY-SEVEN ARGEI

The third witness to the addition of curias is the archaic itinerary of the Argei, long a puzzle in the history of Roman religion, by reason of the fact that its evidence had already become obscure before the end of the third century. Religious observances took place at the Argei in Rome on 16 and 17 March and 14 or 15 May. These days have no notation of rites at the Argei in the official calendars although state officials participated. Of the March day's activities at the stations called Argei we know next to nothing. Of the May rites we are more, if not well, informed. Then a procession of pontiffs, Vestals and praetors went the circuit of the stations, fetched figures of rush, reed and straw worked into human shapes, and proceeded to the Pons Sublicius whence the figures were tossed into the Tiber. Both the stations (*sacraria* or *sacella*) and the figures (*effigies* or *simulacra*) bore the name Argei whose etymology is unknown.[1]

Varro (*LL* 5. 45–54) preserves a partial list of the twenty-seven Argei which he draws from an unidentified ritual manual. What follows is that list without the Varronian comment:[2]

I Suburan Region

    1. Princeps est Caelius Mons.

      (primae regionis quartum sacrarium scriptum sic est:)

---

[1] Ovid, *F.* 3. 791–2: 'itur ad Argeos—qui sint, sua pagina dicet—hac, si commemini, praeteritaque die'. Gellius 10. 15. 30 reports the flaminica went to the Argei (*it ad Argeos*) which Plutarch, *Quaest. Rom.* 86 appears to relate to the May rite. D. H. 1. 38. 3 omits mention of the flaminica as does Ovid, *F.* 5. 621–62. Besides discussion in the handbooks of Roman religion and Frazer's commentary to Ovid, L. A. Holland, 'Janus and the Bridge', *Amer. Acad. in Rome: Papers and Monographs* 21 (1961), 313–31, has contributed an appendix on the Argei in which she discusses chiefly the relation of the Vestals, pontiffs and the *pons sublicius*. For pontiffs and Argei see also Livy 1. 21. 5 and D.H. 1. 38. A relation between the Argei and curias on the basis of Dionysius, *loc. cit.*, has been discussed before me; see, e.g., Gervasio in De Ruggiero's *Diz. Epigr. s.v. curia* pp. 1393–4. See Degrassi, *Inscriptiones Italiae*, vol. 13, fasc. 2, 'Fasti Anni Numani et Iuliani' (Rome, 1963), pp. 424–5, 457–8.

[2] The text followed here is that of Jean Collart, 'Varron: De lingua latina livre V', *Publ. Fac. Lettres Univ. Strasbourg* 122 (Paris, 1954), whose commentary is also worth consulting. The numeration and punctuation of the text is mine for reasons which will be given; I have set within quotation marks what I believe to be the very words transcribed by Varro from his priestly source. These words display a uniform lack of syntax in contrast to Argei I, 1 and 6 which Varro paraphrases in the belief that, for example, *quarticeps* means *quartus*. On the total number of Argei see *LL* 5. 45 and 7. 44 and Collart's comment on the former passage, p. 171.

4. 'Caeriolense. Quarticeps: circa Minervium, qua in Caelium montem itur, in tabernola est.'
6. Eidem regioni adtributa Subura, quod sub muro Terreo[1] Carinarum. in eo est Argeorum sacellum sextum.

II Esquiline Region

(in sacris Argeorum scriptum sic est:)
1. 'Oppius Mons. Princeps: Esquilis uls Lucum Facutalem, sinistra via, secundum moerum est.'
3. 'Oppius Mons. Terticeps: uls Lucum Esquilinum, dexteriore via, in tabernola est.'
4. 'Oppius Mons. Quarticeps: uls Lucum Esquilinum, via dexteriore in figlinis est.'
5. 'Cespius Mons. Quinticeps: uls Lucum Poetelium, Esquilis est.'
6. 'Cespius Mons. Sexticeps: apud aedem Iunonis Lucinae, ubi aeditumus habere solet.'

III Colline Region

(ex Argeorum sacrificiis in quibus scriptum sic est:)
3. 'Collis Quirinalis. Terticeps: uls aedem Quirini.'
4. 'Collis Salutaris. Quarticeps: adversum est Apollinar, uls aedem Salutis.'
5. 'Collis Mucialis. Quinticeps: apud aedem Dei Fidi, in delubro ubi aeditumus habere solet.'
6. 'Collis Latiaris. Sexticeps: in vico Insteiano summo, apud auguraculum aedificium solum est.'

IV Palatine Region

(in hac regione scriptum est:)
5. 'Germalense. Quinticeps: apud aedem Romuli.'
6. 'Veliense. Sexticeps: in Velia apud aedem Deum Penatium.'

This itinerary is here interpreted as the vestige of four processions to sacred areas once used by twenty-seven curias for taking the auspices necessary to curial business. Its present form can be no older than 241 B.C. when the Minervium (I 4) was built. The present state of the itinerary and the disparity of the stations affirms the obscurity of the sites as Argei in the third century and displays an adherence to the four Servian sectors of the city. The lack of uniformity of the then existing occupation of the sites proves the Argei had lost their original purpose at least as early as 466 when the temple of Dius

---

[1] Cf. Varro, *LL* 5. 21: 'terra dicta ab eo, ut Aelius scribit, quod teritur. itaque tera in augurum libris scripta cum R uno.'

Fidius (III 5) stood on one site.[1] Romans of the Republic did not use the Argei as originally intended.

In Regions II and III the sites are noted by place; in Regions I and IV, the regions of Old and New Curias, they are noted by demotics except for Argei I 1 and I 6 whose identification has been paraphrased by Varro in his discussion of Caele Vibenna and of the etymology of Subura. Argei IV 6 in the Palatine Region bears the same demotic as the Curia Veliensis of Old Curias.

Ritual identification of the Argei had been prompted by continuous encroachment upon their land. Four Argei stood in the open beyond grove or temple or along a wall (II 1, II 5, III 3 and III 4). Two Argei apparently had structures of their own (I 6 and III 6). One of these Argei was the solitary building in an augural precinct (III 6). Seven stood within the precincts of a temple building (*apud aedem*), in two *tabernolae* and in *figlinae*. Two Argei beyond temples had yielded ground to the temple buildings (III 3 and 4). Although temples had been built on the lots of the Argei, this concession did not prevent the temple-warders from taking up their post in the Argei proper (II 6 and III 5). Obviously the Argei themselves had been spared at first; then they, too, were occupied. It is no wonder that the processional route had to be preserved in writing and revised according to buildings raised from 466 (III 5) to the later third century (I 4 and IV 6).

Only one Argei still stood on a lot of relatively great extent, an augural precinct in the Colline Region (III 6). Augurs took their positions according to strict rules: the formula was *recte* or *vitio tabernaculum capere* (Cicero, *De div.* 1. 17. 33, 2. 35. 75). The *tabernaculum*, properly speaking, was the site of the augury, the place of the *taberna*. In historical times the Roman augurs did not sit in a *taberna*, but certain Iguvine augurs did sit within a structure of uncertain material called *tremnu* (*Tab. Ig.* VIA 2, 16). These may be huts of thatch. At Rome three famous relics were the thatched *casa Romuli* on the *auguraculum* of the Capitoline *arx*, the *tugurium Faustuli* on the Palatine where Romulus took the augury for founding a city, and the *casa Romuli* of the Palatine with which the *aedes Romuli*, Argei IV 5, invites comparison, if not identification.[2] The

---

[1] For the dates of these temples and others cited in the itinerary the list in G. Wissowa, *Religion und Kultus*[2], pp. 594–5, offers the easiest reference.

[2] See D.H. 1. 79. 11, Festus 17 L., Solinus 1.18, Vitruvius 2. 1. 5: 'item in Capitolio commonefacere potest et significare mores vetustatis Romuli casa et in arce sacrorum

Romans also knew the sites of other royal domiciles. Their tradition may reflect the existence of archaic huts.

Tullus Hostilius' house had once stood on the Velia where in Varro's day the temple of the Penates was standing. Thus, Tullus' house coincides with Argei IV 6. Varro also reports that Ancus Marcius had his home at the Porta Mugionis *secundum viam sub sinistra*.[1] Solinus confirms the site of Tullus' house and puts Ancus Marcius where later stood a temple of the Lares *in summa Sacra Via*. Instead of Ancus, Solinus situates the house of Tarquin I at Porta Mugonia above Summa Via Nova where, in effect, Pliny would have the house of Tarquin II when he says that it stood opposite the temple of Jupiter Stator. The hut which had once stood near this gate and the temple of Jupiter may be one of the missing Palatine Argei. The location of the temple of the Lares remains problematic; it was also in the Palatine Region and perhaps near the arch of Titus. Solinus has Tarquin II's house on the Esquiline above Clivus Pullius at the Fagutalis lacus (presumably a mistake for *lucus*). It coincides with Argei II 1. According to the same authority Servius Tullius' house stood on the Esquiline above Clivus Urbius. This ascent led to the Oppian Mount. Perhaps the hut belonged to Argei II 2 and was its *tabernola*. The last two houses which Solinus discusses are Titus Tatius' on the *arx* and Numa's on the Quirinal. The former may coincide with the augurs' *auguraculum*. The latter is so situated because of the folk belief in Quirinus' origin in Cures, Numa's home town. It may be identified as Argei III 3. Tatius' house on the citadel stood as a pendant to Romulus' Capitoline hut near the Curia Calabra.[2] Finally, independently of the tradition in Solinus the hut of Tullus Hostilius is located somewhere on the Caelian Mount.[3]

The nature of the augural *tabernaculum*, the place of the *taberna* or hut, can best be realized from the following fragmentary commentary on a line of Vergil:

Sabidius commentar. XII vers. Salior. ut in exercitu [signum ad pugnam

stramentis tecta'. Platner–Ashby have a discussion of these sites with more references.

[1] Varro, *De Vita Populi Romani*, Book I in Nonius, p. 852 L. Cf. Cic. *Rep.* 2. 31. 53 and D.H. 1. 68. 1–2. On this gate see below, p. 94, n. 1.

[2] Solinus 1. 21–6, Pliny, *NH* 34. 29; cf. Livy 1. 41. 4, Plut. *Rom.* 20. 5, and Festus 519 L.: 'umbrae vocabantur Neptunalibus casae frondeae pro tabernaculis.' Tatius' house was later the site of the temple of Juno Moneta which Solinus mentions.

[3] Livy 1. 30. 1, D.H. 3. 1. 5.

datum erat. is, penes que]m imp[erium auspici]umque erat, in taber-
naculo in sella [se]dens auspicabatur coram exercitu; pullis e cavea libera-
tis [immissisque in lo]cum circum sellam suam * * * nuntiato a * * *
ullum. * * * [tripudium sinisterum solisti]mum quisqu[is vestrum
viderit], tripudia[tum nunt]iato.' silentio deinde facto residebat et
dicebat: 'equites et pedites nomenque Lati[num * * *]les cincti armati
paludati, * * * [qui ad]estis sic uti [tripu]dium sinisterum solistimum
quisquis vestrum vider[it, nuntiato.' felici] deinde ill[i augurio] nuntiato
diceba[t: 'dii] uti placet a legionibus invocentur, faciantque quod iis
imperabitur [milites] imp[eriumque] fidemque m[eam servent. quod
con]ducat salutareque siet. viros voca, proelium ineant. deinde exercitu
in aciem educto iterum [morabantur, ut immolare]tur. interim ea mora
utebantur, qui testamenta in procinctu facere volebant.[1]

The *tabernaculum* can refer to the commander's tent which, moreover, evidently took its name from the augural term for that place in
which the auspices were regularly taken by commanding officers.
As we shall see in chapter 9, the ceremony which is here reported for
the preliminaries to a battle might have been held at any centuriate
assembly in the Campus Martius. In any event, the *tabernaculum*
doubtless was necessary to augury and auspices.

The material used in the construction of the primitive huts squares
with the reported material of the Argei which were collected and
tossed in the Tiber. Isidore of Seville summarizes some of the pertinent definitions:

tabernae olim vocabantur aediculae plebeiorum parvae et simplices in
vicis, axibus et tabulis clausae....dictae autem tabernae quod ex tabulis
lignisque erant constructae, quae nunc et si non speciem, nomen tamen
pristinum retinent.

Etym. 15. 2. 43 (De aedificiis publicis).

De aedificiis rusticis. casa est agreste habitaculum palis atque virgultis
arundinibusque contextum, quibus possint homines tueri a frigoris vel
caloris iniuria. tugurium casula est quam faciunt sibi custodes vinearum ad
tegimen sui, quasi tegurium, sive propter ardorem solis et radios de-
clinandos, sive ut inde vel homines vel bestiolas, quae insidiare solent
natis frugibus, abigant. hunc rustici capannam vocant, quod unum tantum
capiat. tescua quidam putant esse tuguria, quidam loca praerupta et
aspera.

Etym. 15. 12. 1–3.

---

[1] Schol. Ver. on *Aen.* 10. 241 in Thilo–Hagen 3. 2. 446 and Bruns, *Fontes*[7] 2.77 f.,
followed here. On the formal character of the testamentary ceremony see below, pp. 193–
5. Notice the similarity of the phrase *equites et pedites...cincti armati paludati* to passages in
the Iguvine lustration of the *populus*, above, pp. 41–3.

In fact, the word *tesca* belongs to augural formula[1] and had been confused with the old-fashioned seat of the augur. At Suburan Region I 4 and Esquiline Region II 3 the *tabernolae* remained the survivors of auguries without mention of their *auguracula*. Only the Palatine Region in this itinerary shows no survivor of augury, although the Palatine *aedes Romuli, casa Romuli* and *tugurium Faustuli* point to similar foundations. However Hadrian restored an *auguratorium* on the Palatine which the Regionaries mention.[2] In each of the four Servian regions one augural seat had been preserved. The Roman conscientiously maintained four of the twenty-seven and let the land of the rest receive buildings or shrines.

Ancient authors inform us that these archaic huts were made of stakes (*pali*), branches (*frondes*), twigs (*virgulta*), reeds (*harundines* and *calami*) and straw (*stramenta*). The bundles from the Argei thrown annually into the Tiber consisted of reeds, straw and rushes (*scirpi*). Only rushes are not mentioned explicitly in Roman antiquity as wattle. The Moors, however, used them to build the huts peculiar to Africa (*mapalia*) and the Romans for the frames of wagons.[3] Periodically the *casa Romuli* on the *arx* was renewed. Romulus' Palatine hut was scrupulously repaired when weather and time had taken their toll (Dion. *Ant. Rom.* I. 79. 11). In the early days the Romans had repaired these *tabernolae* once a year after the weather would not harm them. In the winter the reeds were cut and in the

---

[1] For the augural formula see Varro, *LL* 7. 8 (cf. Cicero in Festus 488–9 L.). On the meaning of *tesca* see Kurt Latte, 'Augur und Templum in der varronischen Augurformel', *Philologus* 97 (1948), 152–6.

[2] For references to this *auguratorium* see Lugli's *FTVVRP* vol. 8, nos. 338–42.

[3] On hut construction: Ovid, *F.* 3. 527–9 (*frondea casa; calami*); Isid. *Etym.* 15. 12, quoted above; Dion 1. 79. 1 (wood and reed); Livy 25. 39. 3 (*stramentum*); Vitruvius 2. 1 (*stramentum*). Cf. Livy 27. 3. 2–4. Ovid, *F.* 6. 261–2 says primitive huts were thatched with stubble (*stipula*) and their walls woven with osiers (*vimen*); both words are vague and do not really indicate the exact species of plant. Most probably any pliable branch was classed as a *vimen*. Indeed the rush (*scirpus*) was so considered by Varro, *RR* 1. 23. 5. On wagon of rush see Cato, *Agr.* 10. 2, Varro, *LL* 5. 139 and *RR* 1. 23. 5, Ovid, *F.* 6. 680; on the *mapalia* see Livy 30. 3. 9, Pliny, *NH* 16. 178. On the contents of the Argei, Varro, *LL* 7. 44 (*argei fiunt e scirpeis*) whom Festus 14 L. follows, and Ovid, *F.* 5. 621–2 (*scirpea simulacra*), 631 (*straminei Quirites*), and 637 (*harundiferum caput Thybris*). L. A. Holland in 'Janus and the Bridge', pp. 318–23, tries to reduce the material to the stubble (*stipula*) of the *far* which she considers *stercus*. Conon, *Narr.* 48. 8 describing the hut of Romulus or Faustulus, says it was made of wicker-work and whatever the wind would bring (ἐκ φορυτῶν καὶ νέων φραγάνων). The materials of Italian huts are the same in the twentieth century A.D. as the eighth B.C. See Treccani's *Dizionario enciclopedico italiano* and *Enciclopedia italiana* (with drawings and photographs of huts in the Roman Campagna) *s.v.* *capanna*, which are made of branches (*frascame*), reeds (*canne*), straw (*paglia*), stakes (*pali* and stubble (*stoppie*). The modern Italian huts, as well as the ancient, were designed for dwelling and naturally are larger than those used by augurs.

spring the stubble (*stipula*) of the *far* was available.[1] The old thatching was bundled and thrown into the Tiber just as the *far* of the Campus Martius was once destroyed because the crop was under religious interdict.[2] The bundles shaped as human figures and the aetiology of surrogation of human victims grew from the ancient misunderstanding of the technical name of the bundles: 'depontani senes appellabantur qui sexagenarii de ponte deiciebantur' (Festus 66 L.). The adjectives cognate with the Latin *senes* in Greek and other Indo-European languages mean 'old', and are applied to the crop of previous years; and in one Indo-European language it means the wilted grass of the previous year. The Romans thought these 'old men' had reached their sixtieth year because that was the climacteric year for attaining one's seniority. The word *argei*, I suspect, conceals the primitive significance of thatching which can be applied to hut and figure.[3] Both Ennius, *Ann.* 54 V., and Vergil, *Aen.* 8. 72, paraphrase an archaic Saturnian prayer to the Tiber (*adeste Tiberine cum tuis undis*) which they connect with throwing a man into the river. Servius, who quotes the prayer in commenting on *Aen.* 8. 72, perhaps betrays its source when citing on *Aen.* 8. 95 (Dan.) the archaic meaning of *coluber* ('winding') applied to the Tiber in the augural books (*libri augurum*). The very name of the river Tiber was thought to have been derived from the name of a drowned Tiberinus.[4]

Writing on the Latin language Varro vaguely notes the nature of his copy of the itinerary *in sacris* or *sacrificiis scriptum sic est*. Yet he elsewhere refers to the *libri augurum* which he has before his eyes. He cites a strange spelling (5. 21), thrice quotes them directly (5. 58, 6. 64, 7. 8) and invokes their authority for definitions (5. 33, 6. 76, 7. 51). Also Varro devoted a book to the subject of augurs.[5]

---

[1] On the straw, reeds, and *far* stubble see Pliny, *NH* 18. 52, 240–1, 297–9 and below pp. 97, n. 1 and 98, n. 5 on the *camilli flaminii*. Cf. *Menologium Rusticum CIL* I², p. 280.

[2] Livy 2. 5. 1–4; Plut. *Poplic.* 8.

[3] Festus 450 L. (see Bremer, *Jurisprudentiae Antehadrianae Quae Supersunt* (Leipzig, 1896), I, 107), 452 L.; Varro in Censorinus, *DN* 14. 2. For the etymology of the root of *senex* see H. Frisk, *Griech. Etym. Wörterb.* (Heidelberg, 1960) *s.v.* ἕνος. *Senescere* and its compounds retain the original sense; see, for example, Plaut. *Rud.* 1302; Varro, *RR* 3. 9. 8; Pliny, *NH* 11. 242, 15. 82. Perhaps Martial 3. 58. 7 reflects the very old usage: 'multa fragrat testa senibus autumnis'.

[4] On Tiberinus in the augural books see Cic. *ND* 3. 20. 52 (cf. Festus 284, 296 L.); on the drowning of the man Tiberinus see, for example, Livy 1. 3. 8 and Festus 503 L. Vahlen has collected pertinent parallels in his testimonia to *Ann.* 54, on which see also H. D. Jocelyn, *CQ* 58 (1964), 293–5. See Serv. on *Aen.* 8. 63, 8. 90, 8. 330–1; cf. on *Aen.* 7. 190.

[5] Macr. *Sat.* 1. 16. 19 on which see Bremer I, 124. On Varro's use of the pontifical books see *LL* 5. 23, 5. 98—the only two instances.

In contrast he only twice appears to be using the pontifical books in writing on the Latin language. More telling is his etymology of Caeriolense, Argei I 4: 'Caeriolensis a Carinarum iunctu dictus; pote a caerimonia, quod hinc oritur caput Sacrae Viae ab Streniae sacello quae pertinet in arcem, qua sacra quotquot mensibus feruntur in arcem et per quam augures ex arce profecti solent inaugurare. huius Sacrae Viae pars haec sola volgo nota quae est a foro eunti primore clivo.' Surely other *caerimoniae* might have come to mind. Has chance compelled Varro to mention an augural procession from the citadel through the Sacred Way to the point where the Argean itinerary begins? Or to point out that the Sacred Way was longer than commonly held? Rome's Sacred Way ought to be compared with Iguvium's Augural Way (*vea aviekla, Tab. Ig.* Ib, 14; VIb, 52). The augurs begin their procession at the augural precinct of Rome. They pass from the civic center of the Capitoline through the other civic center of the Forum and thence to the point from which they go into the four regions. Before their college was increased in 300, the augurs numbered four. One augur could have augured at the Argei of each region. In the itinerary after the demotic or toponym, which has no syntactical dependence, stands an adjective also without syntactical dependence: *princeps, terticeps, quarticeps, quinticeps,* or *sexticeps*. The adjectives *princeps* etc. could have modified the implied augur who takes the augury first from this eminence, thirdly from that eminence, etc.[1]

Cicero, *Leg.* 2. 21, ordains that the augurs 'augur' the priests, vineyards, orchards and commonweal and that they maintain free and demarcated the city, fields and sacred precincts ('sacerdotesque vineta virgetaque et salutem populi auguranto....urbem et agros et templa liberata et effata habento'). A hill and a temple, dedicated to Salus, are the site of one of the Argei (III 4). This itinerary follows four routes of the *augurium Salutis* in which the *praetores*

---

[1] Cicero, *Rep.* 2. 9. 16 holds that Romulus created one augur for each of the three tribes and *ibid.* 2. 14. 26 that Numa added two more augurs so that the number came to five. Livy 10. 6, on the other hand, says that there were only four augurs at the time of the Ogulnian plebiscite and he infers that two vacancies existed because he believed that the number of three augurs had been doubled. However, he had no evidence for two vacancies or six augurs for that matter. Furthermore, after 300 the college contained four patrician augurs and five plebeian augurs. Thus, four and four only was the number of augurs until 300. For a reconciliation of Cicero's five and Livy's four augurs see Catalano, p. 55, n. 120, 562–3. For the idiom *augurium capere* see Livy 10. 7. 10; cf. Catalano, p. 53. On the relation of curias and the three augurs see Ambrosch, pp. 11–12, 18–19

maiores et minores found mention.[1] The praetors participated in the May procession (Dion. *Ant. Rom.* 1. 38. 3). Besides the augury of welfare the routes were also followed for the augury of spring planting.[2] The augury of spring planting would have fallen about the time of the procession to the Argei in March. The last connection with augury to be found in the itinerary is the augural wand of Quirinus which probably was kept in the *sacellum* of Quirinus which encroached upon an *auguraculum* (III 3) as did the Temple of Welfare.[3]

Before establishing their relation to the curias we sum up our argument on the Argei. The Varronian itinerary derives from the books of the augurs who followed routes leading to huts from which they took the augury in a fixed order. These huts served as sun-shades and bird-blinds standing in an open space originally near groves where the birds would come (II 1, 3, 4, and 5).[4] After the inclement weather the huts were repaired and the old thatching and wattling solemnly disposed of. Most of the huts disappeared but the Romans continued the solemnities of removing thatch and wattle. Allowing the survival of one hut or augural precinct in each region, the Romans permitted the building of sacred buildings on the remaining open lots because the constitutional ownership of these augural sites was suppressed and forgotten.

The Capitoline *auguraculum* was the principal seat of the Roman augurs who on appointed occasions carried out the augural duties of lesser augurs serving twenty-seven entities. If these entities were private and not public, the state's augurs would not have assumed their duties nor would the vacant lots have fallen to the ownership of the people. Dionysius, *Ant. Rom.* 1. 38. 3, believed thirty figures

---

[1] The college of augurs issued a formal definition of these officers named in their formula (Festus 152 L.). See Catalano, pp. 335–46. Discussion of the *augurium salutis populi* is reserved for treatment of the Septimontium which follows.

[2] Festus 520 L. (Bremer I, 265): *vernisera*, Messala (*MS messalia*), *auguria*. See Latte, *Römische Religionsgeschichte* (Munich, 1960), pp. 66–7 and Catalano, pp. 291, n. 176 and 354. In this connection Symm. *Ep.* 10. 15 = *Rel.* 15. 1 (see below, p. 100 f.) is apposite. The Sacellum Streniae was the point at the end of the Sacred Way where, I believe, the four augurs went their several ways. On Strenia's linguistic antecedents see Plaut. *Stich.* 459–63, 671–2, Festus 410 L. On the shrine of Strenia see also Festus 372 L.

[3] Ovid, *F.* 6. 375; Macr. *Sat.* 6. 8. 1; Serv. on *Aen.* 7. 187. On the *sacellum* see below.

[4] [Oppian] *De Aucupio* 3. 11, 15, 23. Cf. Isid. *Etym.* 15. 12, quoted above. On the Italian bird-blind of today see Treccani's *Enc. Ital. s.v. capanno.* For the importance of trees in augural sighting, see the formula in Varro, *LL* 7. 7–9, recited for both augury and auspication, and Latte, 'Augur'. On augurs and groves see Serv. and Serv. Dan. on *Aen.* 9. 4.

were thrown into the Tiber. He implies thereby a connection with the thirty curias and furthermore tells us that only certain citizens might participate in the solemnities. As we shall see in our discussion of Fornacalia and Quirinalia, those Romans who did not belong to one of the thirty curias were excluded from the former festival. And this prohibition held true for the May rites of the Argei. Thirdly, the Sodales Titii who have previously been associated with one of the three original tribes still practiced augury in the first century B.C. This archaic sodality, upon which the Caesars patterned the Augustales, should now more convincingly be related to the Curia Titia since the Atiedian Brotherhood of Iguvium practiced augury.[1] At the time that the Servian regions were drawn, twenty-seven publicly owned augural precincts could have belonged to only one kind of community and this is the community of the curias.

The curias did occupy the land in the name of the curia.[2] This land does not necessarily coincide with their augural precincts which of necessity were laid out on the hillocks of Rome as it existed under the king who redrew the tribes. The name of the Collis Mucialis, site of Argei III 5, instructs us. It is so named only in the itinerary and might be connected with the plebeian Mucii. The Prata Mucia across the Tiber are relevant here. These meadows, say the authors, the senate awarded to a Mucius early in the fifth

---

[1] Varro, LL 5. 85: 'sodales Titii dicti ⟨ab avibus titis⟩ quas in auguriis certis servare solent'. Cf. Schol. on Pers. 1. 20: 'ingentes Titos dicit Romanos senatores aut a Tito Tatio rege Sabinorum aut certe a membri virilis magnitudine dicti titi. Titos scholasticos, quod sint vagi neque uno magistro contenti et in libidinem proni, sicut aves quibus comparantur, nam titi columbae sunt agrestes.' (The source of the scholia is probably Varro who is cited on Persius 1. 72, 2. 36, 2. 69 and whose opinion on Cures and Juno Curitis is mentioned on 4. 26.) Festus 503 L.: 'Titienses tribus a praenomine Tati regis appellata esse videtur. Titia curia quoque ab eodem rege est dicta.' See Catalano, pp. 359–61. The Sodales Titii accompanied the major Roman priests in an *amburbium* of the City (Lucan 1. 592–604). The attribution of the sodales to Tatius is at least as old as C. Sempronius Tuditanus (cos. 129); see Macr. *Sat.* 1. 16. 32 and Bremer 1, 36. For Iguvine practices see *Tab. Iguw.* IIa, 1–14, VIa, 1–18, and above, chapter 4.

[2] Pliny, *NH* 18. 8: 'is [*sc.* Numa] et Fornacalia instituit farris torrendi ferias et aeque religiosas terminis agrorum.' See Momigliano, 'Interim Report', pp. 110, 112. This statement is often attributed to Cassius Hemina who is explicitly responsible for the preceding sentence. However, in this chapter Pliny repeats Varro's assertion that Romulus gave every Roman colonist two *iugera* of land (see above, chapter 3). Moreover, Pliny reinforces his statement on Fornacalia by adducing the goddesses Seia *a serendo* and Segesta *a segetibus* (cf. Varro, *LL* 5. 37) as proof of the archaic cult. These goddesses are also named by Macrobius (*Sat.* 1. 16. 8) in a chapter full of references to Varro and by Augustine (*CD* 4. 8) who frequently relied on Varro's *Antiquities*. Since Pliny writes on primitive agricultural religion at this point, he may have drawn from Varro's *Antiquities* the information on Fornacalia and the two goddesses rather than from the *De re rustica* which he used for 18. 7 and 18. 9.

century. But C. Mucius Scaevola's exploits in the fifth century are the fiction of a folk etymology of his cognomen, invented by the Mucii who first appear in the Roman Fasti about 220.[1] The award of land bears out the great antiquity of the Prata Mucia, not of the family. The same or similar explanations were adduced for the Prata Quinctia, which may have belonged to a Curia Quinctia, for the Tifata Curia which was a curia probably named Tifata not *tifata* of Curius, and for the Campus Flaminius or Prata Flaminia which belonged to a flamen or flamens (of the curias?).[2] With the exception of the Prata Quinctia which we discuss below, all these places were associated with the families of new men eager for ancestral glory. The Curia Mucia held land across the Tiber and its augur took the augury on the Mucial hill in the Colline Region.

Twenty-seven curias maintained augural seats on the hills of the four regions but these seats did not have to lie within the territory of the curia. Nor did the meeting-house of a curia have to stand near the proper augural seat since the Curia Acculeia evidently stood at the point where the New Way entered the Velabrum, i.e. not on an eminence from which an augur might take the augury.[3] Some time after the Servian reform the augural seats of the curias were plotted in a sacral itinerary which each of four augurs followed severally. The number of Roman augurs until 300 was determined by the obligation to carry out the responsibilities of the curial auguries. The partial intention of the Servian reform was the supersession of the centuries over the curias. The reformer also intended to undermine the curial augurs by introducing the Roman augurs in their

---

[1] Livy 2. 13; D.H. 5. 35; Festus 131 L.; *De vir. ill.* 12. See Münzer, *RE* 16. 1 (1933), cols 412–13 and Mucii nos. 7 and 10; on the *prata* cols 411 and 422. The territory of the Curia Mucia in very ancient times may have been called *Muciona. This is a form of toponym *Mucio-na similar to others discussed below (cf. p. 106, n. 2) and not uncommon. On the Palatine an old gate (*vetus porta Palati*: Livy 1. 12. 3, 8 and Ovid, *T.* 3. 1. 31) next to the temple of Jupiter Stator was called Porta Mucionis or Mucionia which the Romans spelled with *g* owing to the fancied etymology with *mugire*. See Varro, *LL* 5. 164 (and Collart *ad loc.*), *De Vita Populi Romani* in Nonius 852 L.; Dion. 2. 50. 3. Festus 131 L. comes closer to the truth with his notice: 'Mugionia porta Romae dicta est a Mugio quodam qui eidem tuendae praefuit'. Porta Mucionia once opened on the path to *Muciona ('the place of the Mucii').

[2] Varro, *LL* 5. 154: 'item simili de causa Circus Flaminius, qui circum aedificatus est Flaminium campum'; Livy 3. 54. 15, 3. 63. 7. All three passages attest the name prior to the time of Flaminius. See Palmer, 'King'. For a discussion of the archaic use of this field and of the Quinctia and Curia Tifata see below. On the supposed donation of Tifata to Curius Dentatus see Festus, *Epit.* 43 L. (apparently contradicted at 503 L.) and *De vir. ill.* 33. 10.

[3] See Platner–Ashby *s.v. curia acculeia* and below.

place. This suggestion is supported by the story of Attus Navius, the augur who thwarted Tarquinius Priscus' proposed increase in the number of cavalry units. Although Livy 1. 36. 6 implies that Attus Navius belonged to the college of augurs, Dionysius 3. 70. 5 reports that he was not an augur of the city even though he did have public functions. If this augur had curial authority and used it to prevent the creation of new tribes (Dionysius) or centuries (Livy), the successful reformer of tribes and centuries would have seen fit to loosen the bond between augury and the curiate constitution, to transfer some of the responsibilities of curial augurs to state augurs, and to forbid the establishment of any more curial *auguracula* within the city. The appointment of all priests originally belonged to the curias and the ratification of their appointment, according to Dionysius 2. 22. 3 following Varro's *Antiquities* (cf. 2. 21. 2), fell to those who interpret divine law through mantic prophecy (ἐπικυροῦσθαι ὑπὸ τῶν ἐξηγουμένων τὰ θεῖα διὰ μαντικῆς), a unique periphrasis for a Greek who translates 'augur' no less than seven other ways or transliterates it.[1] In the event, the sodality of the Curia Titia continued to perform augural functions. When three more curias which are identified below were added to the curiate system and brought the number of curias to thirty, they did not have *auguracula* officially noted in the augural itinerary although they had *auguracula* that lay outside the four regions which the Roman augurs duly noted (below, p. 138, n. 5).

The structure at one Argei remains to be explained. At the fourth Argei of the Esquiline Region stood *figlinae* (sc. *fornaces*). Because all the other Argei were occupied for sacred purposes, these ovens should not be considered secular. Both the pontiffs and the Vestals had assistants called *fictores* who derived the title from their service of moulding or shaping sacrificial cakes (*liba*). Varro, *LL* 7. 43 f., offers this explanation of Ennius' lines on Numa Pompilius (*Ann.* 120–1 V.): 'mensas constituit idemque ancilia libaque fictores Argeos et tutulatos'. The sacrificial cakes are those made with *far*, commonly rendered by the English 'spelt'. The cake-shapers (*fictores*) of the

---

[1] On Navius see G. De Sanctis, *Storia dei Romani* I, 249 and 373 f. For Dionysius' renditions of *augur* see D. Magie, *De Romanorum Iuris Publici Sacrique Vocabulis Sollemnibus in Graecum Sermonem Conversis* (Leipzig, 1905), p. 144. On D.H. 2. 22. 3 see Catalano, pp. 212–13, p. 230, n. 66. Dionysius can refer to the inauguration of kings and flamens which took place in a 'called' assembly. See Gellius, *NA* 15. 27. 1 and above, chapter 5, pp. 69–70; below, p. 285.

pontiffs are attested by Cicero and inscriptions. The Vestals' shapers are known from imperial inscriptions.[1] An aetiological legend, illustrated by a very common superstition, supports our interpretation of the Esquiline *figlinae* as sacred bakery ovens. Once upon a time in the Esquiline Region a drunken potter (*figulus*) fell asleep while his ovens (*fornaces*) baked his wares. A certain miscreant passed by and through the open door spied a saltcellar on the potter's table. He threw the saltcellar into the ovens. In the ensuing blaze potter and all were consumed. The moral of this story is: 'if you are a potter don't put saltcellars on your table'.[2] Now superstitions about salt and saltcellars reach back into very ancient times but they are meaningful only if the table holds comestibles, not clay.[3] A potter (*figulus*) has entered this story only because of dimly remembered fire in *figlinae* where *fictores*, not *figuli* operated. The saltcellar appears because only the Vestals themselves made the salted meal of spelt (*mola salsa*). What had been a tale of sacrilege—for the *liba* had no salt—became the element for a fantastic aetiology.[4] Argei II 4 did not have a potter's shop, but rather bake-ovens built upon it. The cake-shapers of the priests seem to have been connected with the Argei in Ennius' *Annals*. The destruction of the ovens was attributed in folk-tale to a sacrilege wherein salt somehow defiled the preparation of the sacral cakes. The proper preparation of sacral grain and the use of such cakes in curial sacral suppers are discussed below. The *figlinae* of Argei II 4 pertain to religious practice in early Rome.

In this section I have attempted a new interpretation of the Argean itinerary of the four regions and its relevant rites. Dionysius felt a relation between the bundles taken annually from the stations and the curias which he expressed by giving the number thirty. These bundles, I argue, held the year's refuse of wattle from huts which curial augurs, such as the Sodales Titii, haunted during augural ceremonies for their respective curias. The itinerary recognizes only twenty-seven stations. From this number I infer another stage in the expansion of the curias toward the total of thirty. Certain augural functions of the curias were pre-empted by the

---

[1] *Libum*: Festus 78 and 474 L.; Serv. on *Aen.* 7. 109. See Wissowa, *Religion und Kultus der Römer*[2] (Munich, 1912), pp. 518–19, n. 1. Cf. the Iguvine *ficla* cake (*Tab. Iguv.* vɪa, 56).
[2] Festus 468 L. Cf. Livy 26. 36. 6 and Persius 3. 24–6 and schol. on 3. 24.
[3] See W. Deonna and M. Renard, 'Croyances et superstitions de table dans la Rome antique', *Coll. Latomus* 46 (1961), 14, 27–8, 30–2.
[4] Serv. Dan. on *Ecl.* 8. 82 (next note). Cf. Festus 97, 124 L. Cato, *Agr.* 75 has the recipe and Servius on *Aen.* 7. 109 has a similar recipe for *adorea liba* (cf. next note).

state's four augurs who observed the boundaries of the four urban regions. With the encroachment of sacred buildings only one augural precinct or hut was preserved in each of the regions. Like the Argei of Veliensis the name of the Collis Mucialis, the site of one station, ought to be related to the name of the Prata Mucia, Porta Mucionia and a Curia Mucia which I have inferred from its place in the itinerary. Later, I shall argue similar origins for the names Caelius, Oppius, Cespius, Poetilius, Latiaris and Cermalensis. Finally, one of the Argean stations evidently held a kitchen for the preparation of sacral food which suggests the curial sacral suppers.

FEASTS AND FLAMENS

Of the three days on which the Vestals made salted meal from spelt roasted and ground in May the Lupercalia of 15 February is most important for us.[1] Varro believed that this day was itself a *februatio*, a day of purification. One part of the purification required cakes made of sifted spelt.[2] A lictor performed the purification of certain houses with the roasted spelt. The first sign of curial cult is that the 'houses' which were marked for the lictor's attention were not private residences. Ovid writes *domibus* for metrical reasons and means *atriis*. The words appear in some respects to be interchangeable. For instance, Livy speaks of the *atrium regium* and probably reflects an old pontifical notice in which the *atrium regium* stands for the *domus regia*. The *atria* in question are the dining-halls of the curias.[3] Although it has been conjectured that this lictor belonged to the flamen Dialis involved in the *februatio*, a lictor's participation is the

---

[1] Serv. Dan. on *Ecl.* 8. 82: 'Sparge molam far et salem. hoc nomen de sacris tractum est: far enim pium, id est mola casta, salsa—utrumque idem significat—ita fit. virgines Vestales tres maximae ex nonis Maiis ad pridie idus Maias alternis diebus spicas adoreas in corbibus messuariis ponunt easque spicas ipsae virgines torrent, pinsunt, molunt atque ita molitam condunt. ex eo farre virgines ter in anno molam faciunt, Lupercalibus, Vestalibus, idibus Septembribus, adiecto sale cocto et sale duro.'

[2] Varro, *LL* 6. 13: 'Lupercalia dicta quod in lupercali Luperci sacra faciunt. rex cum ferias menstruas nonis Februariis edicit, hunc diem februatum appellat. februm Sabini purgamentum, et id in sacris nostris verbum; nam et Lupercalia februatio, ut in Antiquitatum libris demonstravi.' *LL* 6. 34: 'ego magis arbitror Februarium [*sc.* mensem] a die februato, quod tum februatur populus, id est lupercis nudis lustratur antiquum oppidum Palatinum gregibus humanis cinctum'. Nonius 164 L.: 'februare positum pro purgare et purefacere. Varro, De Vita Populi Romani lib. 1: "in eorum enim sacris, liba cum sunt facta, incernere solent farris semina ac dicere se ea februare, id est pura facere"'. See Plut. *Rom.* 21. 4–10 where an unidentified Greek elegiac poet connects Lupercalia with Alba Longa. This connection, as we shall see, has historical roots in the Curia Quinctia.

[3] Ovid, *F.* 2. 23–4: 'quaeque capit lictor domibus purgamina certis, torrida cum mica farra, vocantur idem'. The *mica* is the *mica salis* and ought perhaps to be connected with

second clue to a curial cult. The lictor(s) might be the officers of the curias.[1] The third sign of curial cult is the origin of the officiants at Lupercalia, the Luperci Fabiani and Luperci Quinctiales, who we maintain are the priestly survivals of two curias like the Sodales Titii (see below, pp. 135–6). The last and most decisive piece of evidence is the roasting of the spelt. In mid-February the curias met severally for the movable feast (*feriae conceptivae*) of the Fornacalia when spelt was roasted.[2] The last day of Fornacalia was set to fall on 17 February, the feast of Quirinalia, by the curio maximus who posted in the Forum instructions for the curias.[3] If Fornacalia had to end on 17 February, it also had to commence before the Nones of February when the *far* was used for a purification. The lictor, then, can be none other than one of the curiate lictors.[4] The curial priest enjoyed the assistance of acolytes (*camilli*), children of freeborn parents (*ingenui*). An old Latin verse refers to the harvest of *far* by the acolyte: *hiberno pulvere, verno luto, grandia farra, camille, metes*. Certain of these acolytes were set aside for a flamen (*flaminius camillus*) who our source says was the flamen Dialis.[5] However, the

the Vestals' *mola salsa* (see *F*. 6. 309–18) made at Lupercalia. The *far* is that sifted for the *februatio* (above, p. 97, n. 2). Livy 26. 27. 3, 27. 11. 16. Ovid uses only the form *atria*, e.g. *F*. 3. 703, 6. 263, *Metam*. 1. 172, 14. 260, *Her*. 16. 184, *Trist*. 3. 1. 72; in these instances the plural is poetic. See *TLL s.v. atrium* I. 1 for poets' avoidance of the word in certain cases. Martial 1. 70. 4 speaks of the *Vestae virgineamque domum* (also dactyli..) for the Atrium Vestae. See below, p. 120, n. 5 for the same interchange of the words and the *atria* of the curias.

[1] The flamen Dialis is mentioned by Ovid, *F*. 2. 21, in the syllabus of the book and probably belongs to the observance on the Nones. The Dialis was also present at Lupercalia (*ibid*. 2. 282). Besides the curias and flamen Dialis, the Vestals also enjoyed the service of lictors. See Wissowa, *Religion und Kultus*[2], pp. 497–8.

[2] Pliny, *NH* 18. 8, quoted above, p. 93, n. 2; Festus 73, 298, 82 L.: 'Fornacalia feriae institutae sunt farris torrendi gratia, quod ad fornacem, quae in pistrinis erat, sacrificium fieri solebant.' Jacques André, *L'alimentation et la cuisine à Rome* (Paris, 1961), pp. 57–8, points out the necessity of the roasting before eating the grain, and also discusses (pp. 64–5) the late date for commercial bakeries at Rome. Pliny, *NH* 18. 107–8 reports Rome had no commercial bakeries (*pistrinae*) before 171 B.C. This fact, of course, does not preclude a bakery for sacral purposes. Cf. Ovid, *F*. 6. 309–18.

[3] Varro, *LL* 6. 13; Ovid, *F*. 2. 519–32; Festus 302–4 L., 418 L. This coincidence is treated below in a discussion of Quirinalia.

[4] Frazer in commenting on *F*. 2. 23 accepts the emendation *domibus versis* 'swept houses' for the MSS *certis* and *ternis*. *Ternis* is nonsense but is paleographically a possible error for *certis*; *versis* would not yield these scribal mistakes. Then Frazer commences to comment on the *everriae* of Festus 68 L. which gives not the slightest hint at a lictor's participation in a ceremony having nothing to do with Lupercalia or February. The agent mentioned is the *everriator*. To be sure, a *purgatio* is involved in this ceremony but concerns the house of the dead. The use of *certis* here is paralleled by the *certa nota* of the *curio maximus* which he posted in the Forum for Fornacalia (Ovid, *F*. 2. 530). See F. Bömer, *P. Ovidius Naso Die Fasten*, 2 vols (Heidelberg, 1957), who also prefers *certis*.

[5] Festus 82 L.: 'flaminius camillus puer dicebatur ingenuus patrimes et matrimes, qui

curial acolytes doubtless assisted the curial flamens and could perform a similar function.[1] The *far* harvested by the acolyte probably grew in a flaminian field similar to the land on which the censor C. Flaminius laid out his circus in 221. The roasting process at Fornacalia was the second occasion for roasting in order to make the *far* edible. The bakeries (*pistrinae*) mentioned in connection with Fornacalia and the Esquiline ovens (*figlinae*) surely antedate the commercial bakeries at Rome.[2]

Between the roasting of the spelt and the last day of Fornacalia the curias had another religious obligation. Pliny, *NH* 18. 8, says Fornacalia was also devoted to the boundary markers of the fields (*termini agrorum*). Here we must refer to the ritual of the state festival of Terminalia on 23 February when two spelt cakes (*liba*) were sacrificed to each marker (*terminus sacrificalis*).[3] Privately neighbors celebrated their own festival of *terminalia* at a common meal. Three kinds of *terminalia* were celebrated for the boundaries of private fields, of state territory and for such curial territory as the Prata Mucia and Prata Quinctia.[4] The *curiales* roasted the spelt in the curias but the Esquiline bakery points to a curial center for preparing the cakes.

Next after Terminalia came the observance of the new year which commenced 1 March. On that day the doors of the Regia, the several curias, the flamens' homes and Vesta's temple (while her fire was also rekindled) were bedecked with new laurel leaves after the old leaves were removed (Ovid, *Fasti* 3. 135–42, Macr. *Sat.* 1. 12. 6). This change of greenery is an analogue to the removal of

flamini Diali ad sacrificia praeministrabat; antiqui enim ministros camillos dicebant. alii dicunt omnes pueros ab antiquis camillos appellatos, sicut habetur in antiquo carmine, cum pater filio de agricultura praeciperet: "hiberno [etc.]".' The poem is also given by Serv. Dan. on *Georg.* 1. 101 and Macrobius *Sat.* 5. 20. 18. Cf. Serv. Dan on *Aen.* 11. 544, 11. 558.

[1] D.H. 2. 22. 2, and he apparently follows Varro whose etymology of *camillus* (*LL* 7. 34) he repeats. For curial flamens see D.H. 2. 64. 1–2 (giving an etymology of Varro, *LL* 5. 84) and Festus 56 L.; Macr. *Sat.* 3. 8. 6–8; Ambrosch, pp. 22 ff.

[2] See above, p. 94, n. 2 and p. 98, n. 2.

[3] Ovid, *F.* 2. 639–84 and Frazer *ad loc.*; D.H. 2. 74, Festus 505 L. The last two passages Bremer, I, 134, assigns to the *ius Papirianum*. See Magdelain, 'Cinq jours epagomènes à Rome', *REL* 40 (1962), 201–27. Frazer II, 481–8, discusses the *termini sacrificales* and offers supplementary citations. For a purpose of these rites see below on Robigalia and the five-mile boundary.

[4] See Ovid, *F.* 2. 643–58 for private *terminalia* and the banquets accompanying them. Cf. D.H. 2. 74, Festus 505 L., *Röm. Feldmesser* p. 141 L. Discrete curial territory is implicit in D.H. 2. 7. 4 which Dionysius takes from Varro's notion of the colony Roma Quadrata; see chapter 3, especially p. 29, n. 1. On the Terminalia see Degrassi, pp. 414–15.

the wattling and thatching from the Argei. Also it confirms the curial observance of the year which religiously ended with the Terminalia. The same treatment of the curias' and the flamens' doors on this archaic Roman 'Palm Sunday' reinforces the close tie which existed between the curias and certain flamens. Besides alluding to these and other ceremonies on the first day of the year Solinus, 1. 35, says that the senate and people assembled (*comitia agere*) on this day. On 1 March perhaps the curiate assembly was once held for some special religious ceremony since Macrobius informs us that in the month of March the assembly or assemblies (*comitia auspicabantur, Sat.* 1. 12. 7) used to be blessed by auspices or used to take the auspices.

The comitial auspication and the changes of the bay leaves may well be directly related to the curial auspices which I suggested above were taken at the twenty-seven Argei. The shrine (*sacellum*) of Strenia was the point of departure on the Sacred Way from which the itinerary branches out into the Argei of the four regions. Symmachus (*Ep.* 10. 15 = *Rel.* 15. 1) reports as follows:

ab exortu paene urbis Martiae strenarum usus adolevit auctore Tatio rege, qui verbenas felicis arboris ex luco Streniae anni novi auspices primus accepit.

From almost the beginning of Mars' city the custom of New Year's gifts (*strenae*) prevailed on account of the precedent of king Tatius who was the first to reckon the holy branches (*verbenae*) of a fertile tree in Strenia's grove as the auspicious signs of the new year.

Lydus, who cites the authority of an Elpidianus, says that the consuls plucked on 1 January the *strenae* which is a Sabine word for welfare (*hygieia*). The 'Sabine' word accounts for the attribution of the New Year ceremony to Tatius. According to Pliny the *verbena*, a clump of grass twisted out with its soil, was employed for public cures (*remedia*) in rites and embassies. Jupiter's table was swept and houses purified with *verbenae*. According to Festus consuls, praetors and envoys took the *verbenae* from holy places. The reference to ambassadors alludes to the function of the *verbenarius* of the priestly college of state envoys who regularly carried the clump of grass.[1] The auspices of the new year on 1 January were borrowed from the new year ceremony of 1 March, New Year's Day, old style. The month of February was devoted to cleansings like those with the

---

[1] Lydus, *Mens.* 4. 4; Pliny, *NH* 22. 5, 25. 105; Festus 424–5, cf. 494 L. and Aug. *CD* 4. 11, 4. 16 (pp. 161, 165 D.).

verbenae at Jupiter's table and the houses. The month of March and the year's cycle were commenced with a ceremony in which the *verbenae* from Strenia's grove were applied for welfare (*auspices* and *hygieia*, i.e. *salus* in Latin). Later I show that an augury of welfare took place at the December rites of Septimontium on the *dies Agonalis* and that these rites may reach back to curial observances (see below, pp. 122 ff.).

The special assembly of the new year, which Solinus mentions, may be connected with the chief magistrates' taking the auspicious *verbenae* from Strenia's grove. Evidently the *verbenae* were used to cleanse the assembly, or assemblies, and the senate in much the same way as the houses were cleansed for public cures (*remedia*). We know for certain that the houses of the priest king and the flamens and the curias received fresh bay leaves on 1 March. Perhaps Strenia's grove supplied these new garlands. The auspication of the senate implies its meeting house, the Curia Hostilia, which derived its sanctity from the inaugurated Comitium on which it stood. The Comitium was also the location of the curiate assembly. Later in the month of March the Argei were visited. The course of the Argean processions started from the shrine of Strenia, a deity of the new year, of purification and of welfare. The March Kalends have the mark *NP* in the ancient calendars which means that day was not fit for ordinary assemblies of the centuries and tribes. However, the curiate assembly may have been exempt from such a prohibition.[1] I presume that the special new year's assembly was curiate since the centuries and tribes were bound by law to foregather only on days marked *C(omitialis)*. Since another special assembly met on the Capitol at Curia Calabra on the Kalends of every month to hear the priest king's announcements, Solinus' ceremonies of 1 March were peculiar to that day alone. The curias were much involved in the February and March rites which marked the ending of the old year and the commencement of the new. At some point the table (*mensa*) of Jupiter, which was probably set for the banquet in September, was swept with *verbenae*, and on 1 March the curias and the houses of the flamens and priest

---

[1] On the *strenae* of New Year's Day and Strenia see Wissowa, p. 244, Latte, *Röm. Religion*. p. 52, n. 1, and M. P. Nilsson, 'Studien zur Vorgeschichte Weihnachtsfestes', *Arch. f. Religionsw.* 19 (1916–19), 50 ff. = *Opusc. Sel.* 1 (1951), 222 ff. Some of the rites Nilsson discusses always belonged to certain winter festivals, others originally to the spring new year. On the Kalends of March, their ceremonies and the character of the day see Michels, *The Calendar of the Roman Republic* (Princeton, 1967), pp. 32, 34, 46–7, 68–83 and 97–100.

king, very likely the same houses whose cleansing with *verbenae* Pliny remarks, were decorated anew with fresh bay.

At this point we may appropriately turn to an examination of the curial and so-called minor flamens and the sacrificial suppers offered on tables to the gods of the Roman curias. According to the account of Numa in Ennius' *Annals* the king instituted the Argei, sacrificial cakes, cake-shapers, tables and those who wore the *tutulus*. The tables (*mensae*) in this context must be altars which bore that name and also the tables used for such sacrificial meals as were regularly offered in each curia. The Romans also designated tables used by flamens with a special name.[1] Although they were not the only priests to wear the *tutulus*, the flamens and the flaminicas wore this peculiar headdress on sacred occasions.[2] Varro (*LL* 7. 45) cites the titles of lesser-known flamens which he knows also from Ennius' account of the Numan foundations (*Ann.* 122–4 V.): Volturnalis, Palatualis, Fur(r)inalis, Floralis, Falacer and Pomonalis.[3] The Palatualis was surely the priest of the place called Palatium.[4] Except for the Floralis and his deity Flora, the rest can be related to places and families.

On 25 July Fur(r)inalia and on 27 August Volturnalia were celebrated. Their gods Fur(r)ina and Volturnus had no cult unless

---

[1] Festus 56 L.: 'curiales mensae in quibus immolabantur Iunoni quae curis appellata est'. Cf. Dion. 2. 23. 5 and 2. 50. 3. Festus 18 L.: 'adsidelae mensae vocantur ad quas sedentes flamines sacra faciunt'. Cf. Festus 148–9 L. See Ambrosch, pp. 26–30. Varro held the Romans ate in a sitting position because they borrowed the custom from certain Greeks. He had the Dorian public mess in mind and perhaps equated it with the curial feasts as does Dionysius; see p. 19, n. 2 and D.H. 2. 23. Because Juno Quiritis, to whom the meals were sometimes offered, was 'Sabine' for Varro and because the Sabines were originally Spartans, Varro easily discerned the avenue of borrowing.

[2] Dion. 2. 64. 1–2; Festus 484–5 L. (cf. 152, 472–3 L.); A. Gellius 10. 15; Serv. Dan. on *Aen.* 2. 683. Dion 2. 22. 2 speaks of curial *tutulatae* who may be the wives of the curial priests since he also says they performed what their husbands were forbidden to do, or their 'daughters'. The wives, too, must have been titled *flaminicae*. Cf. Ambrosch, pp. 16–17.

[3] Varro continues: 'quae [*sc.* nomina] obscura sunt; eorum origo Volturnus, diva Palatua, Furrina, Flora, Falacer pater, Pomona.' Cf. *LL* 5. 84. Dionysius 2. 64 preserves a variant tradition about the beginnings of civil priesthoods wherein Numa, not Romulus, assigns the state rites to the thirty curions, the flamens (for whose title he gives Varro's etymology in *LL* 5. 84; cf. Festus 87 L.), the commanders of the Celeres, *et al.* He then goes on to remark Romulus' foundation of the curions to oversee thirty hearths which Numa preserved (D.H. 2. 65. 4–66. 1). It is quite probable the curions could not go to war because they, like the Vestals, had to preserve fires on these hearths which Dionysius likens to Vesta's. For this reason I do not entertain the possibility that the curions had been demoted to sacral functions as were the king and tribunes of the Celeres.

[4] Festus 284 L.: 'Palatualis flamen constitutus est quod in tutela eius deae Palatium est'. See Mommsen, *Röm. Staatsr.* vol. 3, p. viii, n. 1 and below on Septimontium.

these feasts and flamens belong to the cult of a god. The word *volturnus* has been understood either as a generic word for river or the survival of an Etruscan family name.[1] An interpretation of this festival and flamen as a Tiber cult fails because the only cult-name of the Tiber known to us is Tiberinus (see above, p. 90, n. 4). The Romans also called a certain wind *volturnus* to which Lucretius (5. 745) ascribes the ominous epithet of Jupiter *altitonans* in a book where he painstakingly explains natural phenomena free from divine interference (5. 76–90).[2] The most famous and least historical augury in Roman history involved the vision and number of vultures.[3]

Fur(r)ina had a sacred grove on the Janiculum, but Varro says her name was all but forgotten.[4] Her cult was revived under the Empire with Oriental overtones and she became nymphs named Forinae. One of the Old Curias was named Foriensis. If the root of this word was *for-*, it is already once removed from that root by the *-i-* which indicates either possession or patronymic or a toponym like Velia(e) which yields the curial name Velienses. I would connect the Curia Foriensis with the goddess Fur(r)ina, her grove, flamen

[1] See G. Radke, *RE* 9A1, col. 864; J. Heurgon, 'Voltur', *REL* 14 (1936), 109–18; Degrassi, p. 503.

[2] On augury and winds see Plut. *Quaest. Rom.* 72; on thunder and lightning as omens which might disrupt the assemblies, see Cic. *Div.* 2. 42 f. For *altitonans* see Enn. *Ann.* 541 V.: 'contremuit templum magnum Iovis altitonantis'. The word *templum* also implies augury. There is no doubt that the word *altitonans* had ominous connotations. Cicero in his poem on the consulship of 63 B.C. retails a list of omens among which was the lightning of the *pater altitonans* (*Div.* 1. 12. 19). Seneca, *NQ* 5. 16. 4, following Varro and Livy: 'ab oriente hiberno eurus exit, quem nostri vocavere volturnum et Livius [22. 43. 10] hoc illum nomine appellat in illa pugna.... Varro quoque hoc nomen usurpat, sed et eurus iam civitate donatus est et nostro sermoni non tamquam alienus intervenit.' The word *Volturna* may also be considered a toponym *voltur-na*, 'place of vulture(s) ?'. One of the names of Capua was Volturnum, the name later given to a colony on the Volturnus River; see Livy 4. 37. 1–2 and 34. 45. 1 and F. Slotty, *Beiträge zur Etruskologie: 1. Silbenpunktierung und Silbenbildung im Altetruskischen* (Heidelberg, 1952) on the Capua tile, line 22, p. 6, and comment p. 133, with n. 64. Both Capua and Volturnum are named for birds; on *capus* see Serv. on *Aen.* 10. 145 and Isid. *Etym.* 12. 7. 57; cf. *Röm. Feldmesser*, pp. 216–17 L., Cato, *Orig.* fr. 69 P., [Asconius] p. 251 St. Picentia, near Etruscan Salernum, may be named after the augural *picus*; see Pliny, *NH* 3. 70. Also Latian Ardea is named for an augural bird; see Verg. *Georg.* 1. 365 with Serv. on 1. 364; Hyginus, *Urb. Ital.* in Serv. on *Aen.* 7. 412, Pliny, *NH* 10. 164, 18. 363 and Isid. *Etym.* 12. 7. 21. In my opinion, there can be little doubt that Volturnus was the god of Volturnum, a place.

[3] The auguries of Romulus and Remus are described at least as early as Ennius, *Ann.* 77–96 V. See Plut. *Rom.* 9; Suet. *Aug.* 7 and 95; Festus 3 L.; Pliny, *NH* 10. 19–20.

[4] *LL* 6. 19, 'Furrinalia a Furrina, quod ei deae feriae publicae dies is, cuius deae honor apud antiquos. nam ei sacra instituta annua et flamen attributus; nunc vix nomen notum paucis.' Cic. *ND* 3. 18. 46, followed by Plut. *C. Grac.* 17 and Mart. Cap. 2. 164, bears out Varro's statement since he believed the word was related to the Furies. The false etymology was doubtless owed to Gaius Gracchus' death in the grove (Plut. *C. Grac.* 17 and *De vir. ill.* 65). Cf. Festus 78 L. On the festival see Degrassi, p. 487.

103

and state festival Fur(r)inalia all of which by Varro's day were obsolescent.[1] During the Empire dedications were made under oriental influence to the *genius Forinarum et cultores huius loci* and to the *nymphes Phorrines*.[2] It is difficult to assess the value of such dedications in the frame of archaic Roman cult. Clearly, no matter what the archaic orthography of the divine name (probably with only one *r*), its pronunciation was *for-*. No linguistic difficulty applies to the derivation of Fur(r)ina and her cult from the Curia Forienses. The cult center was a grove on the Janiculan Hill.[3] Although we need not understand them thus, the *genius Forinarum* and *cultores huius loci* may be referred to a curial *daimon* and the remnants or heirs of the *curiales* of Curia Foriensis. Also the dedication to Lares [C]uriales[4] found on the Via Portuensis near the Grove of Fur(r)ina might be associated with a Curia Foriensis whose central cult was at Palatine Old Curias and whose local cult was on the Janiculan Hill across the Tiber. After Augustus organized the area into an urban region a Vicus Ianiculensis was designated.[5] Before that the area of the *vicus* or, more likely, of the whole region was organized as a *pagus*.[6] Pliny (*NH* 3. 68) says that the community of Janiculum, in archaic times called Antipolis, was one of the lost communities which participated in the Latin Festival. This item ultimately goes back to a Greek. Moreover, the word *antipolis*, which in this context must mean the Opposite City with reference to the Tiber, translates neither Ianiculum nor Ager Vaticanus which is thought to have anciently embraced the Janiculum. Ianiculum is a frequent communal toponym (cf. Ocriculum from *ocri-* 'mountain', Olliculani, Corniculum, etc.) so that we may reckon on a community. A possible original of Antipolis is Forentum, a place name of both Latium and Apulia.[7] A third community of Fore(n)tini or Fore(n)tes may have participated in the Latin Festival before its dissolution.[8] We derive Forentum from **fora* etc.[9] Thus, it might mean 'Outside Town' (cf. Esquiliae) and be rendered Antipolis. An Etruscan rendition of

---

[1] See above, p. 83, n. 1. The unstable orthography of the name is owed less to faulty MS traditions of passages cited on p. 102, n. 3 and p. 103, n. 4 than to varying interpretations of her name. For the oriental cult and the spellings see Wissowa, *Religion und Kultus*[2], pp. 240–1 and Platner–Ashby, *s.v. lucus Furrinae*.
[2] *ILS* 4292 and *ILS* 9282 n.; cf. *CIL* vi, 10200 (*ara Forinarum*) a dedication by a gladiatorial trainer.
[3] See Wissowa, *Religion und Kultus*[2] and Platner–Ashby, *s.v. lucus Furrinae*.
[4] See above, p. 81, n. 2.   [5] *CIL* vi, 975.   [6] *ILLRP* 699, 700.
[7] Pliny, *NH* 3. 64 (Forentani of Latium, Forentani of Apulia).
[8] See below, chapter 7.   [9] See Ernout-Meillet[4] *s.vv. fores, forum* and *forus*.

Forentum could be Furina (cf. Caenina, etc.).[1] We may compare the territory Albiona and the Grove of the Albionae also across the Tiber[2] with the Grove of Fur(r)ina.

In sum, we assume that the Curia Foriensis is related to a sometime community on the Janiculum, called variously Forentum and Furina, and to the festival of Fur(r)inalia and its Fur(r)inal flamen. The *genius Forinarum* with the *cultores huius loci* and the Lares [C]uriales may reflect the vestiges of a local curial cult.

The only ancient relation of the flamen Falacer is the Sabine village Falacrinae where Vespasian was born, although Varro believes there was a *pater Falacer*, perhaps a creature of his desperation.[3] Pomona had no cult and no feast. The word *pomona* is a toponym with which we may compare the Latin town Ortona or Hortona, the Latin colony Cremona, the Etruscan town Cortona and the place *bellona* in the Campus Martius, originally the plot of foreign ground in Roman soil on which the Fetiales might declare war. Pliny, at any rate, uses the word *pomona* to mean an orchard.[4]

---

[1] Iguvine *furu* is considered a borrowing of Latin *forum*; see Ernout, *Le dialecte ombrien*, p. 86. Such 'double' names are known; cf. Volturnum/Capua, above, p. 103, n. 2.

[2] Festus 4 L.; quoted below, p. 106, n. 2.

[3] Suet. *Vesp.* 2. 1. See Nissen, *Italische Landeskunde* (Berlin, 1883–1902) II, 468 who believes the name was (*vicus*) *Falacrinus*. *Falacer* is already adjectival in the priest's title and perhaps derives from Latin *fala* ('wooden tower, scaffold') and Etruscan *falado* ('heaven': see Festus 78 L.). Ernout–Meillet[4] *s.v. fala* also suggest a connection with Falerii and Faliscus. The ending of *falacer* may be the same as that of *alacer*. V. Basanoff, 'Evocatio', *Bibl. Ec. Hautes Etudes, Sci. rel.* 61 (Paris, 1947), chapter 4, maintains a close connection between Pales, Palatium, etc. and Falacer.

[4] At the same time the Latin colonists in Cisalpine Gaul named one colony Cremona, the other Placentia (Polyb. 3. 40. 5). Hortona perhaps means the 'place of the garden (*hortus*)?'. Both the temple of Bellona, vowed in 296 by Ap. Claudius (Livy 10. 19. 17–22, Ovid, *F.* 6. 201–8) and the *columna bellica* by which the Fetiales might declare war presuppose that the plot of land purchased by a soldier of Pyrrhus on which they stood (Festus 30 L., Serv. Dan. on *Aen.* 9. 52), bore the name *bellona* 'place of war'. Bellona underwent apotheosis by analogy with Latona, *matrona*, etc. Toponyms in -*na* or -*n-ia* are common in Italy (e.g. see Poultney on *Tab. Igw.* vib, 52). Some personal names exhibit the same formation with stems in -*o*: Antonius from *anta* ('pillar') (cf. Antium); Apronius from *aper*; Atronius from *ater* or *atrium*; Hordeonius from *hordeum*; Villonius from *villa*. If the name Bononia is derived from the Gaulish tribe Boii (Pliny, *NH* 3. 115), it would mean belonging to the 'place of the "Boii" ' and is comparable in form with Populonia. These toponyms are found elsewhere in Etrusco–Italic country, e.g. Verona among the Gauls and Salona(e) in Dalmatia. *Pomona* means the orchard or the crop in Pliny, *NH* 23. 1. 1, Solinus p. 219 M. and apparently in *ILS* 3593 in which an Augustalis left a sum for adorning a temple with *pomonae* (*ad exornandam aedem pomonis*) and lists the architectural adornment separately (*ex qua summa factum est fastigium inauratum, podium, pavimenta marm-(orata), opus tectorium*). See *ILS* 5409 and 8379 for *pomaria* which adorned shrines. Cf. *ILS* 7870: 'idemque vitium pomorumq(ue) et florum viridiumque omnium generum semini-bus ea loca quae T(itus) p(atronus) decurionibus suis adtribuerat, ex pecunia publica adornaverunt'. The Iguvine god Pomonus Publicus and his 'consort' Vesona (= Verona?)

Two groves across the Tiber supply fine examples of the deification of places. The grove of the 'goddesses' Corniscae was dedicated to crows, augural birds, and was under the protection of Juno.[1] The grove of the Albionae actually took its name from Albiona, the toponym of the field in which it lay.[2] The word looked so feminine that the grove became the sanctuary of the deities. But the grove of a place called Fur(r)ina became the grove of a goddess Fur(r)ina and later of nymphs Forinae.[3] By way of contrast Falacer became a male god, Falacer pater, and differs little from the *patres* Alb(en)sis, Reatinus, Pyrgensis and Latinus who, in fact, proceed from the places.[4] We need consider Volturnus, Fur(r)ina, Falacer and Pomona no more divine than Robigus of Robigalia, Fornax of Fornacalia, Terminus of Terminalia, Ops of Opalia and Fons of Fontinalia. Besides the gods they all worshiped in common, each curia had peculiar 'deities' whose worship Romulus assigned to it (Dion. 2. 23. 1). The character of these peculiar deities may be illustrated by the rites assigned, directly and indirectly, to the Curia Acculeia.

The tissue of religious rites is erratically woven around Curia Acculeia and unravelled with topographical combinations. The curia itself is mentioned only once in our sources in relation to two festivals held every December:[5]

betray the same suffix. But Pomonus has assumed a cult and has a statue at Iguvium. Nevertheless, he remains a vegetation spirit. In Sabine country a derivative toponym is attested *poimuniem* (Conw. no. 248: L. *in pomonio*). The Iguvine god may be no older than Bellona, etc. See Poultney, pp. 30, 89–90 and on *Tab. Iguv.* III, 26; IV, 3.

[1] Festus 56 L.: 'Corniscarum divarum lucus [MS locus] erat trans Tiberim cornicibus dicatus quod ⟨in⟩ Iunonis tutela esse putabantur'. Cf. *CIL* I², 975–6 = *ILS* 2986–7 = *ILLRP* 69–70. For crows as augural birds see *Tab. Iguv.* VIA 1; Plaut. *Asin.* 259–61; Cic. *Div.* 1. 7. 12; Festus 214 L.

[2] Festus 4 L.: 'Albiona ager trans Tiberim dicitur a luco Albionarum quo loco bos alba sacrificabatur'. The word Albio-na would be 'the place of the Albii' like *Muciona. The proper name Lucus Libitina (*ILLRP* 822, 941) proves that the literary variant Lucus Libitinae has made the grove Libitina's whereas Libitina was itself the toponym of the grove.

[3] As a toponym the form of *Fur(r)ina* may be contrasted with that of Caenina ('place of mud' (*caenum*)?) whose priesthood was one of those maintained by the Roman people after the destruction of Caenina (see below, p. 134, n. 4). On sacred groves, their festival and income see Festus 106 L.; *ILLRP* 504–6; on augural groves Serv. Dan. on *Aen.* 9. 4. In the calendars 19 and 21 July are *Lucaria*, 25 July Furrinalia and all are *NP*. Cato, *Agr.* 139 offers the formula for clearing the grove clearing in the Roman rite (*lucum conlucare...Romano more*). See also Festus 104–5 L. for the grove of Laver-na and Varro, *LL* 5. 164 for her altar.

[4] See Degrassi on *ILLRP* 42 and above, p. 63, n. 4. Romulus' divine career probably had similarly simple beginnings. Quirinus is another matter.

[5] Varro, *LL* 6. 23–4. On Divalia and Larentalia see Degrassi, pp. 541–4.

The Angeronalia is named after Angerona to whom sacrifice is made in the Curia Acculeia and whose public feast is that day. The Larentinae, which day some call Larentalia when spelling it out,[1] is named after Acca Larentia to whom our priests publicly offer a sacrifice to an ancestor (*parentant*) on the seventh day which is called black. They (call it) the Larentine day of Acca Larentina.[2] This sacrifice takes place in the Velabrum where it enters the Nova Via at what is sometimes called the tomb of Acca for the reason that near there the priests sacrifice to the Manes of slaves. Both these places were outside the old city not far from the Roman Gate mentioned in the previous book.

With this passage must be treated another discussion:[3]

On the 21st of December is the feast of Diva Angerona to whom the priests sacrifice in the shrine of Volupia.... Masurius adds that the image of this goddess [i.e. Angerona] with its mouth sealed and a finger at the lips was placed on the altar of Volupia because persons hiding pain and anxiety attain the greatest pleasure by benefit of patience.[4] Accordingly Julius Modestus claims sacrifice is made to this goddess because the Roman people were freed from the illness angina after making a vow.... On the 23rd day of December is the feast of Jupiter called Larentinalia about which the following opinions are broadcast because people love to talk. They say that in the reign of Ancus the templewarder of Hercules was idle during the feast and asked the god to shoot dice.... The prize was a dinner and a whore. When Hercules won, the warder shut up in the temple a dinner and the most renowned whore of the day, Acca Larentia.... After the death of her husband she became the proprietor of all his goods and in death bequeathed them to the Roman people. For that reason Ancus had her buried in the Velabrum, the most crowded part of the city and established an annual sacrifice by the flamen for her Manes and he consecrated the festival to Jupiter because the ancients thought that Jupiter gave and recovered souls after death. According to Cato, Larentia became wealthy through prostitution and bequeathed the fields called Turax[?], Semurius, Linturius and Solinius, and on that account she was honored with a splendid tomb and annual ancestor worship. According to Macer's *Histories* Book I, in the reign of Romulus Acca Larentia, the wife of Faustulus and the nurse of Romulus and Remus, married a rich Etruscan named Carutius who left her rich, and she bequeathed her estate to her foster-son Romulus who established the ancestor worship and the feast day.

[1] This refers to the resolution of the abbreviation in the Fasti and indicates the lack of ancient certainty on the proper name of the festival.

[2] The MSS are quite corrupt here. See Degrassi, pp. 543–4. For 'seventh day' see below. The Latin reads: 'parentant ante sexto die qui atra dicitur. diem tarentum Accas tarentinas'. The last word, an archaic genitive, should read *Larentinas*. A. Spengel conjectured *Tarentini* for *tarentum*. The least change is *Larentem*; see below on Carmentis. Both *Larentis* and *Larentinus* are ethnics. Then *dies Larentis* is a variant of Varro's (*dies*) *Larentinae*. On *dies atri* see Michels, pp. 62–6.

[3] Macr. *Sat.* I. 10. 7–17.   [4] Word play on *anxietas/Angerona*, *voluptas/volupia*.

First, we will examine the circumstances on 21 December and then those on 23 December.

Varro says the sacrifice of Angeronalia took place *in Curia Acculeia*, which may mean in the building of the Curia Acculeia, within the group of the Curia Acculeia, or both. Macrobius, however, situates the sacrifice to Diva Angerona in the Sacellum Volupiae and remarks a statue of Angerona on the altar of Volupia. Varro mentions the Sacellum Volupiae in connection with Porta Romana which 'has steps in the Nova Via to Volupia's shrine'.[1] First of all, the feast of Angerona is called Divalia in the calendars;[2] hence, Macrobius' Diva Angerona.[3] Therefore, the oldest evidence on the festival does not explicitly make Angerona the recipient of the cult. Secondly, there is no contradiction between the Curia Acculeia and Sacellum Volupiae. A *sacellum* denotes an open air shrine or precinct,[4] *curia* either a structure or a group of citizens. Thus, by combination, the festival was held in the Curia Acculeia within the precinct of Volupia or by the Curia Acculeia in the precinct of Volupia which was on the Nova Via near the Porta Romana.

The statue of Angerona with sealed lips and finger at the mouth was cautioning all from speaking the secret name of Rome.[5] Her mystery deepens with the fact that Angerona exhibits a common toponym.[6] The name Volupia can also be easily explained as an adjective-derived noun.[7] The proper name of the day Divalia need not have originally referred to a *diva*, for the word is compounded *div-al-*. Nevertheless, Volupia had an altar and Angerona a statue which were connected somehow with a Curia Acculeia. The pontiffs

---

[1] *LL* 5. 164; Varro calls it the Porta Romanula. Cf. Festus 318 L.

[2] See Degrassi, 541–2.

[3] Cf. *deve Declune* of Velitrae, above, p. 63.

[4] See below, p. 123, n. 1.

[5] Pliny, *NH* 3. 65 (cf. 28. 18–19), Plut. *QR* 61, Solinus 1. 4–6. This interpretation contrasts with that given by Macrobius whereby she is concealing her pain.

[6] See above, p. 105, n. 4, G. Capovilla, 'Per l'origine di alcune divinità romane', *Athenaeum* 35 (1957), pp. 89–120, and P. Mingazzini, 'Roma', pp. 3–18.

[7] Cf. *sacellum Streniae* in Varro, *LL* 5. 47 with Aug. *CD* 4. 11. Volupia may be related to the notion of the *heries Iunonis* discussed below, if *volupia* is derived from *volo* (see Ernout–Meillet⁴, *s.v. volup*). A similar aetiology of a tomb like that of Acca's may have been conceived from curial worship. Titus Tatius was thought to lie buried in a bay tree grove (*lauretum*) on the Aventine (Varro, *LL* 5. 152; Festus 496 L.). Since Tatius is usually associated with the Quirinal Hill and *arx* (e.g. by Varro, *LL* 5. 51; Plut. *Rom.* 20), and since the grove lay in a region occupied by the former inhabitants of the towns Tellenae and Politorium (D.H. 3. 43), its connection with Tatius may have been prompted by a function of the Sodales Titii there. Tatius' death at Laurentine hands, of course, is owed to a folk etymology of this Aventine grove (e.g. Plut. *Rom.* 23, Varro, *LL* 5. 152).

sacrificed to Angerona. This supervision cannot detract from the curial connection because the pontiffs also participated in Fordicidia. Angerona can serve a double adjectival function in naming both a place and a deity.[1] Volupia presents a different kind of problem. I believe that it is an *indigitamentum*, semantically the same as *heres/hora*, but, coming from *volup<volo*.[2] The word meant 'willingness' and before deification there were a precinct and an altar of 'willingness'.

Both the name Acculeia and the word *volupia* seem inseparable from the Acca to whom sacrifice was offered on the next regular feast day after Divalia. Acca and the gentilicial names Accius and Acculeius share the same root. Evidently the clan names are derived from Acca.[3]

The cult of the Curia Acculeia and the deity Acca Larentina are reflected in the name of P. Accoleius Lariscolus, the Roman moneyer who put the head of Acca Larentina on his coin.[4] Acca's head recalls Accoleius, Larentina Lariscolus.[5] The names Acca, Acculeia and Accoleius, and the near conjunction of the two festivals in the calendar do not stand alone in establishing a relation between Divalia and Larentalia.

The Sacellum Volupiae stood on the Nova Via near the Porta Romana. The Larentalia took place in the Velabrum where it joins the Nova Via near the Porta Romana.[6] Macrobius and Cicero both confirm the situation in the Velabrum. The latter speaks of pontiffs sacrificing at the altar of Acca,[7] the former of a flamen at the grave of Acca.[8] Plutarch, who suffered no less from the confusion than modern students of the problem, believed that two Acca Larentinas existed.[9] His second Larentina was worshipped in the Velabrum during December while his first enjoyed a Larentalia in

---

[1] Cf. *CIE* 471: 'mi unial curtun'; i.e. Juno Cortona.

[2] See above, p. 108, n. 7 and below.

[3] Cf. Appius/Ap(p)uleius. See Schulze, 'Eigennamen', pp. 427, 453.

[4] See Grueber, *CRR* I. 569 no. 4211 with note and pl. 55. 19 and Sydenham, *RRC*, pp. lxviii and 187, no. 1148 with pl. 29, who dates the coin to *c.* 37 B.C. Also, L. Borsari, *NdS* 1898, pp. 66–7 on this inscription from the Ager Lanuvinus (Groag, *PIR*[2] I, no. 31 confuses *Città Lavinia* with anc. *Lavinium*): 'Bellonae d(onum) d(edit) L. Sextius Eros C. [lib.]. Permissu C. Sex[ti – – –] et P. Accolei Larisc[oli – – –]'. The restorations are mine.

[5] The cognomen also plays on Lares related to the iconography of the coin's important reverse discussed below. The Lares are in no linguistic way related to Larentina; see Mommsen, 'Die echte und die falsche Acca Larentia', *Röm. Forsch.* II, 1–22.

[6] *LL* 5. 164, 6. 24.   [7] Cic. *Ad Brut.* I. 15. 8.

[8] Macr. *Sat.* I. 10. 15.

[9] Hence Th. Mommsen's pioneering 'Acca Larentia' II, 1–22.

April when the priest of Mars sacrificed to her.[1] Fortunately we do not have to take Plutarch at his word. For we know that the priest was in fact the Quirinal flamen and infer that Plutarch has confused this priest's business during the Robigalia of 25 April.

Here belongs a chapter of Gellius (*NA* 7. 7) which elucidates the fables of Acca's origin and profession:

The names of Acca Larentia and Gaia Taracia (alias Fufetia) are famous in the ancient annals. The Roman people bestowed very generous honors on the former after her death and on Taracia while she still lived. The Lex Horatia, proposed on her account, bears witness to the fact that Taracia had been a Vestal virgin. Many honors were given her by the law among which was the right of bearing witness for she alone of all woman was capable of bearing witness (*testabilis*). That word belongs to the Lex Horatia and its opposite is met in the Twelve Tables: *improbus et intestabilis est*. Furthermore, if she would have wished to resign her priesthood and marry after her fortieth year, she received the right and power of being 'exaugurated' and married on account of her generous gift of the Campus Tiberinus or Martius to the people. But Acca Larentia had enriched herself on the sale of her person. According to Antias' *History* she bequeathed her estate to king Romulus and according to others to the Roman people. For this good deed a sacrifice is publicly offered her by the Quirinal flamen and a day named after her was added to the calendar. But Masurius Sabinus in his *Memorialia* Book I follows certain historians and makes Acca Larentia Romulus' nurse. According to him, Acca lost one of her twelve sons. Romulus took his place and called the others Arval Brothers (*fratres*). From that moment on the college of Arval Brothers has numbered twelve. The priesthood's symbols are the crown of wheat and white headbands.

Gellius' information cannot be considered separately from Cato's statement that Acca bequeathed four fields to the Roman people.

Pliny's version of Taracia's story differs slightly. The people voted a statue to the Vestal Virgin Gaia Taracia (alias Fufetia) because, so the annals say, she gave the people the Campus Tiberinus.[2] Pliny also knows Masurius Sabinus' aetiology of the Arval Brothers which he combines with the two *iugera* of land which the first Roman colonists received, and with Numa's foundation of Fornacalia.[3]

In order to ascertain whatever link between Acca and the Arval Brethren the Romans found we must return to Plutarch's mistaken identity of Larentalia and Robigalia. The Quirinal flamen sacrificed

---

[1] *Rom.* 4–5, *QR* 35.
[2] *NH* 34. 25. A third account has the Vestal called Tarquinia (Plut. *Popl.* 8).
[3] *NH* 18. 6–8.

FEASTS AND FLAMENS

a dog in order to ward off the rust (*robigo*), a grain blight. The problem is where this sacrifice took place. The Verrian notice in the Fasti Praenestini situates it at the fifth milestone on the Via Claudia[1] which leaves the Via Flaminia across the Mulvian Bridge. Ovid, however, witnessed the sacrifice in a grove on his return from Nomentum. This is most embarrassing because one did not go from Nomentum to Rome by way of the Via Claudia and because Ovid relies heavily on Verrius Flaccus whose contribution to the Praenestine calendar is well known.[2] The only feasible solution is to assume that the Quirinal flamen sacrificed in at least two places. If the same sacrifice took place at the fifth milestone of the Via Nomentana (earlier called the Via Ficulensis),[3] the grove would lie very close to the defunct town of Ficulea and two miles north-east of the Mons Sacer.[4] This suggestion is made because the Grove of Dea Dia which was the headquarters of the Arval Brothers was situated at the fifth milestone on the Via Campana[5] and, like the site on the Via Claudia, lay across the Tiber. The geographer Strabo (5.3.2, 230 C) reports a five-mile limit which was observed in the rites of Ambarvalia when the fields were purified and their fertility was promoted. Presumably the Arval Brothers were concerned in these or like rites. Although the several stations at a distance of five miles from Rome must have required a sacred itinerary of more than one day's travel at least for the Ambarvalia, the statement of our sources is quite clear on the existence of the five-mile limit. However, in the case of the Robigalia the Quirinal flamen could have sacrificed both on the Via Claudia and the Via Nomentana on the same day. Moreover, his duties may not have precluded the use of a vehicle from one to the other place, for we need assume a proper circuit of the boundaries only for the Arval Brothers (see below, p. 114). Ovid, on the other hand, places one of the sacrifices on the feast of the Terminalia at the sixth milestone of the Via Laurentina (*Fasti* 2.679–82).

According to the discipline of the Etruscan Vegoia whosoever moves a boundary stone invites damage to the crops from rain, hail, heat and the rust. Vegoia enjoyed a reputation as an authority on systematizing territory. The health of a community partly depended

[1] See Degrassi 13.2, pp. 448–9.
[2] *Fasti* 4.905–43 on which see Bömer and his introduction, vol. 1, pp. 22–4.
[3] Livy 3.52.3 in connection with the Mons Sacer (next note).
[4] It was three miles from Rome; Festus 422/4 L.
[5] *ILS* 5048.

111

upon the inviolate boundary markers. This connection recalls the curial observances at their *termini* in February.[1]

By name the Arval Brothers religiously superintended the well-being of plowland (*arva*). Their archaic prayer contains the invocation of Mars and the Lares, and mention of a boundary (*limen*).[2] The Brothers' officers, a master (*magister*) and flamen, were elected in May but held office from Saturnalia to Saturnalia, 17 December to 16 December.[3] Varro is our sole Republican authority on the Arval Brothers, although their hymn attests a great antiquity. Between comments on the Luperci and the Sodales Titii he offers one of his worst etymologies:

Fratres Arvales dicti qui sacra publica faciunt propterea ut fruges ferant arva: a ferendo et arvis Fratres Arvales dicti. Sunt qui a fratria dixerunt. Fratria est Graecum vocabulum pa⟨rt⟩is hominum, ut ⟨Ne⟩apoli etiam nunc.[4]

Whoever had suggested *phratria* before Varro far surpassed him on this point. Furthermore, it seems that Masurius Sabinus' statement about the eleven sons of Acca Larentina whom Romulus called Brothers was not current in the late Republic. Yet someone had connected the confraternity with the Greek phratry which was Varro's equation with the curias. Furthermore, Acca's name, her festival's date and the site of her altar or tomb can be connected with Curia Acculeia, its festival of Divalia and its site. Moreover, it is quite curious that priestly officers, elected in May, took office four days before Divalia and six days before Larentalia. In the notice on Larentalia, translated above, Varro says, 'Our priests offer a sacrifice to an ancestor on the seventh day.' The 'seventh day' is our six days after Saturnalia. Varro has withheld information about the connection which seems to be the assumption of the offices on Saturnalia.[5] Add to these items Plutarch's confusion of Larentalia and Robigalia, the five-mile distances of the groves of Dea Dia and Robigus on two roads across the Tiber.

---

[1] For Vegoia see *Röm. Feldmesser*, pp. 348–51 L. and H. H. Scullard, *The Etruscan Cities and Rome* (Ithaca, 1967), pp. 73–4. Cf. Serv. on *Aen.* 6. 72 for her works preserved at Rome. For the curial *terminalia* see above, p. 99.

[2] *CIL* I², 2 = *ILS* 5039 = *ILLRP* 4.

[3] *ILS* 5037, 5038, 5040.   [4] *LL* 5. 85.

[5] Varro (*LL* 6. 22) says *post diem tertium Opalia Opis* which then means Larentalia was the seventh day by Roman reckoning. However, his MSS have *sexto die* which cannot be right. We assume that *vio* was mistaken for *viio*. Furthermore, *septimo die* differs in sense from *post diem tertium*.

Thus we have returned to the problem of how and why the original Arval Brothers were the sons of Acca Larentia. Surely, the fable of the whore (*lupa*) does not apply. Surely, then, her purported bequest of fields (*agri*) is incidental to the creation of a brotherhood to keep sound the plowland (*arva*). At Iguvium the Atiedian Brothers tended some rites in a field: in a grove they elect their *uhtur* (Latin *auctor*), proceed with victims to the field (*arvamen*) by a customary route, set up their utensils and victims in the field, enter a grove for sacrifice, sacrifice to Jupiter and the public Pomonus, make an offering to the Vesona of the public Pomonus and to both severally, and so forth.[1] We are dealing with comparable Italic cults: the twelve Arval Brothers of Rome, the Atiedian Brothers of Iguvium, a special field to be preserved, and sacrifice in groves. Beyond these details, there is the similar construction of the names Angerona, Puemune, and Vesune. Macrobius (*Sat.* 1. 10. 15) says the Larentalia was also a festival of Jupiter, just as the Atiedian Brothers sacrificed to him. These facts do not prove that the Arval Brotherhood was a curial priesthood in the same way as the Atiedian Brotherhood represented Atiediates I and II. Rather, they demonstrate that they could have filled a similar role. The curial relation of the Arval Brothers rests upon Acca's otherwise inexplicable maternity of the eleven brothers. Unless there was an ancient known relation of the Curia Acculeia to the Arval Brothers, this brood of 'sons' could have been assigned to some other lady than a whore. Further, I assume that Divalia, Larentalia, and Robigalia were originally curial festivals and that the first two were curial festivals of the Curia Acculeia: Divalia because it was held in the Curia Acculeia and Larentalia because of Acca. Both of them had been taken over by the 'pontiffs'. The Quirinal flamen, who we argue, was the priest of Mars Quirinus, Mars of the Quirites or curiate citizens, also participated in Larentalia. Principally the Quirinal flamen was involved in agricultural cults. The Robigalia was mistaken by Plutarch for another Larentalia. This mistake can hardly have begun with Plutarch. In my opinion, the participation of the Quirinal flamen does not satisfactorily explain Plutarch's confusion. We can see that it goes further; in fact, perhaps back to the Groves of Dea Dia and Robigus both of which lay five miles from Rome. In their archaic hymn the Arval Brothers invoke Mars to drive away the blight (*lues*). A *lues* can

---

[1] *Tab. Ig.* III–IV.

attack not only crops but also weapons.[1] In a word, rust was a kind of *lues*.

The Quirinal flamen and Arval Brothers said their prayers five miles from Rome. Mommsen's view that this distance marked the Roman boundary and that the Quirinal flamen made a circuit of this periphery can be accepted only if we acknowledge that the procession was of late date[2] and that such a boundary was artificial to the extent that it never reflected an actual political frontier. A political boundary which crossed the Viae Campana, Claudia and perhaps the Ficulensis at the same distance from Rome presumes too much. A ritual boundary may have been described to facilitate an easy circuit. Perhaps such an hypothetical boundary was thought to demarcate the land of curial Rome.[3]

In any case, the Quirinal flamen appears to have taken over the duties of some defunct curial priests whereas the Arval Brothers maintained this observance for themselves. However, they did not pray on 25 April to ward off *lues* but on 29 May.[4] The Arval Brothers held their priesthood in perpetuity. The master and flamen, however, were elected annually. Since the priesthood, though old, was revived by Augustus, I suspect that the flamen at least had once been the perpetual office of curial flamen. Its tenure would have been changed to give all brothers a chance to have the honor and pay the costs.

If the Arval Brotherhood had been a proper curial priesthood and its flamen a curial flamen, we should note here the Virbial flamen. Virbius was associated with Diana at her grove near Aricia which lies about sixteen miles from Rome. Because of the joint cult and the etymology 'twice man' (= *vir*+*bis*) Virbius was equated with Hippolytus. This syncretism has spelled doom for any knowledge of his earlier divinity. On the road to Aricia but four miles from Rome was the Clivus Virbii.[5] This spot would have been in the territory of

---

[1] Verg. *Aen.* 3. 169; Lic. Mac. fr. 21 from Non. 73 L.

[2] See Bömer on *Fasti* 4. 907, and above, p. 111.

[3] The Fossae Cluiliae, five miles from Rome, could have marked such a boundary; see Livy 1. 23. 3, 2. 39. 4–5, D.H. 3. 4. 1, Plut. *Cor.* 30. 1. Livy 2. 39. 4–5 implies the Fossae Cluiliae lay on the way from Pedum, which means on the Via Gabina, later Praenestina. See De Sanctis 1², 366–7. The Fossae Quiritium may have been the curial boundary of the city; see Livy 1. 33. 7 on which see Ogilvie (cf. D.H. 3. 43) and Festus 304 L. These ditches are identified with the Cloaca Maxima in *De vir. ill.* 8. 3. On the *fossa* of the pomerium, see below, chapter 8.

[4] *ILS* 5039.

[5] Pers. 5. 56 and schol. thereon.

early Rome and would have nearly approximated Mommsen's five-mile limit. A single Neapolitan inscription records the existence of a Virbial flamen. This priesthood may be Neapolitan, Aricine or Roman.[1] Since Virbius belonged to the Latins at the Grove of Diana, it is not astonishing to find his cult anywhere in Latium.

If Mommsen's opinion that Acca's other name was truly Larentina, which was altered to the gentilicial type Larentia, holds good, we are dealing with the ethnic or demotic of a common Italic toponym.[2] The same holds true for Varro's *Larentinae dies*.[3] Since its *a* is long, the root apparently bears no relation to the Lares. Rather, the names of the Samnite town Lārinum and the gentilicial name Lāronius seem to be built upon the same root, the latter exhibits a compound *Lār-ōn* frequently met in toponyms. *Larentum was a place. Whether it was a town's proper name cannot be ascertained. However Acca of *Larentum may have been the eponym of the Curia Acculeia. Since *acca* was a common Indo-European baby word,[4] the Curia Acculeia may have supplied a deity from baby language. It is worth emphasizing that the festival of 23 December was Larentalia or Larentinae, the day of *Larentum, and that Acca is, so to speak, an intruder like Angerona upon the Divalia (cf. Mater Matuta, Mater Mursina, etc.).

Only one other Roman festival bears a comparable name. Like the Larentalia, the Carmentalia was held in the winter, on 11 and 15 January. The goddess on whose behalf the festival was held was called Carmentis and had one or more altars in the Forum Holitorium near the Porta Carmentalis which stood by the end of the Vicus Iugarius.[5] Carmentis or the Carmentalia had a flamen Carmentalis whose functions are totally unknown.[6] The form of the goddess' name closely resembles that of the Latian Laurentes and *populus Laurens*. Some ancients believed that Carmentis or two Carmentes were in charge of child birth. Plutarch retails the fullest and

---

[1] *ILS* 6457. Dessau suggests that the priesthood was Roman. See below, p. 126, n. 3.

[2] See below, on Tarentum and chapter 7 on Forentum. Among the so-called Alban peoples and towns (see chapter 2) are met Bubentani, Carventani, Cusue(n)tani, Laurens (Laurentini, Laurentes), Nomentani.

[3] *LL* 6. 23, translated above.   [4] Ernout–Meillet[4] *s.v.*

[5] On Carmenta see Wissowa, *Religion und Kultus*[2], pp. 219–21, Latte, *Röm. Religion.* pp. 136–7, Degrassi, 394–5, 398, and Bömer on Ovid's *F.* 1. 462. On the sites see Platner–Ashby, *s.vv. Carmenta, Porta Carmentalis* and G. Lugli, *Roma Antica* (Rome, 1946), pp. 12, 559–60.

[6] Cic. *Brut.* 14. 56 (cf. Broughton, *s.a.* 359); *ILS* 1418. See Esperandieu in De Ruggiero's *Diz. Epigr. s.v. flamen*, p. 146.

silliest account of her cult's foundation by and for women.[1] His knowledge goes back to Varro's *Antiquities of Divine Matters* where Varro asserted that Carmenta Prorsa (alias Porrima and Antevorta) and Postverta oversaw forward and backward babes in the birth canal.[2] However these two words are wrongly interpreted. Both *prorsi* and *transversi limites* are known technical terms in land survey.[3] Our authorities describe the Porta Carmentalis as having a *ianus dexter*[4] which implies a *ianus sinister*. There is no doubt in my mind that *prorsa* and *postverta* originally described the direction in which the two doors of the double gate opened: forward and backward or inward and outward. Hence, *prorsa* (i.e., *proversa*) and *postverta* differ little from the Porta Pandana of the neighboring Capitol[5] or Janus' epithets Patulcius and Clusivius (or Clusius)[6] and the name Panda Cela.[7] Varro doubtless took his interpretation from a folk aetiology which remade the doors' names into supernatural intervention in child-bed. On my interpretation, Carmentalia, Carmentis and flamen Carmentalis would have begun as a festival, and goddess of a place *Carmentum, and priest of a place or of foreign rites. If the gate had led to the place *Carmentum, it should have been called Carmentana (cf. Porta Nomentana, Flumentana; the latter is an analogical construction). Furthermore, the Carmentalia etc. should have been called Carmentialia and Carmentialis if directly derived from Carmentis. (*Carmenta* is a back formation, partly based on the folk etymology from *carmen*). *Carmentum is a toponym which may have signified either a cult place like Tarentum (see below), or a town whose cult was transferred to Rome, or a locality within Rome itself.

Although the Porta Carmentalis was located in a defensive wall raised in the fourth century, it was deemed holy and always kept open.[8] Not only was it thought to have been the exit of the Fabii when they went to their destruction at Cremera *c.* 478 but it was

---

[1] *Rom.* 21. 2, *QR* 56.

[2] In Gellius, *NA* 16. 16. 4. See Agahd, pp. 168–9.

[3] See Festus 264–5 L.; Front. *Lim.* p. 29 L. (Varro), Hyginus *Lim. Const.* pp. 167–8 L. (cf. p. 202) in *Röm. Feldmesser* and *ibid.* vol. 2, pp. 289, 342.

[4] Livy 2. 49. 8, Ovid, *F.* 2. 201. Holland, 'Janus and the Bridge', pp. 242–60, devotes a chapter to an unconvincing attempt to show that the two authorities, independent of each other, roughly represent the same notion which has been wrongly interpreted as a double gate. See Ogilvie on Livy.

[5] See Platner–Ashby *s.v. Porta Pandana*.   [6] See Bömer on Ovid, *F.* 1. 129.

[7] Varro, *Men.* fr. 506 Buech.

[8] D.H. 10. 14. 2. The oracular injunction probably comes from the notion of Carmenta as a prophetess.

also connected with a Roman capture of Fidenae. A brief and broken notice on the Praenestine calendar at Carmentalia II says 'Festival for Carmentis for the same reason as that on January 11th. This day is said to have been established by – – – if he would have taken Fidenae on that day.'[1] Even if this referred to Rome's last war with Fidenae (c. 426), it would be too early to concern a gate in the so-called Servian wall. The cult of Carmentis must precede the building of the wall and perhaps the gate itself. If, however, the gate was never closed, it may never have been intended to be part of a defensive wall at all. Furthermore, the two Carmentalia of 11 January and 15 January may have been observed first at one door and then at the other. It is attractive to maintain a connection between the Cermalus and Carmentis. Cermalus was the site of one of the Argei.[2]

In two Roman colonies the name *cermalus* is given to *vici* and itself functions as an adjective.[3] The toponym is unique but resembles an adjective enough that its stem might have seemed to be *cerm-*. The lowering of *e* to *a* before *r* is common outside Latin and the raising of *a* to *e* is met even in Latin under certain conditions. The latter conditions do not exist in the case of Cermalus/*Carmentum. Some isolated examples may support a relation between the Cermalus and *Carmentum: Numerius < *Numarios (cf. unrhotacized Numasioi), *camara/camera* (see *ILS* 7868, 7933a, 8115, and Verrius Flaccus and Lucilius in Charisius 73 B.), the common *carcar/carcer*, *patara/patera*, *phalarae/phalerae* (see *ILS* 2660, 2337). None of these variations occurs in an initial syllable and all may be owed to apophony. To them may be added the Etruscan rendering of *magister* by *macstrna* (*CIE* 5267) which reverted to Latin as the proper names *mastarna* (*ILS* 212) and *masterna* (*ILS* 9272 and a). A closer linguistic parallel is to be found in the older cognomen of the Atilii, Saranus, which exhibits a changed pronunciation in the classical period, Serranus, when consonant gemination was consistently observed by orthography. In neither Carmentum nor Saranus does the accent fall on the first syllable. The accentuation of Cermalus is as unknown as the quantity of its penult. Varro's wrong etymology of *Germalus* < *germanus* implies a long *a* and Varro may have had in mind the honorific agnomen

---

[1] See Degrassi, p. 398 who argues for restoring *institutu*[*s a Romulo*]. There are not a few Roman captures of Fidenae recorded in the tradition.
[2] See above, p. 85.
[3] Vicus Cermalus in *CIL* III S, 6835, *ILS* 6663. Cf. the colonial quarters Vicus Esqelinus and Vicus Palatius (*ILS* 8567, 6301) and Rome's Vicus Tuscus.

Messalla from the town Messana (cf. *corolla*<*corona*). However, Varro's skill cannot decide the matter. If *Carmentum and Cermalus are related, we must explain the retention of *a* in the former word as religious conservation which was perhaps supported by a supposed connection with *carmen*, while Cermalus reflected the spoken language with *a* raised to *e* as in Saranus/Serranus in an unaccented initial syllable. The Atilius who was consul in 136 still called himself by the older Saranus (*CIL* 1², 636, cf. 23). We must conjecture a change in pronunciation after that time. Nevertheless, the linguistic relation between Cermalus and *Carmentum remains a possibility which is not proven.[1] Although not far distant, the Carmental Gate cannot be considered adjacent to the Cermalus.[2] If a religious association between Carmentis and the Cermalus should be made, it cannot rest upon the topology of her cult which Dionysius describes as similar to those for heroes and *daimones*.[3]

Varro who recognized the names of curias were gentilicial or toponymous could not have failed to notice theophoric names among them if there were any. However, he did remark the curias' peculiar gods and *daemones*. The connection of Curia Acculeia with Angerona and *Larentum points a way to assessing the situation of curial religion. A curia could be properly called by a gentilicial name and still its members could worship a deity brought from another place. Thus the curia's flamen might have borne the name of the special deity, irrespective of the curia's name.

Before examining possible curial relations in the legends of Larentia's bequest and Taracia's (alias Fufetia) gift of land, we turn again to P. Accoleius Lariscolus' coin. On the obverse was stamped the head of Acca Larentia. On the reverse are three statuesque ladies; one holds a poppy and another a lily. On a platform or beam which the ladies seem to carry on their shoulders stand five trees. The ladies have been almost rightly identified as the *nymphae Querquetulanae*; almost rightly because *nymphae* was the explanation of the Latin *virae*. And the trees have been identified as the oaks (*quercus*) which gave the *virae* their names.[4] Two lexicographical explanations

---

[1] Clement of Alexandria's *Strom.* 1. 21 (108. 3) has *karmalon* which is not decisive. Other than Varro, *LL* 5. 54 (cf. Plut. *Rom.* 3) all authors and inscriptions have the spelling *Cermalus* which Varro alters to *Germalus* for the sake of an etymology.

[2] The distance from the Cermalus to the purported Porta Carmentalis is between 300 and 350 meters, depending on the exit from the Cermalus and the route taken.

[3] D.H. 1. 32. 2.   [4] See above, p. 109, n. 4.

of *vira* assert its meaning to have been 'woman' (Festus 314 L.; Isidore, *Etym.* 11. 2. 23; compare the archaic *puera*). However that may be, the *virae Querquetulanae* are strikingly unique. Although the title could have been imported into Rome with the deities (see below, chapter 7), the root of *vira* is that of *vir*, a component of *co-viria. Hence, the title may be related to the oldest sense of *curia*. Perhaps the *virae* represent a concept similar to that of the Greeks' heroines although Latin does not retain a term for such spirits or supernatural figures. Instead the Romans called Egeria and her kind nymphs.

The Virae Querquetulanae, so we are told, were nymphs presiding over a growing oak grove (*querquetum virescens*) because they think that kind of grove once stood in the gate called Querquetularia.[1] From another source we learn that Rome's Mons Caelius had been called Querquetulanus before Caele Vibenna settled there.[2] On account of this lore the Porta Querquetularia is situated on the Caelian.[3] However, its location remains in doubt because Varro remarks four points in the boundary of the Esquiline Region: the groves of (Jupiter) Fagutalis, *sacellum Larum Querquetulanum*, the Groves of Mefitis and Juno Lucina.[4] When Pliny mentions the Porta Querquetulana as a place named for a grove, he puts it between Jupiter Fagutalis and the Collis Viminalis. Hence, the gate may equally well, if not better, be located in the Esquiline walls.[5]

The puzzling aspect of the gate's name is that it should have indicated the direction in which the traveler who left the city by it was headed. To be sure, exceptions to this manner of name-giving are known. However, in Pliny's alphabetized list of lost peoples who participated in the Latin Festivals are met the Querquetulani.[6] Did the gate open onto the road to *Querquetulum? The Lares and Virae of *Querquetulum were certainly in Rome. But the -*ulum* points to a discrete communal origin.

The moneyer P. Accoleius Lariscolus had both of his names in mind when his coin was designed. Yet he did not have the Lares

---

[1] Festus 314 L.   [2] Tac. *Ann.* 4. 65.   [3] See Platner–Ashby *s.v.*
[4] LL 5. 49.   [5] *NH* 16. 37. See the map below, p. 308.
[6] D.H. 5. 61. 3; *NH* 3. 69. With them are the Venetulani which exhibits the same verbal composition and the Octulani. With this group also belong Aefulani, Longulani, Cingulani, Verulani, Tusculani and perhaps Aesolani, Abolani, Coriolani, Sisolenses, Ficolenses (< Ficulea), besides the towns Capitulum, Trebula, Suessula, Ameriola, Apiolae. See chapter 7.

depicted. Instead, three Virae and five oaks are stamped on the reverse. Accoleius is the only member of his family known to have held office in Rome or under the emperors. Yet his gentilicial name coincides with that of a curia. An ambitious man with a name of archaic value and without a family of any renown could capitalize on that name and its old, old associations. He could, I believe, make both names suit two curias, the known Acculeia and another of the Querquetulani whose Lares and Virae were worshiped in Rome.

The cult of Acca Larentia was a sacrifice for ancestors called *parentatio* or *parentalia*. The chief function of such a sacrifice was a meal at the grave of the ancestor.[1] Thus, the Romans believed that Acca's grave was the site of her cult. A dinner implicit in her cult closely resembles the curial practices of dining.[2] In fact, a curial dinner for Acca Larentina may have been the point of departure for believing her rites were a *parentatio* at a grave. On certain holy days members of the curias dined together in their curias upon old-fashioned wooden tables and partook of barley cakes, sacrificial cakes, spelt and first-fruits. Dionysius of Halicarnassus saw these dinners with his own eyes. On the same or similar occasion the tables were set for Hera Kuritis or Kuritia. These tables were the *curiales mensae* which we have identified with the *adsidelae mensae* at which flamens sat to offer sacrifice.[3] A dining hall for such a special occasion was an *atrium* which Dionysius calls a ἑστία or ἑστιατόριον and says they were separate from the curia building. In Latin the word for this dining hall is *atrium* and Dionysius was obviously translating *atrium* for he compares the curial hearth with Vesta's.[4] Cato the Censor held the opinion that the *atrium* was an ancestral dining-hall and him-self bought two *atria* and four shops (*tabernae*) in order to build the Basilica Porcia. One of these atria was the Atrium Titium which I propose was the dining hall of the Curia Titia.[5] These curial dinner feasts square well with the ritual at private *terminalia*. Accordingly one curial banquet ought to have fallen some time during Fornacalia

[1] Varro, *LL* 6. 13 and Ovid, *F.* 2. 533–70 on which see Bömer.

[2] On the dinners for the dead and dinners for Juno see Palmer, *Juno*.

[3] See above, p. 102, n. 1. Dionysius equates Greek *zea* with Latin *far*; see D.H. 2. 25. 2 and Diosc. 2. 96 W.

[4] D.H. 2. 23. 2 and 2. 65. 4; according to 2. 66. 1 the *atrium Vestae* was the hearth common to all curias.

[5] Cato *apud* Serv. on *Aen.* 1. 726; Livy 39. 44. 7 speaks of the *atrium Titium*; [Asconius] on Cic. *Div. in Q. Caec.* 16. 50, p. 201 St. calls the other building, the Atrium Maenium, the *domus* of Maenius.

when the curias roasted spelt for use in sacrificial cakes offered at the *termini* of their fields and for the common meal known from the practices of private *terminalia*. The curial banquets probably fell on 16 February, the day after Lupercalia. The curial Fornacalia remained a movable feast because the preparation of sacred foodstuffs, their sacrifice and consumption extended over several days from before the Nones and came to an end on the Quirinalia. Indeed after he notes Romulus' grant of two measures of land to every colonist, Numa's institution of Fornacalia and the sacrifices to the boundary markers in the fields (see above, p. 93, n. 2), Pliny says of the ancient Romans, 'They did not even taste of the new harvest or wines before the priests had offered first-fruits to the gods.' Every year in advance of Fornacalia the curio maximus posted in the Forum instructions (*certa nota*) for each curia (Ovid, *F.* 2. 527–32). Each curia had its own task because by Ovid's day not all curias were religiously intact. Some still had fields (e.g. Prata Mucia and Quinctia) at whose boundary-markers cakes were offered and others had priests serving at Lupercalia (i.e. Luperci Fabiani and Quinctiales) just as one curia evidently had assumed the responsibility of shaping and baking the cakes until its shop on the Esquiline had been consumed by fire. The diminution of curial participation at the beginning of the Empire is further demonstrated by the fact that only four of the seven Old Curias still met on the Palatine for religious observances.

The festival of Fordicidia on 15 April well illustrates the procedure and historical development of the relation between the curial and state religions. This feast of Tellus, the Earth, had a double celebration. In each curia a pregnant cow was sacrificed for the curia and on the Capitoline the pontiffs with the chief Vestal sacrificed a pregnant cow for the entire state.[1] A pattern thus emerges whereby the state priests have assumed on behalf of all the people some of the religious responsibility of the several curias. In March the augurs make a circuit of the former *auguracula* of the curias, in April the pontiffs with the chief Vestal perform a *fordicidium* while the same is done in the curias and in May the pontiffs, Vestals and praetors lead a procession in which the old thatching and wattling of the curial augural huts are taken to the Tiber as religious refuse. We shall see that the same pattern may be applied to Fornacalia and Quirinalia.

[1] Ovid, *F.* 4. 629–72; Varro, *LL* 6. 15. See Degrassi, pp. 440–2, and below, chapter 8.

Let us summarize our conclusions about the major curial rites and priests discussed here. The curias observed the end and beginning of the old style year with sacrifices and banquets. The cleansing during February which took its name from this act, the observances of the curial territorial boundaries and the change of the evergreen bay on the curias' headquarters signaled the change of season. At the feast of ovens the curias prepared spelt for sacrificial use and probably for their own sacral suppers. The slaughter of pregnant cows in the curias brought fertility to the state. In sentiment close to the search for fertility at the Fordicidia and for purification in February are the rites of the Arval Brothers which may be connected with the Curia Acculeia, its festivals of Divalia and Larentalia and the deities Acca, Angerona and Volupia. Likewise, the Robigalia, celebrated by the state's Quirinal flamen, may have been curial in origin. The curias held sacral suppers of first-fruits in their curial dining-halls which were also called *atria*. The curial flamens, assisted by their *camilli* and lictors, presided at the curial rites. Among the so-called minor flamens I have remarked the possibility that the Palatual of the Palatine Hill, Fur(r)inal of the Fur(r)inal Grove, Falacer, Volturnal, Virbial, Pomonal and Carmental flamens originated with curial functions. The festivals of the two Carmentalia, the Fur(r)inalia, and Volturnalia, over which the homonymous flamens ought to have presided, seem to have been ceremonies for certain places and their deities just as the Palatual must have belonged to the Septimontium (see next section). With the knowledge that each curia had its peculiar rites and deities as well as holy places, I have drawn attention to Fur(r)ina of Curia Foriensis, to Angerona, Volupia and Acca Larentia of Curia Acculeia and of *Larentum, to Carmentis (one or two) of *Carmentum, which may be related to the Cermalus Hill, and to the Lares and *virae* of *Querquetulum.

THE SEVEN HILLS

The primitive festival of Septimontium displays a unique remnant of curial observances. The corporations whose members lived on seven hills maintained religious enclosures which evidently appertain to Septimontium.[1] Varro (*LL* 6. 24) unequivocally says that the

---

[1] The corporations (*collegia*) are cited by Cic. *Dom.* 28. 74, *Com. Pet. Cons.* 8. 30. See Mommsen, *Röm. Staatsr.* III, 112–15. On the festival see Wissowa, *Religion und Kultus*[2], pp. 29–31, Latte, *Röm. Religion.*, pp. 112–13, Degrassi, pp. 535–6, Michels, pp. 134–5.

Septimontium was not a public festival (*feriae populi*) and likens it to Paganalia. The Septimontium, however, is noted in some liturgical calendars at 11 December, one of the four Agonia (*dies Agonales*) held throughout the year. Furthermore, Paganalia, Varro's parallel, did indeed have a public character although it was movable and not held on behalf of the *populus* (Festus 284 L.; Macr. *Sat.* 1. 16. 6). The curial feast of Fornacalia belongs to this category of public festivals in which the whole *populus* did not participate. According to the report of Dionysius (4. 15. 3), King Servius Tullius founded Paganalia for which the *pagani* contributed the expenses. In the later Republic the expenses of Septimontium were contributed by the *montani* of the seven hills: 'm[ag(istri)] et flamin(es) montan(orum) montis Oppi de pequnia mont(anorum) montis Oppi sacellum clauden-d(um) et coaequand(um) et arbores serundas coeraverunt'.[1] 'The mayors and flamens of the residents of Mt Oppius have overseen the enclosing and levelling of the sacred precinct and the planting of trees (therein) from the monies of the residents of Mt Oppius.' Besides Mt Oppius the communities of the Septimontium were Palatium, Velia, Fagutal, Cermalus, Caelius and Cispius.[2] The flamen Palatualis whom Mommsen (*Röm. Staatsr.* vol. 3, p. viii) attributes to the rites of Septimontium on the Palatium attained a position in the hierarchy of the lesser flamens but no other known flamen of the seven hills became a member of the college of pontiffs.[3]

[1] *CIL* I², 1003 = VI, 32455 = *ILS* 5428 = *ILLRP* 698. See Mommsen, *Röm. Staatsr.* III, viii, n. 1. *Sacella* are referred to as *loca*, not buildings; cf. Cic. *L. Agr.* 2. 14. 36. For the definition of *sacella* as sacred precincts open to the sky with altar see Festus 422 L. Most pertinent is Cic. *Div.* 1. 46. 104: 'L. Flaccum, flaminem Martialem, ego audivi cum diceret Caeciliam Metelli, cum vellet sororis suae filiam in matrimonium conlocare, exisse in quoddam sacellum ominis capiendi causa, quod fieri more veterum solebat'. Cf. Val. Max. 1. 5. 4., Livy 40. 51. 8 speaks of censors removing easements on public *sacella*, which in context could hardly have been buildings. *ILLRP* 518 (105 B.C.), III 2, however, implies that *sacella* might be built upon.

[2] Festus 474/6 L.: 'Septimontio, ut ait Antistius Labeo, hisce montibus feriae; Palatio cui sacrificium quod fit Palatuar dicitur, Veliae [MS villae] cui item sacrificium Fagutali, Suburae, Cermalo, Oppio, Caelio monti, Cispio monti'. Cf. Festus 458–9 and 284 L., quoted above, p. 102, n. 4. Since there are eight places mentioned here, the Subura which was a *pagus* (Varro, *LL* 5. 48) is usually omitted; see G. De Sanctis I, 176, 185–7. On the corporations of *pagi* see Mommsen, *Röm. Staatsr.* III, 112–15, and the inscriptions cited below, p. 124, n. 1.

[3] Festus 137 L.: 'maiores flamines appellabantur patricii generis, minores plebei'. Cf. Gaius, *Inst.* 1. 115. Festus 144 L.: 'maximae dignationis Flamen Dialis est inter quindecim flamines, et cum ceteri discrimina maiestatis suae habeant, minimi habetur Pomonalis, quod levissimo fructui agrorum praesidet pomis'. No authority says the so-called minor flamens belonged to the pontifical college. Likewise, only the Pomonal flamen is cited among the fifteen besides the Dial, Martial and Quirinal. Though perhaps

Yet the Palatualis could not have differed in origin from the flamen Oppialis and their five unattested counterparts. Except for the Palatium which probably found mention among the Argei of the Palatine Region omitted by Varro, all the places of the Septimontium are to be found in the itinerary. Velia was both an Argei (IV 6) and an Old Curia. Cermalus also had an Argean station (IV 5).

To Dionysius (2. 47. 4) Varro appeared to be the solitary dissenter from the prevalent view that the Roman curias derived their names from Sabine women. Varro stated that the curias were called ἀπ' ἀνδρῶν...ἡγεμόνων and ἀπὸ πάγων. Dionysius, who believed that the Latin *pagus* was the Greek πάγος ('hill') (4. 15. 2), frequently uses the Greek word to mean a 'district'. In this case, however, he has spared himself a precise translation of what Varro must have said. The Curia Veliensis was properly named after a hill (to Varro an obvious fact) and could also have been a *pagus*. Although they are not identical in meaning, a Roman hill might be organized as a *pagus*. For example, at Rome were the Pagi Aventinensis, Ianicolensis and Montanus.[1] At Rome the residents were distinguished as *montani* and *pagani* who sometimes had corporations of their own. What Varro had said was that the names of curias came from men, hills and *pagi*, but Dionysius knew no difference in this context between hills and *pagi*. Two of the Servian tribes, Palatina and Collina, betray apposite names. The tribe Succusana or Suburana, on the other hand, was named from a *pagus*. Plutarch (*Rom.* 20. 3) also asserts that the curias were not named after the Sabine women but many of them had names derived from places (ἀπὸ χωρίων). In this one instance Varro's knowledge of Sabine has served to correct a demonstrably false Roman belief.[2]

Indeed there is reason to believe that the curias were considered *pagi*. Dionysius reports that king Tullius divided Roman territory into

not in late Republican practice, at least in theory there were thirty curial flamens. See Wissowa, *Religion und Kultus*[2], pp. 504–8.

[1] *CIL* xiv, 2105 = *ILS* 2676; *CIL* vi, 2219–20 = 1[2], 1000–1 = *ILLRP* 699–700; *CIL* vi, 3823 = 31577 = 1[2], 591 = *ILS* 6082. The last, on *paacus montanus*, is a *SC* of the second century and concerns the cemetery of the Esquiline region under the supervision of the plebeian aediles. D.H. 2. 55, 4. 15. 2 treats *pagus* as if the same as Greek *pagos*. So, too, Varro (in Aug. *CD* 18. 10) considers the second component of Areopagos to be the Latin *pagus*.

[2] E.g. Cic. *Rep.* 2. 8. 14: Festus 42 L.; Livy 1. 13. 6. On *pagus Succusanus*, see Varro, *LL* 5. 48.

four urban and twenty-six rural tribes (as if they were the thirty curias) according to Fabius Pictor, or into four urban and thirty-one rural tribes (as if they were the thirty-five tribes after 241 B.C.) according to Venonius.[1] In this connection must be understood a fragment of Varro (*De vita populi Romani* 1 in Nonius, p. 62 L.): 'et extra urbem in regiones XXVI agros viritim liberis adtribuit'. Under this entry of *viritim* Nonius cites before Varro Cicero's *Republic* 2. 26 on Romulus' division of land and Plautus' *Aulularia* 108 from the passage on the *magister curiae* (see above, pp. 67 ff.). We know that Varro discussed Romulus and his triple state (Nonius, p. 787 L., obelized) and the *Aulularia* (Nonius, p. 851 L.) in the same book of the *Life of the Roman People*. Moreover, Nonius at p. 851 writes as if he is citing the *Aulularia* directly from Varro. Therefore, Varro very likely related the twenty-six rural regions to the curias. In addition to Nonius' testimony, Pseudasconius (p. 212 St.) quotes *Aulularia* 107–8 and says that Plautus meant *divisores tribuum* by *magistri curiarum*. Pseudasconius or his authority was using a manual on the Roman tribes (see p. 213 St.) which was perhaps Varro's *Liber tribuum* (*LL* 5. 55–6). Since Varro thought that there were thirty *regiones* which were tribes or *pagi*, equal in number to the curias, he may also have believed in a coincidence of some curias and tribes. Such an assumption could have been made if, as we suggest below, Fabia, Claudia and Clustumina were the names of tribes and curias. The assumption was equally valid for curias and *pagi*. Confusion between tribes and curias was bound to arise in the authors because the voting units in towns with the *ius Latii* were called *curiae*, but functioned as the *tribus* in Rome.[2] There was a major difference in that the archaic Roman curias were even in number whereas the 'Latin' curias, if not totalling thirty-five, at least were odd in number (cf. *ILS* 6766: the twenty-three curias of Sardinian Turris Libisonis). The name *curia* could have been applied to 'Latin' units only after the Roman curias ceased to count for much in order to avoid confusion between Roman and municipal tribes and it would have been needed only after the Latin War (338 B.C.).

Mt Caelius, Argei I 1, took its name from an Etruscan Caele Vibenna who according to one tradition migrated to Rome and

---

[1] D.H. 4. 15. See Gabba, pp. 102–7.

[2] See Taylor, 'Voting Assemblies', pp. 11–12. Although the fuller evidence of the Latin usage comes from imperial times, it was a republican institution; see the so-called *lex mun. Tarentini* (*CIL* I², 590 = *ILS* 6086 = *FIRA* I², no. 18).

settled there[1] or whose followers (*Caeliani* or *exercitus Caelianus*) according to another came to Rome with Servius Tullius who settled them on the hill.[2] Calpurnius Piso (cos. 58) destroyed a *sacellum* of Diana, *in Caeliculo*, where senators had annually performed sacrifice for their families.[3] Such a *sacellum* might have been appropriately set aside for the sacrifices of noble families if it were a sacred enclosure belonging to a curia. The word *sacellum* is applied by Varro to Argei I 6 and by the residents of Mt Oppius to their enclosed and levelled plantation. Caeliculum seems to be the name of the place occupied by the Caeliani.

The Fagutal of the Septimontium was a *sacellum* of Jupiter Fagutalis which, in fact, was the grove of beech trees (*fagi*) beyond which lay Argei II 1.[4] This *sacellum* ought not be identified with the *sacellum* of the residents of Mt Oppius, first because both Fagutal and Oppius were included in Septimontium and secondly because the designation according to hills in the Argean itinerary of the Esquiline

[1] E.g. Varro, *LL* 5. 46.   [2] Imp. Claudius, *CIL* XIII, 1668 = *ILS* 212.

[3] Cic. *Har. Resp.* 15. 32: 'L. Pisonem quis nescit his temporibus ipsis maximum et sanctissimum Dianae sacellum in Caeliculo sustulisse? adsunt vicini eius loci; multi sunt etiam in hoc ordine qui sacrificia gentilicia illo ipso in sacello stato loco anniversaria factitarint...a Sex. Serrano sanctissima sacella suffossa, inaedificata...esse nescimus?' The word Caeliculum is comparable with Janiculum in form; see above, p. 104. I believe it is an archaic name of Mt Caelius and not identical with Caeriolum. Two possible reasons for Calpurnius' conduct can be offered. First, Cicero abused Piso's ancestry, a subject on which he may have been sensitive before Cicero's stinging gibes (Asconius, pp. 2–4 KS). Hence, he destroyed the shrine used for noble family sacrifices. Secondly, Piso's spite may also have been engendered by a famous legal case adjudicated by Porcius Cato, father of Uticensis, in which T. Claudius Centumalus sold a high apartment-house on Mt Caelius which the augurs had condemned since it obstructed the auspices which they took from the citadel. The uninformed buyer, P. Calpurnius Lanarius, had to take Claudius to court in order to recover damages after the building had been razed (Cic. *Off.* 3. 16. 66). The apartment-house, I believe, blocked a view of the grove, implied by *sacellum*, by Diana's association with the *nemus* of Aricia and the word *suffossa* used of *sacella* uprooted by Serranus. The grove was a necessary landmark for the augur's demarcation of the land and sky. See above, p. 92, n. 4. The Caelian Field (Campus Caelemontanus: *CIL* vi, 9475) probably belonged either to the curia or the *montani*. Family cult apparently was observed in groves; Cic. *Leg.* 2. 8. 19: 'lucos in agris habento et Larum sedes. ritus familiae patrumque servanto'. Cf. *Div.* 1. 46. 104, quoted above, p. 123, n. 1. See Colini, pp. 18–19, 40, 299, 409–11. Perhaps the Virbial flamen (see above, p. 114 f.) belonged to this cult since Virbius is associated only with Diana's cult (cf. Ovid, *Metam.* 15. 543–6, Verg. *Aen.* 7. 761 and Serv. on *Aen.* 7. 84, 7. 761). There was also a Dianium at the juncture of Vicus Cuprius and Clivus Urbius (Livy 1. 48. 6; see above, p. 87).

[4] Varro, *LL* 5. 152; Festus 77 L.; Pliny, *NH* 16. 37: 'silvarum certe distinguebatur insignibus, Fagutali Iove etiam nunc ubi lucus fageus fuit, porta Querquetulana, colle in quem vimina petebantur, totque lucis, quibusdam et geminis. Q. Hortensius dictator, cum plebes secessisset in Ianiculum, legem in aesculeto tulit, ut quod ea iussisset omnes Quirites teneret.' Serv. Dan. on *Aen.* 11. 316: 'secundum Trebatium, qui de religionibus libro septimo ait: Luci qui sunt in agris, qui concilio capti sunt, hos lucos eadem caerimonia moreque conquiri haberique oportet, ut ceteros qui in antiquo agro sunt'.

and Colline Regions is a later and unsyntactical addition made to facilitate finding the Argei and only goes to prove the fact that the name Oppius had latterly come to include Fagutal.[1]

The *sacellum* of the residents of Mt Oppius may have been on the site of Argei II 2 (omitted by Varro), 3 or 4. Argei II 4 had held the bake-ovens (*figlinae*) which burnt down and consequently had probably ceased to be suitable for a *sacellum* of Septimontium long before the restoration recorded by the Oppian priests. Beyond the Esquiline Grove the augural hut of Argei II 3 still stood when the surviving itinerary was plotted. This precinct is a likely site of the *sacellum* and plantation of the *montani* of Mt Oppius. The Esquiline Grove is not mentioned after the time of the itinerary and a portion of it may have been the site of the new plantation.

The Argean itinerary recorded at least two stations of Mt Cespius or Cispius, the seventh hill of Septimontium.[2] Below, I attribute Argei II 5 beyond the Poetelian Grove to another community. Cespian Argei II 6 lay within the temple precinct of Juno Lucina, built in 375 B.C., in a grove (*lucus*) from which the Juno may have taken her epithet.[3] If Dionysius (4. 15. 5) has correctly understood the annalist Calpurnius Piso, whose report he mentions in connection with the Paganalia, the Romans paid into this Juno's treasure a sum of money for each child born in accordance with the religious dispensation of Servius Tullius. Originally whatever offering was made became the treasure of the residents of Mt Cespius for Septimontium.

Some curial Argei had in the course of time yielded ground to these *sacella* or groves which in turn appear to have been used by the seven communities of Septimontium. The anomaly of a festival which is not of the *populus* but is like a festival which is public can be explained in terms of a festival at seven places originally observed at some time by seven curias and thereafter observed by the residents who succeeded the *curiales* formerly inhabiting these seven hills.

[1] The identification is made by Mommsen, *Röm. Staatsr.* III, viii, n. 1, and is approved by Degrassi, *ILLRP* 698. According to Varro in Festus 476 L. the name of Mt Oppius comes from Oppius, a Tusculan, who aided King Tullus Hostilius.

[2] According to Varro in Festus 476 L. Mt Cespius took its name from the Anagnian Cespius who migrated to Rome in the reign of Tullus Hostilius.

[3] Varro, *LL* 5. 49; Ovid, *F.* 2. 449 connects *lucina* with this *lucus*. Varro, *LL* 5. 69 represents the ancient view that the epithet comes from *lux*, but see Ernout–Meillet[4] *s.v. lucus* and Collart on Varro 5. 69. Cf. Festus 56 L., quoted above, p. 106, n. 1. This Juno as goddess of childbirth may have originated in folk etymology under Greek influence. See Palmer, *Juno*.

The seven curias had shared this religious responsibility because they resided there as seven communities. Gradually the *curiales* moved from the area of their curia buildings and augural seats which became the shrines or plantations of different deities and the precincts for observing the Septimontium. In the event, latterday residents assumed and maintained certain shrines for the sake of the Septimontium. The flamen of Mt Oppius may have been elected by the residents of Mt Oppius or by the Curia Oppia which still functioned and could have supervised and sanctioned the religious observances.

The Septimontium does represent feast days on seven hills but only Varro's vague statement that Septimontium was Rome's first name leads us to suppose that primitive Rome embraced only these hills.[1] The character and purpose of the observances have remained obscure. Trees were required and were a vestige of the plantations necessary to curial augurs, preserved out of piety. The procession around a city of seven hills, comparable with an *amburbium*, makes no sense unless the seven stations reflect the existence of seven gates which surely would not have been likely places for enclosed groves.[2] The explicit evidence of Festus and the implication of Varro's remark on the participants in the festival point to seven distinct and simultaneous sacrifices which were not connected by a procession since state priests did not participate.[3] The name of only one sacrifice, the *palatuar*, has survived (Festus 476 L.). This word is a formation like *lupercal*, *fagutal*, *pomonal*, *Apollinar* and *pulvinar*; all are substantives denoting places. The *palatuar* was the *sacellum* of the Palatium to which the 'goddess' Palatua gave her name. Trustworthy evidence of a procession or exchange of rites among the *montani* is wanting. But when the curias had maintained the rites the purpose of Septimontium was clearly understood.

In an analysis of the *cippus* of the Lapis Niger Georges Dumézil discusses a connection between what he considers a royal inscription and the prohibition against the presence of yoked teams at the procession of the augurs. Although we disagree with his understanding

---

[1] *LL* 5. 41: 'ubi nunc est Roma, Septimontium nominatum ab tot montibus quos postea urbs muris comprehendit'.

[2] Gates are the stopping places for the *amburbium* at Iguvium. See I. Rosenzweig 'Ritual and Cults of Pre-Roman Iguvium', *Studies and Documents* 9 (1937), 26–33, wherein she discusses also the lustration of a hill.

[3] *LL* 6. 24: 'dies Septimontium nominatus ab his septem montibus, in quis sita urbs est; feriae non populi sed montanorum modo, ut Paganalibus, qui sunt alicuius pagi'. Here Varro is discussing December festivals, but gives no date.

of the fragmentary *cippus* in this relation to augury, nevertheless the prohibition appears otherwise certain.[1] At Iguvium the lustration of a hill comprises augury by the Atiedian Brotherhood (*Tab. Ig.* vɪa 1–vɪb 47). When Plutarch (*Quaest. Rom.* 69) says that the same prohibition against the use of pack-animals and teams was scrupulously observed at Septimontium, there is no room to doubt that the *sacella* of Septimontium originally were laid out for augury. Because of the date of Septimontium set for the Agonium or Agonalia of 11 December, first expressly attested in a mutilated section of Festus (458 L.),[2] only one kind of augury suggests the purpose of the festival. An augury for the welfare of the state (*augurium salutis populi*) could be taken only when the Roman people were at peace. By inference such auguries have been thought to take place in the winter. In primitive times the winter was not a campaigning season.[3] The Septimontium can represent the remnants of an *augurium salutis curiarum* or *Quiritium* which was taken over by seven colleges of *montani*. The name *septimontium* must be dated to the time when the *montani* assumed responsibility for the festivals. Only seven corporations of residents, however, continued the curial practice and at some of the remaining twenty Argei other rites were introduced. The Iguvine parallel clarifies the original character of the festivals since the mountains themselves had to be ritually cleansed.

Recently the suggestion has been made that *septimontium*, meaning *septem montes*, was a false etymology born of Varro's ingenuity and that, in fact, the word stands for *saepti montes*. If the interpretation were no older than Varro this suggestion would remove doubt.[4] However, the organization of seven communities (*septem vici*) at the Latin colony of Ariminum (founded 268 B.C.) with names drawn from Roman sites and the two inscriptions recording *vici Esqelinus* and *Palatius* at the Latin colony of Cales (founded 334 B.C.), one of which goes back at least to *c*. 300 B.C., attest quite an early interpretation of *septimontium* as 'seven hills'. The names of the civic *vici* of

---

[1] Georges Dumézil, 'Sur l'inscription du lapis niger', *REL* 36 (1958), 109–11. See also Degrassi, *ILLRP* vol. 2, p. 379, and A. S. Pease on Cic. *Div.* 2. 36. 77.

[2] On the date see Wissowa, *Religion und Kultus*[2], p. 439, n. 6; *CIL* 1[2], 1. 336; and above, p. 122, n. 1; p. 128, n. 3.

[3] Cic. *Leg.* 2. 8. 21; *Div.* 1. 47. 105. See Wissowa, *Religion und Kultus*[2], pp. 133, 526, n. 3 and *RE* 2. 1, cols 2327–8; Catalano, pp. 335–46. On the primitive campaigning season see Livy 5. 2. 1–12.

[4] L. A. Holland, 'Septimontium or Saeptimontium?' *TAPA* 84 (1953), 16–34. A *sacellum clausum* could, of course, be a *mons saeptus*; see Festus 146 L.

colonies, Roman and Latin, also demonstrate an early want of uniformity in designating which of the hills were the canonical seven.[1] The list of seven hills which Festus has preserved reflects evidence of the seven which had maintained the observance and the sites for the observances.

The sacrifices of the Fratres Arvales on behalf of the Public Welfare or the welfare of a member of the imperial house consisted of the sprinkling the victim with the salt-meal (*immolatio*) and of sacrificial banquets.[2] The extravagant offering of sacrificial victims by the Arval Brothers does not reflect usage peculiar to Romans living under emperors. In his *Punic War* Naevius represents Anchises the augur:

> postquam avem aspexit in templo Anchisa,
> sacra in mensa penatium ordine ponuntur
> immolabat auream victimam pulcram.[3]

The emperor Domitian celebrated the Septimontium with spectacles and a great banquet (*epulum*) for the Romans who received various fare according to their social status. No doubt, Domitian's Septimontium differed in many respects from the simplicity of the old festival and he elevated it to the status of a sumptuous state observance.[4] Its occasion, I suspect, was unique. Domitian restored many buildings destroyed in the Neronian fire. Among the Roman buildings of Domitian's restoration were seven *atria*.[5] Domitian observed Septimontium with a grandiose banquet to celebrate the

---

[1] *CIL* xi, 379, 419, 6378; x, 4641; i², 416 = *ILS* 8567 = *ILLRP* 1217 (cf. *CIL* x, 3913). The author is preparing a history of the *vici* at Rome and in the colonies. See Serv. on *Aen.* 6. 783 for a list of different hills and above, p. 117, n. 3.

[2] Immolation for *Salus Publica*: e.g., *ILS* 229. 17, 31, 60; 230. 14, 28, 38; 241. 52, 61, 66, 88; 5035. 44 (Salus rei pub(licae) p(opuli) R(omani) Quiritium). For the banquets: *ILS* 451; 5037. 24 (ex sacrificio epulati sunt); 5039–41; 9522. See also *ILS* 9337. Since the oversight of assemblies to ratify the election of priests belonged to the curias and the Fratres Arvales sacrificed at such *comitia* (*ILS* 241. 70), this sodality may have been curial. See pp. 112–14. The Arvales' *patrimi et matrimi senatorum filii* (e.g. *ILS* 5038, 9522) were of course *camilli*.

[3] Fr. 31 Ma.² = fr. 25 St. from Probus on *Ecl.* 6. 31 (p. 336 H.). References to gilded victims and breads abound in the *acta* of the Arval Brethren.

[4] Suet. *Dom.* 4. 5: 'congiarium populo nummorum trecenorum ter dedit inter spectacula muneris largissimum epulum Septimontiali sacro, cum quidem senatui equitique panariis, plebei sportellis cum obsonio distributis initium vescendi primus fecit'.

[5] *Chron. anni 354* (Mommsen, *Mon. Germ. Hist.* ix, 146): 'hoc imp(eratore) multae operae publicae fabricatae sunt: atria vii, horrea piperataria', etc. Cf. Suet. *Dom.* 5; *CIL* vi, 30837abc and *ILS* 4914. The Sodales Titii commemorated Vespasian's preservation of ceremonies and restitution of temples (*ILS* 252).

restoration of seven dining-halls. Domitian took his precedent for the banqueting from the simple feasts once offered upon completion of the augury of welfare in the dining-halls of the seven curias whose Argei had become the places of Septimontium.

The curias whose Argei had been taken over by the *collegia montanorum* were Veliensis, Cermalensis, Palatina, Caelia, Oppia and Cespia which gave to or took from the places their names just as on Collis Mucialis was the Argei of Curia Mucia. The seventh curia probably did not share its name with the *fagutal* even though the Latian town and possible curias of Tifata and *Querquetulum took their names from oak groves. *Fagutal* only describes the grove at the curial Argei and is unlike the grove of the Fur(r)ina and the Poetelian Grove. Its parallel is seen below in the *pomonal* and flamen Pomonalis of Curia Solonia. The toponym *fagutal* is a later name just as Mons Oppius, applied in the itinerary to it, is an even later extension of a toponym at first given to the place where the Curia Oppia took its augury and its members had once lived.

Their primitive agricultural religion hardly induces us to consider the curias primarily as military units. Furthermore the Romans did not consider the religion of the curias as *sacra privata*; the curial festivals were *sacra publica* or *popularia*. Therefore the *genus hominum* which Laelius Felix calls the basis of the curia could not have been either clan or family.[1] Secondly we have distinguished three discernible stages in the expansion of the curiate organization, namely the Palatine Old Curias of seven curias (not coincidental with the Seven Hills of later days), Caelian New Curias of unknown number and the Argei of twenty-seven constituents arranged according to the four Servian regions. The curias met at these sites for religious purposes and they did not necessarily coincide with the territory occupied by the curias. Men of the curias may have dwelt near these twenty-nine places but their fields and meadows, discrete or not, could not have been on the hills of Rome.

This section I have devoted to the religion of the Seven Hills which embraced no site in the Colline Region. The Velia gave its name to a curia and an Argean station, but it is the only one of the four named Old Curias that coincides with one of the Seven Hills. Two of the Seven Hills are known to have had flamens: Palatium and Mt Oppius. The latter also had a *magister*. So, too, the Arval Brothers

---

[1] See chapter 5.

from Augustus' day onward had both officers. Except for the Palatium, the Seven Hills and their shrines can be found in the surviving segments of the Argean itinerary. Like the Arval Brothers' function the rites of the Seven Hills seem to have concerned groves. Their religion resembled that of the *pagi*. I conclude that the hillmen had assumed a religious responsibility abandoned by the old-time residents of the sites and that these residents were certain curial citizens of archaic Rome. Also I have suggested that the nature of the Septimontium was purificatory and, more specifically, an *augurium salutis* of the several curias' urban holdings in a bygone era.

'KINDS OF ROMANS'

The bonds uniting certain Latins, Albans, Sabines and Etruscans at Rome endured until the *genera* regarded themselves as Romans. Our ancient sources preserve a history of this process of union which resulted in the union of thirty curias. Dionysius, Livy and Pliny record the names of towns and peoples of Latium incorporated into the early Roman state. Following Dionysius' order we read of the conquest of Caenina, Antemnae, Crustumerium, Medullia, Cameria, Politorium, Tellenae, Ficana, Collatia, Apiolae, Corniculum, Ficulea, Crustumerium again and Suessa Pometia. Furthermore we are told that the inhabitants of Caenina, Antemna and Politorium were distributed among tribes and curias. Some Sabines, Veientines, Albans, and the Etruscan followers of Tarquinius Priscus likewise joined tribe and curia. Men of Tellenae and Ficana were transported to Rome.[1] Livy records the migration of Antemnates and Crustumini to Rome, the Roman citizenship of Sabines, the settlement of new citizens from Politorium, Tellenae and Ficana on the Aventine, and the capture of Apiolae, Corniculum, Ficulea Vetus, Cameria, Crustumerium again, Ameriola, Medullia, Nomentum and Suessa Pometia.[2] In addition to some of these towns Pliny lists the defunct communities of Satricum, Scaptia, Amitinum, Norba, Sulmo and Tifata.[3] Tifata may also be the name of a Roman curia.[4] Antemna,

---

[1] D.H. 2. 32–5; 2. 46; 2. 50; 2. 55; 3. 29; 3. 37; 3. 38; 3. 48–51; 4. 22; 4. 50.

[2] Livy 1. 11, 13, 29–30, 33–5, 38, 53, 54.

[3] Pliny, *NH* 3. 68. See chapter 2.

[4] Festus 43 L.: 'curia Tifata a Curio dicta est, qui eo loco [luco?] domum habuerat'. Festus 503 L.: 'tifata iliceta. Romae autem Tifata curia. tifata etiam locus iuxta Capuam.' Cf. Festus 117 L. Compare the name of the curia Rapta for the form of the toponym *tifata*. See chapter 5.

or Antemnae, illustrates the tenacious memory of nearby towns which were absorbed by Rome almost at the outset of its history. Situated four miles from archaic Rome on the old Via Salaria at the Anio's confluence with the Tiber, Antemna seems not to have survived the beginning of Rome on the Palatine Hill. However, knowledge of its priority to Rome, its location and very name lived on.[1] We can interpret such an historical survival in terms of the living monument of Antemna's religion which a curia might have preserved. The community of Antemna died out at Antemna many centuries before the Romans began to write their history.

Dionysius and Livy know the names of Alban families which became Roman. Livy cites Tullii, Servilii, Quinctii, Geganii, Curiatii and Cloelii. Dionysius preserves the names of perhaps the Iulii and Metilii.[2] The critical name in these lists is Curiatius. Münzer suggested that the early patrician family of this name and the officials of 453, 451 and 401 of that name are an interpolated invention or a misreading of Horatius, which Dionysius preserves in their place, because the first securely attested Curiatii appear in the later second century. The gens Curiatia of the fifth century belongs to the realm of the aetiological legend of the triplet pairs.[3] In truth a

[1] Cato *Orig.* fr. 21 P., Varro, *LL* 5. 28, Serv. on *Aen.* 7. 631. On the relation of Antemna's topographical plan to the Palatine settlement and the former's dates see R. Lanciani, *The Ruins and Excavations of Ancient Rome* (Boston and New York, 1897), pp. 110–12 and figs. 42–3.

[2] D.H. 3. 29. 7; Livy 1. 29–30. A Metilius was friend of Dionysius. See chapter 2, p. 18. In his comment on Livy's list which he does not consider to have been arranged in reverse alphabetical order despite his belief that the Julii were a later addition, Ogilvie holds that all the families were patricians, that we should accept the emendation of *Iulii* for the *Tullii* in all the Livian MSS and Dionysius' *Quinctilii* over Livy's *Quinctii*, and that the list was compiled in the early second century to reconcile the purported late arrival of patrician families to Rome. First of all, patrician status can be established only for the Servilii, Quinctii, Cloelii and Iulii, if the last were in Livy's list. The Tullii cannot be reckoned patrician nor Dionysius' *Metilii* (see Appendix III). Late arrival is supposed because of the demotic cognomens of Cloelius Siculus (cos. 498), Geganius Macerinus (cos. 492), Tullius Tolerinus (cos. 500) and the Fidenas of the Servilii, even though the first consul of the Servilii, in 495, was latterly called Priscus. The families' early consulships militate against any ancient feeling of late arrival and the feeling of the clans' late arrival can only have grown out of the list. I prefer to retain Livy's Quinctii, whose first consul in 471 bore the Roman demotic Capitolinus, and Tullii which comports with the notion of a reverse alphabetical order. The Quinctii and the Quinctilii could have pointed to their namesake luperci, a priesthood purportedly originating with Rome itself; the Tullii could have traced their family back to a Roman king. Therefore, I retain and follow the readings of Livy's MSS and reject the conflicts raised by Dionysius' obviously interpolated list.

[3] Münzer, *RE* 4. 2, cols 1830–2. Münzer later changed his mind. He believes they were patrician although the certain evidence of 138 makes them plebeian. Münzer conjectures

gens curiatia, or *curiata*, is a clan which has been made a member of a curia.[1]

The demotic cognomens of the early Fasti help to support the authenticity of Alban families: Cloelii Siculi, Geganii Macerini, Tullius Tolerinus, Servilii Fidenates and Quinctii Capitolini. With them we contrast these member states in the archaic Alban league: Sicani, Macrales, Torienses and Fidenates. The Fidenates were Latin members from a lost city of Latium implicitly according to Pliny and are not to be confused with the citizens of another Fidenae.[2] The attribution of toponymous cognomens cannot be introduced to prove any more than property or residence. But these names attached to Alban families do prove that they could not have been used to draw up a later list of clans from Alba Longa because their evidence did not point to Alba but, rather, to member cities of its league. The absence of the archaic Tullii and Geganii from the Roman Fasti after 500 and 367 respectively makes the derivation of the album of Alban clans from family records and a late collation highly improbable. Much more likely is the survival of lists of families belonging to given curias. Eligibility for the office of curion and flamen would have been determined on the basis of such a record. Since the curias were by all accounts a moribund institution toward the end of the Republic, the maintenance of such a curial list was a continuing necessity. The names of the Alban clans were to be found in the roster of a curia traditionally attributing its origin to fallen Alba Longa. The Alban tradition of the curia may well have been kept alive by the scrupulous observance of the *sacra Albana* and the Alban rite by Romans.[3] The long-time Roman incumbency of priesthoods from foreign towns lends independent support to the continuity of records because men of the appropriate clans should have discharged these offices so long as the clans survived.[4] Another

a transfer to the plebs. The Tullii were not patrician. See Fr. Münzer, *Römische Adelsparteien und Adelsfamilien* (Stuttgart, 1920), pp. 133–4 and, below, chapter 9, p. 205, n. 6 and Appendix III, p. 299, n. 2. For the testimonia on these and other magistrates cited below see Broughton under the appropriate year.

[1] Cf. *libertini centuriati*, Livy 10. 21. 4, and similar usage in *TLL*, *s.v. centurio*. Varro's verb *excuriare* from the *Menippean Satires* in Nonius, p. 53 L. appears to refer to the curia of a senate and to mean to expel from the senate-house (see chapter 9, p. 258, n. 2). See Latte, *Röm. Religion.*, p. 133, and below on the *curiati*.

[2] Pliny, *NH* 3. 53, 3. 69–70, 3. 107. See De Sanctis I, 379, n. 134 and above, chapter 2.

[3] Livy 1. 31. 1–4.

[4] Many priesthoods of this kind survived at Rome, e.g. the *sacerdos Caeninensis*, formerly of Caenina destroyed in the royal period (D.H. 2. 32, Livy 1. 10, Plut. *Rom.* 16) and

example of the availability of these records is discerned in the appointment of a priest king in 180. A Cornelius refused to resign his naval command in order to assume this priesthood and a Cloelius Siculus assumed the office even though the patrician Cloelii do not appear in the Fasti between 378 and 180, a lapse of 198 years.[1]

The name of the Alban curia can be recovered from the title of the Luperci Quinctiales which Mommsen first attributed to the Quinctii who migrated to Rome.[2] We know for certain the name of only one Lupercus Quinctialis and he is the freedman of a Considius.[3] The two named Luperci Fabiani are a [Stlac]cius and a Veturius.[4] Manifestly these are not the sodalities of families. However, two luperci can be connected with the Alban families. A freedman of the late Republic, Clesipus Geganius, was master of the Capitolini, master of the luperci and tribunician runner just as Considius was runner of the plebeian aediles.[5] This Geganius, despite his status, represented the Gens Gegania among the Luperci Quinctiales, the priests of the Alban curia to which the family belonged. In 46 Cicero's nephew Q. Tullius was a lupercus because, I believe, the Tullii from Arpinum could be honorary Albans at least for a Lupercalia in the first century.[6]

Even more telling proof of the Luperci Quinctiales' character rests on Caesar's creation of the Luperci Iuliani among whom M.

Cabensis of the Alban town *Cab-*. See Nissen, *Ital. Landesk.* 2. 560–1, 580–1, Wissowa, *Religion und Kultus*[2], pp. 519–21 and Latte, *Röm. Religion.*, pp. 404–7. An immediate connection between the curias and this kind of priest appears from *CIL* vi, 2174 = *ILS* 5009 in which the *sacerdos Cabensis* is also a Roman curion: 'dis man(ibus) C. Noni C. f. Ursi sacerdotis Cabesis montis Albani, curionis. C. Nonius Iustinus alumno dulcissimo. vix(it) ann(is) LI, m(ensibus) XI, d(iebus) XIII'. Note his age. At Ostia Sodales Arulenses appear to have been survivors of a community incorporated in the colony; see L. R. Taylor, 'The Cults of Ostia', *Bryn Mawr Coll. Monog.* 11 (1912), 44–5. R. Meiggs, *Roman Ostia* (Oxford, 1960), pp. 339–40 holds a different view.

[1] Livy 40. 42. 8–10.
[2] Mommsen, *Röm. Geschichte* 1. 51–2 (cf. idem, *Röm. Staatsr.* III, 566–7 and Marquardt-Wissowa, *Röm. Staatsv.* II[2], 440–2). The form *Quintilii* is attested by Ovid, *F.* 2. 378, Dion. 2. 29. 7 and *OGR* 2. 2. 1 but is also a derivative of Quinctius or Quintus (compare the names Lucilius, Pubilius, Hostilius, Manilius, Sextilius, from praenomens). Festus 78 (and 308 L.) offers Quintiliani.
[3] *CIL* vi, 1933 = *ILS* 1923: 'Q. Considius Q. l. Ero[s]...lupercus Quinctial(is) vetus.'
[4] *CIL* vi, 33421: '[M. Stlac]cio M. l. ...[lupercu]s Fabianus. *CIL* xi, 3205 = *ILS* 4948: Q. Veturius Q.f. Pom. Pexus lupercus Fabianus.'
[5] *CIL* x, 6488 = I[2], 1004 = *ILS* 1924 = *ILLRP* 696 (where see Degrassi's comments).
[6] Cic. *Ad Att.* 12. 5. 1 (46 B.C.). Republican luperci were from noble families (so see Mommsen, *Röm. Staatsr.* III, 566–7) such as the Caelii, Herennii and Tullii: see Broughton *s.aa.* 56 and 46.

Antonius was enrolled for the famous Lupercalia of 44.[1] We need not seek far the purpose of the institution of these latterday luperci. Livy, for one, does not include the Iulii among the Alban families whereas Dionysius perhaps does. Nor was it so much a question of Caesar trying to authenticate an Alban pedigree as of his trying to detract from the renown attaching to the Quinctii of Alba who appeared to have been Alba's most eminent family by virtue of an eponymous curia and priesthood. To create a new curia was unthinkable but a new religious sodality might be founded *ad maiorem Caesaris gloriam*. Publication of the roster of Alban families probably went back no further than Caesar's regime when it was a matter of some importance. Livy's listing by reverse alphabetical order points to Caesar's public librarian Terentius Varro and, I would guess, to his work on Trojan families.[2] The roster's uniqueness we may owe to Caesar. At any rate, Tiberius thereafter had the precedent for establishing the Sodales Augustales whose office called to mind a putative Sabine lineage, a Roman king and the augury of the Sodales Titii.[3]

In discussing the Argei of Collis Mucialis we pointed out the inference which latterday Mucii drew from the name of the Prata Mucia across the Tiber. Likewise a carefully reserved plot of four *iugera* across the Tiber in the Ager Vaticanus was ascribed by the Romans to the great dictator Quinctius Cincinnatus. The Prata Quinctia belonged to the Curia Quinctia and had been preserved for that reason and no other. A part of the Curia Fabia's story will be told in the history of the curiate constitution. For now the names of the Curias Quinctia and Fabia ought to be restored to Roman history.[4]

[1] Suet. *Caes.* 76. 1.

[2] See L. W. Daly, 'A Common Source in Early Roman History', *AJP* 84 (1963), 68–71, and *Contributions to a History of Alphabetization* etc., *Coll. Lat.* 90 (1967), 51–4, who suggests Varro's *Antiquities* on the basis of similar alphabetical lists. One of the lists Daly discusses also might have the same source: the peoples of the Alban Leagues (Pliny, *NH* 3. 69). On the *De familiis Troianis* see Dahlmann, *RE* Supplbd. 6, cols 1241–2. Serv. on *Aen.* 5. 117 cites some Roman families of Trojan origins among whom are the Geganii; this information comes from Varro's work which he explicitly cites on *Aen.* 2. 166 and 5. 704. See below, Appendix III, on research into old families. The reverse alphabetical order in Livy's list may indicate he drew it from a work in which Varro was using the list for a second time. There is no doubt the Iulii were 'Alban'. What is at issue here is their absence from the alphabetical list.

[3] Tac. *Ann.* 1. 54: 'idem annus novas caerimonias accepit addito sodalium Augustalium sacerdotio, ut quondam Titus Tatius retinendis Sabinorum sacris sodalis Titios instituerat' *Hist.* 2. 95: 'caesae publice victimae cremataeque; facem Augustales subdidere, quod sacerdotium, ut Romulus Tatio regi, ita Caesar Tiberius Iuliae genti sacravit'.

[4] For the Prata Quinctia see Livy 3. 13. 10, 3. 26. 8; Val. Max. 4. 4. 7; Pliny, *NH* 18. 20; Festus 307 L. On the Fabia see above, p. 125, and below, pp. 234–5.

Here we must digress for a moment to discuss the implication of the term *curiatius* and the legend of the three Curiatii. In chapter 8 I treat the religious ceremony by which an ethnic group became that part of the Roman people called a curia. According to the legend Roman triplets fought against Alban triplets. The ancients entertained doubts as to which nations the three Horatii and three Curiatii belonged. The received tradition has one Roman Horatius survive their duel only to kill his own sister. Ultimately he was purified of his crime by walking under the beam (*tigillum sororium*) which spanned the Crossroads of Acilius between the altars of Janus Curiatius and Juno Sororia. A 'sister' entered the legend because of a fancied linguistic connection of the adjective *sororium* and the noun *soror*. Horatius' purification evidently belonged to a ceremony whereby young men who had come of age were initiated into their curias. Thus *curia* named the *ianus* whose altar was employed in the rites. The identity of the Curiatii was doubtful in antiquity because the Janus Curiatius was as Roman as the family of the Horatii. Juno, a goddess worshiped in all the curias, was venerated at her altar at the initiation rites because her divinity meant 'youth', the age at which the new members of the curias had arrived (*iuno < iuven-*). The ceremony took place on 1 October after the warring season and harvest. The young men's initiation made them curial citizens (*curiati*) by walking under the beam for which they sacrificed to Janus and upon coming of age for which they sacrificed to Juno.[1] The adversaries of the Romans were Albans in the legend because certain 'Alban' families were found among *curiati* or, to put it in the terms of the Roman tradition, the Curiatii were named among the Albans.

In addition to the annexation of conquered territory and the transportation of conquered peoples the Roman state increased through the process of migration. According to Dionysius (3. 48. 2) Lucumo (Tarquinius) acquired a Roman tribe, curia, homesite, citizenship and a plot of land when he migrated to Rome. Of course this manner of speaking is redundant but renders, nevertheless, a rather accurate account of the lengthy and complex process which

[1] See Ogilvie, pp. 109 ff., on Livy 1. 24–5; Degrassi, pp. 468–9, 515–16 for a collection of the testimonia and the bibliography, especially that of H. J. Rose on the initiation; and Palmer, 'Cupra, Matuta and Venilia Pyrgensis', in *Illinois Studies in Language and Literature* 58 (Urbana, 1969), 294–7 and *Juno*.

led to the formation of the *civitas Romana*. With the last three 'Etrus-can' kings apparently ended the practice of receiving captive peoples into the Roman state. Dionysius' all too fulsome treatment speaks of enslavement, not enrolment. However, Servius Tullius' presumed servile origin which may have suggested the policy of enslavement, stems from his praenomen and not from the fact that Corniculum, his family's town, was conquered by Tarquinius Priscus.[1]

The number of curias stood at twenty-seven at the time the city was redrawn into four regions and four tribes. At the end of the royal period two more towns, Crustumerium and Gabii, were associated with Rome by treaty. Dionysius also informs us that Rome and Gabii shared isopolity.[2] Then the Republic was established and in its infant years the Sabine Claudii and their followers reached Rome as migrants and assumed the responsibilities of Roman citizens. Their early demotic cognomen Inregillensis points to a Sabine provenience yet their Tribus Claudia lay elsewhere.[3] These three *genera*, Crustu-mini, Gabini and Claudii, came to constitute the last three curias. In the year 495 B.C. the number of tribes reached twenty-one. Miss Taylor suggests that this year saw both the Clustumina and Claudia formed.[4] On the other hand the Ager Gabinus enjoyed a peculiar status. The Roman augurs distinguished it from *ager Romanus*, *ager peregrinus* and *ager hosticus*.[5] Romans spoke of both Ager Crustuminus and Tribus Clustumina[6] whereas the Gabini had

[1] D.H. 3. 50–1, 4. 50; Livy 1. 39; Cic. *Rep.* 2. 21. 37. The emperor Claudius tells another version *CIL* XIII, 1668 = *ILS* 212.

[2] D.H. 3. 49; Livy 1. 38. 1–4, 2. 19. 2. D.H. 4. 58 also says that the treaty of isopolity still survived on a wooden shield, covered with ox hide, preserved in the temple of Dius Fidius. See A. N. Sherwin-White, *The Roman Citizenship* (Oxford, 1939), pp. 18–19 and below, chapter 9, pp. 195–7.

[3] Livy 2. 16. 3–5, on which see Ogilvie.

[4] 'Voting Districts', pp. 6, 35–7. On the probable identification of names of some tribes and curias see above, p. 125.

[5] Varro, *LL* 5. 33: 'ut nostri augures publici disserunt, agrorum sunt genera quinque: Romanus, Gabinus, Peregrinus, Hosticus, Incertus. Romanus dictus unde Roma ab Romulo; Gabinus ab oppido Gabis; Peregrinus ager pacatus qui extra Romanum et Gabinum, quod uno modo in his servantur auspicia; dictus peregrinus a pergendo, id est a progrediendo: eo exin ex agro Romano primum progrediebantur, quocirca Gabinus quoque Peregrinus sed quod auspicia habet singularia, ab reliquo discretus; Hosticus dictus ab hostibus; Incertus is, qui de his quattuor qui sit ignoratur.' Cf. the report of Roman augurs at Lake Regillus (Livy 3. 20). The kind (*genus*) of field called Gabinus did not comprise the territory of Gabii only; otherwise it would not have been a *genus agrorum*. It must have included the territory of the three curias, Gabina, Crustumina and Claudia, added after the Servian reform when the number of *auguracula* in the four urban regions was forever closed at twenty-seven. On the purported *devotio* of Gabii see chapter 8.

[6] Pliny, *NH* 3. 52–3. discussed below. See also Varro, *LL* 5. 81, quoted pp. 219–20.

no tribe until quite late. This omission supports the view that the isopolity of Rome and Gabii remained different from what was later called *civitas optimo iure*. The Gabini with their Ager Gabinus belonged to the curiate system but did not belong to the centuriate organization and did not have a tribe because the men of Gabii were not bound by treaty to serve in the Roman infantry. A Roman horseman girded himself in the Gabinian manner when wearing the *trabea*.[1]

Roman augurs distinguished the Ager Gabinus from Ager Romanus. Also the Ager Crustuminus was distinct from the Tribus Clustumina, i.e. from Ager Romanus. Despite Beloch's suggestion and Miss Taylor's agreement with him that this was a townless territory within the old tribe Clustumina and was designated after the Social War, I propose that the Ager Crustuminus was at one time the territory of a curia of that name. In close proximity to Rome lay the Ager Latinus or Latiniensis.[2] Miss Taylor and Beloch consider this also a formation after the Social War.[3] The Latinienses belonged to the Alban League and presumably would have become a Roman curia after the league's dissolution.[4] Nissen, moreover, related the Ager Latinus to the Collis Latiaris, the site of Argei III 6 which antedates the Social War.[5] The Ager Latinus stands in the same relation to the Collis Latiaris as Prata Mucia to Collis Mucialis. A Curia Latia suffices to explain the name of the hill and the field.[6]

[1] For the *cinctus Gabinus* of a horseman see Livy 8.9.9 (cf. 10.7.3) and Verg. *Aen.* 7.612. This style of dress was also peculiar to Roman religious rites. For instance, city founders demarcating a pomerium (Cato, *Orig.* fr. 18 P.) and Pisans sacrificing for the Manes of Lucius Caesar (*CIL* xi, 1420 = *ILS* 139) must be *cincti Gabino ritu*. See A. Alföldi, 'Der frührömische Reiteradel und seine Ehrenabzeichen', *Deut. Beit. z. Altertumsw.* 2 (1952), 38–9.

[2] Cic. *Har. Resp.* 10.20; Pliny, *NH* 3.53.

[3] Beloch, *Römische Geschichte bis zum Beginn der punischen Kriege* (Berlin, 1926), pp. 153–4, 159–62; Taylor, 'Voting Districts', pp. 36–7, 52–3. From the evidence cited in the previous footnote and discussed by Taylor, p. 40, n. 17, it is clear that the Ager Latiniensis lay too close to Rome to be considered in the manner of Beloch. Livy 2.16.5 apparently distinguishes an old and new tribe Claudia: 'his civitas data agerque trans Anienem; Vetus Claudia tribus—additis postea novis tribulibus—qui ex eo veniret agro appellati.' Cf. Suet. *Tib.* 1.1. What is important for this study is the *ager* which must have been called *Claudius* and which belonged to the augural kind of territory called after Gabii. If Latiniensis represents the vestigial parcel of tribal territory, why does it not bear the name of a tribe?

[4] Pliny, *NH* 3.69. Nor is this the only member people who appears to have belonged to the Alban League. See below, chapter 7. See M. Pallottino, 'Le origini di Roma', *Arch. Class.* 12 (1960), 26–31.

[5] *Ital. Landesk.* 2.556 with other ancient references.

[6] Varro, *LL* 5.32 preserves the original name: 'qua regnum fuit Latini, universus ager dictus Latius'. Cf. the Iguvine *agre tlatie* (*Tab. Iguv.* vb 9), and see Poultney *ad loc.* Bernardi, '*Populi Albenses*', pp. 251–2, argues Latini are 'plainsmen', Albani 'mountaineers'.

In contrast to the use of *ager* in this context can be adduced the *regio Ficulensis* containing two *pagi* (*CIL* xiv, 4012 = *ILS* 5387). The conquered and defunct community of Ficulea gave its name to a territory called *regio* which must have been larger than the *agri* under discussion. Indeed, the *ager* of a community fully absorbed into the Ager Romanus ought to have lost its identity. The reason for retention of the old name points to its continued special existence.

Laelius Felix's 'kinds of men' comprised the several Roman curias. By 'kinds' I understand peoples from towns and ethnic groups different from those already constituent of the Roman community until their amalgamation with the latter. Amalgamation took place through the conquest and transportation of near neighbors such as were preserved in the Roman historical tradition, through the migration of unsettled groups or, finally, through the striking of a treaty of union.

I have identified an 'Alban' curia called Quinctia that had a priesthood of luperci. This curia was constituted of clans that came from old members of the so-called Alban League. If there was a Curia Quinctia with Luperci Quinctiales, the Luperci Fabiani point to a curia called Fabia which was also the name of a later Roman tribe. The migrant Claudii had their *tribus Claudia* and *ager Claudius*. The latter parcel of land may have been curial just as the conquered village of Crustumerium gave its name to a tribe and an *ager*. The land of Gabii, which had a special treaty with Rome, also became a special kind of augural land and did not belong to a Roman tribe. I assume that the Curias Claudia, Crustumina and Gabina were the last three curias formed after the twenty-seven whose Argean stations were situated in the city of four regions and that these were excluded from the urban augural sites. Ager Latiniensis seems to be curial land and bears a name related to Collis Latiaris of the Argean itinerary in the Colline Region as Nissen suggested. The question of curial lands which are implicit in the sacrifices at the boundary markers of the *agri* during the curial festival of Fornacalia is quite crucial to any discussion of the curias' history. Among the lands I have reckoned the aforementioned *agri* and the *prata* of Curias Mucia and Quinctia. Doubtless there were other lands and in the next section I discuss their possible identifications and their transfer from curial to private ownership.

CURIAL LANDS

The manner by which the *agri* came to be owned by private citizens raises a serious question. In the case of the Argei we have argued that the augural seats of the curias were encroached upon for the sake of the state religion or to observe the lustration of mountains. Cato the Censor said that the whore Acca Larentia bequeathed to the Roman people from her extensive estate four *agri*, Turax or Turacis, Semurius, Lintirius or Lutirius, and Solonius.[1] In Cato's day these four had obviously been a part of the *ager publicus*. The Turacis or Turax has usually been connected with a legendary Vestal Gaia Taracia or Fufetia who also made a similar bequest to the Roman people although her acquisition of it has remained untold.[2] Her name and the family name Taracius[3] point to a MS corruption of the field's name (*a* to *u*). Dealing with rare and unfamiliar proper names some copyist has also corrupted the name of the fourth field. For the Lintirius and Lutirius I suggest the reading Laterius and cite the family name Laterius and the two demotic cognomens Lateranus and Laterensis.[4] The Curia Lateria's god and *genius* was Lateranus. He is represented by folk etymology as a deity of bricks (*lateres*) in the hearth: *deus focorum et genius* (see Arn. 4. 6). I prefer to see this *genius* as a curial *daimon* and the *foci* as a part of the curial dining-hall.

Some Romans believed the curias were named after the Sabine women and presumably were brought to this view by the name of the Curia Rapta.[5] Accordingly De Sanctis nominated Romulus' Sabine wife Hersilia as a curia's eponym.[6] With a good deal of restraint we

---

[1] Macr. *Sat.* 1. 10. 6: 'Cato ait Larentiam meretricio quaestu locupletatam post excessum suum populo Romano agros Turacem Semurium Lintirium [*vel* Litirium, Linterium, Lintiarium, Lutirium] et Solonium [MSS Solinium] reliquisse et ideo sepulcri magnificentia et annuae parentationis honore dignatam'. Willis in his edition (Leipzig, 1963) retains the readings *Solinium* and *Turacem* though they are patently wrong even if attested by Macrobius' MSS. Cf. 1. 10. 6 MSS *Luciniam* for *Liciniam*, 1. 16. 41 *decimus* for *dicimus*, and 1. 6. 7 *curialem* for *curulem*; all these errors are exhibited in cases where the correct reading would be far more easily recognized than in the case of the four toponyms.

[2] Gellius, *NA* 7. 7. 1–4; Pliny, *NH* 34. 25. Cf. Plut. *Public.* 8. See Mommsen, 'Acca Larentia' and Boehm, *RE* 7. 1, cols 480–3.

[3] *ILLRP* 984.

[4] *Ibid.* 613, 1148. See J. Heurgon, 'C. Mamilius Limetanus à Caere', *Latomus* 19 (1960), 221–4. For the families bearing the cognomen Lateranus see *RE* 12. 1, col. 904; on Juventius Laterensis see *RE* 10. 2, cols 1365–7 (cf. Caelius Latiniensis, *RE* 4. 1, col. 197). The cognomen cannot refer to Volscan Laterium because it would then be Lateriensis. See Nissen, *Ital. Landesk.* 2. 674. Both Laterius and Laterensis come from a root *later-*.

[5] E.g. Cic. *Rep.* 2. 8. 14; Festus 42 L.; Livy 1. 13. 6.

[6] De Sanctis. 1, 223. See above, chapter 5.

may find that the name of a curia is given to a legendary heroine which may be the case of Taracia and of Acca.

Varro held the names of curias were derived from family names and places. In the first class we have Acculeia/Accoleius, Faucia/Faucius, Titia/Titius and Velitia/Velitius. All of these are certain. To them may be added Caelia/Caelius, Cespia/Cespius (Cispius), Claudia/Claudius, Fabia/Fabius, Mucia/Mucius, Oppia/Oppius, Pinaria/Pinarius, Quinctia/Quinctius, and Volturna/Volturnius. In the second class we have only one certain example, Veliensis/Velius, and these already proposed in this study Foriensis/Furinius (Furnius), Gabina/Gabinius, and Latia/Latinius.[1] This sum of seventeen examples illustrates one manner of name-giving to both persons and places. It helps explain the existence of early families bearing the same name which are both patrician and plebeian. It shows how 300 Fabii might die at the Cremera. No one objects to a Gabinius named from a Gabinus or a Latinius from a Latinus. And there is no inherent objection to deriving the family name from the curia. Some Servian tribes are said to have taken their names from families, even from families whose names do not appear in early Roman history.[2] In the case of the lady's bequest we have Lateria/Laterius, Solonia/Solonius[3] and Taracia/Taracius.

Besides Cato's report of the donation of four fields by Acca Larentia a second tradition attributes the donation of the Campus Tiberinus to a Vestal Gaia Taracia or Fufetia.[4] The interpolation of a Vestal probably arose to counter the presence of a whore in the folk legend. Taracia is the eponym of Cato's *ager* whose MS tradition ought to be emended from *agrum turacem* to *taracem* or, better,

---

[1] Schulze, 'Eigennamen', has all these names in his index, *s.vv.*; the relation of personal and topographical names is also discussed, pp. 561–82. For Curia Faucia see Livy 9. 38. 15–16, a most important passage for the history of the curiate constitution which I discuss in chapter 9. The Curia Pinaria is an inference from Festus 264 L. where he is discussing tribe names beginning with *p* and cites a Pinaria. Since Pinaria is no tribe, it has been suggested that it is a curia. See De Sanctis I, 241, n. 56.

[2] See Taylor 'Voting Districts', p. 35. Six of the first Servian tribes have names which are not found in the Fasti of Republican magistrates at all: Camilia, Galeria, Lemonia, Pollia, Pupinia and Voltinia (so Broughton's index). When and if they appear as personal names, they might well be derivatives from names of the tribe itself. The tribe Lemonia, in fact, takes its name from *pagus Lemonius* (Festus 102 L.; Taylor, 'Voting Districts', pp. 6, 38). This adjective denotes the place *Lemona with which one may compare Albiona, *Muciona, etc. See below, Appendix III.

[3] See Schulze, pp. 239, 371, 563. Pliny, *NH* 3. 114 and 116 remarks Solinates and Solonates in Umbria and Region VIII respectively but *ILS* 6656 shows that the Umbrian people also were Solonates.

[4] See above, pp. 106–15.

taracium.[1] The Vestal Taracia was excogitated to explain the name of the field given by Acca. Fufetia is an attempt to reconcile the stories of two donations or belongs to an older story of a Vestal who was dislodged by the eponymous Taracia.

In his study of the Campus Martius Castagnoli proposes to explain Gaia Taracia as the Greek translation of Ager Tarax. For him Ager Tarax is identical with the Campus Tiberinus and the Tarentum, a place of cult in the Campus Martius very close to the Tiber.[2] For him Tarax and Tarentum exhibit a pre-Italic word for 'river' also exhibited in the name of the Lacedaemonian colony Taras which the Romans naturally rendered Tarentum.[3] Although I cannot entertain confidence in the meaning of 'pre-Italic' *tar-*, the linguistic connection of Ager Tarax or Taracius and Tarentum is well founded. Place names in *-entum* are quite common.[4] Indeed Tarentum is not a formation which we would expect to find as a cult term.[5] To Ager Taracius and Tarentum I would add the Latin name of the town Tarracina or Tarricina which was also known in historical times by its Volscan name Anxur.[6]

According to Castagnoli the name Ager Tarax was displaced by Campus Tiberinus which in turn yielded to Campus Martius.[7] The first is a place name, the second gives its location and the third identifies the god to whom it became sacred. Then, Cato knew of the past existence of some public land which he attributed to the estate of the whore Acca. The intended irony of a Vestal virgin Taracia who gave the Campus Tiberinus was based upon the proper identity of the location which in antiquity may or may not have been made with recognition of the word Tarentum's significance. The formation of the name Tarentum and the ancient Ager Taracius render likely the existence of a distinct community which occupied the later Campus Martius.

At Iguvium the unit of Clavernii farmed the *agre tlatie Piquier Martier* and the Casilas farmed the *agre Casiler Piquier Martier* for sacral

---

[1] See above, p. 141, n. 1.

[2] F. Castagnoli, 'Il Campo Marzio nell'antichità', *Atti dell'Accademia Nazionale dei Lincei*, Mem. cl. sci. mor. stor. filol., ser. 7, vol. 1, fasc. 4 (1946), 99–112.

[3] Castagnoli, p. 99.

[4] See above, p. 115, n. 2, and below, chapter 7.

[5] But see above on *Larentum and *Carmentum.

[6] See Walbank on Pol. 3. 22. 11. Cf. Tarrichinensis in *ILLRP* 912 and the cognomen Taravos in *ILLRP* 591.

[7] Castagnoli, p. 111.

purposes.[1] Not only are the names of the two fields instructive but also their nature as corporate property and the god to whom both were dedicated, offer an analogy for Ager Taracius as we interpret it.

Twelve miles from Rome off the Ostian way stood a *pomonal* in the Ager Solonius. This *pomonal* has been thought to bear a relation to the Roman flamen Pomonalis. If indeed the *pomonal* was the site of the flamen's religious duties, then Dionysius' remark on the curias having peculiar gods finds further illustration. Festus thought this *pomonal* worth locating for his users. It may have been no more than a sacred grove of fruit trees.[2] Propertius in an elegy on archaic Rome lends support to the view that the Solonian territory belonged to the Roman people and that the territory was originally a curial *ager* (4. 1. 31–2): 'hinc Tities Ramnesque viri Luceresque Soloni, quattuor hinc albos Romulus egit equos'. The word *Soloni* would be an unnatural genitive and a locative without syntax with *hinc*. It must stand for *Solonii*, nominative plural (cf. *Gabi*, *ibid.* 34), and modify *Luceres*. Dionysius 2. 37. 2 tells us that a Lucumo from Solonium, a *polis*, allied himself with Romulus against Tatius and his Sabines.[3] From Propertius' point of view the Roman tribe of Luceres was Solonian.[4] If the relation is at all historical, the Curia Solonia may have belonged to the old tribe Luceres in which its members served. The existence of a Curia Taracia is supported by a connection with augury. Varro believed the Sodales Titii took their name from the bird *titus* which they observed in augury. The suggestion of a Curia Volturna has been supported by the augural character of the vulture. On the Argei of the Curia Mucia (III 5) the Romans reared a temple of Dius Fidius Semo Sancus whose augural bird the osprey had the technical name *sanqualis*.[5] The *tarax* may be connected with the

---

[1] *Tab. Ig.* vb, discussed above, pp. 45–7.

[2] Festus 296 L.: 'Pomonal est in agro Solonio, via Ostiensi ad duodecimum lapidem deverticulo a miliario octavo'. Cf. the Lanuvinian Curia -amonal(is). On the location of Ager Solonius see B. Tilly, *Vergil's Latium* (Oxford, 1947), pp. 112–19.

[3] Cf. Prop. 4. 2. 51; Festus 106–7 L. *s.vv. Luceres* and *Lucomedi*. A town Solonium may have been suggested by re-analysis. The defunct town may have been *Solona, 'place of low land (*solum*)' whence the Solonius ager is named. Cf. the porta Mucionia and the Solonates of the Transpadane Region VIII (Pliny, *NH* 3. 116, above, p. 142, n. 3). The right reading *Soloni*, instead of the vulgar *coloni*, is confirmed by two Salamancan MSS, one of which preserves *Soloni* and the other *Roloni*, a mistake unlikely if *coloni* were the correct reading. See A. Tovar and M. T. Belfiore-Martire's new edition of Propertius (Barcelona, 1963) *ad loc.*; *Soloni* is also found in Barber's and Camps' texts.

[4] See Palmer, 'King' on the Luceres.

[5] Pliny, *NH* 10. 20; Festus 3, 420 L.

Curia Taracia since it was a water-fowl which might well have tarried in the swampy parts of the Campus Martius, a part of which was Taracia's bequest to the Roman people.[1]

In 200 B.C. the senate voted that the consuls should appraise and sell at a third of its appraised value all public land within fifty miles of Rome in order to pay off the state debt incurred during the Hannibalic War. These parcels may well have included the four fields which Cato later mentions. Cicero owned land *in Solonio* and Roscius was born and reared there. Presumably the Ager Taracius was considered part of the Campus Martius and was not sold. However, we may assume any of the curial *agri* could have been sold in an effort to make the state solvent.[2] Not all the land put on the market in 200 found buyers since the Ager Semurius remained public until 44 when L. Antonius proposed a plebiscite, one clause of which gave the Semurius to Caesar's many military tribunes. Cicero's allusion to the possible allotment of the Campus Martius, partly the bequest of Taracia, points to its close relation to the Ager Semurius and the peculiar status of the Semurius. Furthermore, Sulla is reported to have sold a part of the Campus Martius before leaving for the East, and Cicero may have had this sale in mind.[3] This strange assignment confirms the curial ownership of the land, for military tribunes,

---

[1] The *tarax* is mentioned by Olympius Nemasianus, *De Aucupio* (Bücheler–Riese *Anth. Lat.* 2. 883, lines 1–2): 'et tetracem, Romae quem nunc vocitare taracem coeperunt avium est multo stultissima'. Ernout–Meillet[4] *s.v. tarax* say it is late and borrowed, and cite its Greek cognates and related Latin bird names. Many bird names are onomatopoetic and that means nothing. Besides a flock of cognomens which are Latin bird names, the gentilicial names Titius, Aquilius and Corvius are all derived from birds of omen to which may be added Passerius, ominous only for Greeks, and the praenomen Gaius 'jay'. The difference between birds of augury and auspication was that the former required certain birds, the latter any bird at all (Serv. Dan. on *Aen.* 1. 398 from either the augural *libri* or *commentarii*) cf. Cic. *Div.* 2. 35. 73, 2. 36. 76. On the site of the land bequeathed by Taracia see Castagnoli, pp. 99–112.

[2] Livy 31. 13. 5–9; Cic. *Ad Att.* 2. 3. 3, *Div.* 1. 37. 79, 2. 31. 66; Gellius, *NA* 7. 7. 4. The passage of Cato in Macrobius is usually included in the fragments of the *Origines* (Peter, *HRR* 1², 60) but it may belong to an edict or speech of Cato as censor in 184 which treated the sale or, for that matter, ceased it. At any rate, Cato's interest in the lands may have arisen from the *SC* of 200.

[3] Cic. *Phil.* 6. 5. 14: 'statuerunt etiam tribuni militares qui in exercitu Caesaris bis fuerunt. quis est iste ordo? multi fuerunt in legionibus per tot annos. eis quoque divisit Semurium. Campus Martius restabat, nisi prius cum fratre fugisset [*sc.* L. Antonius]'. Orosius 5. 18. 27: 'namque eodem tempore cum penitus exhaustum esset aerarium et ad stipendium frumenti deesset expensa, loca publica quae in circuitu Capitolii pontificibus, auguribus decemviris et flaminibus in possessionem tradita erant, cogente inopia vendita sunt'. On the latter passage see Castagnoli, p. 114 and Palmer, 'King'. Although no ancient source indicates the site of the Semurius, it must have lain reasonably close to Rome for the legend of the inheritance to have been credible.

as we shall see, were originally the officers of the oldest military organization and were elected by the curiate assembly. The perverted sense of historical ownership subsequent to civil war prompted this unusual allotment. Within Cato's memory the four fields were public land. In 44 the Solonius and Laterius (cf. the Laterenses) were privately owned, the Taracius as part of the Campus Martius still presumably belonged to the Roman people, and the Semurius briefly became the property of Caesar's tribunes.[1]

On the occasion of these three civil emergencies the curial *agri* could easily have been reduced in size to a token plot or have passed wholly into private ownership. It is not at all impossible that curial lands were sold (cf. *atrium Titium*) or rented by the curias themselves at some time since the curions had a treasury which usually means an income (*curionium aes*: Festus 42 L.; cf. D.H. 2. 23. 1).

There remain two more possible curias to be identified on the basis of property and priesthoods which might evince a curial heritage: the Fratres Marcii and Campus Martialis; the Poetelii Libones and the Lucus Poetelius and P⟨o⟩etelinus. The second plebeian elected curio maximus was C. Scribonius in 174. He and his descendants styled themselves Scribonii Curiones in remembrance of the office.[2] Other Scribonii bore the cognomen Libo which certain Marcii and Poetelii also had for cognomen. The meaning of *libo* is uncertain but a connection with *libum* and *libare* is attractive.[3] The fact remains that the Scribonii appear proud of the lowly priesthood of the curio maximus. The *libones* may be considered minor attendants at the obsolescent religious rites of the curias. The cognomen is borne by Scribonii, Marcii and Poetelii.

In 210 the plebeian M. Marcius, the *rex sacrorum*, died. It has been

---

[1] Antonius' agrarian laws were declared void in the next year because of failure to observe the statutory *trinundinum*; see G. Rotondi, *Leges Publicae Populi Romani* (Milan, 1912), pp. 433–4.

[2] Livy 41. 21. 8–9. See Münzer, *RE* 2A1, col. 861. The first plebeian curio maximus was C. Mamilius Atellus, elected in 209 (Livy 27. 8. 1–3), who should not be identified with the plebeian aedile of 208 and praetor of 207, C. Mamilius, since the curions could not serve in the army or perform other *munera*. Rather the praetor of 207 should be identified as the son of C. Mamilius Q. f. Q. n. Turrinus (cos. 239) and brother of Q. Mamilius Turrinus, plebeian aedile of 207 and praetor of 206 who followed his brother in these two magistracies in successive years. The C. Mamilius, surnamed Atellus, is only mentioned as curio maximus. C. Scribonius, curio maximus after 174, never held another magistracy. M. Aemilius Papus, curio maximus until 210, has no other recorded office and that is as it should be. See Münzer, *RE* 14. 1 Mamilii nos. 5, 11–13; and Heurgon, 'C. Mamilius Limetanus à Caere', *Latomus* 19 (1960), 223–29.

[3] G. C. Chase, 'The Origin of Roman Praenomina', *HSCP* 8 (1897), p. 111 and n. 2,

fairly urged that he bequeathed the cognomen Rex to his son. Mommsen denies the kingship of this man because only a patrician might hold the priesthood.[1] However, his tenure falls during wartime and in 209 a plebeian was elected curio maximus for the first time. The Marcii Reges appear as proud of their titles as the Scribonii of Curio—a matter of plebeian pride. An exception to the rules governing the kingship could be made in the case of a family which could trace descent from king Ancus Marcius and boasted membership in the first augural and pontifical colleges to include plebeians in 300.[2] What is more, Marcii traditionally possessed the gift of prophecy. In 212 a prophet (*vates*) Marcius issued two prophecies (*carmina*) which the senate had the urban praetor publish and in accordance with one of the prophecies the Ludi Apollinares were instituted. The prophecies which Livy quotes show marked Greek influence but he implies that some *carmina Marciana* had existed before 212.[3] Servius calls the predictions *responsa* which were preserved in the temple of Apollo (on *Aen.* 6. 70, 72). Isidore says Marcius first composed *praecepta* for the Latins and likens him to Moses and Pliny counts Marcius the equal of Melampous.[4] Servius, Symmachus (*Ep.* 4. 34) and Cicero all speak of plural Marcii *fratres* or *vates*. Cicero's evidence tells us that there was more than one Marcius of this kind. He finds similarities between the words of the Marcii and Apollonic oracles but he also distinguishes the

suggests that *libo* means the official called 'sprinkler' and cites the verb *delibuere* for the quantity (see Ernout–Meillet[4] *s.v. delibutus*). Similar cognomens are *camillus, lupercus, rex*, and *augur*.

[1] See Broughton 1. 284, n. 8.

[2] See Münzer *RE* 14. 2 Marcii nos. 20 and 98 and on their pretensions of royal descent, cols 1535–8, 1543, and below, Appendix III.

[3] Livy 25. 12. 2–4: 'religio deinde nova obiecta est ex carminibus Marcianis. vates hic Marcius inlustris fuerat. et cum conquisitio priore anno ex senatus consulto librorum fieret, in M. Aemili praetoris, qui eam rem agebat, manus venerant; is protinus novo praetori Sullae tradiderat. ex huius Marci duobus carminibus alterius post rem actam editi comperto auctoritas eventu alteri quoque, cuius nondum tempus venerat, adferebat fidem.' The *duo carmina huius Marci* would be unnecessary if these two prophecies were the only Marcian prophecies and this Marcius were the only Marcius. On these Marcii and prophecies see Münzer and Klotz, *RE* 14. 2, cols 1538–42.

[4] *Etym.* 6. 8. 10, 12: 'praecepta sunt quae aut quid faciendum aut quid non faciendum docent....primus autem praecepta apud Hebraeos Moyses scripsit; apud Latinos Marcius vates primus praecepta conposuit. ex quibus est illud: "postremus dicas primus taceas"'. Isidore, of course, understood the verse as apothegmatic and similarities to this sentiment are found in Latin literature; (e.g., see the *dicenda tacenda* of Hor. *Epist.* 1. 7. 72, Ovid, *A.A.* 2. 604; Persius 4. 5) which reflect a Greek apothegm (see the Liddell–Scott–Jones *Greek–English Lexicon s.v.* ἄρρητος, III 3). The Marcian verse does not convey the same meaning. Pliny, *NH* 7. 119: 'divinitas et quaedam caelitum societas nobilissima ex

Marcii from those who dealt in Apollonic responses.[1] Cicero introduces the readers of his work on divination to the Marcii in this manner: 'quo in genere Marcios quosdam fratres nobili loco natos apud maiores nostros fuisse scriptum videmus' (1. 40. 89). I translate, 'From the written tradition we learn that among our ancestors the Marcii, brethren born in high station, belonged in this class [i.e. mantic prophets].' The nobility of these Marcii appears unusual inasmuch as Roman nobles did not practice prophecy in its Greek sense. The Marcian brothers probably lived in different generations (see below). The priestly Arval Brothers were thought to have originated as blood brothers (see above, p. 110). Classical Latin knew no word for confraternity (cf. Varro, *LL* 5. 85), although its idea was expressed by *sodalitas* and *sodalicium*. At his *Roman Antiquities* 4. 8. 1 Dionysius may reflect the true character of the opposition of Ancus Marcius' sons to the reign of Servius Tullius when he writes of the *hetairia tōn Markiōn* which the latter banished from Rome. Accordingly, when Cicero (*Brutus* 45. 166) speaks of L. Marcius Philippus' political prestige deriving from his *nobilitas*, *cognatio*, *sodalitas*, and *conlegium*, he may refer to the sodality of Marcian Brothers in which the clansmen actually participated. A Marcian confraternity that maintained ties with the nobility could have begun in the performance of curial rites such as I attribute to the Arval Brethren of Curia Acculeia and the augural Sodales Titii of Curia Titia.[2] The policies of Servius Tullius might have faced opposition from a curial priesthood in a manner similar to Attus Navius' successful attempt to thwart the reforms of Servius' predecessor.

The earliest Marcius *vates* has been identified with an Etruscan *mantis* Manios who interpreted some omens at Rome in 295.[3] The

feminis in Sibylla fuit, ex viris in Melampode apud Graecos, apud Romanos in Marcio'. Cf. Arn. 1. 62.

[1] Cic. *Div.* 2. 55. 113: 'eodemque modo nec ego Publicio nescio cui nec Marciis vatibus nec Apollinis opertis credendum existimo, quorum partim ficta aperte, partim effutita temere numquam ne mediocri quidem cuiquam, non modo prudenti probata sunt'; *ibid.* 1. 50. 114–15: 'eodem enim modo multa a vaticinantibus saepe praedicta sunt, neque solum verbis sed etiam: versibus quos olim Fauni vatesque canebant [Enn. *Ann.* 214 V.]. Similiter Marcius et Publicius vates cecinisse dicuntur; quo de genere Apollinis operta prolata sunt.'

[2] On the Cretan *hetairiai* as counterparts of phratries see Hignett, p. 58 f. and Andrewes, 'Phratries in Homer', pp. 134–7. Cf. Cic. *Leg.* 2. 12. 31 and Asc. p. 69 C., and Broughton on the augur of 93 B.C. For *sodales* as a *hetairia* see Gaius on the XII Tables where he quotes Solon (*Dig.* 47. 22. 4); cf. Cass. Dio 44. 6, 45. 30 for *luperci* as a *hetairia* and Augustus, *RG* 4. 7.

[3] Zonaras 8. 1 excerpted from Cass. Dio 8. 28. Livy 10. 31. 8 is unusually brief on the

name Manios probably reflects a Greek correction in accordance with *mantis* and *mania*. Neither Manius nor Marcius is an Etruscan personal name. Indeed two of the three surviving Marcian verses reflect augural ritual:

> quamvis noventium   duonum negumat⟨o⟩   (Festus 162 L.)
> postremus dicas   primus taceas   (Isid. *ibid.*)

The first verse (*carmen*) is ascribed by Festus to Cn. Marcius. The *noventius* (*nuntius*) reflects the augural terms *nuntiare, obnuntiare, adnuntiare,* etc.[1] The *negumato* (*negato*) I offer in correction of the MS (corrected to *negumate*: so, too, MS *moventium*) on the authority of the formulas of the Twelve Tables, e.g.: 'hominem mortuum in urbe ne sepelito neve urito' (Cic. *Leg.* 2. 23. 58). By way of paraphrase: *quamvis nuntium bonum ne dicito*; 'Inasmuch as you wish (it), do not speak the good tiding' or '...do not say that the tiding is good' or '...say that the tiding is not good.' Whatever the sentiment of this prohibition it fits a situation both of augural interpretation and of the distinction between the *spectio* of magistrates and the *nuntiatio* of augurs.[2] The second Marcian verse refers to the prescription of silence at augural ceremonies which is followed by spoken announcement that there is silence. Cicero preserves the ritual of auspication by feeding the birds which nevertheless illustrates any similar procedure and supplies a situation in which the prescription *postremus dicas primus taceas* is applicable:

'Q. Fabi, te mihi in auspicio esse volo.' Respondet: 'Audivi.' hic apud maiores nostros adhibebatur peritus, nunc quilibet. peritum autem esse necesse est eum qui silentium quid sit intellegat; id enim silentium dicimus in auspiciis quod omni vitio caret. hoc intellegere perfecti auguris est; illi autem qui in auspicium adhibetur, cum ita imperavit is qui auspicatur: 'Dicito, si silentium esse videbitur.' nec suspicit nec circumspicit. statim

prodigies of the year 295: 'felix annus bellicis rebus, pestilentia gravis prodigiisque sollicitus; nam et terram multifariam pluvisse et in exercitu Ap. Claudi plerosque fulminibus ictos nuntiatum est; librique ob haec aditi'. The *libri* in question may refer to the *carmina Marciana* (cf. Serv. on *Aen.* 6. 72). On the older sense of Latin *vates* see Ennius, *Ann.* 213–14 with Vahlen's testimonia; cf. *Ann.* 380 and *Sc.* 319.

[1] Examples abound; see Cic. *Div.* 1. 16. 29–30, 1. 47. 105, 2. 72; *Phil.* 2. 32. 81, 33. 83; the censors' formula for auspication in Varro, *LL* 6. 86 and Festus 446 L. Donatus on Ter. *Adel.* 4. 2. 9 illustrates both the *noventius* and *duonus* of Marcius: 'qui malam rem nuntiat, obnuntiat, qui bonam, adnuntiat: nam proprie obnuntiare dicuntur augures, qui aliquid mali ominis scaevamque viderunt'. Cf. Prob. in *Ecl.* 9. 13 and Schol. Ver. on *Aen.* 10. 241, quoted above, pp. 87–8.

[2] Festus 446 L. See Mommsen, *Röm. Staatsr.* I³, 109–14, A. Magdelain, 'Auspicia ad patres redeunt', Hommages à J. Bayet, *Coll. Latomus* 70 (1964), 440–1. Cf. the augural *speturie* of the Brothers at Iguvium (*Tab. Ig.* IIa 1, 3).

respondet silentium esse videri. tum ille: 'Dicito, si pascentur.' 'Pascuntur.' quae aves? aut ubi? attulit, inquit, in cavea pullos is qui ex eo ipso nominatur pullarius. haec sunt igitur aves internuntiae Iovis.[1]

The Marcian Brotherhood were probably practicing prophets as early as 295, were consulted officially in 212, and may have spoken out again under the Sullan regime.[2] Their expertise in historical times was mantic but earlier they had practiced augury which the Sodales Titii still practiced in the first century. The suppression of curial augury led to the Marcii's conversion to an Hellenic profession. Dionysius (2. 22. 3, quoted p. 95) offered Varro's opinion that mantic exegetes confirmed the curiate election of the Roman priests. The Marcii fall into this category and exemplify the alteration of the curial sodalities. The primitive Fratres Marcii are comparable in title to the Roman Fratres Arvales and in function to the Fratres Atiedii of the decuria who practiced augury at Iguvium.[3] Their repute and nobility rested upon their curial membership as well as a sometime coincidence with the Gens Marcia. When the Campus Martius was inundated and the Equirria of 14 March could not be held there, the rites were transferred to the Campus Martialis on the Caelian Hill. This field may have been the field of Mars at the time of Old and New Curias, occasionally used on 14 March in a return to older cult, or the land of the Curia Marcia, perhaps named after the god, whose augurs would have held the *picus Martius* particularly auspicious.[4]

---

[1] *Div.* 2. 34. 71–2, on which see Pease's commentary. Cf. Serv. on *Aen.* 5. 71: 'ore favete apto sermone usus est et sacrificio et ludis; nam in sacris taciturnitas necessaria est, quod etiam praeco magistratu sacrificante dicebat. "favete linguis, favete vocibus," hoc est bona omina habete aut tacete'. At Iguvium the priest always pray silently and the proper word is cognate to Latin *tacere*; see Poultney's index *s.v. tases* and VIA 6–7 on silence during the auspices. A comparable ceremony was held before battle; see above, pp. 87–8.

[2] Serv. on *Aen.* 6. 70 reports that some authors say the ludi Apollinares were founded during the Second Punic War and others under Sulla (*tempore Syllano*) which most probably is a wrong identification of the praetor of 212, Cornelius Sulla; see Livy quoted above, p. 147, n. 3.

[3] See p. 93, n. 1; p. 148, n. 2.

[4] Festus 117 L.: 'Martialis campus in Caelio monte dicitur quod in eo Equirria solebant fieri si quando aquae Tiberis campum Martium occupassent'. Cf. Ovid, *F.* 3. 519–23. Colini, pp. 74–5 suggests the identification of the Campus Martialis with Campus Caelemontanus. At Iguvium two fields, evidently owned by two entities, were dedicated to Picus Martius (*Tab. Ig.* vb, 8–18) and their fruits were used for sacral purposes. A Roman epigraphic record of a state paving contract may have cited a building (?) of the curia Marcia (*CIL* I², 809 = VI, 37043 = *ILLRP* 464): 'ab scaleis [– – –]inieis infimeis praeter [– – –] Marcias ad viam [– – –] et pone foros [et aedif]icia C. Numitori etc.'. The noun which *Marcias* modifies must have filled approximately six letter-spaces.

The plebeian family of Poetelii Libones figures prominently in the Fasti of the later fourth century.[1] All the Argei of the Esquiline Region were certainly situated in the proximity of a grove except for Argei II 6 which lay in the temple precinct of Juno Lucina where the grove of that deity stood (Varro, *LL* 5. 49). The Italic peoples held groves in awe. We have suggested that the grove of Fur(r)ina and the *pomonal* bore a relation to the religion of the curias Foriensis and Solonia and that the groves were preserved near the Argei so that birds would flock there and that the corporations of the Seven Hills maintained some as *sacella*. The Lucus Poetelius near Argei II 5 takes its name, I believe, from a curia Poetelia as did the Lucus P⟨o⟩etelinus in the Campus Flaminius. Here, according to the tradition, an assembly tried Manlius Capitolinus for treason. Livy (6. 20. 11) and Plutarch (*Cam.* 36) report this was a change of venue from the Campus Martius or the Forum. In 342 an amnesty for the partisans of a secession and *lex sacrata militaris* concerning legionary rosters and the privilege of military tribunate were passed in the same Lucus P⟨o⟩etelinus (Livy 7. 41. 3). Both cases were extraordinary public assemblies. The sanctity of the place may have assured the voters of divine protection.[2] No matter what the significance of the meeting-place, its communal ownership is certain. Parallels to the naming of a grove after its curia are the hills Latiaris, Mucialis, Caelius, Oppius, Cespius, Cermalensis and Veliensis.

In conclusion, curial lands are identified by their proper names. The four *agri* which legend had Acca Larentia bequeath to the Roman people are Taracius, Semurius, Laterius and Solonius. I have tried to show that these lands at one time belonged to the state because they had been curial. At the end of the Republic the Taracius and Semurius were still public whereas at least parts of the Solonius and Laterius were in private ownership. The change from public to private ownership I would date to after 200 when the government sought to meet its war debts by a sale of public lands within a fifty-mile radius of the city. In this context I put Cato's evidence for the four fields. Also I attribute the Campus Martialis to a Curia Marcia which had a mantic confraternity and the two groves to a Curia Poetelia. Just as the Tarentum of the Ager Taracius was available

---

[1] See Münzer, *RE* 21. 1, cols 1164–7.

[2] I have discussed assemblies and other kinds of meetings in groves in great detail; see 'King'.

for cult, so the Martial field might hold the Equirria and one grove of the Poetelia might be used for public assemblies and the other for an Argean station.

THE THIRTY CURIAS AND THREE TRIBES

In the ancient evidence we have discerned three avenues of admission to the polity already consisting of a nucleus of curias: first, the migrations of peoples under the leadership of a prominent leader (e.g. Lucumones) or family (e.g. the Claudii); the striking of a treaty between Roman curias and a neighboring town (e.g. Gabii and Crustumerium); and thirdly the transporting of defeated enemies to Rome and their subsequent inclusion in the curiate system (e.g. the Albans and Tatius' Sabines). In the last case the procedure of surrender (*deditio*) demonstrates the totality of submission: 'deditisne vos populumque Collatinum, urbem, agros, aquam, terminos, delubra, utensilia, divina humanaque omnia, in meam populique Romani dicionem?'—'Dedimus'—'At ego recipio'.[1] We have already noted the survival of the Alban and Gabinian religious rites which passed into the Roman religion by this procedure.

Ancient and modern interpretation of the interrelation of the thirty curias and the tribes is based upon the notion that the tribes were ethnic groups and the curias were military units. This interpretation is fallacious political theorizing unsupported except for the bald statement of a neat arithmetic scheme. Thus far we have shown that communal augury derived from the curias, that curial officers and priests were, if anything, non-military, and that the curial festivals cared for the communities' agricultural welfare. On the other hand, the three tribes do have military officers, *tribuni militum* and *celerum*, but do not have tribal festivals nor tribal priests.[2] In

---

[1] Livy 1. 38. 2, on which see Ogilvie.

[2] See De Sanctis I, 247–55; De Martino I², 91–4, 106–9. The following notice in the Fasti Praenestini at 19 March proves only that the *tribuni celerum* were present just as consuls might attend a military festival: '[Salii] faciunt in comitio saltu(m) [adstantibus po]ntificibus et trib(unis) celer(um)'. Since the Salii wore the knight's cloak (*trabea*: Dion. 2. 70. 2), the festival certainly concerned the cavalry which the *tribuni celerum* commanded. Miss Taylor has found but a single reference to a religious act in and for the later tribes (a *supplicatio* in Livy. 7. 28. 8). The lustration by the censors was only a lustration of the army (*populus* or *exercitus*) in which, I believe, the cavalrymen were later included *honoris causa*. See Taylor, 'Voting Districts', pp. 74–8. The ceremony of *supplicatio* may very well have been imported from Greeks (see Latte, *Röm. Religion.*, pp. 245–6) and, hence, have little relation to the old tribes.

fact, the definition of *sacra publica* does not embrace *sacra pro tribubus* because none existed. The six Vestals and three (later four) augurs may be related by their number to the tribes but they do not perform rites for the several tribes as such but for the collective community (e.g. Fordicidia) or the several curias (e.g. at the Argei).[1] Although the three tribes may have provided a means to a central government, the political foundation of the state rested upon the curias.

The curias met in an assembly and voted as thirty units; the three tribes did not convene as an assembly nor cast three ballots. The early Romans fought according to three tribes because the infantry and cavalry were each commanded by three state officers and not by thirty officers. Yet no trace of tribal headquarters has survived. The Curia Calabra, *comitium*, Curia Hostilia, *regia* and *auguraculum* of the citadel were situated on the neutral ground, so to speak, of the Capitol and Forum, and represented the central government of the thirty communities. Except for the uncertain and hazardous etymologies of Ramnes, Tities, and Luceres, no trace of an ethnic synoecism of three tribes remains.[2] If we would subscribe to the statement that a curia supplied 100 foot and 10 horse to its tribe, then we must assume the resources of the curias were roughly equal at one time. This assumption presupposes a head-count of men fit to bear arms and the continuing distribution of new citizens equally into all curias and tribes as Dionysius describes the system. But this hypothesis does not explain the religious, political and non-military character of the curias while the three tribes have only a military purpose. If the curias had ever been an artificial unit for a military end, they ought to have been adaptable to the centuriate organization which perhaps represented a shift of emphasis on cavalry warfare

---

[1] Only Festus 468 L. connects the six Vestals with the six tribes of Tarquinius Priscus' reform. See Momigliano, 'Interim Report', p. 108 f. Plut. *Numa* 10 directly precludes any relation with the tribes, for two Vestals learned for ten years from two who taught for ten years while only two performed their sacred duties. Dionysius 2. 67. 1 says their number was originally four. Leaving aside the question of what were the original number of the colleges of Vestals and augurs, we note that originally there was only a single pontiff, later called *maximus*, and the same title is found among the Vestals, *maxima*. Secondly there was no office of augur *maximus* because they were all equal. The number of augurs, three or four, in the royal period, conforms to tribal divisions of territories in which the curias maintained augural seats. Probably, there had been only one Vestal in the beginning, just as there had been only one pontiff, in contrast with the augurs whose number depended on three or four tribes. A plurality of virgins in primitive Rome would have been a luxury which the Sabines could ill afford. See Latte, *Röm. Religion.*, pp. 196–7, 108–10.

[2] See above, pp. 6 ff. and Momigliano, 'Interim Report', p. 108. On the meaning of the Curia Hostilia see Palmer, 'King'.

to that on infantry tactics and a change of infantry armaments, and for which the census was first taken. Such a preponderance of troops already existed in the curiate levies which are the figments of Hellenic stimulation. Yet the coexistence of the curiate and centuriate systems shows that they were not interchangeable and that the creation of new curias towards military ends was plainly impossible. The proliferation of military systems should have meant the sovereignty and autonomy of the later centuriate system whereas, in fact, the centuriate system never was constitutionally autonomous because its commanders' authority had to have at least the symbolic consent of the thirty curias.

If the three tribes were ethnic divisions of equal size as has been believed, then the curias as tenths could be increased only by equal numbers of Latins, Sabines and Etruscans. Accordingly the Latins, Sabines and Etruscans as ethnic tribes of ten curias would have contributed equally to the army. Contemplating the language spoken at Rome we need not dwell on this absurdity. Also absurd is the theory that three social castes of priests, tillers and warriors contributed matched military contingents.[1]

In fine, we have been asking the wrong questions about the character of the three tribes in spite of Varro's explicit statement that they were districts of the Roman territory.[2] In 495 there were twenty-one tribes whose names are derived from either places or families. These tribes, called Servian, are circumscribed territories whence military tribunes levied troops who are assigned to tactical units according to their capacity to supply and bear arms. This military system transformed the army because its planner took into consideration the military capacity of the citizen. The new system had tribal

[1] This is the theory of G. Dumézil, *Naissance de Rome* (Paris, 1944), chapter 2 and *passim*; *L'héritage indo-européen à Rome* (Paris, 1949), chapter 4 and *passim*; 'L'idéologie tripartie des indo-européens', *Coll. Latomus* 31 (1958), chapter 1 and *passim*. See Momigliano, 'Interim Report', p. 113 f. If two tribes were priests and tillers, why did they also go to war under tribunes? The tillers (*coloni*) were the Luceres only according to Propertius 4. 1. 31 but the word *coloni* was a *lectio facilior* for *soloni* (see above, p. 144, n. 3). The presumed priesthood of the tribe Tities, the Sodales Titii, belonged to the Curia Titia which probably gave its name to the tribe. Only in his *Naissance*, p. 111 ff., does Dumézil follow the reading *coloni*. In *Héritage*, p. 193 ff., and *Idéologie*, p. 14 ff., he observes the reading *Soloni* though he does not take it adjectivally as in this paper. Notwithstanding his conversion he pursues his belief in the distribution of men into tribe by station.
[2] Varro, *LL* 5. 55: 'ager Romanus primum divisus in partis tris, a quo tribus appellata Titiensium, Ramnium, Lucerum. nominatae, ut ait Ennius, Titienses ab Tatio, Ramnenses ab Romulo, Luceres, ut ait Iunius, ab Lucumone; sed omnia haec vocabula Tusca ut Volnius, qui tragoedias Tuscas scripsit, dicebat.'

units in common with the old. Since an immediate reformation is assumed, the new tribes must have been in nature exactly the same as the old, namely a circumscribed territory for recruitment and defense. For our purposes it matters not at all what *tribus* meant originally and from what family of languages the word came. In point of fact at a given moment in Roman history the old and new tribe had the same meaning. Yet curias and centuries did not mean the same thing.

Before Servius the Ager Romanus was divided into three districts for the sake of their defense and the convenience of levying troops. Leaving plow and taking arms the fighting men served according to one of the three tribes in which they owned and worked land. Three districts sufficed a small state but not the Rome of the Etruscan period. Answers to where and how the curial *agri* lay with respect to these districts cannot be hazarded. The circumscription of three tribes took into account the situation of existing curias. The annexation and adherence of new *genera* must have complicated the early tribal system and left unclear its demarcations.

Striking parallels to these artificial Roman tribes come from Sicily and Etruria. Fictile bullets, probably belonging to Roman allies in the Slave War at the end of the second century, bear inscriptions of the soldier's name, patronymic, phratry and tribe (*phyle*). Whereas the phratry bears a proper name, the tribes are called 'first', 'second' and 'third'.[1] Siciliote deployment of tribes as military regiments is at least as old as the Athenian debacle in Sicily.[2] The numbered tribes certainly demonstrate old artificial divisions which etymologically the Greek *phyle* does not at all convey. Closer to Rome at Naples the civic divisions were also phratries.[3] A unique Etruscan bullet bears in Etruscan letters PHYLE IL, i.e. the forty-ninth tribe, perhaps from the time of the Social War.[4] It points not only to Etruscan borrowing from Greeks but also to the artificial military character of the Etruscan tribe. The Siciliote and Etruscan examples of noting their tribe and its number finds contrast with similar Roman inscriptions of legion and its number on pellets.[5]

[1] *IG* XIV, 2407 and E. Militello, *Not. Sc.* 15 (1961), 348–9.

[2] Thuc. 3. 90. 2 (Messana) and 6. 100. 1 (Syracuse).

[3] Varro, *LL* 5.85. See also the index of *IG* XIV and Latte, *RE* 20. 1 (1941), cols 747, 758.

[4] C. Zangmeister, 'Glandes plumbeae', *Eph. Epig.* vol. 6, no. 45 in addition to *CIL* IX, 6086 (cf. Degrassi, *ILLRP* vol. 2, p. 298).

[5] For legionary pellets see Zangmeister, 'Glandes plumbeae' and *ILLRP* 1096–8, 1114–17a.

The equations of *tribus* to *phyle* and of curia to phratry were probably published by a Roman historian writing for Greeks well before Dionysius of Halicarnassus. In fact, the similarities between the Roman and Greco-Etruscan systems could have been noticed far in advance of Roman history-writing. In spite of all uncertainties we can be sure that the Latin words *tribus* and *curia* with their Italic cognates do not have Indo-European roots even vaguely implying the birth or kinship which their proposed Greek equivalents do imply.[1]

The etymology of curia accepted in most quarters today is *co-vir-ya* ('a band of men' or 'fellowship').[2] The early and persistent formation of the titles *duoviri*, *decemviri* etc. illustrates the simplicity inherent in this etymology of curia. Furthermore, in light of the character and origins of the curias argued in this book the word is politically neutral. It signifies a community of persons in no way so limited in number as the linguistically unrelated *decuria* and *centuria* which indicate a selection. Its usual Greek translation of φρατρία ('brotherhood') denotes common birth or blood ties which *curia* does not. It does not denote land or territory as *tribus*, *pagus* and *ager*. Lastly it does not denote buildings or town as *vicus* and *oppidum*, though by semantic extension it may mean 'meeting-place'. The bonds of a curia are not defined in the same way as the bond of centuries by number and of tribes by borders. Basically a curia meant an assemblage or congregation cooperating by common consent.

QUIRITES

The curias of a united community represented disparate elements in

---

[1] The equations doubtless go back to the time that *strategos* represented the praetor-consul and *chiliarchos*, the tribune of soldiers. See De Sanctis I, 248, 403–4. The Latin *tribus* has a cognate in Umbrian *trifo* which can only mean the territory of the people (see Poultney on *Tab. Iguv.* ivb, 54). At Iguvium a distinction is observed between the citizen-body (*toto*, Latin *civitas*) and the territory (*trifo*, Latin *ager*); see *Tab. Iguv.* ib, 16, iii, 24–5; 29–30; vib, 53–4, 59; viia, 11–12, 47–8. At the same time a lustration is held and prayers prayed for the army (*poplo*, Latin *populus*) of the citizen-body itself; see *Tab. Iguv.* ib, 2, 5, 10, 40; vib, 61–2; viia, 3, 6, 9 and *passim*. These distinctions only go to confirm our interpretation that the Roman *tribus* was probably always a territorial division (never related to Latin *tres*), the *populus* was originally the infantry, and that the *Quirites*, the primitive *cives Romani*, were by no means corporately identical with the *populus*. See above, pp. 40 ff.

[2] A. Walde and J. B. Hoffmann, *Lateinisches etymologisches Wörterbuch*[3] (Heidelberg, 1938–9), *s.v. curia*, Ernout–Meillet[4] *s.v. curia*. See J. H. Oliver, *Demokratia, the Gods and the Free World* (Baltimore, 1960), pp. 73–4 and above, pp. 67 ff.

the primitive state which had no common generic name unless it be
Rome. Throughout Roman history the citizens of the city had but one
official designation 'Quirites'. For this and other reasons I subscribe
to the opinion that the Quirites designates the members of the curias,
the later *curiales*.[1] The ancient derivation of Quirites from the Sabine
town Cures and the modern derivation from an unattested *Quirium*
are not convincing. In the former case it appears absurd that a state
of admitted racial mixture adopted the name of a minority in order
to express what we call today nationality. The Sabines of Cures
always called themselves *Curenses* so far as we know. Sabine and Latin
are two markedly different tongues. Since the Romans spoke Latin,
we can consider the majority of Romans as Latins and not Sabine or
Etruscan. In favor of *Quirium* little can be said. At least in the case of
Romani we are secure in our knowledge of a *Roma* whether or not we
know what or where Rome was originally. This security is entirely
lacking in the case of *Quirium* particularly because its proposed
location, *collis Quirinalis*, could not have directly derived its name from
Quirium and more importantly because excellent evidence points to
the fact this hill had an earlier name which has nothing at all to do
with a root *quiri-*. On the other hand, a derivation of 'Quirites' from
co-vir-yom or *co-vir-ya* remains hotly argued because it stands in
unparalleled isolation. Linguistically it is possible. For our purposes
the relation of Quirites to curia must be demonstrated in the frame-
work of earliest Roman history.

Clearly the safest means to a definition of the Quirites rests on the
word's use in archaic times and vestigial use in historical periods.
Caesar broke his soldiers' mutiny by calling them 'Quirites' to which
they answered that they were *milites*. Romans apparently ceased to be
Quirites when they were soldiers under oath in the centuriate army.
The appellation of Quirites may have released the soldiers from the
military oath by which they had subordinated their public rights to

[1] Walde–Hoffman, *s.v. Quirites*; Ernout–Meillet, *s.v. quiris*; Leumann, *Lat. Gram.*
(*Handb. Altertumsw.* 2. 2. 1), p. 233. The entire problem is now overcast by the dust of
polemic. See, for instance, J. Paoli, 'Autour du problème de Quirinus', *Studi in onore di
U. E. Paoli* (Florence, n.d.), pp. 525–37. Consequently, some students of history shy away
from the discussion. In defense of the etymology and not of its more vociferous proponents
and their theories, I must say that all evidence points to the use of *Quirites* prior to *populus
Romanus* and by its application to the Iunones (*Quirites* or *curites*) in the thirty curias, at
Falerii, Tibur and Beneventum further points to the curias severally. On *Quirium* see
Latte, *Röm. Religion.* p. 113 and, in general, Poucet, pp. 6–74. See Varro, *LL* 5. 51, 6. 68,
in D.H. 2. 48. 2., Festus 43, 59, 302–4 L.

military discipline.[1] Surely their national character was not altered in the course of verbal exchange. In political assemblies, on the other hand, speakers and president always addressed the citizens as 'Quirites' (never by *Romani*) by which their public rights were acknowledged. The origin of these usages must be sought in the relation between the Quirites and the *populus Romanus*.

The salient difference between the Roman *populus* and the Quirites is that the former is a collective body and the latter are individuals. Some students of early Rome find in the formula *populus Romanus Quirites* a sign of ethnic cleavage which the Romans themselves thought they discerned. If this is true, assembly presidents always put their questions to the Sabines of Rome and never to the Latins (so Festus 59 L.). Although the possibility of collective action by two elements, the Roman *populus* and the Quirites, cannot be denied and although some of our texts preserve the phrase, construed by asyndeton, *populus Romanus Quirites*, the usual and less easily explained phrase *populus Romanus Quiritium* cannot be damned as a *lectio facilior* in our manuscripts.[2] One example suffices to illustrate the three constitutions of Rome: 'ubi noctu in templum censor auspicaverit atque de caelo nuntium erit, praeconi sic imperato ut viros vocet: quod bonum fortunatum felix salutareque siet populo Romano Quiritium [so the MS, the editors notwithstanding here or in other texts] reique publicae populi Romani Quiritium mihi collegaeque meo, fidei magistratuique nostro, omnes Quirites, pedites armatos privatosque, curatores omnium tribuum, si quis pro se sive pro altero rationem dari volet, voca in licium huc ad me!' (Varro, *LL* 6. 86). The censors superintended the citizens' qualifications for military service. Therefore their performance of the census concerns the army (*populus*). Their herald, however, summons three kinds of citizens (who in reality may be the same persons) for rating: the Quirites, the armed and unarmed foot-soldiers and the overseers of the tribes. These are not in apposition. They are the *iuniores* (*pedites armati*) and *seniores* (*pedites privati*) of the centuriate organization, those who keep the rolls of the tribes and the members of the

---

[1] Suet. *Caes.* 70, Tac. *Ann.* 1. 42. For the oath see L. Cincius, *De re mil.* in Gellius, *NA* 16. 4 (Bremer 1. 254 f.).

[2] See Coli, 'Regnum', pp. 160–1, whom I follow, and De Francisci, 'Primordia Civitatis', pp. 737–41 who holds that we have a hendiadys of two nouns in the same case. For certain examples of a dependent *Quiritium* see Livy 1. 32. 11–13, 8. 9. 5–8, 22. 10. 2–6, all quotations of legal formulas.

curiate organization (Quirites). The *equites* have been omitted because they were always rated in the Forum and did not belong to the *populus Romanus*. Mommsen recognizes this passage as the formulary of the *census populi*.[1] What is more it is the census of the *populus* of the Quirites. The *populus* and the Quirites were never constitutionally identical. The Quirites constituted or composed or possessed the *populus Romanus*. It follows that the Quirites precede the *populus*. The *populus Romanus Quiritium*, Servius' centuriate infantry, fought in units of equal complement according to weaponry under king or praetor rather than massed in tribes under king and tribune. The commanders of the centuriate *populus* ultimately derived their Republican *imperium* from the legislative action of the curias (*lex curiata*).[2] This procedure sustains the argument for the precedence and priority of the Quirites and curias over the *populus* and centuries. The tribal army which included foot and horse yielded to the centuriate army which included always only the infantry. As an appendage to the *populus Romanus*, the Roman cavalry served in six contingents under the command of tribunes. The *populus* and Quirites are no more legally identical than *milites* and Quirites. The *milites* constitute the *populus* while Quirites remain Quirites. In the beginning an infantry was drafted from three tribes to which curias may have been assigned but this fact does not prove the curias were even potential military units. The centuriate *populus* was drafted from thirty-five tribes which were certainly not potential military units because of the varying census ratings.

When the Fetiales declare war because the Roman *populus* of the Quirites has so ordered and the senate has so deliberated and voted, they declare war against both the armies of the Prisci Latini (*populi Priscorum Latinorum*) and the Prisci Latini themselves (*homines Prisci Latini*). When a treaty is struck on the battlefield, the parties are the armies (*populi*) of Alba and Rome and the Roman commander-in-chief. Indeed, the Quirites (that is to say, *homines Romani*) and the Albans (*homines Albani*) cannot be party to the treaty even though the war was directed against both *populus* and *homines* because the treaty

---

[1] *Röm. Staatsr.* II³, 359 ff.; Mommsen (p. 361, n. 6) construes *privatos* with *curatores* but this interpretation does not take into consideration the *seniores*. The same distinction prevailed at Iguvium where we meet the *iovies hostatir anostatir* (Latin *iuvenes hastati inhastati*). In this case *iuvenis* stands for any man capable of bearing arms. See Poultney on *Tab. Iguv.* VIb, 59–60.

[2] The *lex curiata* is discussed in chapter 9.

is struck in the field where, on the Roman side, at least, may be marshalled only the centuriate *populus*.[1] No trace of Quirites, in the strict sense, declaring war has been left us because in the historical period the Roman *populus* of the Quirites alone decided whether they would fight. Before the Servian constitution state decisions would have been made according to an entirely different institution.

Quiritary rights (*ius Quiritium*), De Visscher argues, originally segregate the Quirites from the Prisci Latini, mark an early stage in the development of Roman ideas of citizenship and predate the notion of *civitas*. The *ius Quiritium* belonged to members of the curias and laid down the foundation of a civic order, *conubium* and *commercium*, which in the fourth century are distinguished by the *ius Latii* and *civitas sine suffragio*.[2] In the later extensions of a Roman citizenship are seen the shadows of the isopolity which Dionysius says Rome and Gabii shared. Confusion as to whether the Campanians' earliest Roman status was that of *cives sine suffragio* or *socii foederati* arises from imperfect understanding of a treaty of 'isopolity' similar to that granted Gabii and Crustumerium.[3] In the fourth century the Romans conceded to some of their neighbors the rights of Quirites but created no new curias. Nonetheless the curiate citizenship omitted the right to vote because without assignment to a curia or creation of a curia it no longer implied participation in the assemblies of the centuries and the tribes. The one civic duty still required of the curias was cavalry service, precisely the military contribution of the Campanians to the Roman army. A grant of Quiritary rights to the non-Roman had the advantage of legal private ownership of land in the Ager Romanus and legitimate marital and mercantile intercourse while the well-to-do who derived the greater benefit made a minimal contribution of cavalry to the Roman forces and had no obligation to the Roman *populus*.

QUIRINUS

From Quirites we turn to *Quirinus*. *Quirinus* is an adjective. Those who

[1] Livy 1. 24. 4–8, 1. 32. 11–14. L. Cincius preserves the same formula of declaring war (see above, p. 158 n. 1).
[2] F. De Visscher, '*Ius Quiritium, civitas Romana*, et nationalité moderne', *Studi in onore di U. E. Paoli* (Florence, n.d.), pp. 239–51. De Visscher demurs when it comes to defining *Quirites*. These civic rights are discussed in chapter 9.
[3] See A. Bernardi, 'Roma e Capua nella seconda metà del quarto secolo av. C.', *Athenaeum* 20 (1942), 86–103, 21 (1943), 21–31; A. de la Chevalerie, 'Observations sur la

maintain Quirites is an alternative to Curenses believe Quirinus is the god of Cures. Those who believe in *Quirium consider him the god of that place. However he may be viewed in this light, he joins the company of such famous gods and heroes as Romulus, Latinus, Lavinia, and Sabus. Quirinus, the god, cannot derive his name from *collis Quirinalis*, and *Quirium does not parallel Palatium which yields *mons Palatinus*, not *Palatinalis*. The hill ought to have been *collis Quirinus*; it was not.[1]

The festival of Quirinalia belongs to the oldest Roman calendar and is the earliest reliable evidence of a *Quirinus*. The nature of the rites of Quirinalia is totally unknown to us. The last day of the movable curial festival Fornacalia fell on Quirinalia, fixed at 17 February. On this day those who did not know their curias and who had not participated in Fornacalia celebrated Quirinalia, nick-named the feast of fools (*feriae stultorum*).[2] Since the feast of fools is only the nickname which of itself supplies no connection with the curias, the explanation by way of a relation with the curias is un-equivocal and should not be considered an invention.[3] Romans participated in Quirinalia although they did not know the name of their curia and had not observed Fornacalia. This circumstance pre-vailed at the time of Augustus when the Quirites and *curiales* had become distinct. The Quirites, a term by which was then understood all *cives Romani*, participated in Quirinalia whereas at Fornacalia only *curiales* celebrated with their curias. Those who were made Roman citizens after the creation of the thirtieth curia did not have member-ship in the curias even though they enjoyed the *ius Quiritium*. By the first century few Romans might lawfully claim curial ancestry. Accordingly they were excluded from the several celebrations of the curial festival but were included in the state festival of Quirinalia. Furthermore, another instance of curial exlusiveness had been re-corded. In describing the ceremony of throwing the *argei* into the Tiber Dionysius says that the Vestals, pontiffs, praetors and only those who might lawfully (*themis*) attend were present.[4] The same

nature du conubium et la situation juridique des Campaniens', etc., *RIDA* ser. 3, vol. 1 (1954), pp. 271–81, and Sherwin-White, pp. 37–40.
   [1] See Festus 302–4 L.; on Quirinus in general, C. Koch, *RE* 24 (1963), cols 1306–21, and Poucet, especially pp. 22–71.
   [2] Varro, *LL* 6. 13; Ovid, *F.* 2. 475–532; Festus 302–4, 418–20 L.; Plut. *Quaest. Rom.* 89. See Degrassi, pp. 411–12.
   [3] See Frazer on *Fasti* 2. 513 and Latte, *Röm. Religion.*, pp. 113, 143.
   [4] *Ant. Rom.* 1. 38. 3.

holds true for Fornacalia, a movable feast. The Argean rites are not noted in the liturgical calendar because they also may have been movable.

One of the three major flamens, the Quirinalis, most probably participated in the Quirinalia but again there is no evidence. The restrictive taboos applied to the person of the flamen Dialis did not apply to the Martial and Quirinal flamens who occupied a position in the Roman hierarchy after the priest-king and the Dial flamen. The Quirinal flamen officiated at the dog sacrifice during Robigalia, laid an offering on the 'grave' of Larentina during Larentalia and during Consualia brought an offering to the subterranean *consus* along with the Vestals.[1] His religious obligations were discharged at Roman agricultural festivals, and do not explain his title.

One of the most puzzling data in Roman religion has been this lexicographical notice:

> PERSILLUM vocant sacerdo-
> tes rudiculum picatum, quo unguine flamen
> Portunalis arma Quirini unguet. PERSICUM
> PORTUM etc.[2]

What does the flamen Portunalis, whose existence is not otherwise attested, have to do with Quirinus? The answer is nothing. Quirinus is confirmed by Paulus. The MS *portunalis* is a mistake for *quirinalis* made by the copyist who read *portum* at the same place in the next line.[3] The Quirinal flamen evidently had the regular oversight of Quirinus' sacred weapons.

The nature of the Quirinal flamen's supervision can be understood from the proper interpretation of two incidents during the Gaulish assault on and occupation of Rome.

According to the annalistic tradition the Quirinal flamen and the Vestal virgins assumed the responsibility for the *sacra* of Rome which they saved by removing them from the city. On their way to Caere on foot they met a man named Lucius Albinius who generously gave

---

[1] See Wissowa, *Religion und Kultus*[2], pp. 155, 196, 504–6, 516 and above, pp. 106–14.

[2] Festus 238 L. Paulus' excerpt (239 L.) makes no mention of *portunalis*: 'persillum dicebant vas quoddom picatum, in quo erat unguentum, unde arma Quirini unguebantur'. A *rudis* or *rudicula* was a spoon or spatula; see Ernout–Meillet[4] *s.v.* On preserving sacred utensils see Festus 292 L. *s.v. patella* and Serv. on *Aen.* 8. 278, and *ILLRP* 518 (105), II, 3 for applying pitch. On the sense of *vas* in Festus, cf. p. 10 (*anclabris, arferia*), 15 (*arculum*), 44 (*cuturnium*), 55 (*cumeram*), 87 (*guturnium*), 455 (*simpulum*). For *rudiculum* cf. p. 21 *apiculum*. On the form *persillum* cf. p. 23 *auxilla* = *olla parvula, armilla*, and 298 *postillum*.

[3] Holland, 'Janus and the Bridge', pp. 166–70, has an informative but quite far-fetched interpretation of Festus' Portunalis.

them a ride on his wagon. Through his act Rome's *sacra* were preserved from capture.[1] Older than the annalistic tradition is Aristotle's
notice that a Lucius saved Rome from the Gauls.[2] A third source is
the fragment of an inscribed elogium which its last editor Degrassi,
following Borghesi, assigns to the Quirinal flamen whom he leaves as
anonymous as Livy does.[3] However, there is no doubt as to the man's
office, the Quirinal flaminate. Livy's Lucius Albinius *de plebe Romana
homo* and Aristotle's Lucius, who are identical, is the Quirinal
flamen. The name of the consul in 23 B.C., L. Sestius Quirinalis
Albinianus, demonstrates their identity.[4]

The Quirinal flamen's association with the Vestals further supports the identification. First of all, the Quirinal flamen and the
Vestals shared a duty at Consualia.[5] Secondly, there was an indirect
association through the cult of Juno Lucina. According to the
Verrian notice to 1 March in the Fasti Praenestini the sacrifice to
Juno Lucina took place on the Esquiline because on 1 March the
matrons dedicated to the deity a temple which Albinia the [daughter]
or wife of Albinius had vowed if she [would have cherished] her son
and herself [in childbed].[6] There can be no doubt that this lady was
the wife of Albinius, otherwise her name would have been *Albinia
– – –f(ilia)*. A doubt would have perhaps arisen in the mind of
Albinia, mother of Sestius, consul of 23 B.C., since the old system of
nomenclature was already changing. Matrons did not dedicate
temples. This bit of information may also depend on family lore.
The temple of Juno Lucina was founded in 375 B.C. when anarchy
prevailed. The Vestal virgins regularly hung their hair on trees in the
grove (*lucus*) from which the goddess took her cognomen.[7] The
grove probably existed before the temple itself[8] and the Vestals' custom. The wife of Albinius can be the *flaminica* of the Quirinal flamen
c. 390 or the wife of Albinius who was military tribune with consular

[1] Livy 5. 40. 7–10 with Ogilvie's important comments and bibliography.
[2] In Plut. *Cam.* 22. 4. See Sordi, pp. 49–52 and *passim*; and Ogilvie (last note).
[3] *II* 13.3. 11 (also *CIL* VI, 1272 = *ILS* 51): '[cum Galli obs]iderent Capitolium,
[virgines Ve]stales Caere deduxit, [ibi sacra at]que ritus sollemnes ne [intermitte]rentur
curai sibi habuit [urbe recup]erata sacra et virgines [Romam rev]exit'.
[4] See Ogilvie on Livy. The consul of 32 bears an analogous name: L. Arruntius Camillus Scribonianus.
[5] Tert. *Spect.* 5. See Palmer, 'King'.
[6] *II* 13. 2, p. 418: 'Iun[o]ni Lucinae Esquiliis, quod eo die aedis ei d[edica]ta est per
matronas, quam voverat Albin[i filia] vel uxor, si puerum [parientem]que ipsa[m
fovisset]'.
[7] Pliny, *NH* 16. 235; cf. Festus 50 L. See Palmer, *Juno*.   [8] See above, p. 127, n. 3.

power in 379.[1] Furthermore the consular tribune and the flamen may be identical. The vow of the lady is not likely to have been honored unless she herself had some priestly authority. Hence, she would have probably been the *flaminica*. Thus, we have established a second association of the Vestals and the Quirinal flaminate.

The second incident occurring during the Gaulish crisis is the annalistic account of Fabius Dorsuo which only goes to confirm the association of the Quirinal flamen and the Vestals. Livy preserves the story that Fabius went to the Quirinal Hill to take care of some family cult while the Gauls occupied all Rome but the Capitol.[2] Another tradition makes Fabius a pontiff on public business for the religion of Vesta.[3] The second version is fully supported by the circumstances of transporting the *sacra* to Caere. The Quirinal flamen and the Vestals were absent from Rome. Therefore the flamen's attention to Vesta's cult was assumed by a pontiff. In both incidents we see a combination of cult and priesthoods: the priests of Quirinus and Vesta in the one and in the other Vesta's cult on the Quirinal. It is clear that the Quirinal flamen whose role is not in doubt fulfilled a major religious function that could be popularly described as the salvation of Rome. Quirinus belonged not to a Sabine element but to all Quirites and was a national god whose flamen saved the city by saving the *sacra* and *ritus*.

The uncertainty in the story attaches to the name of the Quirinal flamen. However it is easy to see why one of Livy's predecessors has suppressed the name of Lucius Albinius. Albinius was plebeian. One of the certain first plebeian tribunes was L. Albinius Paterculus.[4] The author responsible for the suppression believed only patricians could fill a major flaminate.[5] The culprit was possibly Fabius Pictor who may also have turned the incident of Fabius Dorsuo from one of civil religion to gentilicial cult. Although the Quirinal flamen regularly served an agricultural cult, his position took on a great importance in the hour of danger. This importance rests, I believe, on Mars Quirinus' function not only in agriculture but also in war and peace and his protection of the Quirites.

Entirely separate from the cult practiced by the Quirinal flamen is

---

[1] His praenomen was either Marcus or Lucius; see Broughton, *s.a.*
[2] Livy 5. 46. 1–3, 52. 3, hence Val. Max. 1. 1. 11.
[3] Cassius Hem. fr. 19 P. (= App. *Celt.* 6); cf. Florus 1. 7. 16 and Cass. Dio fr. 25.
[4] See Broughton, *s.a.* 493.
[5] See above, p. 123, n. 3 and below, Appendix III.

the legend of the god Quirinus. The first temple of Quirinus at Rome
was built in 293 on the Quirinal Hill by Papirius Cursor whose
father, Livy (10. 46. 7–8) conjectures, had vowed the temple some
thirty years before. Cursor's spoils went for the adornment of the
temple and a forum. Near the Quirinal Gate stood a shrine (*sacellum*)
of Quirinus whose relation to the grander temple is uncertain.
Modern students have suggested that the *aedes* of Quirinus replaced
his *sacellum*. From the use of the present tense in Paulus and its
restoration to Festus we can plainly see that the *sacellum* and *aedes*
existed at the same time. This interpretation is supported by the
demotic *a Quirinis* ('from the Quirini') and the later *Quirinenses*.[1]
It is difficult not to believe that the *sacellum* had a purpose other than
that of a temple and that no temple of Quirinus stood in Rome before
293. The erection of this temple must be viewed in the political frame
of the era. Papirius Cursor was consul with Sp. Carvilius in 293 and as
consuls for the second time in 272 they again celebrated triumphs.
In the latter year another Papirius and Curius Dentatus served as
censors.[2] Miss Taylor has made the bold and attractive suggestion
that these censors conceived the formation of the tribes Quirina and
Velina. In 272 Quirina was intended to embrace Sabine Cures but
when the formation of the two tribes was deferred to 241 Quirina
took in other territory. Furthermore, the choice of the name Quirina
Miss Taylor ascribes to Curius because he claimed Sabine ancestry
and his gentilicial name approximated the name of Numa Pompilius' hometown of Cures.[3] Since the powerful Papirii had already
displayed an interest in Quirinus twenty years before, both Papirius
and Curius, censors of 272, would have chosen the tribal name
Quirina because it was particularly appropriate to the enfranchisement of Sabines which took place in fact before 241.

Whatever piety motivated the choice of the tribe name Quirina it
coincided with a political advantage for certain men of the early
third century. Although I treat the subject in detail in the history of
the curiate constitution, I note here that the Ovinian plebiscite made
eligibility for conscription into the Roman senate contingent upon
membership in a curia.[4] This requirement in no way impaired the

[1] Festus 302–3 L.; *CIL* vi, 9975, 31895.
[2] See Münzer, *RE* 3. 2, col. 1630; 4. 2, cols 1841–5; 18. 3, cols 1002–5, 1051–6, 1073–4.
[3] 'Voting Districts', p. 342 (index) under *Curius Dentatus*.
[4] Festus 290 L.: '....donec Ovinia tribunicia intervenit, qua sanctum est ut censores ex

legislated qualifications for a magistracy established in 367. Curius is represented by tradition as a champion of the plebeian politician against patrician intransigence during his plebeian tribunate.[1] An effort to authenticate a curial pedigree could have been made indirectly through the claim of Sabine ancestry going back to a time in which the bond of Roman and Sabine was thought to have been very close. Curius certainly and perhaps Carvilius, plebeian colleagues of the patrician Papirii, would have derived no slight benefit from this pretension.

Although Quirinus' prior existence cannot be doubted, his role of patron saint of Sabines cannot be dated any earlier than this time. The word *quirinus* is nothing but an epithet which attained discrete divinity at the beginning of the third century. Janus and Mars bear the epithet but the attribution to the latter is by far the more frequent.[2] Although Mars had no temple within the precincts of early Rome, the Salii preserved his utensils in a Palatine curia. The Palatine Salii conducted worship of Mars as god of war (*Gradivus*) and of vegetation. Another sodality of Salii had its headquarters on the Quirinal Hill. These later bore the title Salii Collini after the name of the region and tribe but their archaic title, found in their archives, was Salii Agonenses derived from Agonus which we are told was the earlier name of the Quirinal Hill. The later name applied to the hill likewise may be no older than the building of Quirinus' temple.[3]

The rituals of the two Salian colleges are undifferentiated in our sources just as the Martial flamen is hardly distinguished from the Quirinal flamen in the nature of his functions. With the chief pontiff the Martial flamen offered the October horse. All three major flamens, Dialis, Martialis and Quirinalis, sacrificed together to Fides Publica on the Capitol.[4] This common worship of the state's trust suggests the origin of the epithet of Mars. Servius attempts to

---

omni ordine optimum quemque curiatim [MS curiati] in senatum legerent'. See below, chapter 9.

[1] Cic. *Brut.* 14. 55.

[2] With Ianus and Mars, Lucilius 19–22 M.; with Ianus, Festus 204 L., Macr. *Sat.* 1. 9. 15. With Mars: Livy 5. 52. 7, 8. 9. 6 (*Mars pater Quirine*); Dion 2. 48. 2; Serv. on *Aen.* 1. 292; Mart. Cap. 1. 46, 1. 50; cf. Martius Quirinus in Arn. 1. 41. On Janus Quirinus see Holland, 'Janus and the Bridge', pp. 108–37. On a threefold sacrifice to Jupiter, Mars, Quirinus or Janus for the *spolia opima* see Varro in Festus 202 L., Plut. *Marcellus* 8, Serv. on *Aen.* 6. 860.

[3] See Wissowa, *Religion und Kultus*[2], pp. 555–9; Latte, *Röm. Religion.*, pp. 114–16.

[4] Livy 1. 21. 4.

explain the peace made by Romulus and T. Tatius by citing the bellicose nature of Mars and the peaceful nature of Quirinus.[1] The cooperation of the three flamens reflects the gods by whom the Romans made treaties: Jupiter, Mars (Gradivus) and (Mars) Quirinus. The oath *equirine* has remained without illustration in Latin literature in which we read the occasional ejaculation of *ecastor*, *edepol*, *mehercule* in trivial matters or *me dius fidius* in a solemn moment. The oath *equirine* never parts the lips of a character in Latin literature because no person in literature strikes a treaty.[2] The Mars Quirinus of Rome, invoked to vouchsafe preservation of treaties, bears the epithet in order that he might be distinguished from the Mars of any other Italic town. He is the Mars of the Quirites, the Mars of the Roman curias which severally swear to a treaty binding all the curias.

The proper imprecations or addresses (*indigitamenta*) of the gods caused no little anxiety to a Roman people removed in time and spirit from their archaic religion. A. Gellius preserves a list of abstract nouns which he has culled from priestly books and prayers.[3] They are probably *indigitamenta*. Romans invoked the *hora* and *virites* of Quirinus and the *moles* and *nerio* of Mars. Latte rightly points out that the *moles Martis* is a Greek borrowing perhaps from Cumae. On the other hand, Festus and Ennius mention a *heres Martea*.[4] The words *heres* and *hora* are cognate with the Italic root of 'will', apparent in Latin *hortor*. The *virites* has been referred to the Latin *vires* until Latte who rightly considers it the doublet of the Latin *virtus*. The derivation of Quirinus' *virites* from *vir* is proved by Mars' *nerio* which is the Sabine equivalent of *virtus* from the Sabine *ner* ('man') and cognate with Nero, cognomen of the one Roman family of certain Sabine extraction, the Claudii. On the tombstone of the Sabine god Quirinus be it graven: 'hic sita virites Romana Sabini Quirini exstincta superataque neriene Sabina Romani Martis'. The Romans called on Mars and Quirinus to lend them manhood and manpower, suitable boons from a god of growth and war.

At first sight *hora* and *heres* have less pertinence to Mars than his

[1] On *Aen.* 1. 292.
[2] Festus 71 L.: 'equirine ius iurandum per Quirinum'. See Walbank on Polybius 3. 26. 6–9, where the treaty oaths by Jupiter, Mars and Quirinus are mentioned.
[3] *NA* 13. 23.
[4] Latte, *Röm. Religion.*, pp. 55–7; Festus 89 L.; Ennius, *Ann.* 104 V. in Gellius, *ibid.* See the *feriale Cumanum* for 24 May (*CIL* x, 8375 = *ILS* 108).

manhood. Gellius however cites the *heries* of Juno which likewise
conveys the sense of Juno's will. Juno Quiris or Curis is the only
deity known to have been worshipped in all the curias.[1] Varro and
his followers, ancient and modern, say Juno Curitis of Falerii bore
the epithet Curitis from the Sabine word for lance.[2] It is curious, to
say the least, that the chief deity of the Faliscans who spoke the
Italic dialect most akin to Latin and who were strongly tinged with
Etruscan culture should have had a chief deity whose epithet was
Sabine. Doubtless this Faliscan goddess bore the same epithet as the
goddesses of the Roman curias, Tiburtine Juno and Juno Quiris to
whom the consul and praetor of the Latin colony of Beneventum made
a dedication.[3] The ritual invitation of Juno to migrate from fallen
Veii to Rome points to a longstanding custom of summoning (*evocatio*) the Juno from her home. Livy, whose generation had lost sight
of this primitive practice, describes the procedure with much less
reverence than his forbears would have given and supplies the pertinent formula: 'visne Romam ire, Iuno?'.[4] The consent sought at
Veii can be none other than the *heries Iunonis* remarked by Gellius.
According to the formula of the surrender (*deditio*), quoted above, the
conquered surrender to the discretion of the Roman commander and
populus all their goods intended for god and man (*divina humanaque
omnia*). Each of the Roman curias worshipped its own Juno whose
willingness had been sought in advance of her worshipper's amalgamation. Each of the curial Junos had once played such a critical

[1] D.H. 2. 50. 3; Festus 56 L., quoted above, p. 102, n. 1. Cf. Serv. Dan. on *Aen.* 1. 17:
'aut certe illud "currus" quod ait ductos alta ad donaria currus. habere enim Iunonem
currus certum est. sic autem esse etiam in sacris Tiburtibus constat ubi sic precantur:
Iuno Curitis tuo curru clipeoque tuere meos curiae vernulas.' See Latte, *Röm. Religion.*,
pp. 105–6, n. 2; W. Eisenhut, *RE* 24 (1963), cols 1324–33.
[2] The Sabine lance (*curis*) is in the *Fasti* of Praeneste (*BC* 1904, p. 277) and of Pole-
mius Silvius (*CIL* 1², vol. 1, p. 259) at 17 February, Ovid, *F.* 2. 477; Festus 43 L. and 55 L.
The immediate source of all these authors was Verrius Flaccus who most certainly drew his
information from the Sabine Varro because Dionysius 2. 48. 4 cites Varro as the authority
of an etymology of Cures from *cures*. The etymology of Juno's epithet must have been
treated in an expanded version of *LL* 5. 74 which Dionysius follows in 2. 50. 1–3. C. W.
Westrup, 'Sur les *gentes* et les *curiae* de la royauté primitive de Rome', *RIDA* ser. 3, vol. 1
(1954), pp. 471–2, goes so far as to suggest that the Quirites were lancers. The adjectival
formation, however, is certainly not comparable with *hastatus, armatus*, etc. Secondly, the
Romans did not consider the Quirites soldiers but, rather, the opposite. See A. Alföldi,
'Hasta—Summa Imperii', *AJA* 63 (1959), 18–20.
[3] *ILLRP* 169.
[4] Livy 5. 22. 3–7; cf. 1. 55. 4 and Festus 180 L., quoted above, p. 83, n. 1. The cult
epithet of this Juno is *regina* which means Juno of the King, not Queen Juno and stands in
contrast with Juno of the Curia. A king ruled the Etruscans of Veii (Livy 5. 1. 3–9,
5. 5. 10). See Sordi, chapter 1 and Palmer, *Juno*.

role in the cooperation of the curias that her annual worship outlived any remembrance of her importance to the communities. Although the Romans ceased to incorporate the conquered into curias, they scrupulously observed the protocol of bringing Junos from Etruscan and Latin towns and that god or goddess under whose protection the army and citizens of Carthage lived.[1]

Similar mental involution brought Roman attention to bear on the *hora Quirini* and the *heres Martea*. The whole of March was intermittently given over to Mars in his capacity for war and vegetation. Apparently the Romans conciliated Mars Gradivus' *nerio* and *heres* to inaugurate the season of growth and military campaigns in what was once the first month of the year. On 23 August, the feast of Volcanalia in the oldest calendar, the Romans enticed (*venerari*) *hora* from Mars Quirinus on the Quirinal hill.[2] Since the notation in the liturgical calendar is written in small letters, this enticement was not at first fixed on a regular date and resembles in this regard the Argean rites.[3] The invocation of Mars Quirinus at a treaty-making and the god's association with peace demonstrate that the consent of Quirinus sought in August appertained to a religious covenant between the Quirites and their Mars to end the military campaign which had commenced in March. Of course, this ceremony would have had no fixed date because the Romans would have acted only if and when a warring season ended in fact and a treaty had been concluded. When it became no longer feasible to end the campaigns at the time appropriate to the annual cycle of primitive Rome, the Romans set a convenient date prior to the harvest which approximated the season for which the Romans and their near Italian enemies had to be free for bringing in the crops. Festus betrays the nature of the ceremonial activity. He reports that the Quirinal flamen anointed the arms of Quirinus. If this occurred on 23 August, the ritual may have been intended to put in sacred storage the arms of Mars. The arms of Mars had been awakened from sleep by the Roman commander in March. The rites of *virites Quirini* may have

---

[1] L. Furius Philus (cos. 136) *apud* Macr. *Sat.* 3. 9. 6–13: 'si deus, si dea est....' Cf. *ILLRP* 291: 'sei deo sei deivae sac(rum). C. Sextius C. f. Calvinus pr(aetor) de senati sententia restituit'. See below, chapter 8.

[2] Ennius, *Ann.* 117 V.; 'Quirine pater veneror horamque Quirini'. Cf. 'precor venerorque veniamque a vobis peto ut vos populum civitatemque Carthiginiensem deseratis' etc. from the formula of *evocatio* in Macr. *Sat.* 3. 9. 6.

[3] See M. Guarducci, *BC* 64 (1936), 32–6; Degrassi, p. 502.

been observed at Quirinalia, 17 February, at the end of the year (old calendar) according to reasoning similar to that which required prayers to Mars Quirinus at the end of a military campaign.[1] The evidence for the feasts of Fornacalia and Quirinalia weighs in favor of an agricultural festival by the curias in behalf of Mars to whom the *far* roasted at Fornacalia was particularly sacred. At Iguvium, for instance, far-cakes were offered only to Mars while Jupiter was worshipped at the same sacrifice without such cakes. Also two Iguvine decurias were under contract to supply the Atiedian Brothers with *far* from two fields sacred to Picus Martius; one of these fields bears the name of the decuria under contract and doubtless was communal land. At Rome the *far* growing on the Campus Martius at the time Tarquinius Superbus was expelled was laid under religious interdict and had to be disposed of ritually in the Tiber.[2]

Ovid couples the *hora Quirini* and a 'goddess' Hersilia whose name resembles only too slightly the word *hora*. This Hersilia, according to popular belief the wife of Romulus, probably takes her name from the Curia Hersilia (see chapter 5). Ovid's connection of *hora* and Hersilia reflects the curial character of the August observance.[3] The annalist Cn. Gellius (*apud* A. Gellius, 13. 23. 13) represents Hersilia invoking Neria, 'wife of Mars', and beseeching her to grant peace between the Romans and Sabines.[4] Perhaps the pontiff Fabius who, substituting for the absent Quirinal flamen, went to the Quirinal Hill under fire, was seeking peace with the Gauls. Such an act accords with the notorious tradition that the Romans bought off the Gauls.

Two flamens and two Salian sodalities superintended the cult of the Roman Mars. The Martial flamen and the Palatine Salii were attached to the cult of Mars (Gradivus) whose rites fell in March and opened the new year of war and vegetation. These Salii maintained a meeting-place (*curia*) on the Palatine where they kept the utensils

[1] On the *termini*, *Terminalia* and February *Equirria*, see Magdelain, 'Cinq jours', pp. 201–227 and Degrassi, pp. 414–15. See Michels, pp. 138–9, on festivals which in early times were set each year according to the occasion and in later times were fixed on a certain annual day.
[2] *Tab. Iguv.* IIa, 10–12; vb, 8–18; vIb, 2; vIb, 44. In the last two instances the *far* cakes are distinct from the *ficla* cakes. See above, p. 90, n. 2 for the produce of the Campus Martius.
[3] *Metam.* 14.829–51. See J. Gagé, 'Hersilia et les Hostilii', *Ant. Cl.* 28 (1959), 255–72; De Sanctis I, 223.
[4] The marriage of Nerio and Mars is as old as Plautus, *Truc.* 515.

for invoking Mars' favor and the augural wand (*lituus*), miraculously saved from the Gauls' havoc, with which Romulus inaugurated the city of Rome. On a height named Agonus outside the limits of what the Romans called the Septimontium stood another storehouse (in the *sacellum Quirini*) which I would assign to the Salii Agonenses. Here, too, an augural wand was preserved perhaps with the arms which the Quirinal flamen anointed each year. The Mars of the Quirites enjoyed a special epithet only because he guaranteed the inviolability of a treaty to which the Roman curias adhered.[1]

A stronger union of the curial communities under a strong king witnessed the centralization of state religious rites on the Capitol and in the Forum. This centralization also wrought a change in the manner of swearing to treaties. Jupiter Feretrius on the Capitol became chief guarantor of treaties to which the *populus Romanus Quiritium* adhered. Even though Mars Quirinus took a decidedly second place in treaty oaths, he was still invoked because the god of the Quirites could not be omitted.

In 388 B.C. the first temple of Mars was built by the Romans but outside the pomerium. Not quite a hundred years later politically ambitious plebeians converted to their advantage the remnants of the Mars Quirinus cult which had languished with the ascendancy of Jupiter Feretrius. These statesmen fashioned a mythology of ancestry in which Romulus, the eponymous founder of Rome, bears the cult name Quirinus betokening the union and accord between the Romans and the Sabines. Severed from its deity, the word Quirinus became a deity in its own right. No longer was he Mars but Romulus, deified son of Mars. No doubt, the Romans were stimulated to these mythopoeic confections by the Greeks whose ancestry was traced back to Dorus, Ion, Achaeus, Aeolus and Hellen. Hazy glimpses into their past induced the Romans to evolve a story of gods and men of the

[1] Varro, *LL* 6. 14; Livy 5. 52. 7; Dion. 2. 70. 1; Ovid, *F.* 6. 375, Festus 9 L., Gellius 4. 6. 1–2; Serv. on *Aen.* 7. 187, 7. 603, 8. 3, 8. 663. The *hierophylakion* of the Agonenses on the Quirinal would be *sacrarium* in Latin, since that is what the storehouse of the Palatini is called. Only the *sacellum Quirini* is attested and perhaps it ought properly to be termed a *sacrarium*. On the Salii, see Latte, *Röm. Religion.*, pp. 114–16; on the *sacellum Quirini* see M. Santangelo, 'Il Quirinale nell' antichità classica', *Atti d. Pont. Accad.* ser. 3, mem. 5, pp. 129–34. After writing the foregoing pages the book of Poucet, cited in the bibliography, was published. On some points he and I have reached the same or similar conclusions. However, I rank myself among the agnostics who know no pre-Capitoline triad that included a simple Quirinus; see Poucet, especially pp. 22–4. Three disparate flamens do not a triad make. For me Quirinus began as an adjectival epithet of Mars; indeed, it distinguished that Mars from other Martes. So I have argued here and continue to hold this view.

two towns of Rome and Cures. At the end of the Republic when Roman insight into the past had grown even dimmer and the political mythology of the third century had acquired the lustre of antiquity, that ingenious Sabine Terentius Varro breathed new life into the Sabine origins of the Tities, Quirites and Quirinus and further injected the Sabine lance (*curis*) into the discussion, for his working hypothesis was 'Scratch a Roman, find a Sabine'.

CONCLUSION

In the last two chapters we treat or mention thirty-one entities which we can consider curias. Now we schematize them in alphabetical order and bring together the details. The evidence is grouped by arabic numbers: (1) territory; (2) meeting-place and Argei; (3) priesthoods; (4) deities; (5) festivals; (6) augural bird; (7) personal names (plebeian unless otherwise noted); (8) members of the Alban League or participants in the Latin Festival.[1] An asterisk before a curia's name denotes a conjectural curia.

I. Acculeia. 1. Angerona, *Larentum(?); 2. Curia Acculeia; 3. Fratres Arvales; 4. Acca Larentina, Angerona, Volupia; 5. Divalia, Larentalia; 7. Accoleius; 8. Accienses.

II. *Caelia. 1. Mt Caelius, Caeliculum, Campus Caelemontanus; 2. Argei I 1; 3. Flamen Virbialis(?); 4. Diana; 5. Septimontium at the atrium, *sacrificia gentilicia ordinis senatorii*; 7. Caelius.

III. *Cermalensis. 1. Cermalus, *Carmentum(?); 2. Argei IV 5; 3. Flamen Carmentalis(?); 4. Carmentis(?); 5. Septimontium at the atrium, Carmentalia(?).

IV. *Cespia. 1. Mt Cespius; 2. Argei II 6; 5. Septimontium at the atrium; 7. Cispius.

V. *Claudia. 1. Ager Claudius; 2. No Argei; 7. Claudius (pat. & pl.).

VI. *Crustumina. 1. Ager Crustuminus, Crustumerium; 2. No Argei; 8. Crustumerium.

VII. *Fabia. 3. Luperci Fabiani; 7. Fabius (pat.); 8. (Fabienses(?)).

VIII. *Falacer. 3. Flamen Falacer; 4. Pater Falacer.

IX. Faucia. 7. Faucius.

X. Foriensis. 1. Lucus Fur(r)inae, *Forentum; 2. Curiae Veteres; 3. Flamen Fur(r)inalis; 4. Fur(r)ina, Lares [C]uriales(?); 5. Fur(r)inalia; 7. Furinius, Furnius.

XI. *Gabina. 1. Ager Gabinus, Gabii; 2. No Argei; 7. Gabinius; 8. Gabii.

XII. *Hersilia. 7. Hersilius.

---

[1] See next chapter.

XIII. *Lateria. 1. Ager Laterius (cf. Laterensis and Lateranus); 4. Lateranus; 7. Laterius.

XIV. *Latia. 1. Ager Latinus etc., Collis Latiaris; 2. Argei III 6; 7. Latinius; 8. Latinienses.

XV. *Marcia. 1. Campus Martialis(?); 3. Fratres or Vates Marcii, Libo; 4. Mars(?); 6. Picus Martius; 7. Marcius.

XVI. *Mucia. 1. Prata Mucia, Collis Mucialis, *Muciona; 2. Argei III 5; 6. Sanqualis; 7. Mucius; 8. Mu⟨c⟩ienses.

XVII. *Oppia. 1. Mt. Oppius; 2. Argei II 3(?); 3. Flamen (Oppialis); 5. Septimontium at the atrium; 7. Oppius.

XVIII. *Palatina. 1. Palatium; 3. Flamen Palatualis; 4. Palatua; 5. Palatuar, Septimontium at the atrium.

XIX. *Pinaria. 7. Pinarius (pat. & pl.).

XX. *Poetelia. 1. Lucus Poetelius, Lucus P⟨o⟩etelinus; 2. Argei II 5; 3. Libo; 7. Poetilius, Petilius.

XXI. *Querquetulana. 1. *Querquetulum; 4. Lares Querquetulani, Virae Querquetulanae; 8. Querquetulani.

XXII. *Quinctia. 1. Prata Quinctia; 3. Luperci Quinctiales; 7. Quinctius (pat.).

XXIII. Rapta. 2. Curiae Veteres.

XXIV. *Semuria. 1. Ager Semurius.

XXV. *Solonia. 1. Ager Solonius, *Solona; 2. Pomonal; 3. Flamen Pomonalis; 4. Pomona; 7. Solonius.

XXVI. *Taracia. 1. Ager Taracius, Tarentum; 6. Tarax; 7. Taracius.

XXVII. Tifata(?). 1. Tifata; 7. Tifatius; 8. Tifata.

XXVIII. Titia. 2. Atrium Titium, Lauretum; 3. Sodales Titii; 6. Titus; 7. Titius; 8. T⟨i⟩tienses.

XXIX. Veliensis. 1. Velia; 2. Curiae Veteres, Argei IV 6; 5. Septimontium at the atrium; 7. Velius; 8. Velienses.

XXX. Velitia. 2. Curiae Veteres.

XXXI. *Volturna 1. Volturnum(?); 3. Flamen Volturnalis; 4. Volturnus; 5. Volturnalia; 6. Vultur(ius); 7. Volturnius.

The number of known curias stands at six. The Curia Tifata, also the name of a town, depends upon the interpretation of Festus' *Epitome* and the Curia Hersilia upon an inference from the folk-tale of the curias' names. I cannot vouch for the authenticity of any of the conjectural curias. Some or all may be wrong conjectures. All cannot be right for I have listed thirty-one. The Pinaria is the suggestion of others basing themselves on a scrap of Festus.

A few words may be said about the known and conjectural curias in other central Italian towns.[1] The Caeretane Asernia exhibits a dedication to its Dei Curiales. Although no exact Roman parallel

---

[1] See chapters 4 and 5.

survives, the Lares [C]uriales which we relate to the Lucus Fur(r)ina
with its Genius Forinarum and thence to Curia Foriensis bear a
resemblance. We suggest that the *meros Sikelikon* of Tibur, which did
have curias, may have been a curia Sicana formed of remnants of
the Sicani who had participated at one time in the Latin Festival.
No such curia is known at Rome (cf. Varro, *LL* 5. 101) but the
Cloelii Siculi, we argue, belonged to a Curia Quinctia which was
originally 'Alban'. Lanuvium contained the Curias Clodia Firma
and -*amonal(is)*. The mutilated name of the latter may be construed
in light of what we have said about the names Angerona, *Solona,
Pomona and *Muciona *inter alia*. Here, too, may belong Deve
Declune in the Volscan inscription of Velitrae which contains the
word *covehriu*. The existence of a Lanuvinian Curia Clodia merely
confirms the tradition that the Claudii who came to Rome were
migrants seeking new homes. Perhaps a similar migration ultimately
carried a Claudius to Mamertine Messina.[1]

The thrust of our analysis of the curiate system rests upon our
view, derived from the meagre ancient testimony, that the curias
incorporated diverse groups into a state which started from a nucleus
which was the first curia. Successful and unsuccessful attempts at
synoecism and unification abound in the ancient world. Attica under
Athens and Lacedaemon under Sparta offer two examples of successful attempts. The later Hellenic leagues offer examples of both
success and failure although the successful ones did not effect a
consolidated state. Also the Roman tradition of absorbed villages
which neighbored Rome is too strong to deny. Their names do not
belong to the work of inventors. Conquest doubtless took place on
some occasions. Yet the Roman mode of imperialism eschewed
oppression in the hour of conquest. Rome's implements of imperialism
were not always finely honed. However, the Romans must have
begun with a rude and simple tool upon their tiny neighbors.
Although knowledge of their precise role and contribution can never
be recovered, many communities joined in that imperial phenomenon
we call Rome.

In this chapter I have attempted to define the character and
origins of the Roman curias and to illustrate their communal
religion. In origin the curias represented communal entities united

[1] See C. D. Buck, *A Grammar of Oscan and Umbrian*[2] (Boston, 1928), p. 369 for the record
in Greek letters of [M]amereks Klavdis Mamerekēis.

and disparate. Four stages in the history of the union can be distinguished: seven curias meeting on the Palatine, an unknown number meeting on the Caelian, twenty-seven curias of the four regions meeting on the Capitol and in the Forum at the time of the Servian reform, and the thirty curias which formed the Republican curiate assembly after 495 B.C. Although the auguries of the state ultimately resided with the curias, the curias lost their actual augural authority when the centuriate army was created. Contrary to ancient theory, the thirty curias were primary, ethnic, non-military units and the three tribes were secondary, military, non-ethnic units. A numerical proportion between the thirty curias and the three tribes did not result from the policy of a Romulus if ever such a proportion was the intention of the Romans but was an accident. Indeed, the tribes may have grown from one to three as the curias grew from one to thirty. Nowhere else in Italy do we have only three tribes. The interchange of certain rights among the united curias led to the most primitive expression of Roman citizenship. At the outset of Roman history, however, the differences between the curias as groups of men were so pronounced that the Romans, who in fact succeeded the Quirites, never forgot that Roman citizenship, however precious, gave no cause to boast of the ethnic purity of a closed society.

CHAPTER 7

ROMAN CURIAS AND THE LATIN FESTIVAL

In chapter 2 we listed the names of all communities, both real and fictional, which were attributed to the so-called Alban League or Latin League and which participated in the Latin Festival on the Alban Mount or the rites at the Nemus Dianae (Lucus Dianius) near Aricia.[1] During our discussion of certain curias we have alluded to their apparent independence as a people. Any testimony on their separate independence comes from one or another list of states belonging to a Latin religious reunion. Since most of the peoples or towns listed by our authorities disappeared even in antiquity, the MS tradition of these sources is far from secure.[2] In the following pages I will discuss ten peoples which are known or presumed to have been closely bound to Rome.

First of all, there are the two known and one likely curias, Foriensis, Veliensis and Tifata:

Foriensis. Pliny: *Foreti*; Dionysius: *Phortineiōn*. Foreti and Fortineii are not normal ethnics. Fortini, Foretini, and Fore(n)tes (cf. Laurentes) are possible. In Pliny stand *Cusuetani* and *Bubetani*, but in Dionysius *Boubentanōn* with the nasal preserved. *Forentum is a normal place-name construction (cf. *NH* 3. 64). Latin Forentani are evidently distinct from Pliny's Foreti. The toponymous suffix is also apparent in Tarentum, Ferent-, Nomentum, Carventum and Flument-(?). Presumably the Forienses name Forentum.

Veliensis. The curia and the people are secure. The identification has already been accepted.[3]

Tifata. This is the name of a likely curia and one of Pliny's lost towns not in the alphabetized list. The name meaning 'oak groves' semantically resembles the Querquetulani (see below).

Seven peoples can be related to the curias suggested in the foregoing chapter: Accienses, Crustumerium, Gabini, Latinienses, Mucienses (MS Munienses), Querquetulani, Titienses (MS Tutien-

[1] See above, pp. 10–13.
[2] In what follows Pliny = *NH* 3. 68–9, Dionysius = *AR* 5. 61.
[3] Pallottino, pp. 26–31, especially p. 27. Bernardi, '*Populi Albenses*', pp. 233, 255.

ses). Two other peoples, Vimitellani (MS Vimitellari) and Fabienses will also be discussed:

Accienses. No identification of this people has been made. The stem is the same as the gentilicial name which we have remarked belongs to the series Acca/Accius/Acculeius. The last is the name of a curia.

Crustumerium. This town disappeared after or with its absorption into Roman territory as a part of the Tribe Clustumina. The preservation of its *ager* bespeaks a special place in the Roman state.

Gabini. The relations of Gabii and Rome which we have detailed above present an anomaly. The Roman augurs considered a certain kind of territory Gabinian. One authority calls 'isopolity' the basis of Romano-Gabinian ties. Gabinian cult is practiced by the Romans. Yet the Gabinians still took part in the Latin Festival in Cicero's day.[1]

Latinienses. Like Crustumerium, the *ager* of this people enjoyed its integrity. However, they did not give their name to a Roman tribe. No name of the town of the Latinienses has survived.

Mu⟨c⟩ienses. Pliny's MSS: *munienses, mumienses*. Usually the Munienses are identified with the Castrimoenienses who still thrived in Pliny's time (*NH* 3. 64). While it is true that he twice lists a lost town and people, Politorium in the analphabetical list and Politaurini among the alphabetized people, he does not knowingly count a people as lost and as surviving. For instance, he has the lost Bolani and existent Bovillae (*NH* 3. 63). We know the Bovillani belonged to a league (D.H. 5. 61). However, Pliny's Bolani may be the Bolani of Bolae whom Livy (4. 49) calls Aequians. This town was near Pedum and Praeneste. Therefore, we doubt the identity of Castrimoenienses and Munienses, especially since the name of the lost people evinces the later vocalization. Pliny's MSS have *caecina* (or *cec-*) for Caenina at 3. 68 (after the Etruscan city of that name); *cerce, cercaei, cerici, cirici* and *cernei* for Circei in 3. 58 while having the correct or nearly correct form of the same city three other times in 3. 57–8. The ethnics in 3. 63–4 are generally transmitted badly as elsewhere in this book. Therefore, I do not hesitate to emend to Mu⟨c⟩ienses on the basis of Collis Mucialis and Porta Mucionia.

Querquetulani. So, Pliny; D.H. *Korkotoulanōn*, alphabetized between P. and S. Bernardi considers that the Querquetulani lived on the Caelian Hill.[2] In any case, they were at one time independent of the Romans who took over some of their gods. Their town whose existence is to be assumed both from the form of their name and the Roman Porta Querquetulana, must have been fairly close to Rome. It bore a name similar in sense to Tifata.

T⟨i⟩tienses. Pliny: *Tutienses*. Some hold that the name is related to the Tutia River six miles from Rome.[3] Pallottino suggests Titienses and identifies them with the archaic tribe.[4] I prefer to identify it with the Curia

---

[1] *Planc.* 9. 23, cf. D.H. 5. 61. 3.　　　　　　　　　　　　　[ancient Querquetulum.

[2] Bernardi, '*Populi Albenses*', p. 232. Modern Corcolle is sometimes identified as

[3] Livy 26. 11. 8. See Bernardi, '*Populi Albenses*', p. 233.　[4] Above, pp. 93, n. 1 and 176, n. 3.

Titia because the two other tribes are not counted in any of the relevant lists while at least one curia (Veliensis) is.

Vimitellani. Pliny: *vimitelari, vimiterali, vinutellarii, vinutelari*. An ethnic ending in -*arii* is unparalleled. Pallottino would relate Vimitellani to Rome's Collis Viminalis.[1] However, *vimitellani is not the right compound and *viminetellani is even more monstrous. The name is hopelessly corrupt except for the initial letter. I cannot consider it a 'Roman' or pre-Roman entity.

In an alphabetical list of the existing Latian towns Pliny *NH* 3. 63–4 has *Gabienses in monte Albano*. They stand between *Cingulani* and *Foropopulienses ex Falerno* and, therefore, the transmitted *g* is incorrect. It has been corrected to *cabi*- and *fabi*-. In support of the former is Dionysius' *Kabanōn* and the *sacerdos Cabe(n)sis montis Albani* (p. 134, n. 4). On the other hand, *Fabienses* are not otherwise attested and should probably be denied.

The fact that ten or eleven communities or peoples can be identified with ten known or proposed curias supports our thesis that the curia ('a fellowship of men'), which one authority defines as a *genus hominum* 'ethnic group', represents the synoecism of various towns and peoples at and near historical Rome.

Pallottino's identification of the Velienses and T⟨i⟩tienses has been accepted here.[2] Bernardi, whose view of the Albans and Latins differs from ours, reckons the Velienses, Querquetulani, Foreti and Latinienses among the 'Alban' Romans.[3] Since all but one of the ten communities discussed here had disappeared by Pliny's day, we cannot ascertain whether a people ceased to participate in the Latin Festival upon becoming Quirites or, having become Quirites, a curia left to the officers of Rome its onetime responsibilities to the Latin reunion. The case of Gabii does not fully settle the question because Gabii was the exception to prove the rule. Moreover, the Gabinians evidently did not migrate to Rome and preserved a marked measure of communal independence to the extent that it may have sided with Rome's enemies in the fourth century.[4] The Romans' imperial

---

[1] Pallottino, p. 27; cf. Bernardi, '*Populi Albenses*', p. 255.

[2] Above, p. 176, n. 3, p. 177, n. 4.

[3] Bernardi '*Populi Albenses*', p. 255 who identifies, p. 232, the Foreti etc. with the *Forcti* or *Forctes*. These men, whom our one source contraposes to the Sanates, were not a people. *Forctis* is archaic Latin *fortis*; *Sanates* may be a real ethnic. See Festus 74, 91, 426/8, 474 L. However, Gellius, *NA* 16. 10. 8 quotes a section of the Law of the Twelve Tables which groups *sanates* with *proletarii* and *adsidui*, i.e. among property classes, or with sureties (*vades, subvades*, etc.).

[4] Livy 6. 21. 9 (cf. 3. 8. 6; D.H. 9. 68. 1), and next chapter where a purported *devotio* of the town is discussed. It never took place. Otherwise, the Gabinians could not have survived and taken part in the Latin Festival.

system was not foolproof. Separatist movements as well as sectionalism occasionally plagued them even in Latium.

The Tiburtine situation may have developed parallel to the Roman. Dionysius' *meros Sikelikon* which we have suggested was an element of the Latian Sicani and perhaps a curia[1] survived at Tibur till the beginning of the Christian era.

At Lanuvium one curia was named Clodia Firma. We have suggested the possibility of a Roman Curia Claudia. The Roman Claudii have no known connection with Lanuvium.[2] Perhaps, the Claudian migration, attested *c.* 500, ended in settlement in more than one community.

The adherence of communities to the Roman curiate system must have been founded upon a formal procedure. In the next chapter we attempt a reconstruction of the procedure. At this point it is worth pointing out that the peoples whose incorporation we have been discussing need not have led a communal life in a city-state as that term is understood or, for that matter, a sedentary communal life before entering into a formal arrangement with a larger community.

---

[1] See above, pp. 62–3, 174.
[2] Lanuvium was in the Tribe Maecia and the Claudii in other tribes. See the index of Taylor's 'Voting Districts', *s.vv.*

CHAPTER 8

COMMUNION AND COMMUNITY

Traces of the process whereby the Roman community grew by the adherence of curial communities remain. Because of the religious character of the process I choose to call the act communion and distinguish three stages: first, evocation of a Juno who thereafter became a Juno Quiritis; secondly, the actual commingling of earth from the land of the new curia with Roman earth; thirdly, the regular reaffirmation of allegiance by unanimous curiate law. To these three acts may be added a probable solemn oath or two.

EVOCATION

The archaic Romans usually invited the chief god of a conquered community which they wished to annex to come to Rome and take up abode in their city. Regularly the chief deity was a Juno. The religious rite was called an evocation.[1] Evocation might take place internally. For our present purpose we recall the record of evoking curias and their religion from Old Curias: '...quae [sc. sacra] cum ex Veteribus in Novas [sc. Curias] evocarentur, septem curiarum per religiones evocari non potuerunt'.[2] It has been my contention that the rites of curias, like most curias themselves, originated outside of the Roman communities. Presumably, then, these sacra had been evoked from several places and transported to Old Curias on the Palatine. At some later date, all curias which existed at the time and were housed together at Palatine Old Curias were removed to Caelian New Curias with the exception of the seven of which four still functioned at Old Curias in the historical period. The priests of the four curias evidently preserved knowledge of the frustrated ceremony of evocation.

The sole deity common to all thirty Roman curias were the thirty Junones Quirites. The universality of her curial cult seems far from coincidence. Rather, I interpret her presence in and protection of

---

[1] I have dealt with general aspects of Juno and evocation in *Juno*.
[2] Festus 180/2 L. See above, pp. 82–4.

every curia as the remnant of her evocation from another place and community to Rome at the time of communion.

In closing a long section on the ceremony of evocation of national gods and cursing (*devotio*) towns, Macrobius writes: 'in antiquitatibus autem haec oppida inveni devota: †Stonios†, Fregellas, Gavios, Veios, Fidenas....'[1] No trace of the conquest and cursing of Gabii is found in Roman history. However, we have seen how the Ager Gabinus occupied a special place in the ceremonial manual of the Roman augurs. Furthermore, the evocation which would have preceded any *devotio* would have yielded Juno Gabina and incidentally brought the *ritus Gabinus* to Rome.[2] A part of the land of the Veientines, whose Juno was brought to Rome, was exploited for the Roman augurs.[3] The historical account of Romano-Gabinian isopolity and the priestly supervision which Roman augurs exercised over Gabinian land can be reconciled with Macrobius' testimony on the assumption that his authority misunderstood evidence of the evocation for proof of a *devotio*.

Since the four towns mentioned by Macrobius all lay close to Rome, the corrupt *Stonios* may also be considered a neighbor of Rome. Could it be *S⟨ol⟩onios*?[4]

THE COMMUNION OF EARTH

Macrobius quotes Scipio Aemilianus' curse of Carthage which closes with the imprecation 'Tellus mater teque Iuppiter obtestor'. Macrobius adds the detail that the commander touches the earth with both hands when he says 'Tellus' and raises his hands to heaven when he says 'Jupiter'.

We should expect some such formal treaty between the actual Romans and peoples about to become Romans as the tradition records between Quirites and Romans under T. Tatius and Romulus.[5] Indeed, the Salian Hymns contained the word 'treaties' (*foedera*) but the context is lacking.[6] The Salian treaties may merely refer to the end of campaigns.

---

[1] *Sat.* 3. 9. 13.

[2] For Juno Gabina, Verg. *Aen.* 7. 682 and Servius thereon. Cf. pp. 138, n. 5 and 139, n. 1.

[3] Festus 204 L. *s.v. obscum*: 'sed eodem etiam nomine appellatur locus in agro Veienti, quo frui soliti produntur augures Romani'. On the evocation of Veientine Juno Regina see Palmer, *Juno*.

[4] Cf. D.H. 2. 37. 2: *ek Solōniou poleōs*.   [5] E.g., in Plut. *Rom.* 19. 9–10.

[6] Varro, *LL* 7. 27.

A formal agreement made between the two parties can be inferred from its implementation. Plutarch preserves a most interesting remark on the subject which has been unjustly condemned. According to Plutarch Romulus decided to build his Roma Quadrata. He sent to Etruria for men adept at certain sacred usages and writings. They dug a circular ditch around the Comitium of Plutarch's time and into the ditch threw first-fruits and necessary goods. Then each man with Romulus took a piece of soil from the land whence he came and threw it into the ditch so that all the soil would commingle. This ditch the Romans called the *mundus* after the sky. From the *mundus* the new city radiated. A pomerium was described. All this took place on the festival day of Parilia. Lastly, Plutarch introduces Varro, Tarutius and the horoscopic computations.[1] Now Varro, who discovered Roma Quadrata, placed it on the Palatine and cannot have been guilty of having primitive Rome radiating from the Comitium.[2] Furthermore, the known *mundus* is inferentially located on the Palatine.[3] And the supporting testimony, which we treat below, speaks of a Palatine ceremony. Since Varro seems to be Plutarch's source for the rites of foundation,[4] either Plutarch has made a mistake or Varro made a mistake. As we shall see, Varro seems to have used a ceremony at Parilia on the Palatine as a point of departure from which he discussed a custom peculiar to the founding of colonies. Here Plutarch may have gone astray. But this likelihood does not and can not explain his explicit identification of the historical Comitium which had a *mundus* of its own. To be sure, the Comitium did not belong to any Palatine community. However, the Comitium was the regular meeting-place of the curias under the kings. I conclude that there were at least two *mundi* at Rome.

Ovid's account of the Parilia gives some help:

apta dies legitur, qua moenia signet aratro;
    sacra Palis suberant: inde movetur opus.
fossa fit ad solidum, fruges iaciuntur in ima
    et de vicino terra petita solo;
fossa repletur humo, plenaeque inponitur ara,
    et novus accenso fungitur igne focus.[5]

---

[1] *Rom.* 11–12.

[2] See above, pp. 20–1, 26–34, 97, n. 2.

[3] Platner–Ashby, *s.v.*

[4] Plutarch's Etruscans are the *haruspices* whose *disciplina* in founding colonies Varro discussed. See above, pp. 26–8.

[5] *F.* 4. 819–24. Like Plutarch, Ovid continues with the description of the pomerium.

Clearly Parilia contained a ceremony quite similar to that related by Plutarch to the Comitium. Ovid's *de vicino terra petita solo* is less informative. The ceremony for all its antiquity, is not obscured in its simplicity.[1] It seems to me that there are two historical instances involved in Plutarch's and Ovid's accounts. First, annually at Parilia the people renewed their accession to curial Rome. The festival of Parilia may be connected with the curias through Fordicidia, a partially curial festival on behalf of Tellus, the Earth. At Parilia the ashes of the unborn calves cremated at Fordicidia were compounded for lustral use.[2] Secondly, whenever a new curia was created the *curiales* of the new curia deposited earth from their homeland in a ditch. The latest curias would have done so at the Comitium where the curiate assembly regularly met.[3] Every year thereafter on 21 April at the Parilia *curiales*, or more likely the curial priests, renewed this symbolic pledge from the curiate land which was that involved in a *terminalia*.[4]

A splendid analogy is found in legal procedure:

similiter si de fundo vel de aedibus sive de hereditate controversia erat, pars aliqua inde sumebatur et in ius adferebatur et in eam partem proinde atque in totam rem praesentem fiebat vindicatio, veluti ex fundo gleba sumebatur et ex aedibus tegula....[5]

According to the old procedure (note the tense) one could not go to law over land without bringing to court a clod of its earth (*gleba*).[6] By the same token a people could not become Roman without commingling their soil with Rome's. Furthermore, the colonial foundation known from the haruspices' manuals could have required the same act. I suppose that this was the way the Latin colonists from different communities of the Latin League threw in their lot with each other.

'When the *mundus* is open', says Varro, 'it is like a door to the underworld and its gloomy gods being open. Consequently, it is contrary to religion to give battle, levy troops, set out on a campaign, launch a ship, and take a wife.'[7] Such a *dies religiosus* was reserved for Roman

---

[1] See Bömer on *F*. 4. 821.   [2] See Degrassi, pp. 440–5.

[3] See below, pp. 217 n., 284–5.   [4] See above, p. 99.

[5] Gaius, *Inst*. 4. 17; cf. Gellius, *NA* 20. 10. 6–10 and Festus 516/18 L.: 'vindiciae...ex fundo sumptae'.

[6] For the *glebae* turned by the plow for a pomerium see Cato, *Orig*. fr. 18 P. from Serv. on *Aen*. 5. 755, and Varro, *LL* 5. 143–4.

[7] In Macr. *Sat*. 1. 16. 18, perhaps from the *Libri augurum* (1. 16. 19).

rites and was reckoned an inauspicious day for other business.[1] The day of peace, the armistice, is paralleled at the Feriae Latinae on the Alban Mount.[2] Divine peace attends the reunion of peoples, and perhaps, forestalls the outbreak of sectional strife. The prohibition against holding an assembly when the *mundus* was open would have allowed or even required assistance at a curiate assembly if a new people were joining the Romans at a solemn public ceremony. All days on which a *mundus* is known to have been opened, 24 August, 5 October and 8 November, were comitial days. The earliest of these three days followed that marked *Hora Quirini* in the calendar. Then the Romans besought from Quirinus his willingness.

THE CURIATE LAW

In the next chapter we discuss the activities of the curiate assembly. One republican act of the curiate assembly, lately represented by merely thirty curiate lictors, was the so-called *lex curiata de imperio* by which the man elected to an imperial magistracy by the centuries received his auspices and command. The law constituted a unanimous curiate affirmation of a centuriate election. Furthermore, we shall argue that the plural *comitia*, rather than *comitium*, reflects originally meetings of the several curias. Latte has proposed that the *lex curiata* was a kind of soldier's oath of allegiance to the new commander.[3] However, a military oath of fealty to consul took place on another occasion and, if it had been appropriate to an assembly, it would have been appropriate to the centuries which elected him and technically served under him. Lastly, the *lex curiata* was not an oath so far as we are told. Despite these misgivings, I believe that there is something basically true in Latte's interpretation of the *lex curiata*. Why vote unanimously on a king what a majority of curias has already decided? The ancient tradition speaks of foreign kings. Rather, the kings probably emerged from curias wedded to Rome. However that may be, a king chosen by political units which had disparate back-

[1] Festus' (124/6) *Mundus Cereris* indicates to me that there were other *mundi*. Festus (144/5) says that it was forbidden to join battle, enroll an army, hold assemblies and generally administer the state when the *mundus* was open. See W. W. Fowler, 'Mundus Patet', *JRS* 2 (1912), 25–33 = *Roman Essays* etc., pp. 24–37; H. Le Bonniec, *Le culte de Cérès à Rome* (Paris, 1958), pp. 175–84; Michels, pp. 63–5.
[2] Macr. *Sat.* 1. 16. 16–17.
[3] K. Latte, 'Lex Curiata und Coniuratio', *Nachrichten von der Gesellschaft der Wissenschaften zu Göttingen* (1934), pp. 59–73.

grounds would have wished a formal grant of his powers by all rather than by many. Leaving aside the curias, we can pose the question with certain examples. How could the Roman leaders be assured of the wholehearted loyalty and support of Attius Clausus and his host of followers or of the Gabini joined to Rome by isopolity? Suppose that the Fabii were to embroil themselves with Veientines over land. Could the king or consul rely on the rest of the Romans to obey his call to battle if he chose to lead all Romans against the Veientines on behalf of the Fabii? In a great modern state the reasons for war can be concealed or distorted. In a small community it would have been difficult to conceal facts in order to have a disagreeable decision carried out by those who disagreed.

Consequently, I assume that the *lex curiata* partly assured the loyalty of the several constituencies wherein separatist tendencies might have engendered civil dissent. This assurance was especially necessary at the choice of a new king. It was continued for centuriate officers not only because the Romans still believed the curiate assemblies were the source of the *imperium* and auspices, but also because the separatist tendency lingered longer than the institution of a republic. It did not affect the centuriate assembly which had a different basis. The basis of the thirty curias would have remained for generations to come. Potential sectionalism would ultimately be removed. Until it disappeared, the king and early consuls could have relied upon the unanimous curiate law.

Finally, we mention *ex hypothesi* the likelihood of some kind of oath whereby new citizens bound themselves to the state. Soldiers swore to obey their commanders and the plebs to defend their sacrosanct tribunes, citizens swore the truth of their census declaration. Unless one supposes that the unanimous *lex curiata* embodied an oath to observe adherence to the Roman state—an improbable supposition—such an oath, both initial and reaffirmative, should have been extracted.

The obvious historical divine candidate for the primitive treaty oath is Jupiter (Feretrius) through the implementation of the flintstone.[1] The form of such an oath of mutual allegiance may have resembled that sworn by certain Latins against the Romans[2] and

---

[1] See Walbank on Pol. 3. 25 and Ogilvie on Livy 1. 24. 4–9.

[2] Varro, *LL* 6. 18: 'dies Poplifugia videtur nominatus, quod eo die tumultu repente fugerit populus; non multo enim post hic dies quam decessus Gallorum ex urbe, et qui tum sub urbe populi, ut Ficuleates ac Fidenates et finitimi alii, contra nos coniurarunt.

by the Samnite *legiones linteatae*.[1] Although Jupiter would have supplied a common ground to the Latins at Rome, he may not have served the Etruscan elements. The archaic oath *eiuno*[2] would have been inviolable by all elements. Furthermore, the universal curial cult of Juno is attested. If our interpretation of the origins of these Junos is nearly correct, then this deity is especially appropriate to the function of a binding national oath.

No discussion of an oath and a treaty of this kind can be complete without a discussion of the priestly college of Fetiales who had charge of the declaration of war and conclusion of peace down to the Second Punic War. The Fetiales through their chief agent, the *pater patratus*, seem to be the representatives of the Quirites.[3] In light of our later discussion of the *patres*[4] the title may be connected in origin with the primitive senate of *patres*, the *patricii*,[5] and the curias. Varro alone, preserved by another, says the Fetiales constituted a sacral college of twenty men.[6] All accounts of the Fetiales agree that they had to reach a decision among themselves before presenting it to the senate or people for a final vote. Therefore, the number of Fetiales is not only unprecedentedly high but also is incompatible with obtaining a majority vote. No other archaic Republican priesthood or sodality exceeded twelve members. The later colleges of augurs and pontiffs had an uneven number of members. Therefore, I propose two alternatives. First, either our authority wrote *triginta* which itself, or its numeral XXX, was corrupted to *viginti* or XX. Or secondly, by Varro's day the number of curiate representatives had dwindled from thirty to twenty. The Fetiales seem to me to represent in an official manner the thirty curias because the Fetiales could summarily try and hand over a Roman citizen found guilty of violating a treaty with another state.[7] Roman citizens, especially noble citizens, did not lightly surrender so grave a power to anybody

aliquot huius diei vestigia fugae in sacris apparent, de quibus rebus Antiquitatum Libri plura referunt'.

[1] See below, pp. 235–6.   [2] Charisius, p. 258 B. See Palmer, *Juno*.
[3] Livy 1. 24. 4–9, 1. 32. 5–14 and Ogilvie thereon. Cf. Varro, *De Vita Populi Romani* in Nonius, 850 L. On *populus Romanus Quiritium*, see above, pp. 156–60. For the Fetiales see Samter, *RE* 6. 2 (1909), cols 2259–65 and Kübler in De Ruggiero, *Diz. Epigr. s.v.*
[4] Below, pp. 197–202.
[5] See D.H. 2. 72, who calls them the élite of the finest families.
[6] Non. p. 529 M. = 850 L.: Varro, *De Vita Populi Romani*, lib. III: 'si cuius legati violati essent, qui id fecissent, quamvis nobiles essent, uti dederentur civitati statuerunt; fetialesque viginti, qui de his rebus cognoscerent, iudicarent et statuerent et constituerent'.
[7] The function of the 'trial' was later taken over by the Fathers. See Varro (n. 6);

but the assemblies. Without knowledge of the religious and legal
bases and particulars it would be rash to say how the Fetiales exercised the power. When they did exercise it, they must have had a
broader based authority than our sources tell. A hint of the Fetiales'
role in internal politics and of a connection with the curias is found in
Dionysius. He reports that the plebs and patricians were reconciled
by a compact which the Fetiales worked during the first secession
before the curiate assembly elected the first tribunes of the plebs.
The persons of the new tribunes were sacred to Ceres. Tradition,
however, attributes a dedication to Jupiter the Terrifier on the Holy
Mount by the plebeians (*AR* 6. 89–90). Jupiter Feretrius regularly
oversaw the keeping of the Fetiales' oath. The purpose of the plebeian dedication to Jupiter *Deimatias* cannot have been what
Dionysius reported, that the god's epithet (which we do not know in
its Latin form) preserved recollection of the plebs' fright. Rather, as a
god of oaths, the Terrifier was expected to strike terror into whosoever failed to keep the compact which the Fetiales supervised. The
rest of the Roman tradition knows the Fetiales as envoys to foreign
peoples. Their participation in the settlement of the secession seems to
me to have been derived from an archaic constitutional representation of their several curias.

If we hold that the Fetiales, as patrician representatives of their
curias, for some time renewed the mutual treaties of communion,
the annual renewal of Rome's treaty with Lavinium, brought to
light in the wake of the Latin War,[1] could have had the curial circumstances as a living precedent.

The oath and renewal of curiate adhesion would have taken place
in the Roman Comitium where new Romans deposited earth from
their previous homelands. The Comitium may once have been planted
with a holy grove appropriate to public meetings[2] and oath-taking.[3]

Cic. *Caec.* 98, *Leg.* 2. 9. 21, *De or.* 1. 181, 2. 137, *Off.* 3. 107–10; Livy 8. 39. 10–15, 9. 8. 6,
9. 10; D.H. 2. 72; Plut. *Cam.* 18. 1–4. See Ogilvie on Livy 5. 35–6.

[1] Livy 8. 11. 15: 'extra poenam fuere Latinorum Laurentes Campanorumque equites
quia non desciverant; cum Laurentibus renovari foedus iussum renovaturque ex eo
quotannis post diem decimum Latinarum [*sc.* feriarum]'. Cf. 1. 14. 2, 5. 52. 8, Serv.
Dan. on *Aen.* 2. 296, Macr. *Sat.* 3. 14. 11. The Lavinians had a special fetial for their part
of the renewal (*CIL* x, 797 = *ILS* 5004): 'pater patratus populi Laurentis foederis ex
libris Sibullinis percutiendi cum p(opulo) R(omano), sacrorum principiorum p(opuli)
R(omani) Quirit(ium) nominisque Latini quai apud Laurentis coluntur'. See De Sanctis
2², 267–8.

[2] See Palmer, 'King'. The emperor Claudius struck treaties with foreign kings according to Fetial Law in the Forum (Suet. *Cl.* 25. 5).

[3] Livy 3. 25. 6–9 with Ogilvie's comment.

In conclusion, this chapter has been devoted to the formal procedure of creating new curias with their new Romans. After parleys and internal discussion on two sides, we imagine, the procedure commenced with the evocation of the Juno which was destined to become Quiritis. With divine assent, the new Quirites commingled the soil of their land with that of the Roman Comitium or of another site before the Comitium became the civic center. This act was annually renewed at Parilia (but perhaps in historical times only by the original Palatine curias who seem to have been the most conservative, viz. Old Curias). At some point Juno was invoked and oaths were exchanged over a treaty. In our sources there survive traces of annual renewals of an oath and a treaty in other connections. Similar renewals may have been made by the curias. In the same vein we have proposed a curial origin for thirty Fetiales because of their extraordinary number, executive competence and role in the first secession. Lastly, the unanimous *lex curiata* which had an entirely different explicit purpose may have carried incidental assurance of every curia's loyalty to the new king or imperial magistrate.

CHAPTER 9

THE CURIATE CONSTITUTION

In the previous chapters on the origins of the curias I argue that the curias represented the sometime disparate ethnic elements which came to constitute the citizenry of historical Rome. The number of curias had increased by migration, transportation of conquered peoples to Rome and adherence to the Roman curiate system by formal treaty. Until the adoption of the centuriate military system which supplanted a threefold military system based upon territorial tribes, the curias maintained their own augurs and exercise of the auspices. At that time the curias numbered twenty-seven. After the Servian reform the last three curias were created. The Curias Crustumina and Gabina participated in the curiate constitution by virtue of treaties of isopolity; Curia Claudia joined the curiate constitution through the migration of the Sabine Claudii. The curias constituted the sole repository of domestic, religious and political authority and exercised this authority in meetings of the several curias. Although the curias had different names and their members might be designated by the name of the curia, all members of all curias bore the official title *Quirites* which betokened the relationship between the individual and the united state and, in effect, the equality of all curial members before the central government which rested upon the consent of the curias.

Roman tradition bespeaks the priority and precedence of the curias as a state assembly (*comitia curiata*).[1] Few of its comitial responsibilities remained clearly defined because the curiate assembly had become a political fossil when students of Roman history began to write. Consequently the evidence pointing to a reason for its political decline and to the approximate time of its subordination to the centuriate and tribal assemblies does not emerge clearly from later Roman attitudes. Although the Romans recognized imperfectly

---

[1] E.g. Cic. *Rep.* 2. 13. 25: 'qui [sc. Numa] ut huc venit, quamquam populus curiatis eum comitiis regem esse iusserat, tamen ipse de suo imperio curiatam legem tulit'; 2. 17. 31: 'mortuo rege Pompilio Tullum Hostilium populus regem interrege rogante comitiis curiatis creavit, isque de imperio suo exemplo Pompili populum consuluit curiatim'.

an historical development of the centuriate and tribal assemblies which exercised certain powers in the last centuries of the Republic never intended at their inception, Roman historians failed to remark any appreciable history of the curiate assembly which they presumed had very nearly lapsed into political inactivity after King Servius Tullius.[1]

In his *Roman Antiquities* Dionysius of Halicarnassus supplies more detail than the briefly explicit and implicit accounts of those authors who had occasion to refer to the curiate assembly. Servius Tullius deliberately transferred the elections, the legislative power and the right to declare war to the centuries from the curias which had exercised that government from Romulus' dispensation (4. 20. 3; cf. 2. 14). Tarquin II proceeded to forbid the religious meetings of curias, *vici* and *pagi* (4. 43). Thereby Dionysius implies that the curias' political meetings had already ceased. However, Junius Brutus could summon the curias in his capacity of tribune of the Celeres (4. 71; cf. 4. 75, 5. 12). The curias, which were supposed to have been suppressed, voted the expulsion of the last king while the centuries proceeded to the election of the new government (4. 84). One of the new magistrates' first acts was the restoration of sacrifice which Servius had allowed to the *phyletai* and *demotai* but which Tarquin had abolished (5. 2. 2). Presumably, Dionysius intends *phyletai* to refer to the curias and *demotai* to the *vici* and *pagi*. In the same first year of the Republic the thirty curias voted on the restoration of Tarquin II to his Roman properties. Dionysius blunders outrageously in saying that Tarquin's property reverted to him by a single vote because the thirty curias could not issue a majority of one if they numbered thirty (5. 6)! Thus we see that the restoration of the Servian centuriate system and its concomitant supersession of the already suppressed curias were thought to have left the curias in a political limbo where they could exercise only religious functions. Such an ancient inference was not only unfounded in fact but contradicted by the evidence on their continuous political authority in certain spheres of government and in civil processes.

This chapter aims at the correction of generally erroneous Roman opinion and at the solution of problems regarding the early constitu-

---

[1] Romans believed the curias had only religious superintendence (e.g. Varro, *LL* 5. 155, 6. 15, 6. 46) and were defunct (Cic. *L. Agr.* 2. 11. 27, 12. 31). For Roman views of Servius' constitution see Cic. *Rep.* 2. 22, Livy 1. 42–3.

tion of the Republic and the cleavage between patrician and plebeian. To put the matter squarely before the reader, I propose to show that down to the Licinio-Sextian Rogations of 367 two constitutions, curiate and centuriate, coexisted and functioned separately. It is only fair to reaffirm at the outset my own credence in the traditional dating of most constitutional decisions and of the lists of the eponymous magistrates. Recent works particularly on the date of the Republic's foundation have done the service of a catalyst to which an anticatalyst may now be applied.[1] The results of archaeological trenches in Rome do not modify the literary tradition unless supported by soundly dated epigraphic evidence.[2] The drastic rearrangement of eponyms in the lists of magistrates has, in the main, simply muddied the waters.[3] The present state of the lists does not evince infallibility, but despite their mistakes the Romans who kept and compiled them had more information at their disposal than we.

THE CURIATE CIVIL SYSTEM

Imperial jurists and antiquarians report and comment on the nonpolitical transactions of the curiate assembly and at the same time report its demise along with a part of its legal heritage surviving in the Republic. From the jurists we learn of the process of adoption, its attendant relinquishment of religious rites and lastly a testamentary formula, all of which fell under the control of the curias. These curiate activities lasted at least as long as the Republic itself.

The procedure of adoption reserved for curiate approval was loosely called an adrogation. The pontiffs presided over an assembly of the curias as *comitia calata*. The person adopted could not be a minor or in the power of his father but had to be a *homo sui iuris*. The person adopting had to have passed the time of siring children to which he swore an oath which also protected the property of the adopted party from the adopter.[4] The question put to the curias was:

---

[1] E.g. R. Werner, *Der Beginn der römischen Republik* (Munich, 1963).

[2] The works of E. Gjerstad are a case in point on which see Momigliano, 'Interim Report', pp. 95–108 and M. Pallottino, 'Fatti e legende (moderne) sulla più antica storia di Roma' *St. Etr.* 31 (1963), 3–37.

[3] See Werner, *Der Beginn der römischen Republik*. (Munich, 1963), especially pp. 264–94 and Momigliano's review of his book in *Riv. St. Ital.* 76 (1964), 803–6.

[4] Cic. *Dom.* 34–8; Tac. *Hist.* 1. 15; Gellius 5. 19. 1–8; Gaius, *Inst.* 1. 98–107, *Epit.* 1. 5, *Dig.* 1. 7. 2; Ulpian, *Tit.* 8, *Dig.* 1. 7. 17. See F. Schulz, *Classical Roman Law* (Oxford, 1951), sections 241–53.

'velitis, iubeatis uti L. Valerius L. Titio tam iure legeque filius siet, quam si ex eo patre matreque familias eius natus esset, utique ei vitae necisque in eum potestas siet, utique patri endo filio est? haec ita, uti dixi, ita vos, Quirites, rogo'.[1] This procedure of adrogatory adoption could be followed only at Rome. What the Romans called a proper adoption (*adoptio*) was transacted before the praetor or another magistrate. In effect, the difference lay in the approving body. The curiate assembly controlled the adrogatory adoption; the officers of the centuriate constitution controlled what is simply called adoption.[2] The *ius* by which the adopted son became as if an actual son was the *ius* of the Quirites to whom the pontiff put the question. The *lex* was the curiate vote by which the adrogation was approved. A freedman could not be adopted by adrogation because he had no curia and therefore a praetor's court was resorted to in his adoption. Our sources tell us that the two parties to the adrogation had to be freeborn. But if they could resort to the praetor, the sources have misunderstood the historical reason for excluding freedmen from adoption by adrogation in the curiate assembly.[3] Both parties had to be freeborn and presumably members of curias. All Quirites, in the strict sense of the word, were freeborn. Manumission did not give the new citizen membership in a curia. A freedman, of course, also was not a *homo sui iuris*.

The person whose adoption was enacted by adrogation in the curias also forswore certain religious rites (*detestatio sacrorum*). Only

[1] Gellius, 5. 19. 9. The very question as well as the term *adrogatio* presupposes comitial action although some modern writers claim a 'called' assembly did not actually vote. See Catalano, pp. 238–46.

[2] See above, p. 191, n. 4 and Cic. *Dom.* 39 and 77 on the authority of the thirty curias. When writing of the praetor's jurisdiction, I understand that the consul exercised the same jurisdiction before 366 since the magistrate later called 'consul' had formerly been called either 'praetor' or 'judge' (*Comm. Cons.* in Varro, *LL* 6. 88, Cic. *Leg.* 3. 3. 8, Livy 3. 55. 11–12, Zon. 7. 19).

[3] Cato and Masurius Sabinus in Gellius 5. 19. 11–14. The Lex Julia Papia permitted adrogatory adoption by conceding *iura ingenui* to freedmen; see Marcellus, *Dig.* 23. 2. 32. Later Romans believed the patricians alone were *ingenui* perhaps in light of the later curiate assembly. Festus 277 L. (= Bremer 1. 253): 'patricios, Cincius ait, in libro de comitiis eos appellari solitos qui nunc ingenui vocentur'. This statement probably arises from the false inference that Romans who resorted to the curiate assembly were patrician. For instance, P. Clodius had himself adopted through the curiate assembly; yet the Fonteius who adopted him was plebeian. So far as we know, *liberti* were not excluded from either the centuriate or tribal assembly. A bronze tablet, found in Rome, may have been posted at a meeting place of the curiate assembly (*CIL* 1², 2388 = xv, 7151 = *ILLRP* 1266): 'l(ocus) d(atus) ingenuiis qui ad subfragia descendunt'. Cf. Livy 10. 8. 10, 34. 1. 4–5; D.H. 2. 8. 3; Suet. *Caes.* 13. On *liberti* and *vernulae* in Italian curias see pp. 59–62, 64.

Cicero who had no keen grasp of the law and ventilated publicly the whole question of Clodius' adrogatory adoption in order to condemn Clodius and embarrass the college of pontiffs[1] specifies that this religion belonged to the family (*gens*) of the adopted.[2] The forsworn *sacra* must have included both the *sacra* of the family and of the curia. Otherwise, the adoption before the praetor would have required a similar forswearing.

The third legislative act of the curias concerning non-political matters was one of the two oldest forms of testament. Since it was transacted in the *comitia calata*, the chief pontiff presumably also put the question and, what is more, he had framed the will according to formula.[3] Gaius says the comitial testament had fallen into disuse by his time along with the other archaic form of will. When the *comitia calata* still approved this kind of will, it was convened but twice a year. The restriction, no doubt, reflects a change at a time when few Quirites resorted to the pontiff and the curiate assembly in order to make their testamentary dispositions. The second archaic form of will depended upon neither the pontiff nor the curiate assembly. Rather it was a ritual statement by the testator to a comrade when they stood in battle-order (*testamentum in procinctu*). Our sources do not clarify how imminent battle was.[4] A Roman probably had the right to make a military will *in extremis* during the period when only the formulary will could be drawn by the pontiff who submitted it to the curias. However it too became a formulated means of circumventing pontiff and curias and could be declared merely in centuriate

---

[1] *Dom.* 34–8. See Schulz, *Roman Law*, pp. 145, 147. On Cicero as a student of law, Schulz, *History of Roman Legal Science* (Oxford, 1946), pp. 44, 68–9. On Clodius' adoption, etc., see also Dio Cass. 37. 51. 1–2, 38. 12. 1–2, 39. 11. One assumes Clodius had belonged to Curia Claudia.

[2] Gellius 15. 27. 3 (cf. 7. 2. 1); Gaius, *Dig.* 50. 16. 238; Ulpian, *Dig.* 50. 16. 40. Cicero, *Dom.* 14. 35, summing up one argument against Clodius, says: 'ita perturbatis sacris, contaminatis gentibus, et quam deseruisti et quam polluisti, iure Quiritium legitimo tutelarum et hereditatium relicto, factus es eius filius contra fas cuius per aetatem pater esse potuisti'. Hissing this sentence, the spell-binder calls attention to the *ius Quiritium legitimum* appertaining to curial business.

[3] Gellius 15. 27. 3; Gaius, *Inst.* 2. 101; Ulpian, *Tit.* 20. 1–2; Just. *Inst.* 2. 10. 1.

[4] *Ibid.* (cf. Isid. *Etym.* 10. 218). On both kinds of will see Schulz, *Roman Law*, sections 361, 431. There and in *A History of Roman Legal Science*, p. 19 Schulz emphasizes the pontiff's role in drafting the adoption and the testament. The ritual is reported by Schol. Veron. on *Aen.* 10. 241 (Bruns[7] 2. 78): 'viros voca, proelium ineant. deinde exercitu in aciem educta iterum [morabantur, ut immolare]tur. interim ea mora utebantur qui testamenta in procinctu facere volebant.' See pp. 87–9. De Sanctis IV, part 2, tome 2, p. 52 suggests this will might have been made in any centuriate assembly. If its procedure had become as much a part of ritual formula as the auspices which were prescribed before it, then it cannot have been so spontaneous and informal as the jurists suggest.

battle-order whether or not battle was imminent. In other words, it parallels the adoption before the praetor just as the adrogatory adoption parallels the testament in the *comitia calata*, for this will was made while the testator was under the command of a centuriate officer.

The third archaic form of testament was the fictitious sale by bronze and balance (*mancipatio per aes et libram*). In this case the formula of sale appears to have drawn partly on the formula recited in the *comitia calata*: 'haec ita ut in his tabulis cerisve scripta sunt, ita do ita lego ita testor itaque vos, Quirites, testimonium mihi perhibetote'. The clause of this formal declaration (*nuncupatio*) pertinent to the comitial procedure of the curias is the last, by which the testator calls on the Quirites to serve as witnesses to the will.[1] All three wills, by assembly, in battle array and by sale, originated in the desire either to make legitimate heir(s) or to avoid bequest to the legitimate heir(s) who were either the nearest agnate or the whole clan (*gentiles*).[2]

The pontiff alone summoned his curiate assembly, specially named *comitia calata*, on the Capitol at the Curia Calabra. This meeting-place was usually reserved for sacral purpose while, if we may judge by the practice of the *rex sacrorum*, the Forum or Comitium held curiate assemblies convoked by the king and the curio maximus.[3] Since the comitial adoption and comitial testament both involved either a transfer of person and property or of property alone from one family to another, it might well be asked why the curiate assembly had to approve the transfer. To answer that both transfers perhaps involved sacred rites suffices to explain only the office of the comitial president. Rather the transactions must have concerned transfers from one curia to another although no ancient authority

---

[1] Gaius, *Inst.* 2. 102–5; Ulpian, *Tit.* 20. 2–9 (cf. Isid. *Etym.* 5. 24. 12 who modernizes). On borrowing the formula from the phraseology in the curiate assembly see C. W. Westrup, *Introduction to Early Roman Law* II (Copenhagen and London, 1934), 129 ff., Schulz, *Roman Law*, sections 423–33, and De Francisci, pp. 584–8.

[2] *Lex XII Tab.* 5. 4–5: 'si intestato moritur, cui suus heres nec escit, adgnatus proximus familiam habeto. si adgnatus nec escit, gentiles familiam [habento]'. According to L. Cincius in Festus 83 L. (= Bremer I, 257) the *gentiles* were those who bore the same name and came from the same *genus*. See Schulz, *Roman Law*, pp. 224–5, 254. On *genus* as another word for *curia*, see chapter 5.

[3] Varro, *LL* 6. 27–8, 6. 31 (cf. 5. 13, 5. 155); Macr. *Sat.* 1. 15. 19. That the curio maximus posted instruction in the Forum in Ovid's day (*F.* 2. 527–30) points to a defunct curiate assembly called by him at the Comitium in order to assign the curias their parts in the Fornacalia. See Taylor, *Voting Assemblies*, pp. 3–5, 41.

suggests this. By the date of the Twelve Tables Roman citizens had certainly found ways to bypass the curiate constitution through the centuriate constitution both in order to make a will and to adopt a son before a magistrate elected by the centuries.[1]

The contrast between curias and centurias is not limited to inheritance and adoption. The division also underlies the kinds of ownership. Romans might own property either in accordance with the *ius Quiritium*, called quiritary rights, or in accordance with the formula *in bonis habere*, called bonitary ownership. In the latter case ownership was protected by the praetor. Furthermore, if litigation over ownership was based upon equally just claims, divergent only with regard to quiritary and bonitary ownership, the praetor found in favor of the bonitary owner. In this instance, the owner under praetorian (i.e. centuriate) law had prior rights over the owner under curiate law. Besides the Roman citizen who alone could enjoy these rights, any non-Roman with a grant of *commercium* enjoyed the same rights.[2]

Although the *ius Quiritium* extended far beyond the right to own property and make valid contracts (*commercium*) and, in fact, was the primitive Roman citizenship, this one article of quiritary rights demonstrates the character of the curial interrelations. Adoptions, testaments and religious rites were subject to curiate review. Other domestic and business matters, however, did not come before the curiate assembly. Ownership of property and contracts equally valid among all Quirites belong to the constitutional agreement among the Roman curias. A constitutional situation in which parties to a contract from different curias had to seek the approval of the curiate assembly would never have promoted a civic unity such as the Romans enjoyed. Secondly, a constitutional situation in which

---

[1] Schulz, *Roman Law*, section 432 interprets Gaius, *Inst.* 2. 101 to mean the testaments in the curiate assembly and battle array went back to the XII Tables. The fictitious sale of a son recorded in the Tables (4. 2) presupposes the father's intention to emancipate the son that he might be adopted; see Schulz, section 249. Since there is no valid evidence of a single citizen's enrollment in a curia after the kings, the Fonteius who adopted P. Clodius should have had curiate citizenship. Yet some Fonteii were Tusculan (Cic. *Font.* 18. 41). On the other hand, the archaic Roman names Tarpeius, Rabuleius and Canuleius demonstrate the possibility of an early Roman family of Fonteii. None of the four parties named by Cic. *Dom.* 35 in two other adoptions is patrician and their families do not go back to fourth-century Rome. Perhaps their cases were heard by a praetor.

[2] Gaius, *Inst.* 1. 32–5, 1. 54, 2. 40–2, 2. 88; Ulpian, *Tit.* 19. See Schulz, *Roman Law*, sections 586–9.

parties to a marriage from different curias had to seek the approval of the curiate assembly would never have conduced to the same unity and ethnic assimilation which must have happened between the arrival of various peoples and the fruitful synoecism of a Roman people. Yet, approval of marriages might have been an analogue to curiate approval of adoption, forswearing religious rites and testamentary disposition that removed person and property from the power and succession of agnates and clan. When Dionysius says that Gabii and Rome concluded a treaty of isopolity, he certainly means the rights of contract and marriage (*commercium* and *conubium*) were exchanged.[1] We should see in these rights the paths to a national fusion and the weakening of curial ties. At the same time, we should not try to discern a conscious effort to promote a national fusion and weakening of curial strength by these means, even if it worked to the advantage of the king and, later, of the centuriate system as I believe it did. The men and their aims were much simpler; and their results, much greater than their expectations.

Recently De Visscher has argued that the right of intermarriage (*conubium*) primarily touches the conduct of private affairs of Latin patrician families.[2] Following Last and Magdelain I believe that the distinction between patricians and plebeians must have been made for the first time after the foundation of the Republic.[3] Hence, *conubium* ought to be related to the primitive *ius Quiritium* as is *commercium*. In early practice, *conubium* is legitimate exogamy, nothing more or less. To be sure, it is a peculiar form of exogamy, exogamy among persons of the same state but not necessarily among persons of the same ethnic antecedents and civil condition. Latins from diverse communal backgrounds, Sabines and Etruscans all composed the state of one Rome. When the authors of the Twelve Tables attempted to impose a developing class distinction by forbidding marriage between patrician and plebeian, they violated the older *ius Quiritium* which allowed marriage between any persons of any curia. Early law often articulated what custom had allowed prior to its infraction. But in this case it was the law which violated custom and right. Accordingly the Canuleian Law of 445 promptly confirmed Quiritary *conubium*

---

[1] D.H. 4. 58. See above, pp. 138–9, 181.

[2] F. De Visscher, ' "Conubium" et "Civitas"', *RIDA* ser. 2, 1 (1952), 401–22.

[3] H. Last, 'The Servian Reforms, *JRS* 35 (1945), 30–4; A. Magdelain, 'Auspicia', pp. 450–73.

and set aside the offending article of the Twelve Tables. Roman tradition explicitly affirms the fact that in some respects the Twelve Tables had violated ancestral custom.[1] The law of 445 imposed upon the patricians themselves the regulation of their peers. From the quarrels over the article in the Tables emerges clearly the fact that *conubium*, as originally conceived, implied a legitimate relationship among Quirites. This right of intermarriage or of exogamy did not grow out of internal castes or international marital ties. Rather, its roots must be followed to the ethnic disparity of the Quirites' diverse customs which could not be publicly recognized in the matter of marriage. Otherwise, Latin might have married only Latin, Etruscan only Etruscan, Sabine only Sabine at Rome. A people's adherence to the curiate constitution involved the surrender of its control over marriage and contract.

'PATRES, PATRICII, PLEBS'

Ancient authors mention the distinction between patricians and plebeians from the beginning of Roman history until Caesar created the former from the latter. Unfortunately these same authorities have not left us a proper definition of the terms. What survive are puerile explanations. Yet the Romans made and observed the distinction although their writers portray quarrels of the two castes in the mold of the *optimates* and *populares*. We have already remarked that the distinction was important in the adrogatory adoption of Clodius, a patrician, by Fonteius, a plebeian, in the curiate assembly and in the control of marriage asserted by the Law of the Twelve Tables. Throughout this chapter we return to the distinction until we reach some conclusions on the nature of the patricians and on the relation of the Fathers to the curias. Before an examination of details necessary to any comprehension of the terms *patres*, *patricii* and *plebs* a few preliminary statements as to how far the terms themselves can inform us seem in order.

The word *pater* bore an honorific sense besides its primitive sense 'father'. So it was applied to gods, particularly Jupiter and Mars, and to the priestly envoy, the Fetiales' *pater patratus*. It was not, however, a common priestly title as it is found in the Roman church. Applied to men it usually had a special significance among members of the

---

[1] Cic. *Rep.* 2. 37. 63; Livy 4. 1–6. See Last, 'The Servian Reforms'.

Roman *senatus*, the 'body of old men', who were sometimes divided into the *patres* and the *conscripti*. Of the senators only the Fathers were lawfully called upon to legitimatize a law or an election by their *auctoritas*, that is by their 'being sponsors' of the law and election, *patribus auctoribus*. At first this happened before the submission of the bill or candidates to the people's assembly when they could withhold approval, but in later times after the enactment or election when they had to accede. The other true power which the *patres* exercised on occasion was the interregnum. When the king was dead or, in the Republic, the major magistracies were vacant, the auspices were said to 'return to the Fathers', who by an elaborate procedure, imperfectly known to us, controlled the election of new magistrates while they themselves provided the government. In determining which men were Fathers, the Romans sought an ex-magistrate who had exercised the *imperium* and who came from a patrician family. At once we must ask what made a patrician family and how a man could be a Father under the Roman kings when to be an interim king, *interrex*, could not have required a former magistrate with the *imperium*. In contrast to these constitutional powers, the Fathers could not participate in a plebeian meeting (*concilium plebis*) and claimed an exemption from the legislation enacted by this kind of meeting (*plebiscita*).

Besides being the Fathers, these men were not members of the plebs. Whereas the notion of the Fathers as potential interrexes must by definition reach back to the royal constitution, the notion of the *plebs* cannot be firmly dated any earlier than the first secession of the plebs in 494 when they elected their own tribunes. The word itself may be related to the root of the Latin verb *ple-* 'to fill' and the Greek noun *plēthos* 'the many'. The meaning of *plebs* is clear enough. The plebs were those who were not the Fathers and were the majority of citizens. We have mentioned the article of the Law of the Twelve Tables around 450 which forbade marriage between the plebs and the patricians, and was set aside by a plebeian enactment in 445. In 367–366 the consulship, the chief magistracy, was opened to plebeians and one-half of the enlarged board of Ten Men for Sacrificing was reserved to the plebeians. In 342 one consul was required by law to be plebeian and in 300 one-half of the augural and pontifical colleges was set aside for plebeians only. What powers did the plebs have? Their assembly could pass laws binding only on themselves

198

and elect tribunes to protect their rights and aediles. Since plebeians could not serve in the interregnum or approve proposed laws which alone were binding on all Romans or pass on candidates to the magistracies of all the people, their powers were indeed slight in comparison with those of the Fathers. However, the strife during the early Republic did not arise between plebs and *patres* as such, but between the plebs and the patricians who were by no means identical with the *patres*.

The *patres* to whom the auspices returned in time of anarchy had to be *patricii* before ever they were magistrates with the *imperium* and auspices. This is, linguistically speaking, preposterous. The word *patricius* is derived from *pater* with a suffix -*icius*, met also in *aedilicius*, *tribunicius*, *sodalicius* etc. Thus, *patricius* implies being 'of the *pater*' and yet a *pater* had to be *patricius*. The royal interrex as *pater* could not have been a former imperial magistrate and the Republican *pater* had to be a former imperial magistrate and a *patricius*. A man did not become a *patricius* as he became a *pater*, he was born a *patricius* into a certain family. In the broadest sense he was not born of a father, a definition countenanced by ancient statements on patrician origins. He was born into a clan which had had a member who was a *pater* in the sense of *interrex* or *auctor* among the senators who were former imperial magistrates. The rules of Roman kingship required *patres* for the transmission of power and the approval of potential laws. Since these *patres* cannot have been former magistrates, the other criterion for a Republican *pater*, namely patrician birth, may or may not have obtained under the kings. If patrician birth was required for service in the capacity of *pater*, the position must precede the class, for a family cannot have been patrician before there was a *pater* from it. Therefore, the *patricii* formed a class of men after the institution and function of the Fathers. What powers did patricians exercise as a body or constitutional element? None. A patrician enjoyed a certain eligibility by reason of birth. He could hold certain offices and perform certain functions that a plebeian could not hold and perform. If we ask ourselves about patrician eligibility during the kingship, we must limit our question to the office of the king himself. If Tullius was a patrician, then one Roman king was patrician. However, the king of the Romans did not have to be patrician.

In his elegant rage against Clodius Cicero tells us what functions were proper to the patricians: the magistracies, the priestly kingship, the flaminates, the Salian priesthoods, one-half of the other priest-hoods, the approval of curiate and centuriate assemblies and the auspices of the Roman people. The *auctoritas patrum* and the auspices of the people inherent in the institution of the interregnum would indeed have died out without *magistratus patricii* as Cicero claims (*Dom.* 14.38). These were the two functions of all the *patres*, not of any *patricius*. The other cases given by Cicero fit the *patricii*, not the *patres*. Nevertheless, we know the name of a plebeian priest-king and are informed of certain flaminates open to plebeians. The half of the remaining priesthoods are doubtless the augurate, pontificate and decemvirate. From another source we learn that the auspices of the patrician magistrates belonged to the consulship, praetorship and censorship (A. Gellius, 13. 15. 4). Not every consul, praetor and censor was patrician. Indeed, one consul and one censor had to be patrician up to certain dates, but a patrician praetor was required only briefly. In this chapter and in Appendix III, I discuss the patri-cian requirements and their temporal limits in detail. For the time being I summarize our knowledge of the terms *patres*, *patricii* and *plebs*.

The Fathers had fixed powers, exercised on certain occasions. They did not act whenever and wherever they wished to act. They were a small part of the group of patricians, for they alone had once had the *imperium* and its attendant auspices. Patricians *qua* patricians also had power only when they were empowered to act by virtue of an annual magistracy or a perpetual priesthood. The Fathers had to act in their capacity of Fathers when the situation demanded that they act. The patricians acted in their capacity of magistrate or priest. Their patriciate did not demand certain functions. Patrician birth meant access to civil powers. The status of a Father implied a residual power exerted on certain constitutional occasions. In a negative way, the patricians maintained themselves exempt from plebeian legislation.

The plebs were bound by all legislation if the Fathers approved or if their own assembly passed it. The plebs had no power by birth or by virtue of a previous magistracy. When plebeians were elected to magistracies or made priests, they had the same powers as their patrician colleagues. Their disability lay in their exclusion from certain magistracies and priesthoods until legislation changed the rules. By the same token they could fill two offices not open to the patricians, the plebeian tribunate and aedileship. A patrician could legally fill these offices only if he legally ceased to be a patrician.

In the early Republic the contrast of castes was drawn between the plebeians on the one side and the patricians on the other. The Fathers as Fathers represent the patricians. However, the Fathers were not the antagonists of the plebs, for their powers were theirs alone and their powers were not exercised by the patricians or the plebeians. When we read of the *patres* in ancient authors, we can determine their powers, know their limitations, recognize their clans and assume their prior imperial magistracies. Men became Fathers while men were born patrician and plebeian. A patrician became a Father under given conditions, a plebeian could never become a Father. A plebeian could never become a patrician; a patrician could become a plebeian. The plebs could prevent a patrician from becoming a Father by withholding their votes and never electing him to an imperial magistracy. The patrician's only means of becoming a Father without the intervention of the plebs was an appointment to the imperial dictatorship.

That only the institution of the Fathers can certainly be proved royal does not mean that the patriciate was not royal. That the plebs first organized themselves after the Republic's foundation does not mean that no plebs existed before 495. However, nothing proves that either patriciate or plebs as castes were recognized under the kings of the Romans. Because the one requirement for being a Father arises from the constitutional order of Republican annual and imperial magistracies, the sole remaining requirement of patrician birth was either a royal requirement or another Republican institution. If it was royal, patrician clans must have had a *pater* in their ancestry. What was the qualification of the first 'father'? The Romans said that Romulus made the patricians and the first senate. How are we to explain the majority of 'plebeian' kings created by 'patrician' Fathers if a king created the senate and the Fathers and the patricians? Marcius, Hostilius, Pompilius, Tullius and Tarquinius, not a single king can be shown to be patrician.

The patriciate was not a demonstrable criterion for eligibility to the one and only office of the royal period whose incumbents are named with any certainty by the Roman tradition. The kings could have been plebeian if, in fact, such a distinction existed. The interregnal Fathers created 'plebeian' kings. Yet time and time again our authorities emphasize the patriciate of the king's political successor, the Republican consul, and a single authority asserts the patriciate of the priest-king, the religious successor.

For the purposes of this study which centers on the question of the Fathers' power and the patricians' eligibility I emphasize the desirability of ascertaining the constitutional origins of the Republican castes. The Fathers alone enjoyed the capacity of presiding at electoral assemblies during the anarchy. Interregnal government has a far more prominent place in early Roman history than is met after the third century.

PROCEDURE IN THE CURIATE ASSEMBLY

Before discussing the political powers of the curiate assembly its procedure must be detailed insofar as our evidence allows. From the point of view of chronology the curiate system laid the foundation for the two assemblies, centuriate and tribal. The most important aspect of the curiate constitution was the vote by discrete units which originally represented diverse peoples incorporated into the Roman state of the Quirites. Each curia met and conducted its own balloting; its meeting (*comitium*) had presumably greater implications than the meeting of a Servian tribe whose balloting as a unit simply followed a pattern laid down by the curiate constitution, because the several curias had business of their own which did not concern all the curias. This we know from the vestiges of curial religious observances in the late Republic. When the curias held meetings to decide matters touching all the curias, the sum of the meetings constituted a state assembly (*comitia curiata*). No matter what the purpose of the several meetings, the curias began their meetings with the taking of the auspices. The twenty-seven Roman Argei originally were augural sites for the curias and, furthermore, the Sodales Titii and Fratres Marcii survived into historical times as augural brotherhoods of the Curias Titia and Marcia. Livy preserves a precious notice of curiate procedure which has been much neglected and recently doubted:[1]

Papirius C. Iunium Bubulcum magistrum equitum dixit; atque ei legem curiatam de imperio ferenti triste omen diem diffidit, quod Faucia curia fuit principium, duabus insignis cladibus, captae urbis et Caudinae

---

[1] Livy 9. 38. 15–39. 1. U. Hall, 'Voting Procedures in the Roman Assemblies', *Historia* 13 (1964), 274–5 says the evidence of the *principium* is uncertain. She has no evidence for her assertion and can adduce none. She discusses curias on pp. 269–71 and the curiate assembly on pp. 273–5. On p. 283 f. she says the curias did not elect the king.

pacis, quod utroque anno eiusdem curiae fuerat principium. Macer Licinius tertia etiam clade, quae ad Cremeram accepta est, abominandam eam curiam facit. dictator postero die auspiciis repetitis pertulit legem.

Livy had two authorities for his account. Both authorities agreed that the auspices taken in the curiate assembly had jinxed the magistrates who commanded against the Gauls in 390 and the Samnites in 321. Licinius Macer, most probably relying on the Linen Books, added a third instance of ill-luck attending the battle at the Cremera when the Curia Faucia had voted first in the assembly. Because of the religious character of the notice Livy's other authority was most probably the pontifical archives which preserved such information.[1] The procedural act of *principium* must be taken in its literal sense. The chosen curia 'took first'. But what did it 'take first'? Surely not the lot since the curias would not have drawn their lots in a fixed order that one of them might 'take first'. An omen was attached to the curia which 'took first' and in this regard the Faucia had become ill-omened (*abominanda*). The one curia was chosen by lot to take the auspices first. The curia was the 'first to take' (*princeps*) the auspices. From this custom arose the later observance of the tribe which balloted first (*principium*) and the century of the first class which was first asked to declare its vote (*praerogativa*) although neither the tribe nor the century ever took auspices. In the period of the curiate constitution before the Servian reform all the curias had taken the auspices at their meetings. However, a curiate augur had interposed his authority in Tarquinius Priscus' attempt to increase the number of civic fighting units. Consequently, the reformer fixed at twenty-seven (the number of curias in existence then) the number of curial precincts for augury within the pomerium. The state augurs thereafter took over some of the responsibilities of curial augury at the twenty-seven Argei and observed special auguries for the three curias added after the reform of Servius.[2] Probably the reformer at the same time

---

What precedent and authority did a republican interrex have for presiding over the election of republican magistracies? For procedure in the curiate assembly see also Botsford, *The Roman Assemblies* (New York, 1909), pp. 152–200 and *passim*, and Taylor, *Voting Assemblies*, pp. 3–5. Botsford can devote much space to the curias because he believes that he can recreate the human behavior of the voter.

[1] On Macer and the Linen Rolls see below. On the pontiffs' institution or, perhaps, only record of the religious character of the *dies Alliensis* see Cass. Hem. fr. 20 P. (from Macr. *Sat.* 1. 16. 21) and Degrassi, p. 484. Cf. Serv. on *Aen.* 1. 373 on the pontifical notices of each day. For a fine discussion of the pontifical *Annales Maximi* see Jacoby, pp. 60 ff.

[2] See above, pp. 84–95. The sense of *princeps, terticeps,* etc. in the Argean itinerary parallels

curtailed taking the auspices in the curias at a curiate assembly at this time and left only one curia, chosen by lot, to take the auspices because the first auspices (*principium*) had an extraordinary significance. Hence in 310 the dictator Papirius had to repeat the auspices for the *lex curiata* on the following day because the auspices of Curia Faucia had proved abominable. The tribal *principium* certainly and the curiate probably had a second purpose. A whole or part of the preamble to three tribal laws records (1) the name of the president, (2) his office, (3) the place of assembly, (4) the date, (5) the name of the first tribe voting (*principium*), and (6) the name of its first voter.[1] In contrast with the preamble of tribal laws is the preamble of the senate's *consulta* and *auctoritates* in which are recorded (1) the president, (2) his office, (3) the date, (4) the place of meeting and (5) the names of those present at the writing of the document (*scribendo adfuerant*).[2] The first tribe with its first voter and the senators present at the writing of the document all served the same purpose: they bore witness.[3] In the tribal assembly the principal tribe and the principal voter, chosen by sortition, bore witness to the proceedings and transactions of the whole assembly. The formula for the testament by fictitious sale by bronze and balance, borrowed partly from usage in the *comitia calata*, includes formal invocation of the Quirites to bear witness (*perhibere testimonium*) to the proceedings.[4] By the end of the Republic the thirty curiate lictors functioned as the entire curiate assembly,[5] and one of these lictors might serve as the principal voter of the principal curia. It is also likely that the principal voter in both the curiate and tribal assembly originally kept the tally of the thirty and thirty-five ballots.

Although doubt has been cast on the possibility of legislative activity in the curiate assembly in the kingdom and Republic,[6] the

this usage. Nichols, 'The Content of the *Lex Curiata*', *AJP* 88 (1967), 260–1, interprets Cic. *L. Agr.* 2. 26–7 to refer to the auspices of the curiate assembly. See below, p. 212, n. 3.

[1] *CIL* 1², 2. 585 = *FIRA* 1², no. 8; *CIL* 1², 2. 589 = *FIRA* 1², no. 11 = *ILS* 38; Frontinus *Aqu.* 129 = *FIRA* 1², no. 14.

[2] *CIL* 1², 2. 581 = *FIRA* 1², no. 30 = *ILS* 18 = *ILLRP* 511; *CIL* 1², 2. 586 = *FIRA* 1², no. 33 = *ILS* 19 = *ILLRP* 512; *IG* vii, 2225 = *FIRA* 1², no. 31 = Ditt. *Syll.* ii³, no. 646; Cic. *Fam.* 8. 8. 5–8 = *FIRA* 1², no. 37.

[3] See O'Brien-Moore, *RE* Supplbd. 6, col. 801 f., P. Fraccaro, 'La procedura del voto nei comizi tributi romani', *Opuscula* (Pavia, 1957), ii, 235–54.

[4] See above, p. 194.

[5] Cic. *L. Agr.* 2. 12. 31 (cf. *Dom.* 29. 77); Gellius 15. 27. 1–2.

[6] See the discussion of De Martino 1², 128–30. On the meaning of *lex* see G. Barbieri and G. Tibiletti, *Diz. Epigr.* 4 (1957), 701–5. Cicero's language, quoted p. 189, n. 1, confirms the normal legislative activity of the curiate assembly.

evidence points to the same procedure for legislation as can be found for the centuriate and tribal assembly. A *lex curiata* does not differ procedurally from *leges* passed in the two other assemblies. The president put the question. In the instance quoted above, he was a dictator. The pontiff put the question to the curias convoked for religious purposes on the Capitol in precisely the same wording as used in other assemblies, 'I ask whether you would wish (and) order, as I have said, that ...'[1] And the response of the curias must have been couched in the same terms as the centuries and tribes returned: 'As you ask' (*uti rogas*) or 'Keep the old' (*antiquo*).[2]

Transactions approved by the curias were the *leges curiatae*. However, those approved during the royal period came to be called specifically *leges regiae*, after their sponsors just as the Romans called the law proposed by Canuleius the *lex Canuleia*.[3] Other transactions than the *lex curiata de imperio* can be discerned from Roman use of the participle *curiatus* and its derivative adjective *curiatius*. When a new people (*genus hominum*) was to be incorporated into the Roman state by the formation of a curia, the matter was put to the curias. Dionysius errs when he attributes this power of enrolling peoples and families into the curias to the kings alone.[4] Dionysius and his Roman authority, no doubt, had in mind the process whereby the Republican magistrate assigned a person and his family or a town to a particular tribe. However, it is clear that the assemblies controlled the greater donations of citizenship.[5] In fact, existent curias voted on the formation of a new curia as the evidence of the Alban families incorporated into the Roman state demonstrates. Among them was the archaic clan of the Curiatii, which we believe is historically spurious. The word *curiati* headed the roster of the Alban families made Roman because the families had been made into a curia with the approval of the curiate assembly.[6] Only the meetings where official action was taken were *comitia curiata*, *centuriata* and *tributa*. The adjective is

---

[1] Quoted p. 192. The pontiff's *rogo* and the question (*adrogatio*) put to the curias proves that even the curiate assembly convened for religious purposes had the same procedure. So, too, the *lex curiata de imperio* was normally passed (*lata*); see A. Magdelain, 'Note sur le loi curiate et les auspices des magistrats', *RHDFE* 42 (1964), 198–203.

[2] See Mommsen, *Röm. Staatsr.* III, 402–3, Taylor, *Voting Assemblies*, pp. 34–5.

[3] Citations and bibliography on *leg. reg.* in Riccobono, *FIRA* I², p. 1.

[4] D.H. 2. 32–5, 2. 46, 2. 50, 2. 55, 3. 58. See above, pp. 132–7.

[5] E.g. Livy 38. 36. 7–9.

[6] Above, pp. 133–7. The name of the later clan Curiatia probably comes from an ethnic *Curiates* (Pliny, *NH* 3. 114). See Ernout, p. 67. If the Roman gentilicial name has an Umbrian origin, then its artificiality in the early Roman annalistic is assured.

similarly applied to a *lex*. The several meetings (*comitia*) and the law became 'curiate' by official proceeding. Janus Quirinus and Janus Curiatius well illustrate the force of the word. Janus Quirinus, the chief *ianus* of Rome, belonged to all the Quirites and its opening and closing marked the Quirites' state of war and peace. Janus Curiatius became at some time the property of a curia or curias.[1] A *ianus* and a Mars are called *quirinus* to distinguish them from others of the same name not peculiar to all the Quirites.[2]

The title of the curias' flamens was *flamen curialis*, of the curias' thirty lictors *lictor curiat(i)us*. The difference between a curial and curiate officer lies in the fact that the lictor had been officially appointed to vote for the curia in the stead of the curia's members whereas the flamen was routinely elected to carry out usual priestly duties. The title *lictor curiat(i)us* emphasizes the irregularity of his appointment for, after all, the curias themselves had at one time met and had only latterly appointed a vicar, a tool of their expedience and symbol of their deteriorated sovereignty.[3]

Before examining the elective procedure in the curiate assembly which relied partly on the interrex, we must discuss the origin and constituents of Rome's senate, the council of elders. According to the Roman tradition Romulus had a senate of 100 members which Tarquinius Priscus raised to 300.[4] These numbers derive from an underlying notion that Romulus had 100 advisers from his tribe (Ramnes or Ramnensis) and that Tarquin increased the number in order to equalize representation from all three tribes, Ramnes, Tities and Luceres. The earlier senate could not have been excogitated on the basis of the number of curias because Roman antiquarians believed that Romulus had created the thirty curias. In his brilliant study of the auspices and the interregnum André Magdelain does not go into the problem of the royal senate. Indeed, the royal senate now presents a problem because of his new interpretation of the Fathers and patricians to whom the public auspices reverted upon the vacancy

---

[1] Cf. Holland, 'Janus and the Bridge', pp. 80–6, 108–37.

[2] See above, pp. 160–72.

[3] Festus 56 L.; *CIL* vi, 1885–92. The inscriptions display an ambivalence between *curiatus* and *curiatius*. See Cic. *L. Agr.* 2. 12. 31 (cf. *Dom.* 29. 77); Gellius 15. 27. 1–2.

[4] Most modern students accept the number 300 as historical. It is. But for what period? Where the ancient authors say the Romulean senate had 200 members, they have reckoned the inclusion of another tribe which could be either Tities or Luceres. For ancient references and modern bibliography see F. De Martino I², 117–20. According to Dionysius 2. 47 the curias chose an inflated number of new patricians from newly added Romans.

of the major magistracies under the Republic. These patricians, in effect, resumed the auspices which they had assumed when previously elected to the consulship or praetorship.[1] In the kingdom, however, there were no former kings to resume their auspices. Who, then, had the auspices to hold the assembly and to preside over the curias in the capacity of interrexes? The answer is the elders (*senes* or *patres*). But who were they and on what authority did they act? Only one officer emerges as candidate for the royal senator. The heads of the curias, the curions, had to be at least fifty years of age; on this account they would qualify as elders. They served for life; on this account they would have provided the continuity. These officers were considered priests; on this account they would qualify to take the auspices.[2] After the discrimination of patrician and plebeian the curio maximus was patrician until the year 209 B.C.[3] And presumably the other curions at one time were patricians also since in practice they had once exercised the right to take the auspices. The royal senate had as many elders as there were curias. This number, small in relation to the traditional numbers, finds a neat parallel in the Spartan *gerousia* of twenty-eight or thirty elders (*gerontes*).[4] In the event, the Fathers superseded the curions in conducting the interregnum because of the peculiar character of their auspices. The Fathers had been elected to an *imperium* for a fixed term but to the auspices for a lifetime (just as the king and the curions). The curions suffered from one important disadvantage, their authority extended only over a single curia whereas the auspices of the Fathers extended over all curias (indeed derived from all curias) and the auspices had never been exercised with an *imperium*. The curions were elected by their curias[5] and this office must have brought membership in the early Republican senate. Perhaps the small plots of land set aside for senate meetings (*senacula*) on the Capitol and near the Comitium and Curia Hostilia bear testimony to this archaic senate of curions.[6] The word *senaculum* has the same formation as *auguraculum* (cf. the Argean itinerary).

---

[1] Magdelain, 'Auspicia', pp. 427–50.

[2] D.H. 2. 21. 3 following Varro's *Antiquities*.

[3] Livy 27. 8. 1–3. See p. 146, n. 2, and below, pp. 209, 275–6.

[4] Needless to say, the Spartan constitution and its numbers are often as bewildering as the Roman. For ancient references, discussion and bibliography see H. Michell, *Sparta* (Cambridge, 1964), pp. 99–100, 135–40.

[5] D.H. 2. 21. 3 following Varro's *Antiquities*.

[6] Varro, *LL* 5. 156; Livy 41. 27. 7; Val. Max. 2. 2. 6; Festus 470 L.

The Roman senate was still based upon curial representation in 312. The Fathers had exercised for many years before 312 an *auctoritas* which means they were the *auctores* of election and legislation.[1] The word *auctor* ought not to be separated from its cognate *augur* and the notion of augury which attended public business.[2] Here we need but recall the *uhtur*, an official of one decuria or *eikvas-* at Iguvium. There the decuria of the Atiedian Brotherhood performed certain augural functions.[3]

At Rome the decurial unit figures in the operation of an interregnum and in the organization of the augural college. A single, mutilated roster of priests, who are very likely augurs, records the existence of decurias wherein there is only one member at a time.[4] Such reckoning in defiance of arithmetic can be understood only as a reflection of practice in an era when the augurate was closely bound to a system whereby ten men fulfilled a certain function later fulfilled by one man. The interregnal system which rested upon continuing auspices conforms with such a system. In his *Roman Antiquities* (2. 57) Dionysius describes Romulus' patrician senate of 200 members who were divided into decurias which cast lots for the establishment of the order of interregnal decurias which changed after fifty days if no new king were obtained. Although these units were doubtless called decurias, they did not always contain ten men. However, repetition by the interrexes was perhaps allowed up to the tenth interregnum of a single decuria. Furthermore, one decuria could repeat the interregnum evidently up to the tenth interregnum of the decuria if necessary. Thereafter a second decuria must have assumed the interregnum when the procedure recommenced. Quite obviously in 355 there were not ten different men for an interregnal decuria; two members of the same clan belonged to the same decuria of six men; and one of these two repeated an interregnum.[5]

When the government of the Roman state reverted to the interrexes because of a vacancy in the magistracies, the Republican Fathers who had held a major magistracy and had had the auspices resumed their auspices in order to elect magistrates. According to interregnal procedure the first interrex could not commence the election of magistrates. Rather, the second interrex was the first to preside at the election during his five-day term. On one occasion

---

[1] See below, pp. 256–7, 269–72.   [2] See Catalano *passim*.   [3] See above, pp. 40–57.
[4] *ILS* 9338 with Dessau's comment.   [5] See Appendix IIIF.

the interregnal power revolved through the entire panel of six interrexes and it was not until the second interregnum of the second interrex that a magistrate was elected. The order was 1–2–3–4–5–6–1–2; hence it is not impossible that the first interrex might have presided ultimately over the successful election.[1] The tenacity with which the patricians held the office of curio maximus and the critical times in which they relinquished it (209) suggest to me that the chief curion originally initiated the interregnum. By the same token, the fact that the office could be held by a plebeian suggests that the office was only later usurped by those called patricians.[2] The decuria of six men evidently had a complement of ten potential members. However, the decuria seems to mean that a decuria controlled ten interregna before another decuria tried to obtain a king or magistrate. During the Republic the ten places cannot be held by representatives of ten curias because in 351 two Fabii serve in the same decuria. Very probably a clan belonged to only one curia. Thence it follows that these decurias were not related to the curias. Because a curion could not hold a magistracy, a curion could not have been an interrex when the interrex was the patrician who had held an imperial magistracy, the auspices of which he resumed during anarchy. But before there was a man who retained imperial auspices, who was the interrex? If the primitive interrex had to have auspices, he will have been a curion. We conclude that the decurias of interrexes belong to the later history of the interregnum when the interrex was a former imperial magistrate.

In the royal period there appears to have been no provision for a regular president of the curiate assembly other than king and interrex. This limitation worked to the advantage of the 'patricians' when the centuriate constitution was set aside in the early Republic. That the curio maximus posted the instructions for the Fornacalia in the Comitium of the Forum may indicate his erstwhile political presidency during the interregnum. The Roman tradition maintained that the curions were captains of a military unit and priests of their

---

[1] Livy 7. 17. 11. See Magdelain, 'Auspicia', pp. 428–50. Without dates we cannot determine the number of *dies comitiales* in an interregnum, if the interrex was bound to observe them.

[2] See below, pp. 293–4. The chief curion probably was not the thirty-first curion. Rather, he was the eldest in point of curionate or the curion of the eldest curia. Some students see in the office a Republican creation to supplant the king. Momigliano, 'Interim Report', p. 112, n. 71 suggests a constitutional dualism. This is unnecessary because the chief curionate accords well with the continuity which interregna facilitated and with the basic

curias. Their sacerdotal functions probably rested upon their original role of ethnic chieftain—for want of a better expression—whose group had submitted to the corporate unity of Rome. Ancient assembly presidents did not break tie-votes in the assembly as do their modern parliamentary counterparts because at Rome, at least, the assembly votes were unit votes. The problem of equal votes for and against a question or candidate never concerned the centuriate and tribal assemblies because the number of units in both assemblies was odd. However, the curiate assembly after 495 had an even number of units. The tie-votes in the centuries and tribes were avoided through the artificial creation of the units. Curias, on the contrary, were natural creations if we may be permitted the use of a very old distinction. A curia, we argue, could not be added to the state unless constituents were available under peculiar circumstances. Furthermore the success of the centuriate reform partly rested upon curtailment of certain curial powers and perhaps the cessation of curial expansion. In the event, curias were not added to the thirty in existence before or shortly after the revolution of 510. Consequently, a tie-vote was a possible outcome in curiate balloting. In this case the Quirites must have looked to the principal, auspicious curia as the unit whose vote had prior authority and thereby broke the tie. This practice would have been followed only when the total of curias was even. Even though the number of curias at the time of the Servian reform was twenty-seven, the reformer could not altogether abolish curial auspication. Hence, the *principium* was retained. The original sense of the curial auspices was surely lost by the time of the censorship's institution. In general, curial augury and auspices may have been moribund by 466 and, for all intents and purposes, dead in 443.[1] The *principium*, however, survived.

As the evidence of the procedure in the *comitia calata* indicates, the legislative procedure of the curiate assembly did not differ markedly from that in the other assemblies. The elective procedure, however, was based upon the nature of its presidency. Only the king, his viceregent and interrex could have held the curiate assembly during the kingship.

notion that the curias through the *lex curiata de imperio* were the ultimate repository of government.

[1] In 466 a building was erected on the augural precinct of a curia for the first time (Argei III 5). In 443 the auspices of the censors were conferred by a *lex centuriata* after their election (Cic. *L. Arg.* 2. 11. 26, quoted below, p. 212, n. 3).

Let us begin with the making of the king. The interrexes, who in other circumstances were the curions, retained the ensigns of the *imperium* and at the same time one interrex exercised the *imperium* for a period of five days. Any of the interrexes except the principal interrex had the power to appoint a new king. A reasonable cause of the first, principal interrex's disability to preside over an election in the first interregnum was the avoidance of the luck or ill-luck such as was attached to the curial *principium* and the centuriate *praerogativa*. The interrex's appointment (*creatio*) took the form of bringing the name of the man appointed (*creatus*) before all the curias. The curias either accepted or rejected the man whom an interrex alone had the power to appoint. Once the appointed king (*creatus*) was made (*factus*) king by a majority of curiate votes, it remained to try the divine will for his approval. The augural interrex by virtue of his power of auspication put an explicit, unequivocal question to the god(s).[1] Upon the observation of an affirmative answer through auspices the divinely approved king (*designatus*) himself officially assumed the office.[2] Thereupon the designated king requested from all the curias an acknowledgement of the divine will. It must be remembered that not all curias had necessarily voted for the king in the second instance. In the last instance the king sought and received universal acceptance by which were conferred upon him the auspices and the *imperium*.[3] A reconstruction of this procedure depends on

[1] On the terminology of what was not an elective process properly speaking, see De Francisci, pp. 406–9, 419–23 (*creare regem*), pp. 409–15 (*facere regem*). Note that the curial 'increaser' (the curion who is *augur*) makes the king 'come to life' (*creare*). In another context, the curions were the *patres auctores*.

[2] *Ibid.* pp. 423–5. The *designatio* of the king depends on the *signa ex caelo* which were also sought at the curiate assembly in which Clodius was adopted (Cic. *Dom.* 39–40). On the king's inauguration see also Coli, pp. 77–98.

[3] The nature of the *lex curiata de imperio* has been, and always will be, subject to discussion so long as we have no text of the law. For discussions and bibliography see: Coli, pp. 66, 165–7 (it asks acceptance from the curias and grants the right to take the auspices and exercise the *imperium*, use of lictors and permission to name quaestors); Staveley, 'Forschungsbericht', pp. 84–90 (it gives the Republican officeholders the right to take the auspices); Momigliano, 'Interim Report', pp. 110–11 (the choice of the kings rests with the curias); and Magdelain, 'Note', pp. 198–203 who argues that all magistrates except censors had to be invested by a *lex curiata* (Val. Messala in Gellius 13.15 and Cic. *Agr.* 2. 11. 26) in order to exercise their magistracies, that there were two investitures, by gods and by curias (sacral and civil), and that the civil investiture was Republican in origin. Against the last point, it is easy to see why the centuriate citizens of Rome in 509 would not have wished curial control of their assembly. If the *lex curiata* had been a Republican institution, the Romans could have easily abolished it but this they could no more do than abolish *patrum auctoritas*. Even in the procedure of electing censors a *lex centuriata* was necessary; see below. Nichols holds that the *lex curiata* provided 'some sort of legitimation'.

what little we know of interregnal procedure in the Republic,[1] upon the practice of electing consuls in the centuriate assembly and their gaining their approval in the curiate assembly[2] and lastly on the singular practice of censorial election and consequent approval. From 443 on censors were proposed by an imperial magistrate to the centuries who could accept or reject the candidates. The two accepted censors then had to be confirmed by all the centuries.[3] The censors enjoyed a limited right of auspices but no *imperium*.[4]

At the last stage came the *lex curiata de imperio* which Cicero says was voted for the sake of the auspices (*auspiciorum causa*). Presumably the auspices and *imperium* became effective only with the passage of this law.[5] At the second and third stage the proposed king (*creatus*) might have failed to receive either the acceptance of the several curias or the divine approval. Because not all curias might have voted for the proposed king, it was felt necessary for all curias to acquiesce in the approval of the gods. Latte has suggested that the *lex curiata* served the function of an oath of fealty or homage of soldiers, that is the *lex curiata* was the soldiers' *sacramentum* or *coniuratio*.[6] For two reasons I believe that this was not the case. First, the curias were not the units of the pre-centuriate army although one authority says they were. Secondly, only certain military tribunes exacted the oath which was made requisite upon all recruits after 216. Polybius and others do not tell us how many tribunes had charge of administering

He makes a number of good points but is imprecise because we do not know the contents of the law. Nichols also asserts (pp. 257–8) that 'there can be no doubt that he [*sc.* Cicero] knew the procedures of the curiate assembly and the form of the curiate law'. If Cicero knew the former, it was from the activity of thirty lictors and if the latter, he has not conveyed it to his audiences.

[1] E. S. Staveley, 'The Conduct of Elections During an Interregnum', *Historia* 3 (1954), 193–211; Magdelain, 'Auspicia', pp. 427–450.

[2] See above, p. 211, n. 1, and next note.

[3] Cic. *L. Agr.* 2. 11. 26–7: 'maiores de singulis magistratibus bis vos sententiam ferre voluerunt. nam cum centuriata lex censoribus ferebatur, cum curiata ceteris patriciis magistratibus, tum iterum de eisdem iudicabatur, ut esset reprehendendi potestas, si populum benefici sui paeniteret. nunc, Quirites, prima illa comitia tenetis, centuriata et tributa, curiata tantum auspiciorum causa remanserunt. hic autem tribunus plebis quia videbat potestatem neminem iniussu populi aut plebis posse habere, curiatis eam comitiis quae vos non initis confirmavit, tributa quae vestra erant sustulit.' The last sentence does not mean that the plebs did not belong to the curiate assembly but that only the thirty lictors in Cicero's day played the curias (2. 12. 31).

[4] Magdelain, 'Auspicia', pp. 434–5; Palmer, 'Censors', pp. 319–24. See above, p. 158.

[5] Cic. *L. Agr.* 2. 11. 27, 11. 29, 12. 31; Val. Messala in Gellius 13. 15 on the interpretation of which see Coli, 'Regnum'; Magdelain, 'Note'; and Oliver, *Demokratia*, p. 81, n. 15. Nichols argues that the *lex curiata* did not concern imperial auspices but curial auspices.

[6] K. Latte 'Lex Curiata', p. 59 ff. See our chapter 8.

the oath. However, the archaic *sacramentum* would probably have been administered by the three military tribunes whose command had once comprised the tribal infantry. The oath was sworn by individuals (Quirites) and not by tactical units.[1] Since the formula of the *lex curiata* has not survived, a more precise definition of this law cannot be hazarded. Nevertheless it may safely be said that the curias formally conferred unanimously what had already been voted by a majority of curias and approved by the gods.[2]

THE POWERS OF THE CURIATE ASSEMBLY

The king reigned by virtue of a power ultimately derived from the Quirites of the curias. He might from time to time propose rules by which ancestral custom was confirmed or changed. These rules consisted in conditions laid down by bilateral accord, being what the Romans called *leges*.[3] The remaining scraps of royal laws concern religious matters since they alone had been in force into historical times.[4] The curias no more formulated, proposed and modified the laws on their own authority than did the centuries and the tribes in the other assemblies. They accepted or rejected questions and candidates just as the centuries and tribes accepted or rejected questions and candidates. While the kings enjoyed an authority deriving from the interregnal auspices which proposed them, from the divine approval subsequent to curiate approval and from the auspices conferred upon themselves, the human power of the Roman king undeniably rested upon the consent of the men of the curias. Otherwise there would have been no curiate assembly and no curiate law which even the republican consuls and dictators had to seek in order to assume the *imperium*.[5]

[1] Polyb. 6. 21. 1–3; Livy 22. 38. 2–5, 28. 29. 12; D.H. 11. 43. 2; Festus 250 L.; Macr. *Sat*. 3. 7. 5 (cf. L. Cincius in Gellius 16. 4. 2–5). See below, p. 215, n. 1 and S. Tondo, 'Il "sacramentum" nell'ambiente culturale romano-italico', *SDHI* 29 (1963), 1–25.

[2] Besides passages already cited, Tac. *Ann*. 11. 22 and the *Lex de imperio Vespasiani* (*CIL* vi, 930 = *ILS* 244 = *FIRA* i², no. 15) may cast some light on the *lex curiata*. Cicero *L. Agr*. 2. 10. 26–13. 32 remains the fullest ancient treatment subject to the cautious use of a pleader's harangue.

[3] Pomponius, *Dig*. 1. 2. 2. 2. See Coli, pp. 99–124 and Tibiletti, *Diz. Epigr*. 4 (1957), 701–5. A *lex curiata* was a *lex rogata et lata*; see Magdelain, 'Note', p. 198.

[4] Collected in *FIRA* i², 4–18 with a bibliography on p. 3. On the authenticity of the laws of king Numa see E. Gabba 'Considerazioni sulla tradizione letteraria sulle origini della repubblica', *Les origines de la république romaine* in the *Entretiens* of the Fondation Hardt, xiii, 133–69.

[5] Momigliano, 'Interim Report', pp. 110–11. In this regard the only discernible

Outside the confines of Roman territory the Roman kings doubt-less exercised greater power than within. So, too, the consuls. The representation of the king's appointment of the Fetialis as royal messenger (*regius nuntius*), based most certainly on consular practice, illustrates this aspect of his unimpeded authority. Furthermore, he most certainly did make treaties in the field.[1] This also may have been excogitated from consular practice. However, the curias did seek the consent of Mars to any peace treaty. This Roman writers apparently did not know. In our discussion of Mars Gradivus and Mars Quirinus I suggest that the Quirites enticed Mars Quirinus to consent to the treaty closing an annual campaign. The oaths by which the Quirites swore to the treaty included Jupiter Feretrius and the Mars who is surnamed Quirinus to distinguish him from the Martes of other Italic communities. Furthermore, the oaths taken by the soldiers to their commander were sworn by Jupiter and Mars Gradivus at the outset of a campaign.[2] The surname of the Quirites' Mars and the consent (*hora*) sought from him in late summer suggest an analogue to the control of the centuriate assembly's control of war and peace. The curias had previously controlled the declaration of war and the making of a peace within the limitations somehow imposed by their Mars. In the centuriate revolution of 510 the Romans who overthrew the king wanted the warriors to have a voice in decisions directly affecting them, or rather, the more important voice. The votes of the curiate assembly respected only the ethnic past; the votes of the centuriate assembly respected the age, property and appropriate military service of the voters. Conceivably the curias could have voted for a war which the centuries did not wish to fight.

Traditionally the Roman kings had the defense of the community as their most important task. From the military organizations of the kingdom emerged the magistrates of the early Republic who had been commanders of the three tribes before the reform and of the legionary centuries after the reform. The two systems observed a cleavage between the mounted soldiery and the infantry. In the

---

distinctions between king and consul were collegiality and term of office. In the works of certain recent scholars *charisma* is fast moving westward earlier in ancient time than had been previously postulated. I know of no Roman doctrine of grace, divine or otherwise.

[1] Livy 1. 24. 5, 32, 38. 1–2 on which see Ogilvie (cf. Cic. *Leg.* 3.3.8); L. Cincius in Gellius 16. 4. 1.

[2] Livy 2. 45. 14, 46. 5. See above, pp. 167–72. The opening and closing of the Quirites' Janus Quirinus are analogous. Cf. Serv. on *Aen.* 12. 198 where Janus is said to be invoked in treaty oaths.

earlier system the three commanders of the cavalry and the three commanders of the infantry had served under the king who provided the unified command. From the fact of their election in the Republican assemblies we infer that the commanders of the three infantry regiments (*tribuni militum*) also were approved by the curiate assembly during the kingdom. If these commanders had to be approved by the curias, so too the three commanders of cavalry regiments (*tribuni celerum*) must have been subject to curiate approval.[1] The king, as commander-in-chief, proposed his own candidates to the curiate assembly who could accept or reject them. Presumably these lieutenants did not have either auspices or *imperium* and the last two stages of the king's appointment might have been omitted. However, some authority must have been exercised by them and conceivably a *lex curiata* was passed by all the curias bestowing a lesser authority such as *potestas* upon them (cf. Cic. *L. Agr.* 2. 11. 28).

To king Servius Tullius the Romans ascribed the alternative military organization of the centuries which did not give equal emphasis to cavalry and infantry. The king or his assistants assigned the Quirites to a unit (*centuria*) of the new infantry (*populus*) according to their physical and material capacity to bear arms. Some of the Quirites were not included in the summons to arms (*classis*) and were, therefore, listed without ranking (*infra classem*).[2] The former territorial divisions of three tribes embracing twenty-seven curias no longer suited the realities of the Ager Romanus so that it was redrawn into new tribes from which the new infantry was recruited.[3] The king now chose probably two subaltern commanders (*praetores*) whom the centuries of the *populus* of the Quirites might accept or reject. Even though the centuries had approved a commander of

[1] The usual Greek translation of *tribunus* is *chiliarchos* (except D.H. 2. 7 where *phylarchos*). There were three consular tribunes in 444, 438–437, 422, 419–418, 408, 368 (Diod.); four in 428 (?), 427–426, 425 (?), 424, 420, 417–414, 407–406, 378 (?), 376 (Diod.); and six from 405 to 380, in 379 (?), 378 (?), 377, 370–369, 368 (Livy) and 367. See Appendix 1. The triple number of *tribuni celerum* is inferred from Varro, *LL* 5.81, 5.91 and D.H. 2. 7, 2. 64. 3. See Kübler, *RE* 6. 1, cols 272–3; Mommsen, *Röm. Staatsr.* II³, 177–8; P. Fraccaro, *Opuscula*, II, 287–306; Bernardi, 'Dagli ausiliari del *rex* ai magistrati della *respublica*', *Athenaeum* 30 (1952), 19–20, 45–46; A. Alföldi, 'Der frührömische Reiteradel und seine Ehrenabzeichen', *Deut. Beitr. z. Altertumswiss.* 2 (1952), 47–8, 89–90, and H. Hill, *The Roman Middle Class* (Oxford, 1952), pp. 1–31.
[2] Gellius 6. 13. See Staveley, pp. 78–9, Momigliano, 'Interim Report', p. 120.
[3] Although it has been recently suggested that levies by tribe are late (see Walbank on Polyb. 6. 19. 5–20. 9), I agree with L. R. Taylor, 'The Centuriate Assembly Before and After the Reform', *AJP* 78 (1957), 337–42 and 'Voting Districts', pp. 7–9 that the tribes were intended from the beginning for the collection of the tribute and the levies. Of course,

the legionary centuries, the curiate assembly reserved the right to bestow whatever power he would exercise.[1]

Any treatment of the Servian reforms must take into account the introduction of hoplite armor and tactics into Etruria and Latium. The armor presupposed a designated class according to wealth. Snodgrass dates complete absorption of the Greek system by the Etruscans to sometime after 650.[2] We have already remarked the Etruscan borrowing of the term *phyle* as a military unit.[3]

Since the king reigned without colleague, he had to appoint in his absence from Roman territory a person to oversee the government at home. His title of prefect indicates that the king himself made him in charge (*praefectus*) of the city.[4] On the other hand if the king for any reason could not fulfill his kingly function, he or an interrex appointed (*dicere*) a viceregal substitute, the master of the infantry (*magister populi*), whose office became the Republican dictatorship.[5] This office was neither a Republican invention nor reversion to the kingly power. We may suppose that an aged, injured or dead king might be immediately and temporarily replaced at any moment. The circumstances of an emergency did not permit the painstaking deliberation and solemn procedure of finding a king for a lifetime. Furthermore an ill or injured king might live to resume his authority. Hence, the simplest procedure was required. Either king or interrex named the master of infantry and he himself alone presented himself to the curias for a *lex curiata de imperio*. Thereby, he obtained a royal command (*imperium*) with temporal limitations of six months, which at the time was the longest conceivable period of a military command. His title (*magister*) implies that his office was 'greater' than others and resembles *magistratus*. His superiority must be related to the military tribunes and the praetors. Similarly, the superiority

the ancient evidence vacillates between levy by tribe and levy by century because you could not have one without the other. Furthermore, in a moneyless economy military service was but a variety of tribute or taxation.

[1] The number of royal and early Republican praetors is a matter of dispute. See Staveley, pp. 90–101 and J. Heurgon, 'Magistratures romaines et magistratures étrusques', *Les origines de la république romaine. Entretiens sur l'Antiquité Classique* XIII (Vandœuvres-Geneva, 1967), 97–127.

[2] A. M. Snodgrass, 'The Hoplite Reform and History', *JHS* 85 (1965), 110–22.

[3] See above, chapter 6, p. 155, n. 4.

[4] According to Livy 1. 59. 12, 60. 3 and Tacitus, *Ann.* 6. 11 a prefect of the city held the first consular elections. On the title see De Francisci, pp. 415, 597 f.

[5] On the *dictio* Magdelain, 'Auspicia', pp. 446–7. On the dictator and magister populi Staveley, pp. 101–7. For the latter title see Cic. *Rep.* 1. 40. 63; *Leg.* 3. 3. 9; *Fin.* 3. 22. 75; Varro, *LL* 5. 82; Sen. *Ep.* 108. 31; Festus 216 L.; Velius Longus, *CGL* 7. 74 K.

of the master of cavalry (*magister equitum*) must be related to the cavalry tribunes. If there is any truth in Servius Tullius' Etruscan title *mastarna* (Latin *magister*), he exercised this office under his predecessor or before his kingship.[1]

The historical priority of the master of the infantry over the master of the cavalry leaves little room to doubt that the new organization of the centuries was intended partially to supplant the old tribal system. But by the time that the kingship had come to an end the centuriate organization had only grown so strong as to lead the revolution and offer itself as an alternative to the curiate constitution wherein the military tribunes would enjoy pre-eminence. The *populus* of the Quirites was recruited from new tribes but the cavalry was perhaps still levied from the old tribes. Whether the units of cavalry numbered six, twelve or eighteen, their numerical basis was the older tribal system of three territories.[2] Presumably they inherited their position in the cavalry. Otherwise the survival of the names of the three Romulean tribes cannot be explained since the description of the three territories would not have been maintained within the greater confines of an Ager Romanus of twenty-one tribes.[3] Although under the centuriate constitution the praetors-consul commanded both infantry and cavalry, the master of the infantry had to follow the same procedure of appointing his master of cavalry as the king or interrex had followed in appointing him. In spite of the change in titulature the republican dictator observed the constitutional niceties of the curiate system. However subordinate the master of cavalry was to the master of infantry in the time of the centuriate constitution, his appointment (*dictio*) was inferior only in the fact that he was appointed after the master of infantry and by the master of infantry.[4] This inferiority supposedly meant that the master of cavalry had an *imperium*, second to the masters of infantry and conferred by the curiate assembly.[5] The dictator was forbidden to use a horse not because of taboo or fear of tyranny: the dictator could command the master of cavalry, he could not command the cavalry.[6] This evidence

---

[1] Imp. Claudius in *ILS* 212. [2] Alföldi, 'Reiteradel', pp. 102–14, Hill, pp. 32–44.
[3] The curiate assembly met at the Comitium in the Forum where the horsemen later passed in review before the censors. Cf. [Asconius] p. 238 St.: 'Comitium locus propter senatum quo coire equitibus R. et populo R. licet'. See Mommsen, *Röm. Staatsr.* II³, 397–400, Alföldi, 'Reiteradel', pp. 41, 111 and below, p. 260.
[4] E.g. Livy 9.38. 15–16, quoted above, pp. 202–3. See Magdelain, 'Auspicia', pp. 446–7.
[5] Mommsen, *Röm. Staatsr.* II³, 178–9; Alföldi, 'Reiteradel', pp. 47–8, 79 n. 174.
[6] Livy 23. 14. 2: Plut. *Fab. Max.* 4. 1 (cf. Zonaras 7. 14). See Alföldi, 'Reiteradel',

makes clear only that under the centuriate constitution the infantry commander took precedence over any cavalry commander and offers confirmation that the tribal horseman for some time remained aloof from the centuriate foot-soldiers. Moreover the evidence demonstrates such an historical cleavage between foot and horse, (three) tribes and centuries, that the question arises whether the *imperium* of the master of cavalry had always been inferior to the master of infantry when they were appointed in the royal period if both offices existed before the Servian reform.[1] If the *dictator* as such were Roman from the first, the new title *dictator* seems best explained as a means of insisting that the master of infantry name the master of cavalry and not *vice-versa*. The title is so closely tied to Latin *dictio* that it is hard to believe that *dictator* is not of Roman origin. On the other hand, tradition makes the earliest cavalry (*celeres*) the king's bodyguard. Moreover, after the expulsion of the king the name of the cavalrymen was changed from *celeres* to *flexuntes*. This change in name (not in personnel) bears out the peculiarity of their royal position and reflects the attachment of the whole cavalry to the king when it survived the abolition of tribal regiments.[2]

The military organization, ascribed to Ser. Tullius, was intended to supplant only the threefold infantry. Beyond its intended aim the centuriate army went forward to the establishment of a constitution based upon their own organization and led by their own elected annual magistrates. Despite their success at a revolution in government the centuries did not abolish the curias nor were they ever technically free from curiate approval in electing imperial magistrates. All the Quirites, by curias, consented to the bestowal of *imperium* in accordance with the ancestral custom concerning the

p. 18, n. 16. When the dictator failed to appoint a master of cavalry in 249, he was compelled to resign (*Fast. Capit.*, Livy *Per.* 19, Suet. *Tib.* 2). In 217 a dispute arose between the dictator and the master of cavalry which led to their joint dictatorship without masters of cavalry. A similar situation occurred in 216. See Broughton *s.aa.* Regardless of their origins we must admit a certain collegiality in the two offices; see Mommsen, *Röm. Staatsr.* II³, 148, 158-9. Possibly only one *magister* was appointed before the Servian reform to command instead of the king, and the two *magistri* were regularly appointed only after the three squadrons of cavalry had ceased to fight severally with the three regiments of infantry. In that case Servius Tullius was simply a *mastarna* without further designation.

[1] A supersession of the master of infantry over the master of cavalry might have led to the convention that the infantry commander did not mount a horse, i.e. assume actual command of the cavalry.

[2] *Celeres*: Livy 1. 15. 8; D.H. 2. 13, 2. 29; Festus 48 L.; Zonaras 7. 4. *Flexuntes*: Varro in Serv. on *Aen.* 9. 603; Pliny, *NH* 33. 35. See Alföldi, 'Reiteradel', pp. 89-90 and Hill, pp. 2-3. The name may have been changed to *flexuntes* in 501 (?) when the title of *dictator*

bestowal of royal suzerainty. The *Populus Romanus Quiritium* had ceased to be merely the infantry. Tradition makes it the first organ of Republican government. In the event there existed two political organs which may be termed constitutions: the centuriate and the curiate. And they were not equal because the centuriate *populus* remained the *populus* of the Quirites and still drew its legal warrant for the public action of its officers from the Quirites of the curiate assembly. In 495 the number of twenty-one tribes was reached with the likely addition of the Claudia and Clustumina.[1] These two units represented the addition of new lands and people to the Roman state and also the last two curias to be created.[2] The curiate system was a constitutional order still to be reckoned with. The following year saw the first secession of the plebs and the election of *tribuni plebis* for 493. Our sources explicitly state that the curiate assembly elected these new tribunes until 471 when the centuriate assembly authorized their election by the tribes.[3] Although it has been doubted that the curias elected the tribunes of the plebs in the beginning,[4] it is difficult to explain Roman reasoning which led to such a fiction. Insofar as Roman historians were able to determine, the curias did not elect any state officers in the Republic (cf. Gellius, *NA* 13. 15. 4). Furthermore, the title of these new plebeian officers is derived from *tribus*; yet none of the traditional numbers of the college (two, four or five, and ultimately ten tribunes)[5] accords with the number of then existing tribes or the Romulean tribes, unless the four plebeian tribunes were elected to serve the tribules of the four urban tribes who were at that time presumably identical with the residents of the four urban regions. The title of tribune is owed to three considerations. First, the only regular officers over whose appointment the curias could have had direct control at that time were the tribunes of the soldiers.[6] Secondly, the latter officers were said to have been instrumental in 494 toward the election of the plebeian tribunes. According to Varro: 'tribuni plebei, quod ex tribunis militum primum

replaced *magister populi* (Livy 2. 18. 1–7, Festus 216 L.). On Momigliano's recent views of the cavalry see below, p. 264, n. 1.

[1] Taylor, 'Voting Districts', pp. 35–7.
[2] See pp. 138–9, 177.
[3] Cicero in Asconius 67–8 KS.; D.H. 6. 89. 1, 9. 41. 2. Livy 2. 56. 2, 58. 1 attests the transfer but is silent on the nature of the earlier assembly.
[4] E.g. by H. S. Jones, *CAH* 7. 453–4. See De Martino I², 289–92.
[5] De Martino I², 278–82.
[6] See next note and below, pp. 223–6.

facti, qui plebem defenderent, in secessione Crustumerina'.[1] I understand this to mean that the military tribunes presided over the creation of this office and the first election of tribunes of the plebs in the meeting-place of Curia Crustumerina which lay outside Rome and furthermore, that the military tribunes had convoked a curiate assembly. Finally at that time the centuriate organization (*populus*) was electing only its own military commanders subject to curiate approval and the tribal assembly had not yet been conceived. Since plebeian tribunes had not the slightest competence in military affairs, the centuries could not have elected them.[2]

After 471 the plebeian tribunes were elected by the tribes and their number was increased from two to four or five.[3] The original number of two perhaps shows a parallel with the two praetors who headed the centuries. Neither of the numbers after 471 reflects another Roman political institution but the number of five plebeian tribunes is the correct one and Diodorus, responsible for the number of four, must have erred if his copyists have not.[4] In 462 a plebeian tribune strove to create a board of five men either to draft legislation on the consular *imperium*[5] or to issue a code of written law.[6] Five years after this tribunician failure the number of plebeian tribunes was raised to ten.[7] In 451 the Romans elected their first board of ten men with consular power to draft the laws (*decemviri consulari imperio legibus scribundis*).[8] Not only did the Ten have the consuls' power, they also replaced the consuls who were not elected for 450 and, in effect, the plebeian tribunes who were not elected for 451 and 450.[9] This was the first certain suspension of the centuriate constitution. The consuls

---

[1] *LL* 5. 81. See De Martino I², 281 and, for discussion of the *secessio*, K. von Fritz, 'The Reorganisation of the Roman Government in 367 B.C.', *Historia* 1 (1950), 21–6.

[2] On the censorship see below, pp. 222–3.

[3] Livy 2. 55–8, D.H. 9. 43–9 for five; Diod. 11. 68. 8 for four. One of my readers suggests the possible connection between four plebeian tribunes and the four urban Servian tribes to which the city residents belonged since they might more easily appeal to their own representatives. See De Martino, pp. 278–82.

[4] Oliver, *Demokratia*, pp. 69–72, for instance, sees in the number five a reflection of the Spartan ephorate. Asconius 68 KS. reports that some ancient authorities asserted five was the original number and each tribune represented one of the five centuriate *classes*! Similarly the four tribunes may have been related to the urban tribes.

[5] Livy 3. 9 on whose mistake Mommsen, *Röm. Staatsr.* II³, 702, n. 2.

[6] D.H. 10. 1.

[7] Livy 3. 30. 5–7; D.H. 10. 30. 6. A parallel without an intervening college of five men are the *duoviri sac. fac.* raised to *decemviri* in 367, evenly divided between plebeians and patricians (Livy 6. 37. 12, 42. 2).

[8] *Ibid.* 3. 32. 6–7. See Broughton, *s.aa.* 451, 450.

[9] Cic. *Rep.* 2. 61–3; Livy 3. 53 (cf. 3. 55. 14); D.H. 10. 58. 1. Cf. *ILS* 212.

were not set aside and the centuriate constitution superseded by an unprecedented office despite the title decemvirate. In 462 the tribune had proposed *quinque viri consulari imperio legibus scribundis*. And why five men in 462 and ten men in 451 ? Because in 462 there were five tribunes of the plebs and in 451 ten tribunes of the plebs whom the Decemvirs supplanted at the same time they supplanted the two praetors-consul. The constitution which it drew up displeased the plebs at least insofar as the clause on marriage between patrician and plebeian was concerned,[1] and the plebs sought and obtained the election of tribunes again in 449 in an assembly convened on the Capitol or Aventine and presided over by the pontifex maximus,[2] an officer who might convene the curias.[3] In turn, the plebeian tribunes sought and obtained the election of praetors-consul for 449 in an interregnal assembly.[4] Overlaid with more than the usual rhetoric, one tradition speaks of the unconstitutional continuance of the decemvirate in this year.[5] Indeed, the Decemvirs might well have asked why they should not have remained in office since they represented a new form of government by prytany. The first phase of civil struggle and disorder ended with the writing of the laws and the termination of the short-lived decemviral magistracy. The second phase opens with the temporary reversion to the centuriate constitution of the praetors-consul which the plebeian tribunes again called into force.

[1] See above, pp. 196 f. and De Martino, I[2], chapter 11 ('Il decemvirato ed il tentativo di una nuova costituzione'). Although the Law of the XII Tables was said to have been enacted by the centuries (Livy 3. 34. 6), they may have been approved by the curias. Sidonius (*Ep.* 8. 6. 7) speaks of a *lex proquiritata* as one which the Decemvirs might have issued: 'per ipsum fere tempus, ut decemviraliter loquar, lex de praescriptione tricennii fuerat "proquiritata" '. See Eg. Weiss, *Glotta* 12 (1923), 82–3 who suggests the verb *proquiritare* means to 'publish' for the Quirites and follows Kretschmer's derivation of *Quirites* from *curia* which I accept.

[2] Livy 3. 54 names the pontiff Q. Furius and says the election was on the Aventine; and Cicero in Asconius 69 KS. names the pontiff M. Papirius and says the election was on the Capitol after a secession to the Aventine. The confusion in names arises from a source who said the pontifex maximus was consul *a.u.c.* 313 (or in a similar fashion) when Papirius and Furius were consuls. See R. Syme, 'Seianus on the Aventine', *Hermes*, 84 (1956), 257–66.

[3] See above, p. 191, n. 4. The tribes could not be convoked because there was no tribune of the plebs. The chief pontiff flayed alive a minor pontiff (i.e. a pontifical scribe) in the Comitium. His crime was religious. See Livy 22. 57. 2 and Cass. Hem. fr. 32 P. The priest king, too, administered justice in the Comitium; see Varro, *LL* 6. 31 and Palmer, 'King'. Both the pontifical and royal activities in the Comitium seem to indicate a connection with a curial meeting.

[4] Livy 3. 54. 14–55. 2.

[5] See Broughton, *s.a.* 450 and for all further references under the given office and year.

Livy opens his fourth book at 445 with the story of Canuleius and his law on intermarriage and the institution of the military tribunes with consular power. In his chapter on the magistracy Mommsen lists all the acts which, he thinks, the consular tribunes could not constitutionally perform. No tribune ever triumphed. Dictators, however, did triumph in years when the consular tribunes were eponymous. I cannot believe that the Romans forestalled a tribune's triumph by appointing dictators. Perhaps it is coincidental or no tribune ever deserved a triumph. Also it is possible that their triumphs were expunged from the record for the same reason Augustus denied Cornelius Cossus the *spolia opima* taken when he was a tribune (see below). The consular tribunes could name dictators (Zonaras 7. 19) and must have done so in 437, 426, 418, 408, 396, 390, 389, 385, 380, 368 and 367 if any of the dictators of these years is authentic. As ex-magistrates consular tribunes could be interrexes. Therefore, the consular tribunate ought to be treated as the magisterial equal of the consulship.[1] For 443 were elected the first censors who assumed from the consuls the responsibilities of the census. The ancients suggest that the censorship was created in order to alleviate the consuls' task for more pressing military functions.[2] This squares well with the ancients' notion that the consular tribunate had a primarily military scope.[3] In this light, the consular tribunate and the censorship belong to the same reformation of the Roman government.[4] The censors had auspices inferior to those of the praetors-consul[5] and, we might add, to the consular tribunes.

---

[1] Livy 4. 1–7. On the various titulature of this magistracy see Mommsen, *Röm. Staatsr.* II[3], 186–90; De Martino I[2], 262–70. As ex-magistrates they could be interrexes; see below, p. 228, n. 1.

[2] D.H. 11. 63; Pomponius, *Dig.* 1. 2. 2. 17; Zonaras 7. 19.

[3] Livy 4. 7. 1–3 who also (4. 6. 6–12) states the office was created to share consular power with plebeians. See F. E. Adcock, 'Consular Tribunes and Their Successors', *JRS* 47 (1957), pp. 9–14. A. Boddington, 'The Original Nature of the Consular Tribunate', *Historia* 8 (1959), 356–64 in effect represents these magistrates as forerunners of the *legati pro praetore* of the emperors although she does not say so. See Fraccaro, pp. 304–6.

[4] M. P. Nilsson, 'The Introduction of Hoplite Tactics at Rome', *JRS* 19 (1929), 4–5. Because the first censors are also given as the (spurious) suffect consuls of 444, their authenticity has been entirely doubted. Yet the office's institution conforms with the outcome of the decemvirate. In the period under discussion the censors very likely rated in 443, 435, 418, 393, 380, 378 and 366. The censorship of 430 is not mentioned in the surviving annals and that of 403 forms part of Camillus' legend. Even if all these censors are accepted, none of the later regularity of the five-year *lustrum* is discernible. See further Broughton *MRR s. a.* 443 and 435. and Ogilvie on Livy 4. 7–8.

[5] Magdelain, 'Auspicia', 434–5; Palmer, 'Censors', 319–24.

The censors were elected by the centuries and after their election the centuries voted a *lex centuriata*, comparable with the *lex curiata* of the major magistrates, since by their auspices they did convoke the centuries for the census.[1] It might well be asked why the censors alone based their auspices on the centuriate law whereas the imperial magistrates based theirs on the curiate law. That such a ratification was still necessary in 443 is quite clear. The censors' lack of *imperium* could explain it. However, it is very probable that the quaestors, who had no *imperium*, also based their power on a *lex curiata*.[2] The election of censors by the centuries and of praetors-consul by the centuries did not have the same scope at all. The centuries elected praetors-consul to the chief magistracy of all the Romans and only the curiate assembly might authenticate such a magistracy because the Quirites of the curias alone enjoyed the citizenship. The centuries elected censors to an office of the centuries and only the centuriate assembly needed to authenticate that office because the soldiers of the centuriate *populus* alone were affected by the census in accordance with which they served. Yet the institutions of censorship and consular tribunate are indeed connected. The intention of the emerging patricians who, we shall see, promoted the new arrangement was the abolition of the praetors-consul elected by the centuriate assembly. The latter magistrates and the king before them had taken the census. The new supreme magistracy, the consular tribunate, had never been in charge of the census. The centuries maintained the right to elect their own magistrates whose powers did not extend beyond the centuriate citizens.[3]

The place and procedure of election of the military tribunes with consular power are by no means certain. Livy has combined evidently two sources so that on one occasion the centuriate assembly elects the tribunes and perhaps on another, the tribal assembly.[4] If the latter case is as interpreted, it commands no credence since the tribes never elected legitimately imperial officers but did elect military tribunes after those officers had ceased to be imperial. The bestowal of the censors' auspices (*lex centuriata*) was legislated by the very same assembly which had just elected them. This procedure appears anomalous beside that whereby praetors-consul were elected

---

[1] Cicero (above, p. 112, n. 3); Varro, *LL* 6. 93.   [2] See below, pp. 240–2.
[3] See Appendix IIID and E. At this time the Fathers still controlled the election of the censors through their *auctoritas*.
[4] Livy 5. 13. 3 (cf. 5. 52. 16). The reference to the tribal assembly is indeed muddled

by the centuries and awarded the authority by the curias. It would not have been anomalous if the procedure of censorial election instituted in 443 paralleled the procedure of election to the consular tribunate supposedly instituted in 444. But the institution of 444 by no means was new in that year and went back to the earlier kingdom.[1] Secondly, the consular tribunate was abolished in 367 by the Licinio-Sextian Rogations.[2] This abolition left mere military tribunes, subordinate to the praetors-consul. Yet in 362, we are told, the six military tribunes were elected for the first time and were no longer appointed by the commanders. Patently this report is in error for the military tribunes (albeit with consular authority) had been elected off and on in some assembly from 444 to 367. Next, we are told that in 311 two offices began to be elected by the people, one of which was the military tribunate whose college now numbers twenty-four (?) for the four legions.[3] Surely the comitial election of military tribunes cannot have commenced in both these years or, for that matter in either of these years. The plebiscite of 311, in fact, raised the number of tribunes to twenty-four to be elected by the tribes (hence the improbable tradition which ascribes the election of consular tribunes to the tribes). The plebiscite (?) of 362 presumably transferred the election of military tribunes from the curiate assembly to the centuriate assembly.[4] When first the Romans chose their own military tribunes, they met by curias. If they had first chosen them

(5. 18. 2–6); see Ogilvie's commentary on Livy, pp. 666–9. Mention of the *praerogativa* seems to indicate the election was in the centuriate assembly and that the elder Licinius had the interrex then convoke the people in tribes for a *contio* so that his election might not be officially announced. Then, after his harangue, the people vote again and elect his son (by tribes or centuries?). R. M. Ogilvie, 'Livy, Licinius Macer and the *Libri Lintei*', *JRS* 48 (1958), 43–4 distinguishes a Source A and Source B in Books IV and V. To Source A, Licinius Macer, he assigns Livy 5. 18. Taylor, 'Centuriate Assembly', p. 339 suggests the tribes and centuries of this period were identical.

[1] Livy 4. 6 (cf. 4. 35. 10).
[2] *Ibid.* 6. 35. 5, quoted below, p. 243, n. 1.
[3] *Ibid.* 7. 5. 8–9 (362) who also says the commanders had been appointing the military tribunes who were called *rufuli* in his day. The consuls of 207 appear to have appointed military tribunes for the first time without election (Livy 27. 36. 14) and the *rufuli* appear even later (probably in 105; see Broughton, *s.a.*). See Fraccaro II, p. 306. For the plebiscite of 311 see Livy 9. 30. 3: 'ut tribuni militum seni deni in quattuor legiones a populo crearentur'. One of my readers points out that the Latin says sixteen tribunes for each of the four legions and suggests *seni* [*deni*] because sixty-four tribunes make an absurdly high number. Six tribunes would have their precedent in the six tribunes-consul. I wonder whether the MSS have not lost an abbreviated -*que* from *deni* ⟨*que*⟩.
[4] The Livian reports, cited p. 224, n. 4, do not rest on any such sound tradition as his notice of the abominable *principium*. Also notable is the fact that it is Livy who remains silent about the election of tribunes of the plebs by the curias probably because he did not

by centuries, they began to elect them after the Servian reform or after the foundation of the Republic. If this is so, the number of military tribunes was not adjusted to the number of praetors-consul or of regiments they commanded, but to the number of abolished regiments.

The curias chose the plebeian tribunes from 493 to 471. Then their selection was transferred to the tribes which only a plebeian tribune might convene. Consequently, in 449 when the plebeian tribunate had been suspended under the decemviral prytany, the chief pontiff held the elections of plebeian tribunes because he had to convoke the curias for the election. If the curias had first elected plebeian officers whom they called tribunes after other officers, then the curiate assembly must also have elected both kinds of tribune, although no ancient authority mentions its archaic election of military tribunes. Also the curiate assembly yielded its competence to elect plebeian tribunes to the tribal assembly.

The plebeian tribunes could not be chosen by the centuries which elected only officers connected with their military service. The military tribune, however, was such an officer and from 362 to 311 was elected, so we argue, by the centuries. Lastly, down to the mid-second century the military tribunes in charge of recruitment held their levies on the Capitol, a site directly connected with the curiate assembly.[1]

Since Livy alone doubly attests the first election of military tribunes and in both cases fails to mention the nature of the electoral assembly, he may have been responsible for the supression of the assemblies' identity. Livy had suppressed the identity of the assembly which originally elected tribunes of the plebs when he wrote that their election was transferred to the tribes. He was also guilty of confusion when he incidentally attributed the election of the consular tribunes to centuries and tribes. I assume that military tribunes, consular and non-consular, were primitively chosen by the curiate assembly and that in 362 their election passed to the centuries which in turn yielded

believe what Cicero and Dionysius knew and not because he did not know; see above, p. 219, n. 3.

[1] Polyb. 6. 19. 6 (on which see Walbank); Livy 26. 31. 11; Varro in Nonius 28 L. The men came to the Capitol because the tribal assembly also met there. See L. R. Taylor, 'Was Tiberius Gracchus' Last Assembly Electoral or Legislative?', *Athenaeum* 41 (1963), 51–69. This is just another example of the tribal assembly assuming the externals, at least, of the curiate assembly.

it to the tribes in 311. Finally, their original number of three and later ordinary number of six conformed to the pre-Servian levy of three regiments and thereby confirms the royal origin of the office which ought to have been controlled by the curias to which the military tribunes assigned the first election of tribunes of the plebs. The *lex centuriata* which confirmed the centuriate election of two censors after 444 was patterned after the *lex curiata* which would have confirmed the curiate election of three consular tribunes, a magistracy which was given new power at the same time the censorship was constituted. The double centuriate ballot does not take its precedent from the electoral procedure of consuls. The first election of tribunes of the plebs was worked in the curiate assembly and was promoted by military tribunes whose simple title was accorded the new plebeian officers.

SOME REPUBLICAN INTERREGNA

No election of consular tribunes under the presidency of a pontiff is recorded.[1] However, the persistent interregnal elections of consular tribunes, reported by Livy, invite our suspicions:

Year	Magistrates in office	Magistrates elected	Livy
445–444	Consuls	Consular tribunes	4. 6. 8–7. 1
421–420	Consuls	Consular tribunes	4. 43. 9, 44. 1
414–413	Consular tribunes	Consuls	4. 51. 1
397–396	Consular tribunes	Consular tribunes	5. 17. 4–5, 18. 1–2
392–391	Consuls	Consular tribunes	5. 31. 6–32. 1
390–389	Consular tribunes	Consular tribunes	6. 1. 8–9
387–386	Consular tribunes	Consular tribunes	6. 5. 6–8
371–370	Anarchy	Consular tribunes	6. 36. 3

In 444 the Romans first elected consular tribunes who abdicated because they had been elected by flaw. Livy remarks that only these eponyms appear in his predecessors and the Fasti, which means they were still considered the only eponyms of this year. Yet Licinius Macer had cited before Livy the authority of the Linen Books and two Roman signatories to a treaty with Ardea in 444 which indicated there were two consuls in this year. Livy has them elected by an

[1] For example, after the decemvirate the chief pontiff presides over the election of the tribunes of the plebs and the interrex over the election of consuls. Livy 3. 55. 1–2, however, does not know the name of the interrex.

interrex whom he names.[1] Certainly the name of the interrex was not on the treaty. Further Livy does not tell us the interregnum was noted by Macer. The interrex must have presided at the election of the three consular tribunes since his name would have been recorded with the eponyms. In order to explain the notice of an interrex and of two 'consuls', whom he wrongly calls suffect to the three consular tribunes, Livy asserts the consular tribunes had been elected by flaw.[2]

According to Livy's annalistic account political dissension in 421, 414 and 397 led to interregnal elections although apparently able-bodied magistrates could have presided. In 392 a censor died and a suffect censor was elected. Livy then explains that the consuls of 392 were compelled to resign because they had contracted the dead censor's illness and consequently the auspices had to be renewed. The ill-omen attached to the matter was the election of a suffect censor which brought the Gauls' invasion of Rome.[3] The government re-verted to an interregnum in 390 through political dissension at a moment when it might have been wiser to have said that they wished to renew the auspices.[4] They renewed the auspices again in 388.[5] The last interregnum reported for this period occurred in 370 after five years of anarchy caused, we are told, by the plebeian reformers, Licinius and Sextius.[6] From seven of the eight interregna recorded from 444 to 370 emerged consular tribunes. Four of them took place in years when six consular tribunes were in office. One of them would surely have been present and able to preside, if that magistrate could preside over the assembly which elected consular tribunes. This is the crux of the matter. The selection of military tribunes went back to the kingship. Then the king or his vice-regent (*magister*) could preside over the curias.[7] In the Republic, the chief pontiff, the curio maximus, the dictator and the interrex, alone might preside.

[1] Livy 4. 7. 10–12, on which see Ogilvie.

[2] Cic. *Fam.* 9. 21. 2 also knows the suffect consulship of Papirius (see p. 244, n. 3). Livy 4. 7. 3 makes the consul of 445 president in the election of consular tribunes because he has employed the interrex in the election of suffect consuls. Since the centuriate assembly is said to have elected these suffect consular tribunes (see p. 222) to the censorship in the next year, their 'suffection' may represent a confusion between the consular tribunes of 444 and the censors of 443. On the records of interregna see Appendix IIIF.

[3] Livy 5. 31. 6–32. 1.   [4] *Ibid.* 6. 1. 4–8.   [5] *Ibid.* 6. 5. 6–7.

[6] *Ibid.* 6. 36. 3. In this year anarchy produced the interregnum. Yet Livy has no record of the interrex's name. No doubt, there were other years (e.g. 449) for which the names of interrexes are lost.

[7] Note that in 390 Camillus is said to have been dictator and yet he does not hold the elections because his dictatorship is fictitious. See De Sanctis II, 172–5 and M. Sordi, pp. 145–51.

From the evidence we infer that the consular tribunes could not superintend the election of their successors in 397, 390 and 388 and the consuls could not preside over the election of consular tribunes in 445, 421 and 392. The consuls might have elected another college of consuls or allowed the government to revert to an interregnum. Political dissension did surround three of these interregna. In 397, 392 and 388 it took at least six days to obtain a college of consular tribunes. In each of these years the names of three interrexes are recorded which means that the assembly met to choose the magistrates at least into the first day of the third interrex.[1]

The interrex followed a comitial procedure that explains the restoration of the curiate system and the control of the imperial offices by certain families. In the curiate assembly under his presidence no prospective candidates appeared. The interrex submitted the names of men to the curias for their acceptance or rejection until he obtained three, four or six consular tribunes for whom a majority of curias had voted yes.[2] If strong antipathy existed, the process of selection might last through many interregna. For example, in 397–396 the election required at least three interrexes and produced five so-called plebeian consular tribunes. The result of dissatisfaction need not have led to the selection of plebeians. Under the same circumstances six patricians were selected for 391 and five patricians for 387.[3] In the latter years, however, a great concession was made to the lower classes by opening the territory of conquered Veii to Roman settlement.[4] By means of procedure the interrex could and did limit the entrance of certain men to the imperial magistracies.[5] Absolute control was impossible and at times the interrex found himself in a situation where he either proposed men belonging to the plebs or he refused to propose anyone. The former situation effected the predominantly plebeian colleges of consular tribunes in 400, 399 and 396 during the lengthy Veientine War. And, again, in 379

---

[1] The interrexes of 397/6 are the first recorded whose auspices derive from the fact that they had been only consular tribunes. A single interrex is noted for the years 445, 421 and 414 who must have been the president successful in obtaining the magistrates. Since at least two interrexes presided in an interregnum (as recorded for 390), this illustrates also the gaps in our records. See Appendix IIIF.

[2] See above, pp. 208–9, 211–12, 214–15.

[3] One of the consular tribunes of 387, Licinus Menenius Lanatus, is considered patrician, but was plebeian. See Appendix IIIA.

[4] Livy 5. 30. 8, 6. 4. 4, 6. 5. 8. See Taylor 'Voting Districts', pp. 47–9.

[5] See Appendix III.

plebeians predominated doubtless because of the agitation that was to bring Licinius and Sextius to plebeian power in 376.[1] The latter situation prevailed from 375 to 371 when no imperial magistrate of either kind was elected and effectually the government was in the hands of the plebeian tribunes.[2]

Anarchy and interregna are adduced to explain the mutability of the official year's commencement during the early Republic. Indeed, the date on which magistrates entered office may instruct us in the constitutional vicissitudes of the period. In chapter 6 we remarked the curial participation in ceremonies ending the old and beginning the new year before 1 January commenced the magisterial year. The adjustment of the magisterial year may reflect unforeseen changes in the eponymous magistrates. However, we ought to expect consistent irregularity, but we do not find it. For instance, according to Livy's rendition of the ill-omen attached to the consuls of 392 the new consular tribunes entered into office on the Kalends of Quinctilis.[3] This date appeared unique to Livy although he shows no like concern when the consuls of 329 succeed the consuls of 330 on the same date.[4] Other dates for the beginning of the magisterial year are known. In 401, for example, the consular tribunes entered office on the Kalends of October and before that on the Ides of December by reckoning that the consuls of 449 took office three days after the plebeian tribunes elected in that year. It is assumed that this abnormality results from varying unusual circumstances such as interregna.[5] Between 392 and 329 had occurred seven recorded interregna and the anarchy. Nevertheless in 392, in 329 and in the interval the normal date for entering an imperial magistracy was set for the Kalends of Quinctilis. Furthermore, the notations in the calendar bear out the assumption that the Kalends of Quinctilis

---

[1] This college had eight tribunes, an unusually large number. Two names are found only in Diodorus. His Erenucius I take as a mistake for Genucius, since the Minucii, the other suggested emendation, are otherwise conspicuous by their absence from the eponyms of 444–367. Furthermore, I prefer his Sestos or Sextos (for Sestius) to Livy's Sextilius, a family not attested in Roman politics until the third century. Lastly, I do not distinguish between Sestii and Sextii (as if Claudii and Clodii) because the Romans of the fifth century made no such distinction in pronunciation or in politics. See Broughton, s.a. 379.

[2] Our sources do not agree on the length of the anarchy after 376. For our purposes that is unimportant since all agree there was an anarchy. The annalistic tradition, of course, attributes the cause of the anarchy to the plebeian tribunes. See Broughton I, 109–10.

[3] See above, p. 227.   [4] Livy 8. 20. 3.

[5] Ibid. 4. 37. 3, 5. 9, 5. 11. 10–11; D.H. 11. 63. Mommsen, Röm. Staatsr. I³, 596–600 discusses other dates. The Ides of December may be only a learned reckoning from the date when the tribunes entered office in 449 and have no tradition behind it.

was recognized as the beginning of the magisterial year. Two days, 24 March and 24 May, bear the notation *q(uando) r(ex) c(omitiavit) f(as)* which means that on that day only the king may transact public business. In the Republic this rule surely applied to the *rex sacrorum*.[1] The king held his assemblies the day following the cleansing of the war-trumpets (*tubilustrium*) which both fell in March and May. 23 and 24 March and May may mark the beginning of military campaigns under the kings in two different periods.

On 5 July the Romans celebrated the feast of the Poplifugia which was thought to have originated in the flight of the Roman people at the time of the Gauls' arrival in 390[2] or a rout of the Roman army by Etruscans.[3] Varro offers another explanation in which he remarks that certain neighbors of the Romans made a common oath against the Romans on the day of the Poplifugia. This brings us closer to the truth. On 5 July the Roman infantry (*populus*) marched out and made ritual feints against ancestral enemies whom they ritually put to flight. Unlike the feast of the Regifugium, the Poplifugia is plural and must be construed as more than just one feint. A *poplifugium* is not the flight of the Roman people but a routing by the Roman infantry. The ancient connection of the feast with the Gauls confirms the meaning of the ritual feint. The Romans declared 18 July a *dies religiosus* because on that day they suffered their defeat at the hands of the Gauls at the stream of Allia. They ascribed this defeat to the failure of Sulpicius, the consular tribune in command at the Allia, to obtain favorable sacrifices on the day after the Ides of Quinctilis (16 July). The Romans chose this date to explain why every first day after Kalends, Nones and Ides is unlucky.[4] The date of Sulpicius' sacrifice was arrived at by aetiology. Yet his sacrifice or auspices might have taken place on the Kalends when he would have entered his magistracy or at the Poplifugia.[5] Piso's statement that the heifer

---

[1] Varro, *LL* 6. 31; Festus 311 L. Both authors assign the king's activity to the curias' Comitium.

[2] Varro, *LL* 6. 18: 'dies Poplifugia videtur nominatus quod eo die tumultu repente fugerit populus; non multo enim post hic dies quam decessus Gallorum ex urbe, et qui tum sub urbe populi, ut Ficuleates ac Fidenates et finitimi alii, contra nos coniurarunt. aliquot huius diei vestigia fugae in sacris apparent, de quibus rebus Antiquitatum libri plura referunt'.

[3] See below, p. 231, n. 1.

[4] Livy 6. 1. 11–12. See Michels, pp. 62–6, 133.

[5] Livy does not say Sulpicius' college resigned in order to renew the auspices (6. 1. 1–6) but he anticipates the consular tribune's want of piety (*nec auspicato nec litato*) and recklessness (*non loco castris ante capto, non praemunito vallo*) at 5. 38.

of victory (*vitula victoria*) was offered on the day after the Nones of July[1] confirms the religious and military character of this beginning of the archaic magisterial year. On 5 July the Romans made their ritual rout when Rome's ancestral enemies ritually made common cause against them. Three days later an imperial magistrate sacrificed the heifer of a ritual victory. The new year had begun for the new magistrates and the new infantry.

The month of July had begun neither the liturgical nor a curiate year. Quinctilis had once been the fifth month from the beginning. When the year began in March and ended in February, the infantry did not ritually put to rout Rome's enemies. In 402–401 the consular tribunes entered office on the Kalends of October. Livy says the former college was compelled to abdicate.[2] Not at all. In 403 the magistrates had decided to press the siege of Veii through the winter over plebeian remonstrance. Concessions were made[3] but the greatest concession seems to have been the shifting of the beginning of the official year to October, after the harvest, so that new magistrates could go to Veii with fresh levies for the winter siege. The year begins on the first day of July after Veii had fallen. Now it was normal to begin the year after spring planting and the harvest of winter crops in June. The campaigning season commenced at a time much more convenient to the Roman farmer. In 329 the consuls launched their attack on Privernum immediately after 1 July.[4] The year which began on 1 July had its origins in the demands of the centuriate army which would not gladly commence a campaign in late March or May and miss the spring planting and harvest.

The implication of these changes has a bearing on the demands of the centuriate *populus* for a convenient commencement and term of the annual military service and no bearing on the interregnal government. The oldest discernible official year began in March when the patrician Salians, garbed as soldiers, performed such rites as the Tubilustrium. This ceremony later fell also in May where it was fixed in the calendars a second time. The month of October

---

[1] Macr. *Sat.* 3. 2. 14: 'Piso ait vitulam victoriam nominari. cuius rei hoc argumentum profert quod postridie nonas Iulias re bene gesta, cum pridie populus a Tuscis in fugam versus sit—unde Poplifugia vocantur—post victoriam certis sacrificiis fiat vitulatio.' The Etruscans have intruded themselves in the aetiology because the *dies Alliensis* was also the *dies Cremerensis* (see below, p. 235, n. 3). I discuss the Poplifugia, Nonae Caprotinae and the *vitulatio* in *Juno*.
[2] Livy 5. 8–10 who mentions such a dearth of manpower that the *seniores* were called up.
[3] *Ibid.* 5. 2. [4] *Ibid.* 8. 20. 2–5.

contained the sacrifice of the horse to Mars on the 15th and a purification of weapons on the 19th. These rites seem to point to the end of the military season which had begun in March and not to the briefly observed official year commencing on 1 October. On the other hand, the official year which began on 1 July, Kalends of Quinctilis, was observed by the Poplifugia, the heifer of victory and, as we shall see below, by the parade of cavalry on 15 July. The last ceremony also had religious implications so that the second day after 15 July appears the appropriate occasion for marching forth against the enemy. The shifts in the beginning of the magisterial year and military seasons meant new commanders and new levies. In this context the convenience of the soldier–citizen was being consulted where practical. The centuriate army decided the questions of when and with whom it would go to war.

THE CONSULAR TRIBUNATE

Six years after the restoration of the curiate constitution of 444 consular tribunes were again elected. In the following year, 437, the Fasti records the election of consuls and that magistracy marked the years till 434 when the consular tribunate is again filled. The nearly unanimous tradition before Livy claimed that in 437 A. Cornelius Cossus in single combat slew and despoiled the king of Veii, Lars Tolumnius. The spoils of this king he dedicated in the temple of Jupiter Feretrius where they still hung in Augustus' reign. Yet Livy was troubled by this tradition because Cossus was only a military tribune at the time and these spoils (*spolia opima*) could not be won by other than the Roman commander with the auspices from any other than the enemy's commander. Since consuls were the eponymous officers of 437, Cossus could not have been a consular tribune according to tradition. The two sources dissenting from the traditional record were the emperor Augustus and Licinius Macer. Augustus had seen the linen corselet of the Etruscan king which noted Cossus had been consul when he took it. Invoking the authority of the Linen Rolls Macer dates a consulship of Cossus to the seventh year after 437 when he was consul with T. Quinctius Poenus.[1] In 431 the latter was indeed consul but not with Cossus.[2] On the

[1] Livy 4. 19–20. Serv. Dan. on *Aen.* 6. 841 alone calls Cossus a military tribune with consular power. See Broughton, *s.a.* 437.
[2] Livy 4. 26. 1.; Diod. 12. 65. 1. It is possible that Cossus was a third consular tribune

other hand, the two men held the imperial magistracies together in 428, 427 and 426. The Fasti for these years are not clear because some clever man has tampered with them. In 428 Cossus and T. Quinctius are said to have been consuls by the main chronographical sources which include Diodorus. Yet Diodorus also records a second college of consuls, L. Quinctius and A. Sempronius. Livy and Diodorus record the names of the consuls, C. Servilius and L. Papirius, for 427 but Livy also indicates that Cossus and T. Quinctius were again consuls in 427. Although neither 428 nor 427 is the seventh year after 437, one of these two consulships of Cossus and T. Quinctius might be related to Licinius Macer's report of the Linen Books. In 426 Cossus and T. Quinctius were two of the four so-called military tribunes with consular power.[1] That political exigencies which prompted the consulships of these two men belong to the policy of Augustus Caesar has been long recognized.[2] Augustus took pains to prove his claim that none but the magistrate with the auspices was entitled to a triumph. To his mind the deed of Cossus in the capacity of military tribune (with or without consular auspices) boded ill for the Princeps' claim. And he had good authority for his claim that Cossus was consul when he took the spoils and celebrated his triumph. The corselet of Tolumnius, the Linen Books and Licinius Macer unequivocally said that Cossus was consul when he bested Tolumnius.

Confusion prevails also in the Fasti for 434. Diodorus lists three consular tribunes, Ser. Cornelius, M. Manlius and Q. Sulpicius.[3] The oldest annalists knew of this college of consular tribunes but they had been set aside on the authority of the Linen Books. Licinius Macer saw C. Julius and L. Verginius noted in the Linen Books as consuls of 435 and 434. Valerius Antias and Aelius Tubero, however, named M. Manlius and Q. Sulpicius the consuls of 434. Furthermore,

in this year. Livy 4. 27. 1 mentions an A. Cornelius as pontifex maximus in 431 which might account for Macer's miscalculation, although the *viimo* of Livy might be textually corrupt.

[1] See Broughton, *s.aa.* 428–426.
[2] Mommsen *Röm. Staatsr.* 1³, 128, 11³, 190, basing himself on Zonaras 7. 18, laid down that consular tribunes could not triumph. Cassius Dio is certainly not reliable on this score. See H. Last, *CAH* 7. 507–8; M. P. Charlesworth, *CAH* 10. 125; R. Syme, *The Roman Revolution* (Oxford, 1939), p. 404; T. J. Luce, 'The Dating of Livy's First Decade', *TAPA* 96 (1965), 209–40; and E. Mensching, 'Livius, Cossus und Augustus', *Mus. Helv.* 24 (1967), 12–32. Despite the weak tradition of early triumphs, the triumph of Cossus enjoyed a wide acceptance which Livy attests.
[3] Diod. 12. 53. 1 (cf. Livy, next note).

233

Tubero also derived this college of consuls from the Linen Books.[1] Both Macer and Tubero cannot be right and presumably the former had misread the writing on linen. The consuls, Manlius and Sulpicius are also members of the college of consular tribunes, otherwise known to Macer and Tubero. The coincidence tells much.

Autopsy of the linen corselet and Linen Rolls produced the names of consuls. Yet Roman tradition also makes clear that the title consul alone did not exist in the fifth century to designate that magistrate which we and the Romans knew as consuls. The title was *praetor* to which the adjective *consul* was attributed.[2] The conclusion is unavoidable that from 444 to 367 the adjective was also applied to the tribunes of the soldiers whose proper title was *tribuni consules*. And this title was also abbreviated to *consul* alone. The archivists of the Linen Rolls and Cornelius Cossus noted only the title *consul* which signified the magistrate later known as the *tribunus militum consulari potestate*. The later designations were born of a desire to avoid confusion with the magistracy of two men, restored in 366 and called simply *consules*.[3] The eponyms were tribunes-consul or praetors-consul. In Appendix I is a revision of the Fasti for 444, 437, 434, 428 and 427. Following the nearly unanimous tradition, we place Cossus' triumph in 437 when he was tribune-consul, the magistracy which he held again in 428 and 427. In truth, I believe that he never was praetor-consul. The year 426 marks in the present Fasti the first college of four tribunes-consul. In my revision a college of four tribunes-consul appears first in 428.[4]

Licinius Macer offered Livy additional information on the ill-omen of the Curia Faucia which was the principal curia to vote the *lex curiata* for the magistrates who commanded at the Caudine Forks and at the capture of Rome. The auspices of the commander K. Fabius who commanded at the Cremera had been confirmed first by the Faucia. The abominable Faucia could have become abominable only after repeated *principia* in whose consequences commanders

---

[1] Livy 4. 23. 1–3. On the misreadings owed to illegibility see Ogilvie, '*Libri Lintei*'.

[2] *Comm. Cons.* in Varro, *LL* 6. 88; Cic. *Leg.* 3. 3. 8; Livy 3. 55. 11–12; Zon. 7. 19. See Mommsen, *Röm. Staatsr.* II³, 74–9; De Sanctis I, 403–6; and Heurgon, 'Magistratures romaines et magistratures étrusques', *Les origines de la république romaine*, pp. 97–127.

[3] See Mommsen, *Röm. Staatsr.* II³. 188–90 and below, p. 235, n. 2.

[4] The two Quinctii, T. and L., are confused in the tradition of the Fasti of 420 and may be confused also in the 'division' of the consular tribunes of 428 into consular praetors. In that case, there were only three tribunes-consul in 428 and in 427 the first college of four.

saw forebodings of defeat. Using a source outside the pontifical tradition, Macer relied on the Linen Books for his information that the Faucia voted first for the auspices of K. Fabius. The story of the defeat of Fabius has been overlaid with legend, yet a defeat it was. It happened either in 479 when Fabius was consul or in 478 when he was proconsul.[1] Since the proconsulship is first dated to 326, the second office is clearly impossible. The possibility remains that in 478 K. Fabius was one of three tribunes-consul. The most puzzling aspect of the tradition has been the death of no less than 300 Fabii at the Cremera. In chapter 6 I suggest that Luperci Fabiani were the sometime priests of a Curia Fabia and that members of curias might take their gentilicial name from the name of their curia. K. Fabius, tribune-consul of 478, enlisted his army in accordance with the old military system and drew on the curias for soldiers and did not deploy the centuriate army. The curia from which he drew the greatest support evidently was the Curia Fabia. Three hundred members of that curia fell at the Cremera, not 300 members of the Gens Fabia.[2] This apparent reversion to the curiate constitution and, what is more, to the threefold tribal army, for the moment dealt a blow to the curiate system and forever ended the tribal army.[3]

Before discussing the command of the tribunes-consul over the centuriate army we must explain the nature of the magisterial archives on linen. The Linen Books contained material ranging from 478 (the curial auspices at the Cremera) to 428 or 427 (the supposed consulship of Cossus and T. Quinctius).[4] They were deposited in the

---

[1] See Broughton, s.aa. and next note.

[2] See pp. 133–6, 142. Only Dionysius 9. 16. 3 calls Fabius proconsul (anthypatos), a title he also applies to the tribunes-consul (11. 62. 1) as does Zonaras 7. 19. Varro in Gellius 14. 7. 5 and Livy 4. 7. 1 and 5. 2. 9 use pro consule and proconsularis. It is remarkable that the first authentic proconsul, Q. Publilius, triumphed without constitutional difficulty (Livy 8. 23. 12, 26. 7). It is obvious from the ancient circumlocutions for the consular tribunate that the Roman historians were incapable of understanding the precise character of the magistracy. Macr. Sat. 1. 13. 21 equates the military tribunes with consular power with the consuls; see Ogilvie on Livy 4. 7. 10.

[3] See P. Frezza, 'Intorno alla legenda dei Fabii al Cremera', Scr. di dir. rom. in on. di C. Ferrini (Milan, 1946), pp. 297–306, Momigliano, 'Interim Report', p. 121. Roman superstition thrived on repetitions and coincidences such as the omen of Curia Faucia. Hence, I am inclined to accept the report that the dies Alliensis was also the date of the defeat at the Cremera (Livy 6. 1. 11, Tac. Hist. 2. 9. 1). One defeat on one date hardly made an omen. Furthermore, the two campaigns under tribunes-consul would have commenced at nearly the same time after Poplifugia.

[4] In addition to the passages already discussed, Livy 4. 13. 7 cites the Linen Books in support of the prefecture of L. Minucius in 440 and 439. Livy calls him praefectus annonae but the Linen Books may have called him only praefectus. He could have been in charge of

temple of Juno Moneta on the Arx. This temple was vowed in 345 and dedicated the following year.[1] The cult of this Juno may be older than 345 but a temple which housed the Linen Books can be no older.[2] The archives of the Linen Books documented the tribunes-consul and yet our evidence permits us to bring their record only down to 427, whereas the consular tribunate continued to 367 when it was abolished by the Licinio-Sextian Rogations. Most likely the Linen Books were transferred in 344 from somewhere near the Comitium or Capitolium where the curiate assembly met to a new temple of the one goddess worshipped in all the curias. The reason for the transfer of the archives is not far to seek. After the abolition of the tribunes-consul in 367 and the establishment of the election of the military tribunes by the centuriate assembly in 362 curial archives of any officer became impossible and unnecessary.[3] Memory of the oldest Roman cavalry uniform states that the soldier fought in loincloths.[4] Lars Tolumnius still fought in traditional linen garb.[5] As late as 293 the linened legion (*legio linteata*) of the Samnites met in a linen tent and swore a solemn oath according to the archaic formula written on a linen roll that they would fight the Romans to the death.[6]

Linen was reserved for or prevented from certain uses. The Roman Fetials and wives of flamens were forbidden to wear linen garments.[7]

the city. The pontifical annals recorded grain shortages (Cato *Orig.* fr. 77 P.). However, the Linen Books were not pontifical. See Ogilvie on Livy, pp. 550 ff.

[1] Livy 4. 7. 12, 4. 20. 8, 7. 28. 4–6.

[2] Tradition places T. Tatius' and Manlius Capitolinus' houses on the site. See Platner–Ashby, *s.v. Iuno Moneta*.

[3] Ogilvie on Livy 4. 7. 12 holds that the Linen Books contained a full list of magistrates from 509.

[4] Polyb. 6. 25. 3–4. 'Loincloths' is the exaggeration of a *laudator temporis acti*, although they wore so little in training (see Walbank on Polyb.). Rather, the horseman's tunic, worn under the *trabea*, may have been of linen. See Alföldi, 'Reiteradel', pp. 36–53.

[5] His *thorax linteus* (Livy 4. 20. 7) recalls the Homeric *linothorax* (*Il.* 2. 529, 2. 830). The proper Latin word was *lorica* which might be of linen when worn for sacrifice (by the *tribunus celerum*?); cf. Suet. *Galba* 19. 1. Ernout–Meillet[4] suggest a connection between the Greek and Latin words despite the Romans' etymology of *lorica* from *lorum*.

[6] Livy 10. 38 (cf. 9. 40. 3); Festus 102 L. See Tondo, pp. 71–103. The Samnites' oath differs little from that of the Ficuleates and Fidenates (above, p. 230, n. 2). E. T. Salmon, *Samnium and the Samnites*, pp. 104–5, 146, n. 3, 182–6, 270–2, discusses these legions and their oath. He holds that the Linen Books (not the linen military garb) belong to romantic historiography because writing was not traditional among the Samnites *c.* 300. However, Salmon acknowledges that the Samnites signed a treaty with the Romans in 354. Furthermore, writing was common enough in priestly or religious circles of Rome (e.g. *libri pontificum*), Etruscans (e.g. *libri rituales*) and even Samnites (viz. the Agnone tablet) in relatively early times. On the legions' armor I agree with Salmon.

[7] Serv. on *Aen.* 12. 120.

The ladies of the Gens Atilia Serrana, a Campanian family in origin, did not don linen.[1] While touring, Marcus Aurelius wrote to his teacher Fronto:[2]

...we turned off the main road and went about a mile to Anagnia. Then we visited that ancient town which, although a tiny place, holds many antiquities, temples and an unusual number of religious rites. No corner was without a chapel or a shrine or a sacred precinct. Moreover, there are many linen books which concern religious matters. As we departed, we remarked a notice, posted twice on the gateway:

Flamen, sume samentum!

I asked a native what the last word meant. He said that in Hernican *samentum* is the hide of a sacrificial victim which the flamen puts over his apex when he enters the city.

As late as the fourth century A.D. linen still had a special quality. At a magical séance linen clothing and boots were worn.[3] Therefore, I propose that the stuff of the Roman *Libri Lintei* had once been that of the tunics or the tunics themselves of commanding tribunes who kept alive their deeds upon the garb which had once protected them.[4]

The Linen Books have confounded ancient authors and modern historical critics. Ogilvie's view that they represent a later Republican compilation of older material commends itself by reason of the fact that the forgery of this kind of document did not benefit any person or faction insofar as we have received information from and about them. Forgeries ought to be clear to all users. The Linen Books clearly were not clear. Their want of clarity may be attributed to the misunderstanding of the old material. I have demonstrated above how one cause of obscurity in the tradition was the indiscriminate application of *consul* to both praetor and tribune. Moreover, the stuff of the books had a special quality not found in ordinary records. Here the rolls resemble the famous Etruscan ceremonial written on linen which was turned into a winding cloth. Perhaps the Zagreb cloth has survived because of the treatment of its mummy. However, if a compilation of the Linen Books was made around 150, as Ogilvie argues, it seems to me likely that the records were transcribed

[1] Varro in Pliny, *NH* 19. 8.
[2] Corn. Fron. p. 66 N., 1. 174 *LCL*.
[3] Amm. Marc. 29. 1. 29–32, an outlandish mixture of Mediterranean superstitions.
[4] The wooden frame, shaped like a shield and covered with the hide of the sacrificial ox, which records the treaty between Rome and Gabii (Dion. 4. 58. 4) is a document apposite to the dedicated linen corselet

to the same kind of stuff which had preserved them since their inception. The prominence of the tribune-consul in what is left to us and the date of the temple of Juno Moneta point to a series of notices pertinent to the defunct magistracy. The presumed record of the Curia Faucia, first abominable from the defeat at the Cremera River and evidently kept separate from the pontifical archives, suggest archives of the curiate assembly. Elsewhere I have argued that this assembly condemned Manlius Capitolinus whose house was razed and upon whose ground was reared the temple of Moneta. His confiscated ground may have fallen to curial control. At any rate, the temple itself is not directly connected with any curia. The temple was dedicated by the dictator L. Furius Camillus with whom another Manlius Capitolinus served as master of horse (Livy 7. 28).

The chief curion posted the obligations of the several curias for the Fornacalia:

> curio legitimis nunc Fornacalia verbis
>   maximus indicit nec stata sacra fecit:
> inque Foro, multa circum pendente tabella,
>   signatur certa curia quaeque nota.
>
> (Ovid *Fasti* 2. 526–30.)

If he kept records for his annual notice of the movable feast, the chief curion could have been in the habit of preserving curiate determinations. The priest king, too, must have kept records in order to make the appropriate monthly announcements at the Curia Calabra. It was at his former house that the chief pontiff posted the annalistic notices on whitened boards. The chief pontiff certainly presided over the curiate assembly. The Linen Books apparently differed in content as well as in the manner of preservation from the pontifical archives of the Regia. Chief curion or pontiff or the priest-king might have kept the Linen Rolls. No writer before Licinius Macer is known to have made use of them. However, before their compilation or late redaction comparable with that of the *annales maximi* the Linen Books may have been little accessible and, what is more, hardly intelligible.[1]

The ancients believed that the election of tribunes-consul instead of praetors-consul was motivated either by military exigencies or by the political strife of the day. Recent modern students of the consular

---

[1] See H. Peter, *HRR* I², CCCLV–CCCLVII; Münzer, *RE* 13. 1, cols 424–8; Schanz-Hosius I⁴, 28, 320–1; Ogilvie, '*Libri Lintei*'; and Palmer, 'King' and *Juno*.

tribunate have accepted the former purpose and the evidence tends to support them.[1] As for the latter motive, the evidence only partially vindicates Livy's view that the new magistracy was created in order to make room for plebeians.[2] The problem of patricians and plebeians in the Fasti from 509 to 367 is much too complex to be stated so simply.

The generally accepted view on the size of the centuriate army holds that the original number of the one levy (*legio*) was 6,000 and that after the institution of the dual praetorship two legions were enlisted with about one-half the original number.[3] The last attempt to field the old tribal army of 3,000 about 478 had proved a military disaster at the Cremera. When the curiate constitution was revived, its proponents certainly intended to retain the centuriate army and to that effect created the censorship so that the citizens might be rated for military service. Fraccaro maintains that the number of the consular tribunes did not bear any relation to the numbers of legions and that not all the tribunes commanded troops.[4] Between 428 or 427 and 406 the usual number of consular tribunes was four. However, in 418 only three tribunes were elected. For two of them a special levy was conscripted from only ten of the twenty-one tribes.[5] This means that from roughly one-half of the citizen-body two tribunes drew their regiments and that from all the tribes four tribunes would have drawn their regiments if four had been elected to military command. Traditionally the number of tribunes-consul could not be less than three, but military exigencies could not always be anticipated. Occasionally, one or more tribunes might remain in the city and assume no command.[6] One tribune would have remained at home in 418, a year in which no need for a college of four tribunes had been anticipated. The contemporary increase of the number of quaestors to four suggests that this became the greatest number of regular regiments levied in this period. However, if the

[1] See above, p. 222, nn. 3–4.
[2] Livy 4. 6. 6–12 with which compare a similar reason given for the increased number of quaestors (see below, p. 241, nn. 3–4).
[3] Fraccaro, *Opuscula* II, 287–306, has shown that the single and sole levy (*legio*) of 6,000 foot-soldiers goes back to Servius and is pre-republican only, and that the reduction of the size of the centuries which accompanied the enlistment of two legions reflects the dual consulship.
[4] *Ibid.* pp. 304–6.
[5] Livy 4. 46. 1. See Taylor, 'Centuriate Assembly', pp. 340–2.
[6] Fraccaro, *Opuscula* II, 305–6.

government could anticipate the number of regiments to be levied by setting the number of tribunes, it could also anticipate the number of consular tribunes needed at home for civil administration. From 405 on the usual number of consular tribunes was six.[1] After the restoration of the centuriate magistracies in 367 the business of some of these tribunes would have been transferred to the one praetor and two curule aediles.[2] Rome's wars with Veii, the Gauls and her neighbors would account for her willingness to levy four regiments while at the same time arranging for the civil administration. The multiple command of the consular tribunate had an advantage over the dual consular praetorship.[3] The oligarchy employed the consular tribunate in its struggle with plebeian leaders over the major magistracy. The number of tribunes in each college was dictated by military exigencies which the oligarchy dared to neglect no more than they dared to neglect the civil administration. Not until the height of Roman war with Veii did the plebeians attain a majority in a college of tribunes (see below). In the event, the plebeian leaders could take advantage of the hostilities to become consular tribunes while they wanted most of all to have the magistracy abolished (see below, pp. 247–50).

Besides the censorship and consular tribunate a third elective office was perhaps instituted and surely expanded during the politically critical years after the decemviral magistracy. The quaestor never played a prominent role in Roman politics, for he was a minor functionary. His duties were closely bound to the command of his superior, a praetor-consul or tribune-consul. The latter magistracy seems to have prompted the expansion of the number of quaestors and probably the extent of their functions. At any rate, the annalistic represented by Livy evinces an explanation of its expansion similar to that given for the institution of the tribunes-consul. The origin of the quaestorship goes back at least to the beginning of the Republic when two quaestors served under the two praetors-consul. Romans believed that the quaestorship had its beginnings in the royal period, although they do not agree as to whether the kings appointed the quaestor or had him elected. Tacitus says the *lex curiata* sought by

---

[1] See above, p. 215, n. 1. This number indicates that four tribunes were normally in the field and two at home.

[2] Fraccaro, *Opuscula* II, 305; von Fritz, pp. 40–4.

[3] On the wars of this period see De Sanctis II, chapters 15, 16, 18.

Brutus proved the kings had founded the office.[1] In a lost work on the power of magistrates Junius Gracchanus says the kings had created the quaestors by election.[2] In Tacitus' view the first election of two quaestors took place in 446. This date falls between the abolition of the decemvirate and the restoration of the consular tribunate and squares with the political agitation of the period. In 421 the number of the quaestors was raised to four in order, we are told, to open the office to plebeians, and to ensure the presence of two quaestors in the city.[3] The first election of four quaestors was held by a tribune-consul in 420 and four patricians were returned.[4] Not until 409 did the Romans elect plebeian quaestors.[5] In that year praetors-consul presided over the election. Evidently the magistrates elected these subalterns in the assembly in which they themselves were elected: the tribunes-consul in the curiate assembly and the praetors-consul in the centuriate.[6]

The doubling of the magistracy in 421 had nothing to do with plebeian political aspirations. The second reason offered by the ancients is an administrative division of urban and military quaestors, but little commends it. The number of four quaestors comports with the number of four tribunes-consul. The mistaken interpretation arises from the ancients' failure to distinguish between the quaestor who served the military magistrate in the field and the *quaestor* or *quaesitor* who presided over criminal investigations (*quaestiones*).[7] The quaestor who was annually elected from 446 and whose number reached four in 420 is the so-called *quaestor aerarii*, the military paymaster. Neither in 446 nor 421 could the quaestors have served in the capacity of paymaster since military pay was instituted shortly before or after the outbreak of war with Veii about 405.[8] The title *quaestor*, however, has no particular pertinence to the non-existent Roman money. Rather, the quaestor was the likely purveying quartermaster of the general. Although the soldier-citizen then

---

[1] Tac. *Ann.* 11. 22. See Nichols, pp. 270–4.

[2] *Dig.* 1. 13. 1 pr., which has been rejected as the fantasy of the *populares* along with Plut. *Poplic.* 12. See Wissowa, *RE* 10. 1, cols 1031–3, Mommsen, *Röm. Staatsr.* II³, 528 ff., De Martino I², 231–4.

[3] Livy 4. 43, Tac. *Ann.* 11. 22.   [4] Livy 4. 44. 2–5.   [5] *Ibid.* 4. 54. 2–3.

[6] Cic. *Fam.* 7. 30. 1 is the only clear reference to the tribal election of quaestors. Cf. Messala in Gellius 13. 15. The first certain election of military officers by the tribes is legislated in 311.

[7] See W. Kunkel, 'Untersuchungen zur Entwicklung des röm. Kriminalverfahrens in vorsullanischer Zeit', *Bay. Akad. Wissensch. Phil.-hist. Kl. Abh. n. F.* 56 (1962), 37–45.

[8] Livy 4. 60 (cf. Florus 1. 6. 12).

armed and fed himself at his own expense, some officer of responsibility looked to the provision of arms and food. Had a hungry soldier lost his arms in battle, he could hardly be permitted indefinite leave to seek new arms and food immediately after battle. Indeed, the citizen provisioned himself but the command had to supply the soldier's needs. Another function of the quaestor which has every likelihood of being archaic was the sale of conquered land that was designated *ager quaestorius*.[1] Although the first extraordinary increment of Roman territory occurred in 396, the land of Roman neighbors had gradually been annexed through conquest. Around 426, for example, Veii's ally, Latian Fidenae, fell to Rome. The immediate post-war responsibility of the field commander would have been the orderly distribution of newly acquired territory through sale. This business could have been entrusted to the quaestors. The four quaestors, then, served the army during the war and the state after the war.[2]

In this section I have argued that the magistracy of three, four or six tribunes who were the annual eponyms known to the Romans as military tribunes with consular power were titled *tribuni consules*. The title could also have been expressed by the simple *consul* which was so recorded on the linen corselet of the vanquished Lars Tolumnius and on the Linen Rolls. The Linen Rolls preserved the names of curial *principia*, eponymous magistrates, and extraordinary officials such as prefects and interrexes with their interregna. Moreover, I suggest that the Linen Rolls had been curial archives which were rendered unnecessary after the year 366 and were deposited *c.* 344 in the new temple of Juno Moneta. The number of four tribunes-consul can be related to the tribal levies of troops in such a way that at one moment a tribune commanded conscripts from five tribes. Likewise the same number of tribunes-consul can be related to the expansion of the quaestorship. Four quaestors were needed for service to four tribunes-consul. Their duties included purveying, confiscating conquered territory and *c.* 400 the disbursement of payment to troops serving at Veii. Plebeian access to the quaestorship was obtained under one of the rare consular praetorships in the period under discussion. I inter-

---

[1] See *Röm. Feldmesser*, pp. 115–16, 152–4 L. and Rudorff, II, 285 ff.

[2] The quaestors are said to have been increased to eight in 267 (Livy *Per.* 15) which is the doubling mentioned by Tac. *Ann.* 11. 22. The number is, in fact, restored to the *Periocha* which says: 'quaestorum numerus ampliatus est, ut essent....'

pret this event as the result of their election in the assembly which also elected the praetors-consul. Conversely the earlier patrician elections to the expanded quaestorship is explained as the result of curiate election since, I argue, the curiate assembly controlled the election of the archaic officers, the military tribunes, who became the normal chief magistrates after the decemviral magistracy and then bore the title tribunes-consul.

THE FATHERS AND THE PLEBS

The laws proposed by the plebeian tribunes Licinius and Sextius included the abolition of the consular tribunate and made the re-stored consular praetorship (thereafter the consulship) accessible to the plebeians.[1] Magdelain's thesis on the formation of the patriciate rests upon the theory that the persistent election of members of the same families to magistracies with imperial auspices created a political élite at Rome.[2] The statistics which emerge from the Fasti between 509 and 367 present difficulties in defining the patriciate. In Appendix II are listed the seventeen families whose members held an imperial magistracy between 509 and 445 and whose members did not hold an imperial magistracy between 444 and 367. Seven of these seventeen families disappear from our sight forever after. Four of these seven families are represented as having held plebeian tribunates. The remaining ten families emerge after 367 as plebeian. Of these ten six families are represented as having held the plebeian tribunate. In total, ten of the seventeen families held the plebeian tribunate between 493 and 367. Not one family is demonstrably patrician. The outstanding family in the list is the Minucia whose members obtained six imperial offices. Between 444 and 367 they do not have the *imperium* but twice have the plebeian tribunate. Likewise striking is the tradition that the two consuls of 454, Sp. Tarpeius and A. Aternius, are co-opted plebeian tribunes in 448. The story is doubted but may well explain their families' disappearance.[3]

In Appendix IIIA are listed the forty-one families whose members held 294 imperial magistracies from 444 to 367. Only sixteen families in Appendix IIIC were indisputably patrician and these held 219

---

[1] Livy 6. 35. 5: 'tertiam [*sc.* legem] ne tribunorum militum comitia fierent consulumque utique alter ex plebe crearetur'. See von Fritz, pp. 1–44 on the legislation of 367.
[2] Magdelain, 'Auspicia', pp. 450–73.
[3] Livy 3. 65. 1 (cf. 3. 31. 5 on which see Ogilvie) and Cic. *Rep.* 2. 60.

imperial magistracies. Four families may be considered patrician since evidence is lacking that they held a certain patrician or plebeian office after 367. Their members would bring the total of imperial magistracies held by patricians to 240. Of these twenty families only two, the Papiria and Folia, did not have a magistracy before 444. The evidence of the Papirii accords with Magdelain's thesis. The Folii destroy it. In 433 M. Folius Flaccinator was tribune-consul. In 318 his namesake is the patrician consul. These are the only Folii in all the Fasti. The family certainly did not persistently have the *imperium* and auspices from one generation to the next. Yet the Papirii and Folii have another thing in common. A member of their families was chief pontiff.[1] However a Minucius may also have been chief pontiff in this period.[2] The Papiria is the only family which we know was called a patrician *gens minor*.[3] Most probably the Gens Folia also belonged to this group. Hence we may define a *gens minor* as a patrician family whose sons were elected to an imperial magistracy after 444 and held the chief pontificate. The two consular tribunates of the Cloelii in 444 and 378, followed by their family's obscurity for almost 200 years, of the Claudii Crassi in 424 and 403 hardly approach the record of other patrician families. The Nautii with four imperial magistracies come closest to the Cloelii and Claudii.

On the plebeian side between 444 and 367 are twenty-one families. Ten of these families appear for the first time as imperial magistrates after 444. All ten of these families had members who served the plebs and may be safely considered plebeian. The Aquilii, Antonii, Duillii, Genucii, Menenii, Sempronii, Sextii, Verginii and Veturii

---

[1] See above, p. 221, n. 2 and Livy 5. 41. 3.

[2] Plut. *Moralia* 89 F (*Inim. util.* 6); cf. Livy 4. 44. 11–12. According to my estimation, argued in Appendix III, the Verginii and Veturii were plebeian. A Verginius was augur in 463 and a Veturius in 453, when plebeians presumably could not occupy that priesthood. Their office resembles the interregnum of Sempronius in 482; see Appendix IIIE.

[3] Cic. *Fam.* 9. 21. 2: 'sed tamen, mi Paete, qui tibi venit in mentem negare Papirium quemquam umquam nisi plebeium fuisse? fuerunt enim patricii minorum gentium, quorum princeps L. Papirius Mugillanus, qui censor cum L. Sempronio Atratino fuit, cum ante consul cum eodem fuisset, annis post R. c. CCCXII....post hunc XIII fuerunt sella curuli ante L. Papirium Crassum, qui primum Papisius est vocari desitus', etc. The first question which comes to mind is whether Cicero was drawing on a *liber magistratuum* or a history of the Gens Papiria. If the former, it must have been one of the Linen Books since the ordinary eponyms of 444 did not record the *consules suffecti*. Yet Cicero never cites Macer or the Linen Books (cf. Cic. *Leg.* 1. 2. 7). Most likely then, Cicero used a family history in which the *princeps gentis* was styled consul. On the *princeps gentis* see Magdelain, 'Auspicia', pp. 466–7.

all occupied imperial magistracies in the two periods 509–445 and 444–367. Yet the evidence from two directions indicates their plebeian character. The Duillii, Genucii, Menenii, Sextii and Verginii contributed tribunes to the plebs between 493 and 367. The Duillii, Genucii, Menenii, Sempronii and Veturii fill plebeian offices in the later fourth century; the Aquilii, Licinii, Lucretii and Sextii in the third century. The Verginii were an illustrious family in the fifth century. After 389 we meet a solitary Verginius as military tribune of 207 with whom the family's hope seems to have come to an end. All these families surpass the Papirii and Folii in the antiquity of their renown; none could help exceeding the record of the Folii, Cloelii and Claudii from 444 to 367. The Duillii, Lucretii, Menenii and Verginii even held the consular praetorship in this period. The Claudii, Cloelii, Fabii, Nautii, Postumii and Servilii held only consular tribunates and yet they were indubitably patrician. Neither an imperial magistracy with its auspices nor its repetition by a member of the same family proves the origin of the patriciate. The plebeian tribunates held from 493 to 367 tell more. Fifty-eight families are represented in Appendices II and III. Twenty may be patrician. Twenty-three of the remaining thirty-eight families had plebeian tribunes according to the tradition. If we reckon that nearly 1,000 plebeian tribunates could have been filled from 493 to 367, the random mention of only 72 plebeian tribunes for given years (some of which must be fictitious or repetitions) is all the more astonishing.

In effect, certain Roman politicians excluded themselves and their families from the patriciate by serving the plebs as tribune. Those politicians whose family had never been contaminated with plebeian office choked the political life of certain fellow Romans who had dared to protect the plebs. The plebeian families outnumber the patricians in the magistracies between 444 and 367 insofar as families go. But the patricians far outnumber the plebeians in magistracies held: the ratio is 4 to 1. Politically speaking, twenty-one plebeian families ought to have more friends among the voters than twenty patrician families. The patricians alone could hardly begin to fill the army of 6,000, let alone 12,000, every year if need arose. This point the seceding plebs made amply clear. Yet the plebeians elected only fifty-six magistrates from their own in contrast with the 240 patrician magistrates. The explanation of this situation is the interregnal procedure of accepting or rejecting nominees to the consular tribunate in the curiate assembly. Now we are confronted with the question of why the former plebeian magistrates did not serve as interrexes. They, too, had been elected to perpetual auspices in the terms stated by Magdelain. This we cannot deny them.[1]

Iteration of an imperial magistracy by itself never bestowed upon a man and his family the right of the perpetual auspices of the interrex. Already we suggested that the curions of the curias exercised the interregnal auspices after a king's demise and that the Fathers supplanted the thirty curions in the Republican interregna. In a sense this is true. However, the interrex could not be wholly divorced from the curionate. Therefore, the qualifications for a Republican interrex, which we propose, must have been that he himself have already held an imperial magistracy, that he or an ancestor have been a curion and, finally, that no member of his family had ever been a plebeian officer. We know nothing of the procedure of election within one curia but we do know the combined qualifications for the curionate and curial flaminate. These officers had to be at least 50 years old, wealthy, well-born, and free from bodily defects. Lastly, the curion could fill no longer a public magistracy.[2] In a word, the curionate was a political *cul-de-sac* which required property and a minimal age in addition to the doubtless religiously inspired physical qualification. The political qualification of the curionate was certainly inspired by the Roman king whose sovereign authority was not to be undermined by a chieftain with religious and political power in his curia. In the royal period there had been no patrician and no plebeian.

In 483–482 a Sempronius was interrex, in 463 a Verginius augur, in 453 a Veturius augur and in 420 perhaps a Minucius chief pontiff. The first was a Father, the rest filled patrician priesthoods. Yet they were members of clans that were plebeian after 367 except for Verginius whose contemporary relatives served as tribunes of the plebs (see Appendix III). The plebs could recognize itself in 494. The Law of the Twelve Tables knew a distinction between patrician and plebeian and forbade their marriage. In 445 the plebeian Canuleius legislated the legitimacy of such a marriage in a tribal meeting from whose acts the patricians claimed immunity. Yet in succeeding generations intermarriage took place (Livy 6. 34). The Law of the Twelve Tables was well known to later

---

[1] Above, p. 228, n. 1.　　　　　　[2] D.H. 2. 21. 3. See pp. 80–1, 208–10.

educated Romans. No word of a clause on the definition and discrimination of patrician and plebeian survives to us or apparently survived to them who otherwise would not have dated the institution of castes to Romulus and supplied us with quite silly statements on the meaning of *patricius*.

The Licinio–Sextian Rogations opened the consulate to the plebeians. Before these enactments many men had been praetors-consul and tribunes-consul whose clans were destined to be plebeian after the legislation when, at last, Roman records grant us a valid criterion for ascertaining the caste of a family. If they could not be patrician and yet they could be chief magistrates, some grave failing must have been found in them which was adduced by the Fathers as a cause for their political disability. The abolition of the consular tribunate should have altered their opportunity for magistracies. Plebeians believed that the dual consulship would be open to them with greater ease. In my view, this supposed easier access lay through the centuriate assembly. The plebeians were mistaken, for over twenty years later another law was necessary to assure them one consulship every year. The legislation of 367 demanded half the places in the college of *decemviri sacris faciundis*, now expanded from a college of two, be plebeian and further recognized the patricians' sole access to the new praetorship and two new aedileships (Livy 6. 42). The plebeians had legitimate claims only on a half of one priestly college according to their own legislation. Plebeians' ancestors had been priests in 'patrician' colleges, once a Father, masters of horse, major magistrates and even kings of the Romans. The question remains why the plebeians could not assert their ancestral rights if the patricians asserted theirs. Perhaps the plebs had asserted such rights. But the assertion had no validity among all the Romans. In 367 rules must have been formulated for the distinction between the two castes. No previously formulated distinction could have obtained in 367 if 'plebeians' had access to the offices just mentioned. The castes were recognized only for the purpose of exclusion under certain conditions. Furthermore, the plebs accepted the exclusion. The cumulative evidence of plebeians' prior access to the offices demonstrates their eligibility and admissibility before 367. Their disability was lodged in the minds of those who would have excluded them. These were the Fathers who display to us no 'plebeian' after 483. Their clans were patrician. The

Fathers must have had a qualification besides patrician blood and a former imperial magistracy.

Since patricians descended from a Father and the first Fathers were not former magistrates, the Fathers of the royal era must have had an office connected with the auspices necessary for holding an assembly to elect the king. Throughout the Republic all imperial magistrates ultimately received their auspices and *imperium*, the right to rule, from the curias and from curias which no longer had effective power. The several chief officers of the curias, the curions, seem to have been eligible to perform the interregnum which the Fathers later carried out. A lack of consistency in occupying certain magistracies and priesthoods before 367 according to castes which Magdelain has remarked is a sure sign of the lack of a coherent, continuing rule for caste participation before that date. Although the Fathers and their families may have known which clan belonged to which caste, the voters and magistrates did not, indeed could not, impose a rule of ineligibility before 367. Patrician birth was defined once and for all in 367: a forebear had held an imperial magistracy before 367, a forebear had been a curion and a Father, and no forebear had been a plebeian officer. After 367 a plebeian might become consul and curion but it did not make him a patrician.[1] Thereafter, only sixteen families qualified for the patriciate beyond the shadow of a doubt. The curiate magistracy was subordinated to the centuriate magistracy in 367 but the ancestral authority of the curiate constitution was far from negligible. The curias still formally granted the *imperium* and the auspices; the curions and descendants of curions comprised the senate in which the Fathers controlled interregna and the acts of the curiate and centuriate assemblies.

Until 367 the cause of the internal quarrels was which clans had a right of access to the major magistracies and the major priesthoods which especially served an important civil or religious function. The Decemvirs unsuccessfully attempted to impose a legal detriment upon certain clans which was based upon a distinction between those who descended from the Fathers, viz. the patricians, and all the other citizens. Oligarchs resorted to the assertion of ancestral control of the auspices which, I argue, derived ultimately from the several curias through both curial chieftains and curial priests. Neither the

[1] See below, pp. 274–6.

Many nor the Few considered these rights to reach back to time immemorial. The families of the Fathers had to plead their case before the Many who certainly were free neither from religious scruple nor economic dependence upon the magnates. Their argument never went beyond ancestry as the word *patricius* implies. Furthermore, the criteria were determined after the fact. Somewhere along the line the Sempronii, for instance, lost the quality of being patrician. But they certainly did not wittingly transfer themselves to the plebs. I doubt that such transfers brought any political advantage until the third century. It seems to me likely that the Roman people wanted to know in 367 exactly what made a patrician different from a plebeian.

Because no list of tribunes of the plebs has survived, we cannot ascertain when a given family came to be considered plebeian. Manifestly plebeian families were being excluded from the magistracies. First of all, seventeen families have the *imperium* before 444 and either do not appear again in the Fasti or reappear as plebeian (Appendix II). Secondly, the patricians outnumber plebeians in the sum of participation in the censorship, consular praetorship and tribunate by 4 to 1, a ratio which obtains even if we omit the censors. On the other hand, six patrician families elected to the censorship by the centuriate assembly also held the majority of consular praetorships from 444 to 367 (Appendix IIID). Of these the Papirii and Furii can be counted among the friends of the plebs. The pontifex maximus who presided over the revival of the plebeian tribunate came from one of these families.[1] The first predominantly plebeian college of consular tribunes in 400 included a Furius and a Manlius. There followed a college containing all plebeians if at that time the Veturius was plebeian.[2] Five plebeian tribunes-consul were elected for 396 under the presidency of Furius Camillus as interrex; the sole patrician is another Manlius.[3] In 379 the college is again predominantly plebeian; two Manlii and a Julius are the patricians.[4] Finally, it was Furius Camillus who accepted the bills of Licinius and Sextius whereby the curiate magistracy was abolished.[5] Furthermore, the famous Manlius Capitolinus who made an attempt to

---

[1] Above, p. 221, n. 2.

[2] Livy 5. 12. 9–10, 13. 3. On the Veturii see Appendix III.   [3] Livy 5. 17. 4, 18. 2.

[4] *Ibid.* 6. 30. 2 has six tribunes (three plebeian); Diod. 15. 51. 1 names eight (five plebeians). See above, p. 229, n. 1.

[5] Livy 6. 42.

overthrow the government at the head of a popular movement and was executed in 385 or 384 was the only one of his family to be elected praetor-consul which is his only recorded office. It was probably the centuriate or tribal assembly which first refused to convict him and his trial was transferred to a grove which suggests a conviction in the assembly of curias.[1] A slightly higher percentage of plebeians attained the consular praetorship than the consular tribunate even though the patricians far outnumbered them.[2]

The notable obscurity of the Cloelii and Claudii between 444 and 367 invites attention. A Cloelius was one of the three tribunes-consul in 444 along with the plebeian Atilius and Sempronius (Appendix II). The only other Cloelius who is an imperial magistrate is the tribune of 393, a year in which a third Cloelius is censor. Thereafter the family passes into the shadows. The Claudii fared worse in this period: consular tribunates in 424 and 403. Before 451 the family had held three consular praetorships. The decemvirate of 451–450 made the difference. No matter how legend may represent the decemvirate its one secure result, the writing of the laws, can hardly be interpreted as inspired by the small group of men who would have been the aristocracy of the day. Probably four of Claudius' colleagues in the first decemvirate should be classed as plebeian.[3] Six of the second decemvirate belong to the same class.[4] The decemvirate appears to have been a revolutionary compromise which attempted the inclusion of 'new men' in a magistracy combining the imperial authority of the praetors-consul and the

---

[1] Livy 5. 31. 2–4 (his consulship). Diod. 15. 35. 3 puts his execution in 385; Livy 6. 15–16 his arrest by the dictator Cornelius Cossus in the same year. Livy 6. 18–20 and Plut. *Cam.* 36 date his trial and execution to 384. The majority of authorities (see Broughton, *s.a.* 384) state the plebeian tribunes were responsible for his conviction. Livy 6. 20. 12 knows another tradition which lays the responsibility on *IIviri perduellionis*. Though his story is encrusted with popular legend, Manlius' aims belong to plebeian agitation and policy (Livy 6. 14 f.). Hence, the opposition of the tribunes of the plebs, Menenius and Publilius, should be viewed as spurious; rather, they assisted their partisan. Camillus' role in the change of venue is quite fictitious (De Sanctis II. 195–6, H. S. Jones, *CAH* 7. 524). The curiate assembly was certainly a court of appeal as implied in Cicero's citation of the XII Tables (*Leg.* 3. 4. 11, 19. 44 on the *comitiatus maximus*). The curias' recall of Camillus from exile makes it explicit (Livy 5. 46. 10). On the Lucus P⟨o⟩etelinus above, p. 151 and below, p. 252. I discuss this trial and similar assemblies in this and other groves in 'King'.

[2] See Appendix IIID.   [3] Genucius, Veturius, Sextius and Romilius.

[4] Minucius, Poetelius, Antonius, Duillius, Oppius and Rabuleius. The increase in plebeians would suggest that the restoration of the praetors-consul in 449 was prompted by patrician reaction against the new mode of government, supported by the plebs and led by Ap. Claudius (the only Xvir in both years).

number and scope of the plebeian tribunes. In 444 oligarchic reaction followed the political reverses of 451–449. The revenge of the oligarchs took its toll. Between 444 and 367 the Claudii attain only two consular tribunates, the Genucii three, the Horatii[1] two, the Antonii one, the Sextii one, and the Duillii a consular praetorship and tribunate. The Romilii and Rabuleii pass into oblivion. Only after 367 the Oppii, Minucii and Poetelii emerge again in the imperial magistracies. The fortunes of the Claudii likewise are revived after the restoration of the centuriate constitution.[2] They differ from the others in that they remained patrician. Patrician rank did not necessarily mean oligarchic tendency. Two Claudii were named dictator and master of the horse in 337. The reason given for the office is military. But the emergency was not so pressing that the two were declared by the augurs invalidly appointed. It just happens that in the same year the 'first' plebeian praetor was elected. The dictator Claudius may well have been appointed by the plebeian consul to hold the elections and then forced to resign by the augurs on account of his political sympathies.[3]

For ten years after the restoration of the centuriate magistracies a plebeian was one of the two consuls. For 355 two patricians were elected in the eighth interregnum.[4] Again in 353 the government reverted to interregnum and in the twelfth interregnum a consular college of a plebeian and patrician was finally elected for 352.[5] In that year the government again reverted to an interregnum and two patricians were elected consuls, one of them being an interrex. This followed the appointment of a dictator who unsuccessfully tried what the interrexes accomplished. In the same year the 'first' plebeian was elected censor.[6] Again in 350 a dictator was named to preside over the election of two patricians of whom he was one. In the next two years dictators were named to hold the elections.[7] Not until 342 did the plebeians assure themselves by plebiscite a consulship each year and forbid the tenure of two magistracies at the same time or their repetition within ten years.[8] At the same time a mutiny

---

[1] Horatius, not Curiatius, was a Xvir of 451. See Appendix III, p. 299, n. 2.

[2] See Appendix III. Claudius Crassus was named dictator in 363 (Livy 7. 6. 12) and elected consul for 349 in which year he died of old age (Livy 7. 24. 11, 25. 10).

[3] Ibid. 8. 15.   [4] Ibid. 7. 17. 10–12, 18. 1.   [5] Ibid. 7. 21. 2–4.

[6] Ibid. 7. 21. 9–22. 10.

[7] Ibid. 7. 24. 11–25. 2, 26. 11–12; Fasti Cap. for 348 (not in Livy).

[8] Livy 7. 42. 2 states that both consuls could be plebeian. Rather, one consul had to be plebeian. See von Fritz, pp. 7–8, 25–28.

(*secessio*) broke out in the army. In consequence of the mutiny an amnesty was passed in the very grove where Manlius Capitolinus had been convicted and sentenced to death. Thereupon a *lex sacrata militaris* was passed which forbade the deletion of any unwilling citizen's name from the roster of soldiers and the demotion of a military tribune to the rank of centurion.[1] The prohibition of the deletion of the soldier's name cannot be related to possible recriminations after the secession since the amnesty anticipated reprisal. Rather, it concerns the integrity of the rosters which held the names of centuriate citizens. Obviously, the voters in the centuriate assembly were being subjected to a special scrutiny. Although the military tribunes at this time were being elected by centuries, any effort to curtail their activity must be referred to the patricians. This interpretation of the legislation of 342 finds support in the legislation of Pubilius Philo, the outstanding plebeian of the era, who was dictator three years later. First, one of the censors must be plebeian. Henceforth, the patricians will not so easily tamper with the citizen-roster. Secondly, the Fathers must give their approval (*patrum auctoritas*) to all laws proposed in the centuriate assembly before their enactment. This law alone proves that the patricians continued in opposition to the decisions of the centuriate assembly.[2] In 337 the same Publilius became the first plebeian praetor, the patrician consul notwithstanding.[3] This was the year in which the augurs declared that Claudius Crassus had been faultily appointed dictator. In 334 the augurs declared the appointment of another dictator invalid.[4] The consuls of 332 were elected under the fifth interrex.[5] In 327 when both consuls, Publilius and Cornelius, are in the field, the latter appoints Claudius Marcellus dictator by letter to hold the elections. The augurs declare his appointment invalid and the government reverts to interregnum. The fourteenth interrex (that is, after at least forty days) presides over the election of the consuls for 326.[6] In 321 the two consuls who surrendered to the Samnites at Caudine Forks resigned. Two dictators and, at least, two interrexes, attempted

---

[1] Livy 7. 41–2. See von Fritz, 'Leges Sacratae and Plebei Scita', *Studies...D. M. Robinson* (St. Louis, 1953) pp. 893–905 and Tondo, *passim*. The danger to the plebs may be gauged by the circumstances of the passage of the law on the manumission tax (Livy 7. 16. 7–8).

[2] Livy 8. 12. 12–17. The third law made plebiscites binding on all citizens. Although the later *lex Hortensia* decided this issue once and for all, similar legislation may have been passed before it and gone unheeded.

[3] *Ibid.* 8. 15. 9.   [4] *Ibid.* 8. 17. 3–4.   [5] *Ibid.* 8. 17. 5.   [6] *Ibid.* 8. 23. 13–17.

to have consuls elected for the next year.[1] Yet again two dictator-ships are recorded in the next year; their purpose is not certain.[2]

Clearly, the patricians were willfully allowing anarchy in order to employ interrexes in the election of only patrician consuls. Next, they struck upon the plan of naming a dictator who himself would preside over the election of patrician consuls or would resign and leave the government vacant for an interregnum. Then we find a dictator set aside by the augurs in 337, the year when Publilius succeeds in opening the new praetorship to the plebeians. The dictator appointed in the next year to hold the elections names Publilius master of the cavalry.[3] The augurs nullify the appointment of the dictator of the following year. So, too, the augurs set aside the plebeian Claudius Marcellus in 327 and thereby cause an interreg-num. The patricians are trumped by their own device: now dictators are being named in order to ensure a college of consuls acceptable to the plebeian nobility. Then the patricians respond with augural edict. Before plebeians could obtain the augurate, however, they had to gain entrance to the senate.

THE NEW SENATE

Traditionally, the Roman senate derived its membership from the curias, on the principle of equal representation.[4] I proposed above that the earliest senate comprised the thirty curions. Furthermore, the curionate was one of the criteria for distinguishing the patriciate. At the beginning of the Republic every Roman would have enjoyed citizenship by virtue of his membership in curia. His citizenship, *ius Quiritium*, derived from the curia. After 495, however, no new curia was created. Yet more people were made Roman citizens. To certain states the Romans granted the citizenship without the vote or right to a magistracy (*civitas sine suffragio*). In effect, this grant bestowed *conubium* and *commercium* which, in turn, meant the *ius Quiritium*. Since the new citizens did not migrate to Rome, they could not have been organized as a curia even if Roman policy had en-visaged new curiate organizations. Consequently, only migration to a domicile within a Roman tribe would give the new citizen full citizenship (*civitas optimo iure*). The creation of new citizens could be effected by the formation of new tribes, resumed in 387 when four

---

[1] *Ibid.* 9. 7. 12–15.　　[2] *Ibid.* 9. 15. 9–10 and *Fast. Cap.* for 320.
[3] Livy 8. 16. 12.　　[4] E.g. D.H. 2. 12, 2. 47. 1–2.

tribes were circumscribed in the former territory of Veii. Residence in these tribes and in those which were formed after them became the criterion of full citizenship which entailed the right to vote in both the centuriate and tribal assemblies. These two assemblies were accessible to new citizens whereas the curiate assembly contained only those men whose ancestors had been Roman citizens since 495.[1]

The neighbors of Rome who enjoyed the *ius Quiritium* may not have supplied infantry to the Roman centuriate army because they did not belong to the centuriate–tribal system. On the other hand, the rights of valid marriage and contract were not bestowed without some contribution on the part of the citizen who did not enjoy the right of voting. If we may judge by the example of the Gabini who were not incorporated in the tribal–centuriate system at this time and of the Campanians who had some kind of an alliance with Rome after the middle of the fourth century, the citizen without the vote contributed cavalry units to the Roman army.[2] Hence the much later Roman practice of relying mainly upon non-Romans for cavalry service.[3] The difference in the status of the Gabini and Campanians lies in the fact that the former constituted a curia before 495 (and were not in a tribe) and the latter enjoyed only the *rights* of curiate citizens.

Roman tradition attributes the first *lectio senatus* to the censorship of 312.[4] Although this idiom does imply the 'reading' of a list, it further implies the 'choosing' of senators (not *patres*) whose names are recorded. Accordingly, the *adlecti* and *conscripti* of the Roman senate, distinct from the *patres*, were those chosen and enrolled in the senate. The legislation which enabled the enrollment of senators was proposed by an Ovinius whose plebeian tribunate is usually dated to the time between the censors of 318 and 312. Festus alone records the content of the law: 'ut censores ex omni ordine optimum quemque curiatim in senatum legerent'.[5] 'The censors are to choose for the senate curia by curia the wealthiest man from every rank.' The censors make their choice according to three criteria: (1) the man belongs to a curia; (2) he is enrolled in a rank (*ordo*) of the centuriate army,[6] i.e. he belongs to a century and lives in a Roman tribe; and

---

[1] Cf. Sherwin-White, *Roman Citizenship*, chapters I-II.
[2] See above, pp. 160, 187 n. and below, p. 260, n. 4.
[3] Polyb. 6. 26. 7–9.   [4] Livy 9. 29. 7, Diod. 20. 36.
[5] Festus 290 L. *s.v. praeteriti senatores* (cf. 6 *s.v. adlecti*, 36 *s.v. conscripti*, 304 *s.v. qui patres qui conscripti*).
[6] *Tab. Heracl.* (*CIL* I², 2. 593 = *ILS* 6085 = *FIRA* I², no. 13) lines 120–1; Plaut.

(3) he meets a property qualification.[1] Although this tribunician law would not have required the *patrum auctoritas*, the patricians maintained independence from plebiscites. Therefore, the first prerequisite would have been the basis of a compromise between the patrician and the plebeian politicians. Not all plebeians would be eligible for admission to the senate. Nothing is said of enrolling former magistrates, because not all former magistrates would have been eligible. For instance, L. Fulvius Curvus, consul in 322, derived his full Roman citizenship from his Tusculan origins. Tusculans, however, would not have belonged to a curia although they were enrolled in a tribe and served in the centuriate army.[2] The elaborate comitial machinery for curial testaments, adrogatory adoption and forswearing of rites makes sufficient argument against any belief in assignment or distribution of citizens into curias. Patrician domination of the curias bespeaks the limited and old constituencies. Therefore, Fulvius and Romans of similar origin were not eligible for the senate according to the Ovinian Law because their families' citizenship did not go back to 495. Consequently, we witness 'new men' claiming for their families the Sabine ancestry of Roman citizens at the beginning of the third century.[3]

Magdelain correctly dates the distinction of *praetorii* and *aedilicii* among senators to *c.* 250. More precisely it may be dated to the censorship of 252 when sixteen were expelled from the senate.[4] At that

Amph. 219–24, 241; Cic. *Leg.* 3. 3. 7, 3. 19. 44, *Flac.* 7. 15, *Har. Resp.* 6. 11, *Pis.* 20. 45 22. 52 (cf. 22. 51), 36. 88, 40. 96; Livy 22. 30. 5.

[1] *Optimus*, first attested in the sepulchral inscription of L. Cornelius Scipio cos. 259 (*ILLRP* 310), means 'rich' and has nothing to do with virtue. See J. Hellegouarc'h, 'Le vocabulaire latin des relations et des partis politiques sous la république', *Publ. Fac. Lettres Sci. Hum. Univ. Lille* 11 (1963), 496–500 who defines *optimus quisque* 'qui sont l'élite social du groupe' of the wealthy and powerful. The *optimi* belong to the *adsidui* of the XII Tables and both may be contrasted with the *proletarii* who were quite *infra classem* (frr. 1. 4, 1. 10).

[2] Cic. *Planc.* 8. 20. See Taylor, 'Voting Districts', pp. 216, 300–3 and below, p. 276, n. 2. There is no reliable evidence that new Roman citizens were enrolled in curias although the tradition says that the kings assigned newcomers to curias; see above, p. 205, nn. 4–6. According to Ovid the festival of fools took its name from the fact that a stupid part of the people did not know what its curia was. Ovid implies that every man had a curia. But we have argued that all the people actually did not belong to curias. The 'fools' who celebrated the curial festival of Fornacalia only on the last day of the series could have joined in the entire observance if they had been members of curias. See above, pp. 161–2.

[3] Above, pp. 164–6. Conversely, the plebeian Marcii, who had perhaps legitimate ancestral connection with Ancus Marcius, would have gained in prestige through the Ovinian Law by resuming a place among their former peers.

[4] Livy, *Per.* 18. Alföldi, 'Reiteradel', p. 100 remarks that these censors also stripped the horsemen in four of the oldest six centuries of cavalry of their public horses. Wartime

255

time the censors began to take into consideration the former magistracies of those men who were eligible for the senate. If the consular praetors and tribunes had chosen senators before the Ovinian Law as our sources indicate, their choices lay solely within the *ordo equester*.[1] This order comprised only those men wealthy enough to contribute cavalry service to the army. Their divisions were based upon multiples of three and reflect their origin in the curiate tribal system.[2] Furthermore, the archaic *equites* did not belong to the Servian army, for the sole, and later first, *classis* comprised the richest infantrymen. Nor did the military reformer intend to integrate the infantry and cavalry since the master of infantry and master of cavalry both had imperial auspices. Finally, the censors down to the end of the Republic kept distinct their census of infantry and cavalry.[3] Since the centuries of cavalry participate in the centuriate assembly before the middle of the third century, the *equites* must have become voters in that assembly between 443 when the censorship was instituted and that time. The number of equestrian centuries probably reached eighteen before the reform of the centuriate assembly but only six of these, called the 'six votes' (*sex suffragia*), had constituted the destinating, prerogative centuries of the centuriate assembly before the reform. The six centuries represented the doubling of tribal cavalry regiments before the Servian reform.[4] In other words, they were the aristocratic élite of royal Rome. Roman authors believed that the equestrian centuries had always voted first in the centuriate assembly.[5] However, their votes in the centuriate assembly after the institution of the censorship, controlled by the *patrum auctoritas*, perhaps were unnecessary because the aristocracy had created that office in hopes of resuming the curiate constitution. Therefore, the prerogation of the six equestrian centuries may have been established after 367. Likewise, all the equestrian centuries may have been introduced into the centuriate assembly after the restora-

exigencies perhaps prompted expansion of the senate. During the next Punic War a dictator, taking the place of censors, enrolled into the senate men who had never held office (Livy 23. 23. 5–6; cf. 29. 37. 1).

[1] Magdelain, 'Auspicia', pp. 453–465.

[2] *Ibid.*, and Alföldi, 'Reiteradel', pp. 87–123.

[3] *Cens. Tab.* in Varro, *LL* 6. 86 on which see above, pp. 158–9. On the census of *equites* see Hill, chapter II.

[4] The oldest reliable report of the equestrian prerogative is Livy 10. 22. 1. On the *sex suffragia*, Cic. *Rep.* 2. 22. 39–40; Livy 1. 43. 9; Festus 452 L. (cf. 290 L.). See Alföldi, 'Reiteradel', pp. 93–102 and Hill, pp. 7–16, 39–41.

[5] E.g. Livy 1. 43. 10–11.

tion of the centuriate constitution. The prerogation itself followed the practice of the curial *principium* and was accorded in later times the same ominous interpretation despite the fact that then the prerogative century was drawn from the first class of infantry and the *sex suffragia* had been demoted to a fourth stage in voting after the prerogative of the first class, the remaining centuries of the first class and the other twelve equestrian centuries.[1] The law of the dictator Publilius in 339 required the Fathers to grant their *auctoritas* in advance of legislation by the centuriate assembly. Here is the occasion for giving the six archaic equestrian centuries the courtesy of prerogation by way of compromise. Then the old hereditary aristocracy surrendered their unlimited control over centuriate legislation in 339, having acquired the prerogative votes in addition to their control over the election of consuls, censors and praetors in the centuriate assembly.

The censors of 312, empowered for the first time to choose new senators and elected for that purpose, were Ap. Claudius and C. Plautius. They could now enroll wealthy Romans of centuriate rank into the senate so long as the new senator belonged to a curia. The nickname of senators who had no right to speak in the deliberations of the senate was *pedarii*. This word's original significance remained so obscure that the ancients offered conflicting explanations of its application. What is quite clear is that it does not resemble in formation the later designations of senatorial ranks (*consulares, praetorii*, etc.). On the contrary, substantives in -*arius* are attested in Republican Latin mainly in a military sphere and in the Empire mostly in the analogous sphere of spectacles.[2] The *pedarii*, always with pejorative connotation, were called so by their equestrian colleagues who looked upon the *conscripti* as footmen with all the scorn which this English word still has and the medieval *infans* once

[1] Because there were six units voting first there could never be a *principium*. On the order after the reform (Cic. *Phil.* 2. 33. 82) see Taylor, 'Centuriate Assembly', pp. 337–54. On the ominous quality of the later prerogative infantry century Cic. *Mur.* 18. 38, *Div.* 1. 45. 103, 2. 35. 74–5. The deliberate demotion of only the six votes indicates their priority and aristocratic birth whereas the remaining twelve equestrian centuries never had enjoyed such superiority nor had been aristocratic.

[2] Gellius 3. 18. To wit, *proletarii, rorarii, triarii, ferentarii, ordinarii, extraordinarii* (Polyb. 6. 26. 6), *causarii, sagittarii, ballistarii, beneficiarii, praesidiarii, subitarii, tumultuarii, voluntarii, vexillarii, cibarii, duplicarii* and the idioms (*aes*) *vasarium, hordearium, (frumentum) honorarium, aurum coronarium, aerarius, primarius, veterarius, catervarii, gregarii.* Cf. the rare *pedatus* 'infantry charge'.

had. When this rank of senators found their voice in the senate, their nickname was given to others.[1]

The following passage from Aulus Gellius suggests that he did not know what Varro intended by the strange expression *equites pedarii*:

M. autem Varro in Satira Menippea, quae Ἱπποκύων inscripta est, equites quosdam dicit pedarios appellatos videturque eos significare, qui nondum a censoribus in senatum lecti senatores quidem non erant, sed, quia honoribus populi usi erant, in senatum veniebant et sententiae ius habebant.[2]

Evidently Varro's *equites pedarii* meant the 'cavalryman on foot'. His title *Marebitch* reflects such a state of affairs. If there was a cavalryman who bore a formal designation *pedarius*, he must have been one of those with the infantry census who had volunteered himself for cavalry service.[3]

In commenting on Cicero's use of a tribal designation Pseudasconius writes: 'Moreover, it used to be customary to designate a Roman citizen by his praenomen or name or cognomen or his kinship or the tribe in which he was rated or his curia or his census as if he were a senator or Roman knight.'[4] The practice of using the curial affiliation of senators and knights accounts for the spurious tradition that Tarquin I assigned places in the Circus Maximus to the thirty curias and to the senators and knights.[5] The Ciceronian scholiast makes clear that only senators and knights were at one time known by curia. Perhaps the mark was made in drawing up the list of senators.

The tradition on the orthography of rhotacized Latin medial *s* supports the view that Appius Claudius and his censorial colleague first drew up a written list of new senators. Cicero reports that L. Papirius Crassus was the first of his family to abandon the form *Papisius*.[6] Crassus was consul in 336 and 330 and perhaps the father of the censor in 318. Varro also remarked a change from Valesii and

---

[1] Gellius *NA* 3. 18.

[2] *NA* 3. 18. 5 = Varro *Men.* fr. 220 Bue. The only other fragment of this satire also refers to the senate. Fr. 221 Bue. from Non. p. 53 L.: 'Apollonium ideo excuriant quia nihil habebat'.

[3] See Hill, pp. 16–23.

[4] [Asconius] p. 213 St. We have argued above that this commentator derived his information on the tribes from Varro, pp. 68–9 and pp. 124–5. Cf. [Val. Prob.] *De notis iuris* 2 on abbreviation of the name of curias.

[5] D.H. 3. 68. 1. Livy 1. 35. 8–9 says senators and knights had fixed seats. But see Pliny, *NH* 8. 21; Tac. *Ann.* 15. 32; Suet. *Claud.* 21, *Nero* 11; Dio Cass. 55. 22, 60. 7.

[6] Cic. *Fam.* 9. 21. 2.

Fusii to Valerii and Furii[1] which was attributed to Appius Claudius.[2] The emperor Claudius' interest in the alphabet perhaps arose from his ancestor's action.[3] Varro could have found his examples in the censorial records which he used (LL 6. 86) since he took his other examples of rhotacism from the Salian Hymns (7. 26–7). Varro seems to have treated rhotacism in the work on names which was used by the author of De praenominibus. The Sabine Valesius is cited there. The notice from Festus on the Valesii, Papisii and Sabine Auselii may also go back to Varro.[4] Since no Aurelius is met in the list of consuls before 252, Varro must have drawn on local Sabine lore for Auselii. Although Appius Claudius is credited with the discovery of the letter r, he was no philologist. Therefore, we assume that he insisted on writing the names of senators as they were pronounced rather than as they had been spelled theretofore. Secondly, the archaic gentilicial names which have been recorded as examples are those of patricians who presumably had belonged to the senate before the Ovinian Law.

The Republican senate was divided into decurias,[5] a grouping which perhaps goes back to the units of the cavalry.[6] Decurion became the standard title of municipal senators. If we accept the tradition that the primitive senate was based upon curial representation,[7] then the senatorial decurias can reflect a limit of ten senators from each of the thirty curias after the senate was constituted of ex-magistrates rather than of the patricians.[8] Such a limited representation which reflected a desire to equalize the role of each curia also maintained legal regard for the rights which were derived from the pre-eminence of the curias. The decurial representation of curias may be dated to c. 312.[9]

[1] ARD in Macr. Sat. 3. 2. 8, cf. Varro in Praen. 1 on Volesus Valesius. Quint. Inst. 1. 4. 3 has the same examples which he probably took from Varro; cf. 1. 4. 4, 1. 6. 12, 1. 6. 37. Varro discussed rhotacism in LL 7. 26–7. Cf. Livy 3. 4. 1 for Fusii.
[2] Pomp. in Dig. 1. 2. 2. 36. Cf. Mart. Cap. 3. 261 on z which Appius was thought to have removed from the alphabet. Its place was taken by g. See Teuffel's Gesch. röm. Lit. 1⁶, pp. 148, 160.
[3] Cf. Quint. Inst. 1. 7. 26, Mart. Cap. 3. 245.
[4] Praen. 1; Fest. Epit. p. 22 L., cf. p. 232. According to Dionysius 1. 74. 5 the descendants of censors preserved censorial records.
[5] Livy 1. 17. 5–6 (ten decurias of interrexes), D.H. 2. 57–8 (twenty decurias, each in succession an interregnal committee), [Asconius] p. 210 St.
[6] See above, pp. 8–9, 152–4.
[7] Cf. D.H. 2. 12, 2. 47.
[8] See above, p. 206, n. 4 and below, pp. 274–5.
[9] It was in 310 when the first ballot of the Curia Faucia caused the dismissal of the

In the second censorship after Claudius' and Plautius', Fabius Rullianus and Decius Mus set aside the tribal rosters of Claudius and Plautius whereon the sons of freedmen had been enrolled in the rural tribes.[1] This action, we are told, resulted from the indignation of the knights who had come before the censors and surrendered their gold rings and ornaments, the trappings of the archaic cavalry.[2] Nor was this all Fabius and Decius accomplished. Fabius also 'instituted' the parade of cavalry on the Ides of Quinctilis.[3] This means that Fabius and Decius were the first censors to evaluate qualifications for the cavalry.[4] Thus the equestrian order ceased to be hereditary and to be somehow under the control of the curiate organization, and in 304 was subjected to officers of the centuriate assembly.[5] The knights' remonstrance was in fact directed against their subordination and has nothing to do with freedmen in the tribes.

Senators and knights were sometimes listed with a designation of their curias. The senate, reconstituted in accordance with the Ovinian Law, was drafted according to curial representation. Soon after the censors had been charged with control of the senate rosters, the knights were put under control of the censors. The traditional

curiate assembly. This act indicates that the assembly and its *lex de imperio* were not yet regular formalities whose outcome could go unheeded.

[1] Livy 9. 46. The story of the son of an ex-slave in the senate who was Claudius' henchman is of a piece with other fictions of hatred felt for Claudius by all patricians and plebeians who also kept electing him to office.

[2] See Alföldi, 'Reiteradel', pp. 17–35.

[3] Livy 9. 46. 15, Val. Max. 2. 2. 9. The date falls just after the beginning of the old official year which had shifted with the interregnum following the consuls' abdication after surrendering at Caudine Forks in 321 (Livy 9. 7–8. 1). Hence both the parade and its date precede Fabius' 'institution'.

[4] Dionysius 6. 13. 4–5 and Plutarch, *Pomp.* 13 imply the high antiquity of the parade (see Momigliano, 'Procum Patricium', *JRS* 56 (1966), 16–24). The former states that after attending sacrifices the knights parade by tribe and *lochoi* (curia or decuria or *turma*; cf. Dion. 2. 7. 3–4) as if coming from battle. Plutarch says the knights seek discharge from active service at this ceremony. This proves that the term of service and the official year by which it was reckoned had just ended before the Ides of Quinctilis. Presumably the knights remained in service after 1 July in order to participate in Poplifugia and the sacrifice of the heifer of victory, 5 and 8 July. The observance is related to the cult of Castor and Pollux, divine patrons of the cavalry, Dionysius 6. 13. 4–5. According to Livy (8. 11. 16) the Campanian knights put in the Roman temple of Castor a bronze plaque commemorating the citizenship they had received in 340. See above, p. 217, n. 3. See Alföldi, 'Reiteradel', pp. 41–3, 111–12 and Hill, pp. 37–9.

[5] The censors of 304 must have been enabled by a law to pass the knights in review. Since the *tribuni celerum* still functioned as priests in the late Republic (D.H. 2. 64. 3, *Fasti Praen.* at 19 March), they most likely participated in the sacrifices of the official year beginning 1 July and had formerly passed the knights in review. See p. 236, n. 5.

origin of senators before 312 and their relation to the military forces have been challenged of late (see below). Because the senate's membership was bound to the curias as late as the Ovinian Law and the cavalry was bound to the three archaic tribal divisions, a re-examination of the few ancient traditions on the nature of the older republican senate and army appears desirable.

The texts of the main Latin authorities with translations follows.

1. Cicero, *Orator* 46. 156: quam centuriam fabrum et procum, ut censoriae tabulae loquuntur, audeo dicere, non fabrorum aut procorum.

(I would not have said so willingly...) as I dare to say a century of smiths and of 'frontmen', as the censors' records state (in contrast with the modern genitive plurals *fabrorum* and *procorum*).

2. Festus 290 L.: procum patricium in discriptione classium quam fecit Ser. Tullius significat procerum. i enim sunt principes.

In the formulary of the classes of the levy which Servius Tullius instituted 'of the patrician frontmen' means of the *proceres*. For they were the men of the first line.

3. Festus, *Epitome* 251 L.: principalis castrorum porta nominatur quod in eo loco est in quo principes ordines tendunt.

A camp's principal gate is so called because that is where the men of the first line direct their ranks.

4. Livy 8. 8. 6–11 (condensed): robustior inde aetas totidem manipulorum, quibus principibus est nomen, hos [*sc.* hastatos] sequebantur scutati omnes, insignibus maxime armis....ubi his ordinibus exercitus instructus esset, hastati omnium primi pugnam inibant. si hastati profligare hostem non posset, pede presso eos retro cedentes in intervallo ordinum principes recipiebant. tum principum pugna erat; hastati sequebantur; triarii sub vexillis considebant....si apud principes quoque haud satis prospere esset pugnatum, a prima acie ad triarios se sensim referebant; inde rem ad triarios redisse, cum laboratur, proverbio increbuit.

Thereafter a stronger force of the same number of maniples, called the men of the first line, follow [the spearmen], all armed especially well and equipped with shields....When an army had been drawn up in these ranks, the spearmen were the first to engage. If the spearmen were unable to rout the enemy, they withdrew in order between the spaces in rank and the men of the first line received them. Then the fighting fell to the men of the first line; the spearmen followed; the men of the third line held themselves in rank under the banners....If the fighting did not go well with the men of the first line, they gradually fell back on the men of the third line. From that manoeuver grew the proverb 'The outcome has returned to the men of the third line'.

Cicero's citation of the *centuria fabrum et procum* intends to give an indefinite example, to wit, 'a century of'. An effort to establish the number of the centuries of *proci* can yield no result. The censors recognized one century of *proci*. Festus tells us that the same archaic genitive plural belonged to the formulary of the Servian infantry classes and that the word equals *proceres*. Elsewhere I have tried to demonstrate that the formation of *celeres*, *luceres* and *proceres* ('men on chargers', 'men of the grove(s)', and 'men of the front line') are archaic military terms.[1] Since some *proci* were designated patrician, it follows that there were also plebeian *proci*. In other words, *proci* were recruited from no one caste. Festus believed that the *proceres* and *proci* indicated the *principes* which in this passage can mean either 'men of the first line' or 'chief men of the state'. Festus' *Epitome* has an entry recalling the principal gate named after the military *principes*. The Roman camp had two gates and one street named after the *principes* (see Walbank on Polybius 6. 27 ff.). These *principes* fought in the second rank under the reformed army described by Livy. Their very name, reinforced by that of the *triarii*, indicates their original tactical position in the first line of battle. (See Walbank on Polybius 6. 21. 7–8.) In this sense the *proci* of the centuriate classes were the *principes* of the archaic infantry. The evidence of Festus and Cicero makes clear that part of the infantry's first rank was at one time patrician and that the censors still employed an archaic term in their formulary which signified these patricians. By inference the same evidence cannot mean that all *proci* were patrician and says nothing about the other contemporary ranks in battle array that are implicit in the designation of a first line.

5. Livy 2. 1. 10–11: deinde quo plus virium in senatu frequentia etiam ordinis faceret, caedibus regis deminutum patrum numerum primoribus equestris gradus lectis ad trecentorum summam explevit, traditumque inde fertur ut in senatum vocarentur qui patres quique conscripti essent; conscriptos videlicet [novum senatum] appellabant lectos.

Thereafter in order to increase the strength of the order in a full senate meeting he [*sc.* Junius Brutus] filled out the number of 300 senators with chosen leaders of the equestrian rank since the number of Fathers had been decreased by the king's massacre; and it is therefore said to be traditional that those who were Fathers and those who were Conscripts were summoned to senate meetings. This interpretation means that they used to call the men so chosen the Conscripts.

6. Festus, *Epitome* 6 L.: adlecti dicebantur apud Romanos qui propter

---

[1] Palmer, 'King'.

inopiam ex equestri ordine in senatorum sunt numero adsumpti. nam patres dicuntur qui sunt patricii generis; conscripti qui in senatu sunt scriptis adnotati.

Among the Romans the Chosen used to be called those who were added to the number of senators from the equestrian order on account of dearth. For the Fathers are called so after their patrician birth; the Conscripts after their notation on the senate's rolls.

7. Festus, *Epitome* 36 L.: conscripti dicebantur qui ex equestri ordine patribus adscribebantur ut numerus senatorum expleretur.

Conscripts are those so called who were added from the equestrian order to the Fathers in writing so that the number of senators would be filled out.

8. Festus 304 L.: qui patres, qui conscripti vocati sunt in curiam? quo tempore regibus urbe expulsis P. Valerius consul propter inopiam patrici-orum ex plebe adlegit in numerum senatorum C et LX et IIII ut expleret numerum senatorum trecentorum et duo genera appellaret [esse].

Which are the Fathers, which the Conscripts summoned to the senate-house? At the time the kings were driven from the city P. Valerius the consul was prompted by a dearth of patricians to choose from the plebs 164 men and add them to the number of senators so that he filled out the number of 300 senators and called them two kinds.

9. Festus 290 L.: praeteriti senatores quondam in opprobrio non erant, quod, ut reges sibi legebant sublegebantque, quos in consilio publico haberent, ita post exactos eos consules quoque et tribuni militum consulari potestate coniunctissimos sibi quosque patriciorum, et deinde plebeiorum legebant; donec Ovinia tribunicia intervenit, qua sanctum est ut censores ex omni ordine optimum quemque curiati⟨m⟩ in senatum legerent. quo factum est, ut qui praeteriti essent et loco moti, haberentur ignominiosi.

At one time passed-by senators were not held in disrespect because, just as the kings used to choose for themselves or to choose substitute men to serve them in state counsels, so after their expulsion the consuls and the military tribunes with consular power used to choose for themselves their closest patrician friends and later their closest plebeian friends until the tribunician law of Ovinius was passed by which it was made law that the censors were to choose for the senate the richest men from every rank according to curia. This enactment brought about the change wherein those who had been passed by and moved from their position were reckoned of no account.

According to Livy, Junius Brutus chose the leaders of the cavalry to fill out the depleted ranks of the Fathers. Hence the senators were summoned by the formula of address 'Fathers and Conscripts'. Festus' Epitome on *adlecti* gives the same definition as Livy and as itself on *conscripti*. Festus' definition of the phrase *qui patres qui conscripti* attributes the act to P. Valerius, the cause to a dearth of patricians (as opposed to Fathers), the source of the new senators to the plebs in the number of 164. Finally, we possess Festus' discussion of 'passed-over senators' which contains the gist of the Ovinian plebiscite. All he tells us about the kind of senator in question comes at the end of the entry where we learn that they were passed over and moved from their position. This apparently means that they were expelled by the censors from the senate or were left out of the position they had occupied in the previous censorship. Perhaps that position belonged to the protocol in asking senators their opinions by the ranks *consulares, praetorii*, and so on, or to a combination of rankings.

The earlier, respected *praeteriti* have the same origin as the *adlecti* who were added by consuls or consular tribunes to the Fathers. Conscripts were *adlecti* from the equestrian order or the plebs. Since there were *proci patricii* and thus presumably *proci plebeii* in the infantry, the early horsemen could be either patrician or plebeian. Although they agree on the nature of the titles of address, Livy and Festus do not agree on who chose the first Conscripts and from what group they were drawn: Junius Brutus and P. Valerius; *equites* and *plebs*. Of course, neither authority can be trusted on the identity of the consul. Brutus is likely apocryphal; P. Valerius Poplicola's deed comes out of Valerius Antias. The plebs as a source of the new senators belonged to the portrait of the *poplicola*. Antias, an authority on the number of Sabine women and a specialist on the Sabine Valerii (see above, pp. 29–30), excogitated the unreliable number of 164 plebeian senators which cannot be used to excogitate 136 patrician families.[1] The Conscripts, distinct from the Fathers, could have been either patrician, plebeian or both. The late Republican and early imperial need for a definition of the phrase *qui patres qui conscripti* shows the lack of common knowledge of its significance. The Conscripts, however, seem a later institution than both the

---

[1] But see A. Momigliano, 'Procum Patricium', where he discusses the nature of the early infantry, cavalry and their patrician members; 'L'ascesa della plebe nella storia arcaica di Roma', *Riv. St. Ital.* 79 (1967), 297–312; and 'Osservazioni sulla distinzione tra patrizi e plebei', *Les origines de la république romaine* in *Entretiens* of the Fondation Hardt, XIII (Geneva, 1967), 197–221 in both of which he puts forth his views on the caste distinction, argues for *conscripti* as a social caste with military origins, attempts to redefine the relation between *populus* and *plebs* and re-examines the character of the senate's constituents. Many of the views which he expresses in the two later articles I cannot accept.

Fathers and the *adlecti*. The latter are the chosen senators. The Conscripts took their name from the written roster of 312. The *adlecti* seem to have been the *patricii*, those descended from Fathers, who were added to the Fathers, those who had been imperial magistrates with the auspices, in order to create a Republican senate of Fathers and 'chosen' patricians shortly after the founding of the Republic. Imperial adlection of patricians at first derived its authority from laws and from archaic precedent. Thus Tacitus (*Ann.* 11. 25) reports:

Claudius Caesar chose the eldest senators and those of illustrious ancestry for the body of patricians because there still survived few members of those clans which Romulus had called major and L. Brutus minor and because those families Caesar had 'sublected' according to the Cassian Law and Augustus according to the Saenian law had almost died out.

The consuls and consular tribunes chose some patricians, scions of clans whose ancestors had been Fathers according to the royal dispensation. The Ovinian plebiscite not only assigned this task to the censors but also empowered them to enroll the wealthiest of every rank according to curia. These, I assume, were the Conscripts. By 'every rank' the bill intended men from the centuriate ranks who had the property rating. Thus the censors could choose from cavalry-men, *proci patricii*, *proci plebeii* and so forth. The well-known imperial term *adlectus inter patricios* substantiates the later Roman view that a man was chosen for the patriciate. The pre-Ovinian senate had Fathers and patrician *adlecti*. The post-Ovinian senate had Fathers, the long-established patrician *adlecti* and the new plebeian Conscripts. Hence the phrase *qui patres qui conscripti* was spoken to convoke all senators. The *patres* refer to Fathers and patrician senators, a class to which all Republican Fathers belonged, and the *conscripti* to those enrolled in the senate from the wealthiest of every centuriate rank.

By way of illustration of the *adlecti* I cite the Papirii, a patrician *gens minor*, which in the early Republic did not attain a major magistracy. The Papirii, descendants of the royal Fathers, were chosen and added to the Republican Fathers who had exercised an imperial magistracy. Thus was created a senate of Fathers and patrician *adlecti*.[1] In 312 the senate was expanded to include the

[1] See especially Cic. *Rep.* 2. 20. 35, Livy 1. 35. 6, Augustus, *RG* 8. 1, Tac. *Ann.* 11. 25 Suet. *Iul.* 41. 1, *Aug.* 1. 2, Dio Cass. 43. 47. 3, 49. 43. 6, 52. 42. 5 on this kind of *gens minor* and imperial adlections, and above, p. 244 on the Papirii.

likes of the Maenii, Plautii, Publilii, Marcii. A hint of this situation comes from Livy's two reports of the censorship where Ap. Claudius performed a notorious and contemptible reading of the senate (*infamis atque invidiosa senatus lectio*) which included the sons of freedmen or the *humiles*. The sons of freedmen have been introduced into the annalist's account of the enrollment into the senate through confusion with the same censors' enrollment of freedmen into any tribe.[1] The censors defiled the senate by a *lectio* consonant with the Ovinian plebiscite. Since I argue that freedmen had no place in the curias (above, pp. 161–2, 191–2) and the new senators were enrolled from certain groups according to certain considerations, the objection to the censorial enrollment would have been based upon the inclusion of those from every centuriate rank, that is the plebeians or *humiles*. For students of Roman institutions who reject a relation between military service and senatorial standing I point to the case of the special appointment of a dictator without a master of horse in 216 (Livy 23. 23. 5–6):

recitato vetere senatu, inde primos in demortuorum locum legit qui post L. Aemilium C. Flaminium censores curulem magistratum cepissent necdum in senatum lecti essent, ut quisque eorum primus creatus erat; tum legit qui aediles, tribuni plebis, quaestoresve fuerant; tum ex iis qui ⟨non⟩ magistratus cepissent, qui spolia ex hoste fixa domi haberent aut civicam coronam accepissent. ita centum septuaginta cum ingenti adprobatione hominum in senatum lectis extemplo se magistratu abdicavit.

This enrollment, extraordinary in the nature of its supervisor, fell less than a century after the creation of the new senate which included the lowborn.

The title of the Conscripts is officially met only in the summons to a senate session and the frequent address *patres conscripti* in senatorial harangues. The *patres* were not a caste of the people, but a senatorial group with unique powers. Thus the Conscripts were simply a group of senators, not a caste of the people, either patrician or plebeian.[2] There is no sign of the Conscripts outside of the senate. Indeed, the archaic formula for summoning all senators to a meeting alone alerted the later Romans to the fact that *patres* and *conscripti* were distinct from each other and that the participle did not modify the noun. The oldest surviving use of *conscripti* in an official docu-

---

[1] Livy 9. 29. 5–8, 46. 10. See Taylor, 'Voting Districts', pp. 132–7 and above, p. 257.
[2] Quite otherwise Momigliano, 'L'ascesa' and 'Osservazioni'.

ment seems to be the *decretum patrum conscriptorum* voted *c.* 273 to enable three Roman ambassadors to retain gifts from Ptolemy Philadelphus to whom they had gone on diplomatic mission (Val. Maximus 4. 3. 9; cf. Dio Cassius 10 fr. 41, Zonaras 8. 6). The *decretum* stands in contrast with the *auctoritas* of the Fathers.

The crux of the problem is the origin, patrician or plebeian, infantry or cavalry, of the pre-Ovinian senate. Momigliano has demonstrated that there were patricians in the early republican infantry, and he would have us believe that the cavalry was a special armed service originally of the king's henchmen in no way patrician. Our sources on the senate of Fathers and *adlecti* indicate that the new members were equestrians who became patricians. The Conscripts were indeed plebeian in 312, but not in 508. According to Momigliano the cavalry's service for payment puts cavalrymen in a special category of henchmen. However, the cavalrymen of the archaic army who were always detailed in accordance with the divisions of the three *tribus* had the highest property qualification along with the first, single Servian centuriate *classis* even before the institution of a proper *census equester*.[1] Their payment appears quite incidental to the social or economic status. Scipio Aemilianus' praise of the Roman constitution reminds us that the cavalry included Roman senators when it voted among the centuriate *classes*, or so Cicero tells us (*Rep.* 4. 2. 2, cf. Q. Cicero, *Com. Pet.* 8. 33). Varro's satirical term 'infantry cavalrymen' (*equites pedarii*), who had been magistrates but were not senators although they attended and addressed the senate, signifies ex-magistrates serving regularly with the cavalry who had the same social station as footmen. In other words, the cavalry at one time consisted of both hereditary knights and volunteers from the ranks of the infantry.

Were the patricians closely tied to the archaic cavalry? The tribunes of the Celeres, who were merely priests at the end of the Republic, participated with the pontiffs in the patrician Salians' ceremony for Mars in the Comitium.[2] The Dial flamen, who had claims on a senate seat by virtue of his priesthood, could neither be transported by horse nor look upon the centuriate *classis* drawn up outside the pomerium (A. Gellius 10. 15). His right to senate membership arose from his patrician priesthood which makes the Dial

---

[1] See Pol. 6. 20. 9 with Walbank's important comment, Cic. *Rep.* 2. 22. 39, and D.H. 4. 18. [2] See above, p. 152, n. 2.

flamen one of those patrician *adlecti* who could not be a *pater* since he could not be an imperial magistrate at a centuriate assembly (see below, pp. 274–5). No hereditary senate comprised only cavalrymen and infantrymen. If the infantry or cavalry was drafted from only one of the two castes, we should expect their *magistri*, the dictator (= *magister populi*) and master of horse (*magister equitum*), to reflect such a distinction. The first dictator in 501 or 498 was a Larcius, the master of horse a Cassius. In 499 the dictator was a Postumius, the master of horse an Aebutius. In 458 the dictator was a Quinctius, the master of horse a Tarquitius. After 367 when we can judge a clan's caste, the Cassii and probably the Aebutii were plebeian. The status of the Tarquitii and Larcii cannot be ascertained. The Quinctii and Postumii were patrician. Since a Sempronius could be a Father in the fifth century and his clan was plebeian after 367, we cannot prove that the Sempronius who was master of horse in 380 was patrician or plebeian or that the Cassius in 501 and the Aebutius in 499 had one or the other status. Between 367 and 342, after which year one consul had to be plebeian, we encounter only one certainly plebeian master of horse, a Plautius, serving under the first certainly plebeian dictator, a Marcius in 356 (see Appendix III for these families). The status of the two extraordinary commanders cannot be ascertained from the nature of their commands. Our ancient sources inform us of newly created senators who were patricians of lesser clans at the end of or immediately after the kingship. In truth, their military service is unknown and equally unimportant in this discussion. After the determination of major and minor clans came the modification of the senate by the *lectio* of 312 worked under the Ovinian Law. This new senate received members from among the wealthiest of all ranks according to curia. Hence, the conscript *pedarii* entered the senate which had previously comprised Fathers and patrician *adlecti* drawn from the equestrian ranks. Finally, I repeat my belief that before the Republic of annual magistrates the Fathers, interrexes or elders were the thirty curions and that only after the foundation of the Republic did there exist a senate of Fathers and chosen patricians. In any event, only the Fathers exercised any constitutional powers as we saw at the beginning of this chapter. The senate which was a council to advise the magistrates had only so much influence (not power in a constitutional sense) as the same magistrates wished to accord it.

THE DETERIORATION OF PATRICIAN DOMINATION

The senate now received citizens from the plebeian ranks of the infantry and the knights came under censorial scrutiny. The authority of patrician augurs was yet to be tried. In 300 the brothers Ogulnii successfully proposed a plebiscite which created a plebeian majority of five in the college of augurs and a minority of four in the college of pontiffs so long as the chief pontiff was patrician.[1] Now *augures* and *auctores*, divided by Ser. Tullius, had become irreconcilably separate.

Next the authority of the interregnum was weakened and disgraced. Livy (10. 11. 10) reports that Ap. Claudius and P. Sulpicius were interrexes in 299 and that the latter presided at the election of consuls. According to Cicero Curius Dentatus interposed his tribunician power when Claudius refused to accept a consular candidate from the plebs and he compelled the Fathers to grant their *auctoritas* before the centuriate election.[2] Livy (10. 15) has a different story in which Fabius Rullianus, consul of 297, refuses to permit Claudius demand that he and another patrician be elected to the consulship. Instead, Claudius and Volumnius, formerly consuls in 307, are elected for 296. Claudius had been and remained popular with the voters in the centuriate assembly.[3] The anti-Claudian annalistic does not tell even a part of the truth, for Volumnius presided at the re-election of Fabius and his consular colleague of 308 and 297 to the consulship of 285 and the re-election of Claudius to the praetorship.[4]

---

[1] Livy 10. 6–9. A Verginius was augur in 463 (Livy 3. 7. 6) and a Veturius in 453 (Livy 3. 32. 3). Papirius, chief pontiff in 449, had not held an imperial magistracy and therefore was not a patrician, strictly speaking (above, p. 221, n. 2). A plebeian Minucius was perhaps chief pontiff in 420 (above, p. 244, n. 2). Popillius Laenas was flamen Carmentalis in 359 (Cic. *Brut.* 56) but plebeians could hold the minor flaminates (Festus 137 L.). On the authority of Varro (2. 21. 3) Dionysius 2. 22. 3 asserts all Roman priests and sacrificants had been elected by the curias and their election approved by augurs who, I assume (above, pp. 94–5), were curial augurs. It was this manner of election which ensured patrician occupancy of the major priesthoods until 300. The first plebeian pontifex maximus was elected (*creatus*) in 254 (Livy, *Per.* 18). So, too, the new plebeian priests of 300 were elected (*creantur*, Livy 10. 9. 1–2) and not co-opted. See Mommsen, *Röm. Staatsr.* II³, 24–32.

[2] Cic. *Brut.* 14. 55: 'M'. Curium, quod is tribunus plebis interrege Appio Caeco diserto homine comitia contra leges habente, cum de plebe consulem non accipiebat, patres ante auctores fieri coegerit: quod fuit permagnum nondum lege Maenia lata'.

[3] From the *elogium* of Claudius (*CIL* XI, 1827 = *ILS* 54 = *II* 13. 3, no. 79; cf. no. 12) we learn that he was elected censor, consul twice and praetor twice by the centuriate assembly; elected quaestor and curule aedile twice by the tribal assembly. Furthermore, he was interrex and military tribune three times and dictator once.

[4] Livy 10. 22. 9. Furthermore, Decius and Fabius were proconsuls under Claudius and

If ever Curius Dentatus did oppose an interrex, that interrex was not Claudius who had been a friend of the plebeian nobility since 312 and had enjoyed their continued support in the centuriate and tribal assemblies.

In 292 L. Postumius Megellus presided over his own election to the consulship in the capacity of interrex. His consular conduct marks the end of the era in which interregna are employed by the patricians.[1] He attempted to dismiss the Fabii from a command against the Samnites, he quarrelled with his plebeian colleague, he celebrated a triumph which had not been voted him, he employed citizen–soldiers on his own estates, he was condemned and fined by the tribal assembly.[2] His career set a precedent.[3] Postumius committed the last patrician outrage before the last secession of the plebs.

According to the scrappy notices of the Livian epitome the last secession of the plebs took place some time between 289 and 286 after numerous insurrections over debt. The event of the sedition was the appointment of the plebeian Q. Hortensius to the dictatorship.[4] Hortensius' previous career remains wholly unknown and his

Volumnius who, in turn, was proconsul under Decius and Fabius in 295 (Livy 10. 16. 1, 30. 6–7). Nor did this collaboration begin so late. Claudius and Volumnius had been elected consuls for the first time under either Decius or Fabius (Livy 9. 41. 1, 42. 2). In this consulship Fabius was proconsul; Livy 9. 42. 2 reports Appius' opposition to this proconsulship but that is an illogical fiction. Lastly, the consul Decius of Campanian origin remained in Rome during the first year of Claudius' censorship (Livy 9. 29. 3) when he was planning or having laid a road into the heart of Campania. Despite the facts that Fabius modified Claudius' tribal lists and that under the Ovinian Law Claudius could not make Decius a senator, the careers of these four men are too closely meshed to deny their collaboration.

[1] Magdelain, 'Auspicia', p. 450 notes that between 292 and 82 B.C. there are recorded only three interregna. In 193 the senate was reluctant to allow an interregnum which the consul to whom the elections were allotted suggested rather than return from the front. The senate advised the other consul to return home; and he returned. See Livy 35. 6. The decision of both the senate and the consul may have been influenced by the unusual plethora of patrician rivals for the one patrician consulship. See Livy 35. 10. 1–10 and below, Appendix III, p. 296. The consul who returned was a Cornelius. His family and faction were much concerned with these elections.

[2] Livy, Per. 11; D. H. frr. of Books 17–18; Dio fr. 36. 32. Postumius is a very likely interrex against whom Curius would have interceded.

[3] Livy 27. 6. 8.

[4] Livy Per. 11: 'coloniae deductae sunt, Castrum, Sena, Hadria. triumviri capitales tunc primum creati sunt. censu acto, lustrum conditum est. censa sunt civium capita ducenta septuaginta duo milia. plebs propter aes alienum post graves et longas seditiones ad ultimum secessit in Ianiculum. unde a Q. Hortensio dictatore deducta est; isque in ipso magistratu decessit.' The undated dictatorship of Claudius may be a substitution for the dead Hortensius; see Broughton, s.a. 285.

alleviation of the debtors' plight can be only inferred.[1] Hortensius' claim to fame rests upon the passage of a law which once and for all determined the authority of the tribal assembly whose laws hereafter had force over all Roman citizens irrespective of birth and rank.[2] From this law we may infer that Hortensius' other legislation was passed by the tribal assembly and that the projected debtor legislation would otherwise have been neglected by the Fathers who asserted their independence from tribal legislation. Only an unequivocal law on the matter would have sufficed for the seceding plebs. In 342 an amnesty had been granted the seditious soldiery by an assembly in a grove which stood near the River Gate (*Porta Flumentana*). Likewise, the *lex Hortensia* was passed in extraordinary session in an oak grove (*aesculetum*) which probably stood in the same area; they are most probably one and the same.[3] These meetings, then, may have been curiate assemblies held outside the city because of the sedition.[4] So long as the Fathers continued to claim exemption from plebiscites, a plebiscite itself could not impose its own validity upon them. If the centuriate assembly had passed the Hortensian Law, it is hard to explain why that assembly did not meet in its regular place, the Ovile of the Campus Martius. Lastly, a curiate law would have guaranteed in perpetuity the universal validity and application of the Hortensian Law on plebiscites. Although the precise nature of plebeian complaints over debts and their immediate relation to the Fathers elude us,[5] another cause of insurrection may be seen in the foundation of three maritime colonies of Roman citizens on the Adriatic coast a year or two before the last secession.[6] The citizens who were sent out may well have become involved in litigation over debts left behind them in Rome. Hence an Hortensian Law made more days open to legal action.[7]

---

[1] See below, n. 7.

[2] Pliny, *NH* 16. 37: 'Q. Hortensius dictator, cum plebes secessisset in Ianiculum, legem in aesculeto tulit, ut quod ea iussisset omnes Quirites teneret'. Cf. Gellius 15. 27. 4; Gaius, *Inst.* 1. 3; Pomponius, *Dig.* 1. 2. 2. 8; and above, p. 252, n. 2. The tribal assembly was not subject to the *patrum auctoritas* (Cic. *Dom.* 14. 38).

[3] Above, pp. 249–52. See Palmer, 'King'.

[4] Compare the first *secessio Crustumerina*, above, pp. 219–20.

[5] The law severely limiting the *nexum* had been passed either in 326 or 313; see Rotondi, pp. 230–1. Before it laws governing debt had been passed in 367, 357, 347, and 342 (Rotondi, pp. 217, 222–4, 226). See P. Noailles, *Fas et Jus* (Paris, 1948), pp. 91–146.

[6] Livy, *Per.* 11, quoted above, p. 270, n. 4.

[7] Granius Licinianus in Macr. *Sat.* 1. 16. 30. See Michels' important discussion, pp. 103–6. The election of the IIIviri capitales before the secession (above, p. 270, n. 4) may

Some time between 291 and 219 a tribune Maenius successfully proposed the law which required the Fathers to give their *auctoritas* to elections by the centuriate assembly.[1] Since the Fathers might have withstood such a plebiscite before the Hortensian Law, it may have been passed after the Hortensius' dictatorship. In 275 or 274 the censor C. Fabricius expelled the consular patrician P. Cornelius Rufinus from the senate. This is the earliest attested expulsion from the senate. Our authors attribute it to the greed and luxury of Cornelius while they admit the fact that Fabricius had accepted and supported Cornelius' candidacy to a second consulship in 277.[2] Whatever the reason the censors made part of their record, it appears most unlikely that the censors would have been bold enough to humiliate a patrician consular unless the Maenian Law had already been passed.[3]

The laws of Publilius, Hortensius and Maenius reduced the power of the Fathers to the merest tokens except in the cases of infrequent interregna. The centuriate assembly remained independent of control by the old aristocracy. Still comparatively untouched was the curiate assembly which had ceased to elect major magistrates in 367. In two instances, however, the curiate assembly had voted on legislation since 367. Furthermore, the curiate assembly maintained until Cicero's day the final word respecting imperial auspices of the magistrates. The arrangement of the thirty curiate lictors who acted instead of the actual curias is a sign of political atrophy rather than outright curtailment. The lasting distinction between the curiate assembly and the tribal assembly which had fallen heir to the former's political power rested upon the necessity of the *patrum auctoritas* for legislation in the curiate assembly in advance of a bill's proposal and the ratification of curiate acts by the priests and augurs.[4] The priests

point to a new severity in the punishment of debtors who could be imprisoned or executed (*Lex* xii, *Tab.* iii, Livy 8. 28, Varro, *LL* 7. 105, Cic. *Rep.* 2. 34. 59; see De Sanctis ii, 490–3). The IIIviri came to be elected by the tribes later in the third century (Festus 468 L.); see Rotondi, p. 312. Had they previously been elected by the curias? See Kunkel, 'Untersuchungen zur Entwicklung des röm. Kriminalverfahrens in vorsullanischer Zeit', *Bay. Akad. Wissensch.* (1962) pp. 37–45, on their functions.

[1] Cic. *Brut.* 14. 55, quoted above, p. 269, n. 2; Rotondi, pp. 248–9.

[2] Varro in Nonius 745 L.; Gellius, *NA* 4. 8, 17. 21. 39 (other references in Broughton *s.a.* 275). Fabricius became the archetype of frugality and severity.

[3] Before the Maenian Law all magistrates elected in the centuriate assembly were subject to the *patrum auctoritas*. Expulsion of a patrician from the senate would have been perilous for any censor's later career. Neither Fabricius nor his colleague appears to have held office after 274.

[4] D.H. 9. 41. 3, 49 who calls the *auctoritas* a *probouleuma*. Cf. Cic. *Dom.* 14. 38. See

in question were doubtless the curions, whom the later Romans considered priests, and perhaps the curial flamens and such remnants of curial priesthoods as the augural Sodales Titii and Fratres Marcii.[1] No author, on the other hand, mentions the participation of priests in the passage of the *lex curiata de imperio*. A plebeian majority among the public augurs after 300 may have been able to effect a symbolic ratification by that college, at least, until the augurs were consulted at curiate assemblies no more than the curias themselves.[2]

The requisite *patrum auctoritas* for rogations in the curiate assembly goes back to the royal period and may also have been needed for curiate elections in the royal period just as they were needed for centuriate elections until the Maenian Law. Had it been an institution of the Republic, it would have been as easily abolished as established. Magdelain clearly distinguishes the difference between the *patres* and the *patricii*. The latter are a Republican hereditary aristocracy which embraces the *patres* who are a smaller group of men that had held the imperial magistracies.[3] The latter qualification could not obtain in the Rome of the king. The *patres* whose birth held such authority in royal Rome had not been mere fathers, or for that matter, heads of families. Rather they had been the primates of their clans. Their position in Roman curias they owed to their position among their own people before they became a Roman curia. The *princeps* of the *gens Claudia* migrated to Rome with his many clients.[4] The clients of the ruling families regarded the family patriarch as the *patronus*. Originally the Roman *patroni* were the very few and the *clientes* the very many in the curias. Neither word involves citizenship or slavery. Surely, the client had his own *gens* but he was not a member of the ruling clan. The Law of the Twelve Tables still reflects the reciprocal relation of patron and client.[5] The law made social habits civic institutions. Although the patron and his client were

---

H. S. Jones, *CAH* 7. 483. Dion. 2. 14. 3 says the *patrum auctoritas* preceded the passage of curiate laws in his day but had once followed it. Presumably a law similar to the Maenian, if not the Maenian, had reversed the procedure. See Gabba, pp. 209–16.

[1] Above, pp. 92–5, 146–50.

[2] In 215 the augurs voided the election of Claudius Marcellus after it thundered. They claimed the gods did not like the election of a second plebeian consul (Livy 23. 31. 12–14). On the augurs' role in assemblies see Taylor, *Voting Assemblies*, pp. 7–8, 55, 72–8.

[3] Magdelain, 'Auspicia', pp. 467–70.

[4] Livy 2. 16. 4–5; D. H. 5. 40. 3–5; Suet. *Tib.* 1 who calls him a *princeps gentis*; Serv. on *Aen.* 7. 706, *Sabinorum dux*.

[5] *Lex XII Tab.* 8. 21 in Serv. on *Aen.* 6. 609: 'patronus si clienti fraudem fecerit, sacer est'. On *sacer* Tondo, pp. 26–58, especially pp. 33, 41.

distinguished in ancestral usage, intermarriage must have taken place. The word *sodales*, applied to the Titii and Luperci Quinctiales and Fabiani, conceals a root which implies intermarriage. Their name comes from their curia and not from a family which had once solely constituted the priestly order.[1] The original *patres* had enjoyed the political incumbency of their respective curionates. Livy tells us the patricians controlled the votes of their clients to the extent that the tribunes of plebs demanded the transfer of their election to a new assembly of tribes.[2] To be sure, clients remained clients in the tribal assembly as well as in the centuriate assembly. However, we know nothing of the manner in which the Quirites voted in each curia. And we do know that the patricians were excluded from the *concilium plebis* which elected the plebeian tribunes and aediles.[3] Lastly, we do not know what a patron might ask of his clients in a curia's meeting which usage sanctioned. The plebs' constant agitation for debtor legislation and the limitation of the *nexum* suggests that a patron's prestige was reinforced economically. Service in the Servian infantry no doubt helped to improve the condition of clients. However, their political independence could be asserted only with the neutralization of the curiate assembly and the curial aristocracy of the Fathers. After the third century the Fathers might exercise a rare interregnum and monopolize certain priesthoods.

The three major flaminates of Jupiter, Mars and Quirinus, the sacral kingship and the chief curionate had patrician incumbents until some time before 210. The *rex sacrorum* who died in that year was a plebeian Marcius.[4] Noteworthy is the first sacral king, M.' Papirius in 509, whose family attained political office sixty-six years later.[5] The year 209 saw the taking of a new Dial flamen and the election of the first plebeian curio maximus. The new flamen refused the appointment of the chief pontiff and after an appeal to the tribunes ultimately was admitted to the senate although no flamen of

[1] Ernout–Meillet[4] *s.v. sodales* and above, pp. 132–6.
[2] Livy 2. 56. 3–4, 58. 1 (cf. D. H. 9. 41. 5).
[3] See De Martino 1[2], 313–15. The patricians could hardly have comprised a numerical majority in the curiate assembly because the number of patrician families, securely recognized after 342, is less than the number of curias.
[4] Livy 27. 6. 16. No other plebeian king is known. Cic. *Dom.* 14. 38 says the kings had to be patricians but he says the same of flamens, of whom only three out of fifteen were patrician (above, p. 269, n. 1).
[5] D. H. 5. 1. 4. Another Papirius was said to be chief pontiff in 509 (D. H. 3. 36. 4) to which office the sacral kingship was subordinate (Livy 2. 2. 1–2). See Münzer, *RE* 18. 3, Papirii nos. 1–5, 10, 20.

Jupiter in the two preceding generations had been in the senate. Precedent, however, favored his seat in the senate.[1] When this flamen was later elected to the curule aedileship, his priesthood prevented his taking an oath to obey the laws so that only after a plebiscite his brother, then praetor designate, took the oath on his behalf.[2] The oath alone did not keep the Dial flamen from office for he was also forbidden to see the centuriate army under arms or ride a horse. Nevertheless, the priest had been in the senate in the fourth century. His patrician birth had formerly given him his senatorial rank. After 312 neither his priesthood nor his family ensured him a seat and the priesthood may have been made a certain political dead end by forbidding his participation in military activities.[3]

The first plebeian curio maximus was C. Mamilius Atellus whom C. Scribonius succeeded in 174.[4] The next chief curions of whom we hear were Calvisius Sabinus and Statilius Taurus, Augustus' marshals.[5] Since the plebeian tribunes had referred the complaint of the patricians against Mamilius' candidacy to the senate which in turn left it to the discretion of the assembly, the election of a plebeian does not at all appear to have been a matter of pontifical jurisdiction or sacral law. The patricians had argued only from precedent. Consequently, we are not justified in supposing that religiously or legally a plebeian was excluded from the office. More serious is the eligibility of Mamilius on the grounds of membership in a curia. The Mamilii were Tusculan and presumably no Tusculans had Roman citizenship before the fourth century. The Mamilii, however, claimed that an ancestor, Octavius Mamilius, had married the daughter of Tarquinius Superbus with whom he also shared guest-friendship.[6] The authenticity of their claim may be supported by the tower to which they gave their gentilicial name and from which they took a cognomen.[7] The plebeian chief curion, at any rate, might have cited the existence of this tower to support a pretension of archaic *ius*

---

[1] Livy 27. 8. 4–10.

[2] *Ibid.* 31. 50. 6–9. Could he not swear at all or swear to obey all laws or to obey laws passed in the centuriate and tribal assembly?

[3] Gellius 10. 15 lists the taboos binding the flamen Dialis. It is no wonder the flamen botched a sacrifice in 211 (Livy 26. 23. 8) and that it took over a year to find his unwilling successor.

[4] *Ibid.* 27. 8. 1–3, 41. 21. 8–9.   [5] *ILS* 893a and 925.

[6] Livy 1. 49. 8–9; Dion. 4. 45; Festus 116 L. See Taylor, 'Voting Districts', p. 229.

[7] Platner–Ashby, *s.v. turris Mamilia*.

Quiritium (given for the sake of the *conubium*) because it figured in the very ancient festival of the October Horse.[1] The survival of their pretension in the histories of Livy and Dionysius points to a claim for an extraordinary purpose which did them no service in Tusculum.[2]

Elsewhere I have proposed that the cognomen *libo*, borne by the Marcii, Poetellii and Scribonii, reflects a minor sacrificial attendant in the curias.[3] The origins of the Scribonii are not anywhere attested.[4] Calvisius Sabinus and Statilius Taurus, the chief curions of the Augustan principate, certainly had not either Roman or Latin ancestry.[5] By that time, however, patricians were again being made, not born.

CONCLUSION

The foregoing chapter has been devoted to a description and history of the curiate political system during the Roman kingship and Republic. A summary of the curiate organization is given in the following chapter. Here I summarize my arguments on the history of curial political activity in relation to the centuriate assembly in the first two centuries of the Republic.

Toward the end of the sixth century the king who ruled the Romans was expelled and his official duties were supplanted by those of a perpetual priest-king and an annual, collegial magistrate. The change in government was marked by the Roman pontiffs who have preserved a list of eponymous magistrates from the year 509 B.C. At

[1] Festus 117, 190, 191 L.

[2] In the annalistic accounts Mamilius is a henchman of Tarquinius. Cicero, *Planc.* 8. 20, cites only the Fulvii, Porcii and Coruncanii as illustrious Tusculans. Perhaps, the Mamilii were not illustrious enough for Cicero or their citizenship put them in a different class. Tacitus, *Ann.* 11. 24 says the Coruncanii came from Cameria. This divergent tradition may have been invoked in the third century in order to establish T. Coruncanius' curial citizenship for the sake of a place in the senate and his candidacy for the chief pontificate. See Münzer, *RE* 4.2, cols 1663–4 and Syme, 'Sejanus on the Aventine', *Hermes* 84 (1956), 264.

[3] Above, pp. 146–7.

[4] Münzer, *RE* 2A1, cols 858–9 to the contrary. For the formation of the name compare Sempronius. H. Rix, 'Die Personennamen auf den etruskisch-lateinischen Bilinguen', *Beitr. z. Namenforschung* 7 (1956), pp. 168–9 wrongly asserts the Etruscan origin of the name. He repeats others' demonstration that a man had an Etruscan gentilicial name derived from the Etruscan root 'to write' which he rendered into Latin Scribonius. The Etruscan probably adopted an existing Latin name which seemed the best translation of his Etruscan name. The process does not make Scribonius Etruscan. American Smiths and -smiths are sometimes formerly German Schmidt, -schmidt and -schmied, but not all Smiths, etc. are of German ancestry.

[5] Syme, pp. 199–200, 237–8.

first two in number and bearing the later title of consul, the eponyms betray no drastic departure from the institution founded in 509 until the middle of the fifth century when a decemviral board replaced the double eponyms for two years. Thereafter the list of eponymous magistrates displays a vacillation between the double consular praetorship and the boards of consular tribunes of three, four, six and sometimes eight members until 367 when the magistrates, whom the later Romans usually called military tribunes with consular power, were abolished. The two praetors were always elected by an assembly of military units called centuries, for they commanded the centuriate *populus*. However, the curiate assembly alone could confirm and bestow the praetors' auspices and ruling power. In contrast to the praetors, the tribunes-consul had commanded regiments of an earlier royal army divided into three regiments or tribes. I have argued that these tribunes, whose office antedates the praetorship and the legions under the praetors' command, were both elected and confirmed by the curiate assembly just as the centuries later controlled both stages of censorial election and confirmation.

The revolution of 509 had wrought the overthrow of the kingship and the foundation of an annual collegial magistracy which was filled by the men of the centuriate army. The centuriate army, the *populus* of the Quirites, did not contain all Romans but only those fit to bear arms according to their census. The elective and legislative activity of the centuriate assembly, like that of the curias, was restricted by a subsequent ratification on the part of the small group of ex-magistrates, the Fathers, for the Republic's first 200 years. The political and religious implementation, *auctoritas patrum*, was greatly resented as we can securely infer from the fact that it was required in advance of elections and legislation. Furthermore, the very fact that the Fathers could and did thwart the will of the *populus Romanus* expressed in the centuriate assembly and formulated by that assembly's presidents, the consular praetors, demonstrates the openness and liberality of the centuries in contrast with the curias. Unfortunately our surviving evidence of archaic centuriate legislation is indeed slight. It is nevertheless indisputable that the Publilian and Maenian Laws laid the blame for conservative obstruction on the Fathers and not on the centuriate voters themselves. Roman authors of the later Republic knew the centuriate assembly as a legislative

T

277

and elective body, more conservative and aristocratically dominated than the tribal assembly. It was and is a mistake to assume the same relative political tendency in the early Republic since the efforts to release the centuries from fetters imposed by the Fathers aimed at attaining centuriate elections and legislation without subsequent review. The tribal assembly might legislate in place of the centuries after the Hortensian Law, but it could never elect the chief magistrates.

By way of compromise a political settlement was reached in 367–366. Then tribunician legislation imposed the abolition of the military tribunes' *imperium* and the eligibility of plebeians to the two permanently restored praetorian consulships. Although the plebeians had filled the consular tribunate especially in times of stress when their candidacies could have been overlooked only at the risk of secession, they were not pleased to extend the life of that magistracy. They hoped to be elected to the dual consulship. This hope, no doubt, was based on the knowledge that the centuries were more likely to produce plebeian magistrates and more agreeable legislation. Their beliefs were mistaken and their hopes frustrated but this does not reflect upon our view of their confidence and assumptions before 367. The Fathers countered their aspirations through their *auctoritas*, interregna, dictatorships and augural decrees so that the plebeians were forced to weaken these institutions. If the plebeian politicians could have hoped for the same outcome from the continuance of the consular tribunate in 367, they would have voiced no objection to that magistracy which they had occasionally exercised. On the contrary, the plebeians wanted centuriate chief magistrates. Hence, I contend that the consular tribunate, which chronologically precedes the centuriate army, was filled by the curiate assembly voting upon candidates put forth by the interrexes who were the Fathers.

The revolution of 510–509 had been promoted by the Roman *populus* whose military commanders assumed charge of the government. The centuries elected them and quite probably voted on their legislative proposals. The Fathers assumed control of the elections and legislation and the curiate assembly continued to exercise its right of conferring upon the magistrates their auspices and rule. In the early fifth century the plebs organized itself among the curias, the only non-military collective organs of government. The plebs' officers took their title from the tribunes of the soldiers. Curiate election of tribunes of the plebs proved so unsatisfactory that some twenty years later the plebs met according to the new divisions of Roman territory, the Servian tribes, and chose their leaders who could seek the decision of the plebs (*plebis scitum*) on matters which presumably concerned only the plebs. If at that time a goodly number of Roman *curiales/Quirites* still resided on or near their curial land holdings, the creation of the twenty-one tribal meetings was no great break from the curial tradition of thirty curiate meetings. However, the tribal assembly at least contained a larger, less restricted number of voters. In response to the Fathers' sway over centuriate and curiate matters the citizen body sought and obtained the first general writing of the state laws. The decemviral codification was worked by a new magistracy which combined the power of praetors-consul and the number of the tribunes of the plebs, and thereby supplanted and suspended both offices. Members of both castes served on the decemviral board and the second decemvirate with a 'plebeian' majority conceded to the Fathers their cherished hope of a caste untainted by marriage with plebeians even though this article of the Twelve Tables went against tradition. The concession failed to safeguard the existence of the new decemviral magistracy. It was set aside and the former system of praetors and plebeian tribunes was restored in 449. Whereas the praetors could be revived by an interregnum, the interrupted plebeian tribunate had to seek its renewal through the chief pontiff who was ever empowered to convoke the curiate assembly. After a tribune of the plebs obtained the plebs' decision in favor of legitimate marriage between plebeians and patricians in 445, the Fathers and their clans moved to revive the powers of the military tribunate to which was granted the *imperium* and the auspices and to create a new magistracy of censors which would perform the census for rating centuriate service, a function never within the purview of military tribunes. Based upon the pattern of curiate election and curiate confirmation of military tribunes, the censors were elected by the centuries and confirmed in their auspices by the centuries.

The Fathers also persevered in their control of centuriate election when it occurred and legislation if it was enacted. The consular tribunate proved a magistracy of more limited access for the plebs unless mostly war-time exigencies rendered the patrician oligarchy

279

agreeable to plebeian petitioners. The consular tribunate, for a long time an enigmatic eponymous magistracy in the development of the Roman constitution, extended the political vigor of the curiate assembly. Its proponents were the patrician oligarchy led by the Fathers who controlled the interregnal elections. After 367 the military tribunes ceased to receive auspices and the ruling power. Their election was first transferred to the centuries since they were military officers and thence to the tribes in 311. In the wake of the Licinio–Sextian Rogations of 367 two 'new' magistracies were created. The single judicial praetorship and the dual curule aedileship were to be filled only by patricians. However, the praetorship was later thrown open to plebeians although the praetor was always elected by the centuries since he had both auspices and ruling power. The curule aedileship was very soon granted to the plebeians in a compromise whereby each caste held it every other year. Like the plebeian aediles, the curule aediles were elected by the tribal assembly since they had no auspices and ruling power. Also, if my interpretation of the quaestors' election in the elective assembly of their superiors, praetors-consul or tribunes-consul is accepted, the quaestors' election was granted to the tribes some time after 367, perhaps when the office was expanded in the third century. Evidently the censorship was not touched by the rogations of 367 and continued to be held by patricians until they overtly tampered with the military rosters. Thereafter one censor had to be plebeian in accordance with a new law. The requirement of certain plebeian magistracies rendered the patrician control by *auctoritas patrum* most difficult. However, elections could be voided by the college of augurs. Consequently that college and the college of pontiffs with its control of certain curiate assemblies and other legal matters were expanded to receive a possible plebeian majority in the pontiffs' case and a certain plebeian majority of augurs.

The history of the patricio-plebeian strife has never been and never will be fully clear to us. We are ill-served by what little evidence we have. The Fathers, and not the entire patriciate, must have been the repository of patrician domination as they were the repository of interregnal government and of legislative and elective review. I have attempted to relate the origins of the Fathers and the senate to the curions of the royal curias. The consular tribunate I have attributed to a reversion to the curiate constitution dominated by the Fathers in their capacity of *interreges* and *auctores*. The notion of interregnal auspices and of the 'increase' gained through the *auctores* and augurs are religious. The fonts of Roman civil religion were the several curias. Even if we leave aside suggestions made in chapter 6, we are indubitably informed that the curias granted the Republican magistrates their auspices and *imperium* and that all priests and office-holders were at first chosen by the curias whose selections were ratified, in Dionysius' words, by those who interpret divine matters by divination. In chapter 6 I have argued that the Sodales Titii and Marcian Brothers, whom I consider curial, would have fulfilled such a qualification. An assembly that bestowed religious authority on magistrate and priest, that approved testamentary dispositions and adoptions, and that had elected kings, wielded great power. In the early years of the Republic the curiate assembly was the patrician instrument of power and the centuriate assembly was the hope of the plebeians for full participation in the government.

CHAPTER 10

A SUMMARY OF THE CURIATE
CONSTITUTION

Properly speaking, some curias existed before Rome itself. They were independent communities which maintained their own government and observed their own religious customs. Curia meant merely a group of men which was later defined as a *genus* ('stock'). The unification of communities in and around the site of historical Rome took place gradually. A national leader, the king, ruled the united states which continued to uphold their own integrity in the selection of chieftains, the curions, and in their own religions and priests. As units of a united state, the curias severally approved the king's selection and bestowed upon him the right of rule because they reserved to themselves the auspices.

The curias, by definition equal to one another, had their own gods and rites and shared, so far as we are told, only the deity Juno who was worshipped by all the curias. The differences among curias are reflected in the ancient tales about the Alban, Latin, Sabine and Etruscan origins of archaic Romans. The earliest kings whose historicity can be claimed were T. Tatius and Numa Pompilius. Both were considered Sabine and the name of the latter is Sabine in contrast with the Latin Quinctilius. The last kings were reckoned Etruscans and the name Tarquinius fully supports this ancient opinion. Although the historical Latin language is Latin, it contains Etruscan and Sabellian vocables which are very old. Presumably Romans were mainly Latin from the beginning but were surely not entirely Latin. The question why the early Romans were dominated by non-Latins cannot be answered for want of knowledge of the primitive state. Nevertheless, the fact remains to be pondered.

The curias met severally for religious and political purposes. Each had its own place of reunion for communal suppers in the presence of its gods. We believe this place was an *atrium* or a curia. Each curia selected its own curion. We have argued that twenty-seven curias had their own augural plots in the city during the kingship. The curiate

282

assembly was based upon the several meetings of the curias. On that account it and the other assemblies voted by units and one assembly was always a plurality of gatherings (*comitia*).

Toward the end of the kingship a reform of the state took place traditionally under Servius Tullius. This reform arose from a reorganization of the Roman military force which had formerly been organized in three regiments. According to our reckoning, the curial governments through their control of augury and auspices had successfully thwarted or retarded a military reorganization by Tarquin I. His successor wrought the change by curbing and limiting the authority of curial religion. The newly founded military system assumed the civil rule upon expulsion of the king and replaced the authority of the king with that of their own officers, the praetors-consul. Nevertheless, the latters' power still rested upon curiate confirmation and the Fathers' assent. Both of these factors could not be omitted because of their deeply rooted religious implications.

For almost 150 years the Republic was governed by two systems, one centuriate and progressive, the other curiate and highly conservative. The most serious limitation upon the centuriate constitution remained its military character. The curiate constitution, on the other hand, could enable other actions such as the institution and election of plebeian tribunes. Only gradually did the tribal assembly, which was closely patterned upon the curiate assembly, assume the authority which the centuries were unable to take over because of their military basis. The few families that intended to concentrate the government in their hands could control election and legislation in the two older assemblies through the *auctoritas patrum*. The tribal assembly was not fettered by this necessary ratification although for two centuries the patricians insisted that they were not bound by tribal legislation despite plebeian bills which commanded universal legitimacy. In addition to control of centuriate business, the oligarchs restored the officers of the old tribal army to prominence by working the election of three, four or six tribunes-consul in the curiate assembly. These tribunes were endowed with the annual magisterial powers which the praetors-consul had received from the centuries after the king's loss of political power. Constitutionally this change was facilitated by the possibility or fact of withholding both the Fathers' assent to centuriate election or the curiate denial of the *imperium* to the praetors-consul.

The great weapons of the plebs, short of civil war, were the act of secession and in the course of time the plebeian tribunes' intercession. The received tradition concentrates our attention mainly upon the plebeian demand of the right to govern by occupying the offices of state. Undoubtedly, political rivalries and personal ambitions played a part. But that is not the whole story by any means. Equally undoubted traces of economic conditions adverse to the plebs are visible in the annals. Unfortunately, almost all details are lacking to us as they were to the Roman historians who probably would not have pursued such matters anyway. Closely connected with the economic conditions, I believe, were the questions of land tenure, expansion and annexation of territory and the colonial settlements which differ somewhat from the Greeks' in purpose and activities. Related to this complex problem is the crucial matter of Roman imperialism, which some may term incipient, although I, for one, believe imperialism deeply ingrained at Rome. It was not my purpose to deal with imperialism in this work. However, students of Rome's early history must ask which politicians advocated the expansion and annexation of territory. Frank and his followers beg the question. Although our evidence on early imperialistic motives and policy is slight indeed, the evidence that there was no motive and no policy in the acquisition first of Latium and then of Italy is abundant if we count Roman silence and our ignorance as evidence. Therefore, from the events I infer that wars and conquests are fit subjects for discussion of the internal strife in early Republican Rome.

In 367 the Romans abolished the election of magistrates in the curiate assembly. Of course, they did not abolish the office of military tribune. Nor had they abolished the kingship, the curiate assembly, and the Fathers' *auctoritas*. They did not need to abolish these institutions because the old oligarchy which they supported gave way to a new oligarchy which, in its turn, endured till 27.

The curiate assembly could meet in a number of places. No meetings at Old or New Curias are recorded. The Comitium off the Forum was its historical meeting site. There, also, the king, the praetor and his referees sat in judgement,[1] the chief pontiff flayed a

---

[1] Varro, *LL* 5. 155; *Lex XII Tab.* 3. 5 (= Gellius, *NA* 20. 1. 46–7), Plaut. *Poen.* 805–7; Titius in Malcovati, *ORF²*, pp. 201–3 (= Macr. *Sat.* 3. 16. 15–16). See Palmer, 'King'.

sinning scribe,[1] the chief curion posted instructions for Fornacalia and adrogatory adoptions took place.[2] Although the senate convened in the building called the Curia Hostilia, all Republican senate decisions record its meetings in the Comitium which was the inaugurated ground on which the building was erected.[3]

On the Capitol near the Curia Calabra the curias met every first of the month until *c.* 304 to hear the minor pontiff proclaim the priest king's declaration of the Nones and Ides. The Curia Calabra was near Romulus' hut which, we argued, was a remnant of the place for taking the auspices.[4] The curias witnessed the inauguration of the king and flamens in the presence of the pontifical college.[5] The testament and forswearing of rites may have taken place under the same circumstances.

We have discussed possible fifth-century curiate assemblies in the Curia Crustumina during the first secession and on the Capitol (in the Area Capitolina?) or the Aventine to elect plebeian tribunes, and fourth- and third-century curiate assemblies in the grove(s) of the Campus Flaminius to try a citizen and enact legislation. We have argued that the Lucus P⟨o⟩etelinus was a curial site and identical with the *aesculetum* where this Hortensian Law was passed. During the last Republican civil war the Pompeians acquired land in Thessalonica for taking the auspices, but the consuls did not propose a *lex curiata de imperio* and no new magistrates were created.[6] We know that the Roman augurs had sacred land in the Ager Veiens.[7] Such land would have been necessary for the patrician consul to hold a tribal assembly near Sutrium in 357. Later the plebeian tribunes had this kind of assembly forbidden by a subsequent law.[8] However, the Romans had a marvelous facility for constitutional circumvention.

---

[1] Livy 22. 57. 2.

[2] Ovid, *F.* 2. 527–30, Suet. *Aug.* 65. Both mention the Forum which evidently refers to the Comitium. See Taylor, *Voting Assemblies*, pp. 4–5. Gaius, *Inst.* 1. 98–107 says that the adrogatory adoption had to take place in Rome.

[3] See Palmer, 'King'.

[4] Varro, *LL* 6. 27–8; Macr. *Sat.* 1. 15. 9–13. Cf. Fest. *Epit.* p. 42 L., Serv. Dan. on *Aen.* 8. 654.

[5] Gellius, *NA* 15. 27. Cf. Fest. *Epit.* p. 42 L.

[6] Dio 41. 43 who also says 200 senators were on hand. I take this to mean that the Fathers could have granted their *auctoritas*.

[7] Festus 204 L., *s.v. obscum.*, quoted above, ch. 8, p. 181, n. 3.

[8] Livy 7. 16. 7–8. See Rotondi, pp. 221–2 and Botsford, p. 297. See Livy 3. 20 who reports that the augurs were ordered to go to Lake Regillus to inaugurate a plot of land where an assembly could be held with the proper auspices.

We need only recall the piece of foreign ground in the Campus Flaminius where the Fetials could bring war. The Romans at Thessalonica could have made curial ground if they had wished.[1]

Presidents of the curiate assembly were the priest-king,[2] the tribune of the Celeres,[3] the military tribunes who, we argued, first helped elect the plebeian tribunes and their own quaestors, dictators who presided over the grant of their own and their cavalry commander's *imperium* and over legislative assemblies, the chief pontiff at the election of plebeian tribunes in 449 and at assemblies which approved wills, adrogatory adoptions, and transfers to the plebs, interrexes who only presided over elections, and the regular consuls and praetors who saw to the passage of curiate laws on their *imperium*.

According to our sources the curiate assembly acted on declaration of wars,[4] which we have linked to the college of twenty Fetials, the election of the kings, proposed laws on making new curias, on the recall of Camillus from exile, on the exile of the last Tarquin,[5] on the matters of wills, adoptions and transfers to the plebs and, above all, on grants of auspices and *imperium*. For a while the curias elected the plebeian tribunes. We maintain that under the Republic the curiate assembly still legislated until 287, tried a case of *perduellio*, and elected the tribunes-consul and their quaestors until 366.

In the foregoing discussion we have distinguished four stages in the history of the curiate constitution. Under the kings it was the only mode of civic expression for the Quirites. Very early in the Republic the curiate military system suffered an infamous defeat which ended the old tribal infantry but did not terminate the potential power of the tribal commanders. After a short-lived attempt to harmonize the political elements of the state through the decemviral prytany the oligarchy imposed the curiate constitution upon the people whereby they monopolized the magistracy of the tribune-consul by means of interregnal procedure. The third stage begins with the restoration of the praetors-consul. Then the patricians attempted to dominate that magistracy again by interregnum, electoral dictatorships, the Fathers' approval of centuriate legislation and elections, and by augural edict. These political instruments the plebeians circumvented or brought into disgrace. The fourth stage

---

[1] Cf. Nichols, pp. 269–70.
[2] See above, p. 284, n. 1 and p. 285, n. 4.
[3] D.H. 4. 71. 4–6; cf. 4. 75. 1–2, 5. 12. 3.
[4] *Ibid.* 2. 14, 4. 20.
[5] *Ibid.* 4. 84. 2–4.

witnesses the end of patrician monopoly of the sacral kingship and occupancy of the chief curionate and, finally, the admission of Roman citizens to the latter office who did not even bother to claim ancestors among the oldest Romans. In the august principate the jurists and antiquarians could point to the quaint traces of Roman beginnings in private law under the curiate constitution. Latium and Italy now lived in one house under one law.

REVISED FASTI OF YEARS WITH EPONYMOUS TRIBUNES-CONSUL

478 L. Aemilius Mamercus
C. Servilius Structus Ahala
K. Fabius

444 A. Sempronius Atratinus
L. Atilius Luscus
T. Cloelius Siculus

437 M. Geganius Macerinus
L. Sergius Fidenas
A. Cornelius Cossus

434 Ser. Cornelius Cossus
M. Manlius Capitolinus

Q. Sulpicius Camerinus Praetextatus

428 A. Cornelius Cossus
T. Quinctius Poenus Cincinnatus
L. Quinctius[1]
A. Sempronius

427 A. Cornelius Cossus
T. Quinctius Poenus Cincinnatus
C. Servilius Structus Ahala
L. Papirius Mugillanus

[1] See p. 234, n. 4.

IMPERIAL FAMILIES WITHOUT RECORD BETWEEN 444 AND 366 B.C.

The following list contains the families which held imperial magistracies before 444 and which did not hold imperial magistracies between 444 and 366. In the second column is the number of tribunates of the plebs traditionally held by members of the family between 493 and 366; in the third column the number of consular praetorships; in the fourth the number of decemvirates; in the fifth the total of imperial magistracies; and in the sixth the family's status after 366 if it can be determined by the occupancy of the plebeian tribunate or aedileship or the patrician and plebeian consulship from 342 on. The names of the early tribunes of the plebs survive without cognomen; those of praetors-consul are replete with cognomens. The Minucii, for example, are called Augurini even though the surname derives from a priesthood evidently held first in 300. On that account I make no distinction in family branches in this list.[1]

Family	Tr. Pl.	Pr. Cos.	Xvir.	Total	Status after 366
Aternius	1	1		1	Disappear
Cassius	1	3		3	tr. pl. 137
Cominius		2		2	tr. pl. after 313
Curtius		1		1	tr. pl. 57
Herminii		2		2	Disappear
Iunii	3	1 ?		1 ?	pl. cos. 325
Larcii		4		4	Disappear
Minucii	2	5	1	6	pl. cos. 305
Numicius		1		1	tr. pl. 320
Oppius	1		1	1	tr. pl. 215
Poetelius	1		1	1	tr. pl. 358, pl. cos. 326
Rabuleius	1		1	1	Disappear
Romilius	1	1	1	2	Disappear
Sicii or Sicinii[2]	10	1		1	aed. pl. 185
Tarpeius	1	1		1	Disappear
Tullius		1		1	Disappear[3]
Volumnius		1		1	pl. cos. 307

[1] The list has been compiled with the invaluable aid and guidance of Broughton. The writer is quite aware that the earliest Fasti may be interpolated and the sums derived therefrom are only approximate. On the other hand, it is equally difficult to uphold a view that almost all the names were interpolated since not a few names appear which cannot be ancestors of later Roman politicians.

[2] The sources' MSS vary from person to person and Sicinius might also be mistaken for Licinius. The number of plebeian tribunes may well be inflated. The plebeian aedile of 185 is Cn. Sicinius; no Siccius is met after 454.

[3] None of the latterday Tullii is a probable descendant of the consul of 500.

THE PATRICIATE

Our work has not been primarily concerned with persons and families. However, Magdelain's pioneering work on the auspices and our own foregoing studies have touched upon the patriciate. We have inherited no clear idea of what made a man patrician. Livy, for instance, could not recognize a patrician.[1] Cicero, in his famous remark on the falsification of triumphs, consulships, clans and transfers to the plebs, held that M.' Tullius, consul in 500, was patrician.[2] However, no proof existed since his and others' sole criterion for judgement was a consulship held before 366. So long as the Romans held that any descendant of Romulus' senate was patrician, no reliable criterion was needed.[3]

In the following pages I follow the lines drawn by Last and Magdelain to ascertain which Roman families were patrician. It is my contention that a distinction between patrician and plebeian was gradually formulated between the decemvirate and the Licinio–Sextian laws, that is between 451 and 367. To be sure, one of the clauses in the Law of the Twelve Tables forbade marriage between a patrician and a plebeian. Not only the prohibition but also the social distinction was new. Furthermore, the distinction was not fixed at that time. For instance, a Sempronius was interrex in 483–482, but the family is plebeian after 366.

Like every other aspect of early Roman history, the origins of families were bedevilled by the antiquarian research in the last century before Christ. At that time Romans sought to authenticate either Trojan origins mediated through Alba Longa or Sabine origin. Perhaps the first to compose a family history was T. Pomponius Atticus. He treated the Junii, Claudii Marcelli, Cornelii Scipiones, Fabii Maximi and Aemilii Pauli.[4] Of Terentius Varro's work on Trojan families we know a bit more. He handled the Nautii and Julii for certain.[5] Other families which were reckoned as Trojan were probably also discussed by Varro.[6] Ascanius (i.e. Iullus) had two sons, Julius and Aemylos.[7] The remaining Varronian Trojans were companions of Aeneas who became eponyms of Roman families: Cloanthus of the Cluentii, Gyas of the Geganii, Sergestus of the

---

[1] Livy 3. 27. 1 (Tarquinius). Cf. Ogilvie's commentary on Livy, pp. 539, 540, 542, 652–3. Compare D.H. 5. 29. 3–4 (Mucius).

[2] *Brut.* 16. 62.   [3] E.g. Livy 1. 8, D.H. 2. 8–10, 2. 62.

[4] Nep. *Att.* 18. See Peter, vol. II, pp. xxviii–xxviiii.

[5] Serv. on *Aen.* 2. 166 (cf. on 5. 704 and 3. 407, and D.H. 6. 69. 1, Fest. *Epit.* 165 L.) is the only fr. which Peter, II, 9, directly attributes to the work.

[6] See Peter II, xxxii–xxxiii.   [7] Fest. *Epit.* 22 L.

Sergii and Mnesthus of the Memmii.[1] To them may be added Junius,[2] Caecas of the Caecilii,[3] and Clonius of the Cloelii.[4] The author of the short work on praenomens drew on Varro for the name Tutor Cloelius.[5]

Finally we have the two lists of Alban families which we discuss above:[6] Livy's Tullii, Servilii, Quinctii, Geganii, Curiatii, Cloelii,[7] and Dionysius' Julii (?), Servilii, Geganii, Metilii, Curiatii, Quinctilii, Cloelii.[8] Dionysius has included the Metilii for personal reasons.

A contemporary of Atticus and Varro, M. Valerius Messalla Rufus, also wrote a work on Roman families in which he included material on family religion.[9]

Finally, C. Julius Hyginus, Caesar's freedman in charge of the Palatine library, followed in Varro's footsteps and wrote on Trojan families. His surviving fabrication is the Trojan hero Entellus whose name is derived from the Sicilian town.[10] Since Entellus figures in the *Aeneid* and in the very book in which Vergil seems to have used Varro,[11] the poet and Hyginus perhaps took Entellus from Varro.

Varro's *Trojan Families* probably also spread abroad the report that all Alban noble families had migrated to Rome.[12] Of the thirteen Albano-Trojan families the Julii, Nautii, Aemilii, Servilii, Quinctii, and Cloelii were certainly patrician, and the Memmi, Cluentii, Junii, Caecilii and Tullii as well as the intruding Metilii were plebeian. The Geganii and Sergii may have been patrician but there is no certainty. Livy's and Dionysius' lists omit the Nautii, Memmii, Sergii, Cluentii, Junii, Aemilii, Caecilii and, perhaps, the Julii. For this reason and others given above (see above, p. 136, n. 2) I have concluded that the list was drawn from an official record of a Curia Quinctia.

Besides the Albano–Trojan families the Romans reckoned certain Sabines among their ancestors. The most famous was Volesus Valesius.[13] Mettus Curtius, who belonged to the Roman Sabine faction,[14] may have been considered an ancestor of the consul of 445. The third name contained in Dionysius *tallos turannos* is corrupt. The praenomen must be *tullus*. The author of the work on praenomens reports Varro on the Sabine

---

[1] All are to be found in the *Aeneid*. See 5. 117–22 and Serv. on 117; see above, p. 290, n. 5.

[2] D.H. 4. 68. 1; cf. p. 290, n. 5.

[3] Fest. *Epit.* 38 L. Cf. Vergil's Caeculus, founder of Praeneste.

[4] Fest. *Epit.* 48 L. Cf. *Aen.* 9. 574.

[5] *Praen.* 1; cf. Cato, *Orig.* fr. 22 P., D.H. 3. 3, Livy 1. 22–23 and Fest. *Epit.* 48 L.

[6] See pp. 133–7, 205–6. On the Curiatii see above, p. 205, n. 6, p. 251, n. 1, and below, p. 299, n. 2.

[7] 1. 30. 2 on which see Ogilvie.

[8] 3. 29. 7. The order is that of all but one of the MSS. See p. 133, n. 2.

[9] Peter II, LXXVIII, 65.　　　　　　　　[10] *Ibid.* CVI, 76.

[11] 5. 387–472; see above, p. 290, n. 5, p. 291, n. 1.

[12] Serv. on *Aen.* 1. 7; cf. on 5. 598, 6. 773, 7. 716. See p. 18.

[13] Varro in *Praen.* 1, D.H. 2. 46. 3, Plut. *Num.* 5; cf. Val. Max. 2. 4. 5 for Valesius of Sabine Eretum.

[14] Varro, in *Praen.* 1, D.H. 2. 46. 3.

origin of *pustulanum lauranum*, which is also no name. The former must conceal *tul⟨l⟩um* or *p⟨o⟩stu⟨mi⟩um*. The latter may be Lauranius or Luranius or Laronius, none of which is old or common at Rome. Dionysius' *turannos* may be Turranius, also a late name at Rome. Another possibility is *t⟨a⟩ra⟨ki⟩os*. Another Sabine of Varro's is *alium fumusilleaticum.*[1] Here we surely have Avillius, the son of the Sabine woman Hersilia and Hostilius.[2] Thus I would read *a⟨vil⟩lium f⟨ili⟩um ⟨he⟩rsil⟨i⟩(a)e* but can make nothing of *aticum*. The Avillii have no part in Roman history unless they are the unlikely relatives of the Aulius who was consul in 323 and 319.

Outside the legendary origins are the tradition of Sabine Aurelii of the middle Republic[3] and the famous patrician Claudii. Their story was probably preserved by the clan itself and stands apart from learned research.[4] Folk-tale preserved a Sabine origin for the kings Numa Pompilius and T. Tatius. To them Varro may have added Ancus Marcius.[5]

Only two Sabine families, the Valerii and the Claudii, can be properly considered patrician.

The disquisitions on names and families cannot help us in ascertaining the identity of patrician families. Furthermore, not one Roman king bears an indisputably patrician name.

Since Mommsen's pioneering work on the patricians[6] some weight has been given to the names of Roman tribes which coincide with family names. Ten tribal names are also borne by early consular families: Aemilia, Claudia, Cornelia, Fabia, Horatia, Menenia, Papiria, Romilia, Sergia and Voturia.[7] There is no certain evidence that the Sergii and Romilii were patrician. We shall show that the Menenii and Veturii were plebeian at least after 366. Furthermore, six more old tribal names coincide with plebeian names if they are borne by persons at all: Camilia, Galeria, Lemonia, Pollia, Pupinia and Voltinia. At any rate, no man bearing one of these names ever attained a Roman Republican office. Finally, the three known curial names which are also recognized as gentilicial are plebeian: Faucia, Titia, Velitia.

Therefore, I conclude that such names have no bearing on patrician status.

One may well wonder what made a patrician. The Romans tell us certain priesthoods had to be occupied by patricians. One was the chief curionate but plebeians occupied that priesthood during the Second Punic War when a plebeian priest-king appears although we are told that no plebeian might hold that office.[8]

Actually political office supplies a better index to a man's condition. A man who was plebeian tribune or plebeian aedile was or became ple-

---

[1] Only in *Praen.* 1.   [2] Plut. *Rom.* 14. 8.   [3] Fest. *Epit.* 22 L.

[4] See Livy 2. 16. 4–5; D.H. 5. 40; Suet. *Tib.* 1; App. *Reg.* 21; Plut. *Pobl.* 21 and Serv. on *Aen.* 7. 706.   [5] In *Praen.* 4, cf. 1.

[6] T. Mommsen, 'Die römischen Patriciergeschlechter', *Rh.M.* 16 (1861), 321–60 (= *Römische Forschungen* 1, 69–127).

[7] See Taylor, 'Voting Districts', pp. 35 ff. Only the Claudia was formed after 509.

[8] See pp. 274–6.

beian. So, too, his descendants were plebeian. Every other year after 366 the college of two curule aediles was plebeian.[1] After 342 one consul was plebeian. After 300 there were five plebeian augurs in a college of nine and four plebeian pontiffs. Interrexes were always *patres*. We have followed these criteria in assessing the status of a family.

Some clans contained branches of both sorts. The Claudii are the best example of this. On the eve of the Second Punic War Servilii Gemini were both patrician and plebeian.[2]

Nor is this the only pitfall in assessing a clan's social condition. Some plebeian families asserted that they had originally been patrician but had transferred themselves to the plebs. Among these are the Minucii. They claimed their transfer, worked in 439, was a reward. The entire story is a late fabrication.[3] The earliest reliably recorded *transitio ad plebem* seems to be that of some Servilii Gemini.

Our criteria cease to be valid at different times. The Fasti Capitolini report the college of consuls of 172 was the first constituted of two plebeians but Livy who usually notes violation of law and precedent does not remark the novelty.[4] In fact, a departure from the law on plebeian consulship first occurred and was validated in 206 although it had occurred before in 215 (see below). Neither the elections for 206 nor for 172 were followed by constant repetition. Not until the first century B.C. did the college of pontiffs alter the rule on filling its vacancies according to social condition. In 73 Julius Caesar succeeded his plebeian mother's kinsman Aurelius in the pontificate.[5] Finally in 53 a Caecilius, patrician by birth and plebeian by adoption, served as interrex. By the last date many, many old rules had been broken.

Fortunately we can speak of the gradual dissolution of the old rules on patricians and plebeians in the Second Punic War. The times demanded something more than traditional scruples.

The Second Punic War witnessed no less than twenty extraordinary incidents which had serious constitutional ramifications. We list them by years in order to see the progress of change. In 217: the first election of a dictator in an assembly; the dual collegiality of the dictatorship without masters of cavalry; the election of new consuls by interrexes while a suffect consul lived, after the augurs prevented a dictator from presiding. In 216: a dictator without master of cavalry to revise the senate roster instead of censors; the enlistment of slaves as legionaries. In 215: centuriate election of a second plebeian consul which the augurs voided; an attempt to elect the Quirinal flamen consul for 214. In 212: the election of a patrician consul for 211 who had never held a curule office. In 211: the ex-censors

---

[1] Livy 6. 42. 12–14, 7. 1. 6.
[2] See Mommsen, 'Die römischen Patriciergeschlechter', *Rh.M.* 16 (1861), 117–19.
[3] *Ibid.* p. 124.
[4] Livy 42. 9. 8. Between 339 and 131 one of the censors had to be plebeian. Livy (8. 12. 15–16) records the law of 339 and (*Per.* 59) the departure from the law.
[5] In 91 B.C. a similar selection may have been made. See Broughton, *s.aa.* 91, 73.

are to be *cum imperio* with ex-dictators and consulars in defense of the city; the military tribune in Spain assumes the title of pro-praetor after an election but lacks the *patrum auctoritas*; a *privatus* who had advanced only to the curule aedileship is sent to Spain as pro-consul. In 210: the consul is ordered to name a dictator in Italy to hold elections but refuses; a plebeian priest-king dies and it takes two years to find a successor. In 209: a Dial flamen is chosen against his will, demands admission to the senate and in subsequent years attains magistracies; a plebeian is chosen curio maximus. In 207: the patrician consul shares in the triumph of his plebeian colleague; the former names the latter dictator to hold elections for 206 although as consul he already was fully empowered to hold elections. In 204: the censors first take charge of the census of twelve recalcitrant Latin colonies; two plebeian tribunes are sent from the city to investigate charges brought by Locrians. In 203: the dictator was named to keep the consul from exercising his magistracy in going to Africa.[1]

The Roman electorate had willingly elected a second plebeian consul in 215 because the people wanted him. His policy apparently troubled the augurs more than his social condition. Fabius Maximus, an augur, was elected to the twotime vacancy which Claudius Marcellus could not fill because the augurs said nay. The next attempt to fill the consulship with two plebeians would have to be made with the least chance of interference.

The Gens Veturia was very old at Rome. Its name was shared with one of the pre-republican tribes.[2] One of its members was consul as early as 492. Yet after 366 the first Veturius to attain the consulship in 334 and 321 is the plebeian consul. A century later L. Veturius Philo appears in the consulship. Unfortunately, two consular colleges are recorded for 220 and no reliable historical account survives.[3] In 217 the same L. Veturius Philo was named dictator to hold elections. At the time there were two consuls and two dictators besides Veturius. He was declared faultily appointed after fourteen days in office and interrexes held the election.[4] In 210 the two plebeian curule aediles are L. Veturius and P. Licinius Varus.[5] It was then customary for recent curule aediles to reach the praetorship usually after one or two years.[6] Therefore, the praetor of 209, L. Veturius Philo, ought to be identical with L. Veturius, plebeian curule aedile of 210, just as P. Licinius Varus, the praetor of 208, is identical with

[1] Livy 22. 8–10, 22. 25–6, 22. 34, 22. 57; 23. 22–3; 23. 31, 24. 7–9; 25. 40, 26. 2, 25. 37–9, 26. 2, 26. 18; 27. 5, 27. 6. 16; 27. 8 (cf. 31. 50. 7, 32. 7. 14), 27. 6. 16, 28. 9, 28. 10; 29. 37; 29. 20; 30. 24 (cf. 30. 26).

[2] See P. Fraccaro, 'La tribus Veturia e i Veturi Sabini', *Athenaeum* 2 (1924), pp. 54–7 = *Opuscula* II, 1–3.

[3] See Broughton, *s.a.* Besides explanations of the two colleges found here, we suggest that two of the men may have been *suffecti*.   [4] Livy 22. 33. 9–34. 1.

[5] *Ibid.* 27. 6. 19; see Broughton, *s.a.* with note on Veturius and *Supplement*, p. 69.

[6] Cf. Claudius, cur. aed. 217, pr. 215; Sempronius, cur. aed. 216, cos. 215; Laetorius, cur. aed. 216, pr. 210; Fabius, cur. aed. 215, pr. 214, cos. 213; Fulvius (cos. 211) and Sempronius (cos. 204), cur. aed. 214, pr. 213; Cornelius, cur. aed. 213, pr. 211; Licinius, cur. aed. 212, pr. 208, cos. 205; Servilius, cur. aed. 208, pr. 206, cos. 203; Caecilius, cur. aed. 208, cos. 206; Servilius, cur. aed. 207, pr. 205, cos. 203; Livius, cur. aed. 204, pr.

the curule aedile of 210. If the praetor of 209 was the curule aedile of 210, he is a plebeian. L. Veturius Philo proceeded to the consulship of 206 in a highly unusual manner. In 207 L. Veturius Philo, P. Licinius Varus and Q. Caecilius Metellus were sent ahead by the two consuls to announce their glorious victory at the Metaurus. After both the consuls, C. Claudius Nero and M. Livius Salinator, came to Rome and the latter triumphed, the cavalry greatly praised Veturius and Caecilius and urged the people to elect both of them to the succeeding consulship. The consuls joined the cavalry in recommending these two men. Thereafter, C. Claudius named M. Livius dictator to hold elections. The dictator was himself consul and his colleague was in Rome with him! Livius named Q. Caecilius master of cavalry. Caecilius and L. Veturius Philo were elected consul.[1] The only explanation of this procedure which can be offered is that an ordinary president could not have brought about the election of the two men whom the consuls favored. Since the augurs had voided the election of a second plebeian consul in 215 and since, we argue, Veturius was a plebeian, in 207 one consul named the other dictator for the sole purpose of working the election of their favorite candidates, both of whom were plebeian.

Next we meet Ti. Veturius Philo who succeeded the patrician Aemilius Regillus as the Martial flamen. The year is 204, six years after the death of a plebeian priest-king and five years after the election of a plebeian curio maximus.[2] Ti. Veturius Philo was probably replaced by P. Quinctilius Varus who died in 169.[3] Although the Quinctilii had a praetor-consul in 453 and a tribune-consul in 403, there is no certain evidence that the clan was patrician. Therefore, I conclude that both Veturius and Quinctilius were plebeians in a priesthood ordinarily held by patricians.

In 184 M. Porcius Cato was censor. One of his censorial acts was an attack upon a knight, L. Veturius, from whom he took the public horse.[4] One of the fragments of this speech comes from Nonius (p. 217 L.):

plebitatem, ignobilitatem. Cato pro [lege de] Veturio: 'propter tenuitatem et plebitatem.' Hemina in Ann.: 'quicumque propter plebitatem agro publico eiecti sunt.'

The plebitas of Hemina has but one possible meaning and the sentence one explanation. The meaning is literal and the sentence refers to the expulsion of plebeians from public land.[5] Also Cato must have been talking about the same condition of the Veturii: they were plebeian.

In 174 Ti. Sempronius left a plebeian vacancy in the college of augurs which was filled by a kinsman Ti. Veturius Gracchus Sempronianus who had been adopted into the Gens Veturia.[6] The place may have been

202; Valerius and Fabius, cur. aed. 203, pr. 201; Fulvius, cur. aed. 202, pr. 200; Quinctius and Valerius, cur. aed. 201, pr. 199. The careers of plebeian aediles are quite similar; cf. the pl. aed. of the years 210, 208, 207, 205, 203, 201.
[1] Livy 27. 51. 3–6, 28. 9. 18–10. 3.   [2] See Broughton, s.aa. 210, 209, 204.
[3] See ibid. s.aa. 179, 169. A patrician Postumius followed Quinctilius.
[4] See Malcovati, ORF[2], pp. 34–6.   [5] See Peter on Cass. Hem. fr. 17.
[6] Broughton, s.a. 174 with note, inclines toward the view of Münzer that the Veturii

Veturius' because he was by blood a Sempronius. However, he could not have been eligible if he had been adopted by a patrician.

The cumulative evidence on the Veturii after 366 points to their being plebeian without a patrician branch.

Although we propose that both consuls of 206 were plebeians, clearly this college did not shatter precedent. Livy makes it clear that a patrician consul was necessary in 193.[1] However, the Hannibalic War was over. Even though the purportedly first plebeian college of consuls in 172 was followed by like colleges in 171 and 170, a patrician consul was elected in thirty-one of the forty-one years between 172 and 131 when both censors were plebeian. Thus, the election of 172 also did not destroy the old or create a new and binding precedent. Cicero (*Dom.* 37–8) held that there were still patrician magistracies and priesthoods.

Much more difficult to assess are the Livian assertions that certain families were patrician. Clearly, Livy had no clear criteria.[2] This lack of knowledge or state of confusion prevailed among his predecessors. For instance, Livy (8. 37. 2–3, cf. 9. 15. 11) prefers to make an Aemilius the consul of 323 instead of the Aulius whom some annals record. Since the colleague is a patrician Sulpicius, a second patrician, Aemilius, is out of the question. Sometimes Livy is correct in calling a man patrician.[3] When he says Cornelia and Sergia are patrician ladies, we do not have to take his word on the former. However, no record of a Sergius holding a necessarily patrician office survives.[4] The fact that there was a Tribus Sergia is not conclusive, as the case of the Menenii by itself demonstrates.

One example from Livy suffices to illustrate the annalists' ignorance and the manner of falsifying an old family's condition. After the early fourth century the Verginii drop from prominence. Between the election notice of 296 and the cursory (pontifical) report of the aediles' activities in that year, Livy describes the foundation of an altar for Pudicitia Plebeia. What had very likely been a brief notice in pontifical annals Livy has expanded into an account of how the patrician Verginia was excluded from worship of Pudicitia Patricia because of her marriage to plebeian Volumnius, consul in 296. According to Livy she established the shrine of Pudicitia Plebeia in her own home.[5] In fact, Verginia was plebeian. Although we might infer her condition from the cult's institution, we know her ancestors had been plebeian tribunes.[6]

were patrician and of Geer that the man's name ought to read in our MSS of Livy 41. 21. 8–9 Ti. Sempronius Gracchus Veturianus.

[1] Livy 35. 10. 1–9.
[2] See above, p. 290, n. 1.
[3] E.g. 6. 11. 2 (Manlius), 35. 10. 2–3 (Cornelius, Quinctius, Manlius).
[4] Livy 8. 18. 8. Sallust *CC*, 31. 7 and Asconius 58, 73 KS. also assert Sergius was patrician.
[5] Livy 10. 22. 9–23. Cf. Festus 270–1 L. Livy's story closely resembles another on the two Fabias who had married a patrician Sulpicius and a plebeian Licinius. Livy attributes the Licinio-Sextian laws to the ambition of Licinius' patrician wife. See 6. 34.
[6] See Broughton *s.aa.* 461–457, 449, 395, 394.

The evidence from the list of interrexes in all cases but one support the results derived from the criteria of office-holding.[1] Two interrexes are reported for the election of magistrates for 482: A. Sempronius Atratinus and Sp. Larcius Flavus. Because the Larcii disappear after this year, we cannot properly speak of a patrician condition being proved. However, the Sempronii were plebeian at least as early as 310 (see below, p. 298, n. 3). Therefore, we must suppose that later the family was plebeian according to the unimpeachable evidence. Yet in 482 the family was not plebeian. Since Sempronius, like Larcius, had twice been praetor-consul, he could participate in an interregnum. Sempronius was a Father. But were he and his family patrician? In other words, did such a distinction exist in 482 for the sake of interregna or of office-holding? In chapter 9 we have argued that the distinction acquired the force of custom in the fifth and early fourth century, but did not have legal force until 367–366.

A. IMPERIAL FAMILIES BETWEEN 444 AND 367 B.C.

The following list contains the names of all families which held imperial magistracies between 444 and 367. In the second column is the number of tribunates of the plebs traditionally held by members of the family between 493 and 367 which is noted beside the last entry of the family; in the third the number of consular tribunates; in the fourth the number of consular praetorships; in the fifth the total of imperial magistracies for the branch; in the sixth the total for the *gens*; in the seventh the status after 366 if it can be determined by the occupancy of the plebeian tribunate or aedileship or the patrician and plebeian consulship from 342 on.

Family and Branch	Tr. Pl.	Tr. Cos.	Pr. Cos.	Branch Total	Gens Total	Status
Aebutius Helva			1		1	tr. pl. ?[2]
Aemilii Mamercini		13	1		14	patr.
Albinius	1	1			1	
Antistius	2	1			1	tr. pl. 319
Antonius Merenda		1			1	tr. pl. 167
Aquilius Corvus		1			1	tr. pl. ?[3]
Atilius Luscus		1		1		
Atilius Priscus		2		2	3	tr. pl. 311
Claudii Crassi		2			2	patr.
Cloelii Siculi		2			2	patr.[4]
Cornelii		3			3	
Cornelii Cossi		14	1		15	
Cornelii Maluginenses		12	2		14	
Cornelius Scipio		1			1	33	patr.
Duillius			1		1	
Duillius Longus	2	1			1	2	pl. cos. 336
Fabii Ambusti		9			9	

[1] I omit Lucretius, interrex of 509. [2] See Broughton II, 468.
[3] *Ibid. s.aa.* 286 (and vol. 2, p. 641), 211 and 55.
[4] The family does not reappear until 180 when P. Cloelius Siculus was elected sacral king. On the family's later history see T. P. Wiseman, 'T. Cloelius of Tarracina' *CR* 17 (1967), 263–4.

Family and Branch	Tr. Pl.	Tr. Cos.	Pr. Cos.	Branch Total	Gens Total	Status
Fabius Ambustus Vibulanus		1		1		
Fabii Vibulani		5		5	15	patr.
Folius Flaccinator		1			1	patr. cos. 318
Furius		1		1		
Furii Camilli		6		6		
Furii Fusi		2	2	4		
Furii Medullini		13	2	15	26	
Geganii Macerini		3	2		5	Disappear
Genucii Augurini[1]	2	3			3	tr. pl. 342
Horatius		1		1		
Horatius Pulvillus		1		1	2	
Iulii Iulli		9	2	11		
Iulius Mento			1	1	12	patr.
Licinii Calvi Esquilini	10	2			2	pl. cos. 236
Lucretii Tricipitini		6	2		8	tr. pl. 210
Maelius Capitolinus	2	2			2	tr. pl. 320
Manlii		5		5		
Manlii Capitolini		4	1	5		
Manlii Vulsones		2		2		
Manlii Vulsones Capitolini		3		3	15	patr.
Menenii Lanati	2	6	2		8	tr. pl. 357
Nautii Rutuli		4		4		patr.
Papirii Crassi		4	3	7		
Papirii Cursores		2		2		
Papirii Mugillani		7		7	16	patr.
Pinarius Mamercinus		1			1	?[2]
Pomponius Rufus	3	1			1	tr. pl. 362
Postumii Alb. Regillenses		7			7	patr.
Publilii Philones	3	2			2	pl. cos. 339
Quinctii Capitolini Barbati		1	3	4		
Quinctii Cincinnati		8	1	9		
Quinctii Cincinnati Capitolini		5		5	18	patr.
Quinctilius Varus		1			1	
Sempronii Atratini		4			4	tr. pl. 310[3]
Sergii Fidenates		11	1		12	
Servilii Axillae (Ahalae)		6		6		
Servilii Fidenates		9		9		
Servilius Structus		1		1	16	patr.
Sextius[4]	11	1			1	aed. pl. 203
Sulpicii Camerini seu Praetextati		8	1	9		
Sulpicius Longus		1		1		
Sulpicius Peticus		1		1		

[1] See above, p. 229, n. 1.
[2] See Palmer, 'Censors', p. 307.
[3] The Sempronii Blaesi, Gracchi, Longi, Rutuli, Sophi and Tuditani are all plebeian. The tr. pl. of 310 was a Sophus who became one of the first plebeian pontiffs in 300. A L. Sempronius Atratinus appears again at the end of the Republic, evidently the first of his family in office since 380, if he did indeed descend from that family. He may have succeeded a patrician in 40 B.C. (for what it's worth; see Broughton, s.a.). At any rate, he was an adopted Sempronius (see Syme, p. 269, n. 4). Sempronius' cognomen Sophus does not necessarily indicate a family different from the Atratini since his patrician colleague in the consulship is a Sulpicius surnamed Saverrio, borne only by him and his son.
[4] See above, p. 229, n. 1.

Family and Branch	Tr. Pl.	Tr. Cos.	Pr. Cos.	Branch Total	Gens Total	Status
Sulpicii Rufi		4		4	15	patr.
Titinius Pansa Saccus	2	2			2	tr. pl. 192
Trebonii	2	2			2	tr. pl. 55
Valerii Lactucini Maximi		2		2		
Valerii Poplicolae		5		5		
Valerii Potiti		9	1	10		
Valerii Potiti Poplicolae		6		6	23	patr.
Verginii Tricosti	8	2	1		3	
Veturii Crassi Cicurini		6			6	pl. cos. 334[1]

Totals	263	31		294
Patricians	215	24		239
Plebeians	48	7		55

B. FAMILIES NOT IMPERIAL BEFORE 444 B.C.

The following families were not imperial before 444. Those marked with one asterisk had members who served as tribune of the plebs; with two asterisks members who were chief pontiff:

*Albinius	*Licinii	*Publilii
*Antistius	*Maelii	*Titinii
Atilii	**Papirii	*Trebonii
**Folii	*Pomponius	

C. OFFICEHOLDING FROM 444 TO 366 B.C. ACCORDING TO STATUS

Patrician

Certain		Uncertain	
1. Aemilii	14	1. Geganii	5
2. Claudii	2	2. Horatii[2]	2
3. Cloelii	2	3. Pinarii	1
4. Cornelii	33	4. Sergii	12
5. Fabii	15		—
6. Folii	1	Total	20
7. Furii	26		
8. Iulii	12		
9. Manlii	15		
10. Nautii	4		
11. Papirii	16		
12. Postumii	7		
13. Quinctii	18		
14. Servilii	16		
15. Sulpicii	15		
16. Valerii	23		

Total 219

239 patricians = 81 per cent

Plebeian

Certain		Uncertain	
1. Albinii	1	1. Aebutii	1
2. Antistii	1	2. Quinctilii	1
3. Antonii	1		—
4. Aquilii	1	Total	2
5. Atilii	3		
6. Duillii	2		
7. Genucii	3		
8. Licinii	2		
9. Lucretii	8		
10. Maelii	2		
11. Menenii	8		
12. Pomponii	1		
13. Publilii	2		
14. Sempronii	4		
15. Sextii	1		
16. Titinii	2		
17. Trebonii	2		
18. Verginii	3		
19. Veturii	6	55 plebeians
	—	= 19 per cent

Total 53

---

[1] This includes a Veturius or Rutilius of 417. The latter name is first attested in 169.
[2] Reluctantly I list the Horatii as uncertain patricians since the tribune of the plebs in

D. FAMILIES ELECTED IN THE CENTURIATE ASSEMBLY

1. Censorial Families (including the censors of 366)

Family	Censorships	Cons. Praetorships	Cons. Tribunates
Cloelii	1		2
Cornelii	1	3	30
Furii	3	4	22
Geganii	1	2	3
Iulii	1	3	9
Papirii	5	3	13
Pinarii	1		1
Postumii	3		7
Sempronii (pl.)	1		4
Servilii	1		16
Sulpicii	2	1	14
Total	20	16	121

2. Praetorian Families

Family	Censorships	Cons. Praetorships	Cons. Tribunates
Aebutii (pl.)		1	
Aemilii		1	13
Duillii (pl.)		1	1
Lucretii (pl.)		2	6
Manlii		1	14
Menenii (pl.)		2	6
Quinctii		4	14
Sergii		1	11
Valerii		1	22
Verginii (pl.)		1	2
Total		15	89

E. PARTICIPATION IN MAGISTRACIES ACCORDING TO STATUS

	Magistracy	Plebeian	%	Patrician	%
20	Censorships	1	5	19	95
31	Cons. Praetorships	7	22.6	24	77.4
263	Cons. Tribunates	48	18.2	215	81.8
314	Total	56	18	258	82

F. LIST OF KNOWN INTERREXES FROM 509 TO 52 B.C.

The following list contains the interrexes whose names are known and who are assigned to a year. The year is given according to Broughton who has placed them among the officers of the year over whose election they presided. Since the interrex was in effect an eponymous office, his name was very likely included in the pontifical annals.[1]

401 (Livy 5. 11. 4), P. Curatius, may well be read as Horatius; see above, pp. 133 ff. and pp. 205, n. 6, 251, n. 1.

[1] See SHA 27 (Tac.) 1. 1 = Peter Ann. Max. fr. 2 P.; Serv. on Aen. 1. 373.

Some of the interrexes are plausibly dated to a known interregnum without names while the notice of the man's participation comes from his *elogium*. These are marked with a question mark. It is not necessary to assign some interrexes to different years. For instance, Q. Servilius and M. Fabius served twice in 356–355. They could have deemed this service double duty. See below, n. 1.

In 53 Q. Caecilius Metellus Pius Scipio Nasica became the only recorded plebeian interrex. By birth he was a patrician Cornelius. The first interrex or, at least, the identity of the first interrex is very likely apocryphal.

LIST OF INTERREXES

509	Sp. Lucretius Tricipitinus?		M. Fabius (Ambustus)
482	A. Sempronius Atratinus	340	M. Valerius
	Sp. Larcius Flavus		M. Fabius (Ambustus or
462	P. Valerius Poplicola		Dorsuo)
444	T. Quinctius (Capitolinus)	332	M. Valerius Corvus (the
	Barbatus		5th interrex)
420	L. Papirius Mugillanus	327	L. Aemilius (Mamercinus
413	Q. Fabius Vibulanus		Privernas) (the 15th
396	L. Valerius (Potitus)		interrex)
	Q. Servilius Fidenas	320	Q. Fabius Maximus (Rul-
	M. Furius Camillus		lianus)
391	M. Furius Camillus		M. Valerius Corvus
	P. Cornelius Scipio	298	Ap. Claudius (Caecus)
	L. Valerius Potitus		P. Sulpicius (Saverrio)
389	P. Cornelius Scipio	291	L. Postumius Megellus
	M. Furius Camillus *iterum*[1]	?222	Q. Fabius Maximus Ver-
387	M. Manlius Capitolinus		rucosus
	Ser. Sulpicius Camerinus	216	C. Claudius Centho
	L. Valerius Potitus		P. Cornelius (Scipio) Asina
355	Q. Servilius Ahala	?208	Q. Fabius Maximus Ver-
	M. Fabius Ambustus		rucosus
	Cn. Manlius Capitolinus	82	L. Valerius Flaccus
	Imperiosus	77	Ap. Claudius Pulcher
	C. Fabius Ambustus	?55	M. Valerius Messala (Niger)
	C. Sulpicius Peticus	53	Q. Caecilius Metellus Pius
	L. Aemilius Mamercinus		Scipio Nasica
	Q. Servilius Ahala		M. Valerius Messala (Niger)
	M. Fabius Ambustus	52	M. Aemilius Lepidus
352	L. Cornelius Scipio (the		Ser. Sulpicius (Rufus) (last
	12th interrex)		interrex)
351	C. Sulpicius Peticus		M. Valerius Messala (Niger)

[1] The editors have excised *iterum* from Livy 6. 1. 8. However, Furius could have been interrex for the second time in that interregnum. Cf. year 355.

The fifteen clans whose members were interrexes are:

Aemilii	Larcius	Quinctius
Claudii	Lucretius (?)	Sempronius
Cornelii	Manlii	Servilii
Fabii	Papirius	Sulpicii
Furii	Postumius	Valerii

BIBLIOGRAPHY

AGAHD, R. 'M. Terenti Varronis Antiquitatum Rerum Divinarum libri I XIV XV XVI', *Jahrbücher für classische Philologie*, Supplbd. 24 (1898), 1–220, 367–81.

ALFÖLDI, A. *Early Rome and the Latins.* Ann Arbor, n.d. [1965].

— 'Der frührömische Reiteradel und seine Ehrenabzeichen', *Deutsche Beiträge zur Altertumswissenschaft* 2. Baden-Baden, 1952.

AMBROSCH, J. A. *De Sacerdotibus Curialibus.* Bratislava, 1840.

ANDREWES, A. 'Phratries in Homer', *Hermes* 89 (1961), 129–40.

— 'Philochoros on Phratries', *JHS* 81 (1961), 1–15.

BELOCH, K. J. *Römische Geschichte bis zum Beginn der punischen Kriege.* Berlin, 1926.

BERGER, A. *RE* 12.1 (1924), col. 416, *s.v.* Laelius no. 17.

BERNARDI, A. 'Dai *Populi Albenses* ai *Prisci Latini* nel Lazio arcaico', *Athenaeum* 42 (1964), 223–60.

BLUME, FR., LACHMANN, K. F. W. and RUDORFF, A. A. F. *Die Schriften der römischen Feldmesser*, 2 vols, Berlin, 1848–52.

BOEHM, F. W. *RE* 7. 1 (1910), cols 480–3, *s.v.* Gaia Taracia.

BÖMER, F. *P. Ovidius Naso Die Fasten*, 2 vols, Heidelberg, 1957.

BOTSFORD, G. W. *The Roman Assemblies.* New York, 1909.

BROUGHTON, T. R. S. *The Magistrates of the Roman Republic*, vol. 1, New York, 1951; vol. 2, 1952; supplement, 1960. [Usually cited herein by the year (*s.a.*) *B.C.*]

BUCK, C. D. *A Grammar of Oscan and Umbrian.* Corrected ed., Boston, n.d. [1928].

CASTAGNOLI, F. 'Il Campo Marzio nell'antichità', *Atti dell'Accademia Nazionale dei Lincei*, Mem. cl. sci. mor. stor. filol., ser. 7, vol. 1, fasc. 4 (1946).

CATALANO, P. 'Contributi allo studio del diritto augurale I', *Università di Torino, Memorie del Istituto Giuridico*, ser. 2, mem. 107 (1960).

COLI, U. 'Regnum', *SDHI* 17. 1 (1951), 1–168.

COLINI, A. M. 'Storia e topografia del Celio nell'antichità', *Atti della Pontificia Accademia Romana di Archeologia*, ser. 3, mem. 7 (1944).

COLLART, J. 'Varron: De lingua latina livre V', *Publications de la Faculté des Lettres de l'Université de Strasbourg*, fasc. 122. Paris, 1954.

DAHLMANN, H. *RE* supplbd. 6 (1935), cols 1172–1277, *s.v.* M. Terentius Varro.

DE FRANCISCI, P. 'Primordia Civitatis', *Pontificium Institutum Utriusque Iuris Studia et Documenta* 2 (1959).

DEGRASSI, A. *Inscriptiones Italiae*, vol. 13, fasc. 2, 'Fasti Anni Numani et Iuliani'. Rome, 1963.

DE MARTINO, F. *Storia della costituzione romana*, vol. 1, 2nd ed. Naples, 1958.

DE SANCTIS, G. *Storia dei Romani*, vol. 1, Turin, 1907; 2nd ed., Florence, 1956: vol. 2, Turin, 1907; 2nd ed., Florence, 1960: vol. 4, part 2, tome 1, Florence, 1953.

EISENHUT, W. *RE* 24 (1963), cols 1324–33, *s.v.* Quiris, etc.

ERNOUT, A. *Le Dialecte ombrien*. Paris, 1961.

ERNOUT, A. and MEILLET, A. *Dictionaire étymologique de la langue latine*. 4th ed., Paris, 1959.

(FONDATION HARDT). *Les origines de la république romaine. Entretiens sur l'Antiquité Classique*, vol. 13. Vandœuvres–Geneva, 1967. Articles by E. Gabba, J. Heurgon, A. Momigliano and others.

FRACCARO, P. *Opuscula*, 4 vols. Pavia, 1957.

GABBA, E. 'Studi su Dionigi di Alicarnasso, I: La costituzione di Romolo', *Athenaeum* 38 (1960), 175–225.

HEURGON, J. *See* Fondation Hardt.

HIGNETT, C. *A History of the Athenian Constitution*. Oxford, 1952.

HILL, H. *The Roman Middle Class*. Oxford, 1952.

HOLLAND, L. A. 'Janus and the Bridge', *Papers and Monographs of the American Academy in Rome* 21 (1961).

JACOBY, F. *Atthis: The Local Chronicles of Ancient Athens*. Oxford, 1949.

KÜBLER, B. *RE* 6. 1 (1907), cols 272–312, *s.v.* Equites Romani.

LAST, H. 'The Servian Reforms', *JRS* 35 (1945), 30–48.

LATTE, K. 'Zwei Exkurse zum römischen Staatsrecht: 1. Lex Curiata und Coniuratio', *Nachrichten von der Gesellschaft der Wissenschaften zu Göttingen*, philol.-hist. Kl., n. F. 1 (1934–6), 59–73.

—— *RE* 20. 1 (1941), cols 745–58, *s.v.* Phratrie.

—— 'Augur und Templum in der varronischen Augurformel', *Philologus* 97 (1948), 143–59.

—— *Römische Religionsgeschichte*. Munich, 1960.

MAGDELAIN, A. 'Cinq jours epagomènes à Rome', *REL* 40 (1962), 201–27.

—— 'Auspicia ad patres redeunt', Hommages à J. Bayet. *Collection Latomus* 70 (1964), 427–73.

—— 'Note sur la loi curiate et les auspices des magistrats', *RHDFE* 42 (1964), 198–203.

MERKEL, R. *P. Ovidii Nasonis Fastorum Libri Sex*. Berlin, 1841.

MICHELS, A. K. *The Calendar of the Roman Republic*. Princeton, 1967.

MINGAZZINI, P. 'L'origine del nome di Roma ed alcune questioni topografiche attinenti ad essa: La Roma Quadrata, il sacello di Volupia, il sepolcro di Acca Larenzia', *BC* 78 (1961–2), 3–18.

MIRSCH, P. 'De M. Terenti Varronis Antiquitatum Rerum Humanarum Libri XXV', *Leipziger Studien zur classischen Philologie* 5 (1882), 1–144.

MOMIGLIANO, A. 'An Interim Report on the Origins of Rome', *JRS* 53 (1963), 95–121.

— 'Procum Patricium', *JRS* 56 (1966), 16–24.
— L'ascesa della plebe nella storia arcaica di Roma', *Riv. St. Ital.* 79 (1967), 297–312.
— 'Osservazioni sulla distinzione tra patrizi e plebei', *Les origines de la république romaine* in the *Entretiens* of the Fondation Hardt, vol. 13 (1967), 197–221.
MOMMSEN, Th. 'Die Echte und die falsche Acca Larentia', *Römische Forschungen*. 2 vols Berlin, 1864.
— *Römisches Staatsrecht*. Vol. 1, 3rd ed.; vol. 2, 3rd ed.; vol. 3. Leipzig, 1887.
— *Römische Geschichte*. Vol. 1, 9th ed. Berlin, 1903.
MÜNZER, FR. *RE* 3. 2 (1899), col. 1630, *s.v.* Carvilius no. 9.
— *RE* 4. 2 (1901), cols 1830–2, *s.v.* Curiatius; cols 1841–5, *s.v.* Curius no. 9.
— *RE* 2A1 (1921), cols 858–9, *s.v.* Scribonius; col. 861, *s.v.* Scribonius no. 8.
— *RE* 13. 1 (1926), cols 419–28, *s.v.* Licinius no. 112.
— *RE* 14. 1 (1928), cols 956–8, *s.v.* Mamilii nos. 5, 11–13.
— and KLOTZ, A. *RE* 14. 2 (1930), cols 1538–42, *s.v.* Marcius no. 2.
— *RE* 16. 1 (1933), cols 412–23, *s.v.* Mucius and Mucii nos. 7 and 10.
— *RE* 18. 3 (1949), cols 1002–8, 1011, 1051–6, 1073–4, *s.v.* Papirius and Papirii nos. 1–5, 10, 20, 53 and 72.
— *RE* 21. 1 (1951), cols 1164–67, *s.v.* Poetelii nos. 1–8.
NICHOLS, J. J. 'The Content of the *Lex Curiata*', *AJP* 88 (1967), 257–78.
NISSEN, H. *Italische Landeskunde*. 2 vols in 3, Berlin, 1883–1902.
O'BRIEN-MOORE, A. *RE* supplbd. 6 (1935) cols 660–812, *s.v.* Senatus and Senatus consultum.
OGILVIE, R. M. 'Livy, Licinius Macer and the *Libri Lintei*', *JRS* 48 (1958), 40–6.
— *A Commentary on Livy Books 1–5*. Oxford, 1965.
OLIVER, J. H. *Demokratia, the Gods and the Free World*. Baltimore, 1960.
PALLOTTINO, M. 'Le origini di Roma', *Arch. Class.* 12 (1960), 26–31.
PALMER, R. E. A. 'The Censors of 312 B.C. and the State Religion', *Historia* 14 (1965), 293–324.
— 'The King and the Comitium', *Historia* Einzelschriften Heft 11 (1969).
— *Juno in Archaic Italy*. Philadelphia, forthcoming.
PLATNER, S. B. and ASHBY, T. *A Topographical Dictionary of Ancient Rome*. Oxford, 1929.
POUCET, J. 'Recherches sur la légende sabine des origines de Rome', *Université de Louvain Recueil de Travaux d'Histoire et de Philologie*, ser. 4, fasc. 37 (1967).
POULTNEY, J. W. *The Bronze Tables of Iguvium. American Philological Association Monograph* 18 (1959).
RIX, H. *Das etruskische Cognomen*. Wiesbaden, 1963.
ROTONDI, G. Leges Publicae Populi Romani. Estratto dalla *Enciclopedia Giuridica Italiana*, Milan, 1912, reprinted with the author's 'Postille all' opera *LPPR*', *Scritti Giuridici* 1 (Milan, 1922), 414–32. Hildesheim, 1966.

SAMTER, E. *RE* 6. 2 (1909), cols 2259–65, *s.v.* Fetiales.

SCHANZ, M. and HOSIUS, C. *Geschichte der römischen Literatur bis zum Gesetzgebungswerk des Kaisers Justinian*, vols 1 and 2, 4th ed., Munich, 1927–35.

SCHULZ, F. *Classical Roman Law*. Oxford 1951.

— *History of Roman Legal Science*. Oxford, 1946.

SCHULZE, W. 'Zur Geschichte der lateinischen Eigennamen', *Abhandlungen der Königlichen Gesellschaft der Wissenschaften zu Göttingen*, philol.-hist. Kl. 5. 1 (1904).

SHERWIN-WHITE, A. N. *The Roman Citizenship*. Oxford, 1939.

SORDI, M. *I rapporti romano-ceriti e l'origine della civitas sine suffragio*. Rome, 1960.

STAVELY, E. S. 'Forschungsbericht: The Constitution of the Roman Republic', *Historia* 5 (1956), 74–122.

SYME, R. *The Roman Revolution*. Oxford, 1939.

TAYLOR, L. R. 'The Centuriate Assembly Before and After the Reform', *AJP* 78 (1957), 337–54.

— 'The Voting Districts of the Roman Republic', *Papers and Monographs of the American Academy in Rome* 20 (1960).

— *Roman Voting Assemblies from the Hannibalic War to the Dictatorship of Caesar*. Ann Arbor, 1966.

TONDO, S. 'Il "sacramentum" nel ambiente culturale romano-italico', *SDHI* 29 (1963), 1–25.

VETTER, E. *Handbuch der italischen Dialekte*, vol. 1. Heidelberg, 1953.

VON FRITZ, K. 'The Reorganisation of the Roman Government in 367 B.C.' *Historia* 1 (1950), 3–44.

WADE-GERY, H. T. 'Demotionidae', *CQ* 25 (1931), 129–43 = *Essays in Greek History* (Oxford, 1958), pp. 116–34.

WALBANK, F. W. *A Historical Commentary on Polybius*, vol. 1. Oxford, 1957.

WALDE, A. and HOFFMANN, J. B. *Lateinisches etymologisches Wörterbuch*, 2 vols. 3rd ed., Heidelberg, 1938–9.

WISSOWA, G. *Religion und Kultus der Römer*, 2nd ed., Munich, 1912.

— *RE* 10. 1 (1918), cols 1031–3, *s.v.* Junius no. 68.

Old Latium

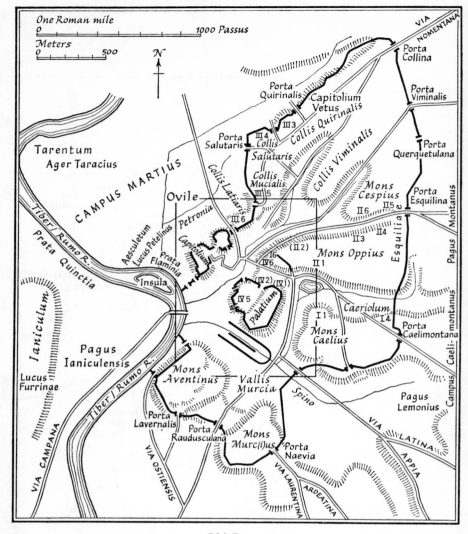

Old Rome

The Argei of the Four Regions

I	1	Mons Caelius = Caeliculum
I	4	circa Minervium
I	6	in Muro Terreo Carinarum
II	1	uls Lucum Facutalem = casa Tarquinii Superbi
(II	2)	= casa Servii Tullii
II	3	uls Lucum Esquilinum = sacellum Montis Oppii
II	4	uls Lucum Esquilinum
II	5	uls Lucum Poetelium, Esquilis
II	6	apud aedem Iunonis Lucinae
III	3	uls aedem Quirini
III	4	uls aedem Salutis
III	5	apud aedem Dei Fidi
III	6	apud auguraculum
(IV	1)	= aedes Larum = casa Anci Marcii
(IV	2)	= casa Anci Marcii sive Tarquinii Prisci sive Superbi
IV	5	apud aedem Romuli = casa Romuli = tugurium Faustuli (?)
IV	6	apud aedem Deum Penatium = casa Tulli Hostilii

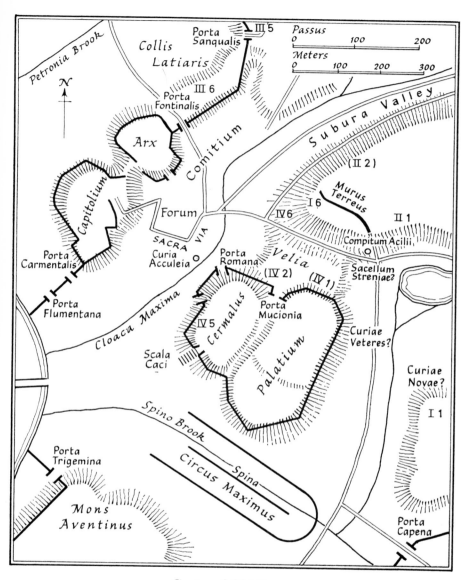

Center of Old Rome

INDEX

NOTE. All Romans, including authors and excluding emperors, are listed under their gentilicial names. Under an author's name is found a list of his passages quoted or discussed here. Epigraphic evidence is found under 'inscriptions', except the 'Tabulae Iguvinae' and 'Fasti Praenestini'. Religious ceremonies with their dates are found in alphabetical order, but special Roman days are found under 'day'. Republican political figures are identified by the year of their highest office. Almost all places on the maps are indexed here by the map's page.

Antemna(e), 132–3, 207
Antevorta, 116
Antias, *see* Valerius
Antiochus of Ascalon, 23
Antipolis, 11 n., 104
Antistius Labeo, M., 69, 123 n.
Antonii, 244–5, 250–1
Antonius, L. (cos. 41), 61, 145–6
Antonius, M. (cos. 44), 135–6
Anxur, 143
apatouria, 68, 81 n.
Apiolae, 132
Apollinar, 85
Apollo, 147–50
Aquilii, 244–5
Ardea, 12, 103 n., 226, 307; treaty with, 226
Argei, 13, 84–100, 102, 117, 121, 124, 126–8, 131, 136, 138–41, 144, 151, 161–2, 202–3, 210, 308–9
    augural itinerary, 89–95, 101; its date, 85
Aricia, 10, 12, 76, 114–15, 307
Ariminum, 129
Aristotle, 14–16
    Ath. Pol. (fr. 385, Rose), 15–16, 34
    on the origins of Rome, 17–18; source for M. Terentius Varro, 21; in Plutarch, *Cam.* (22. 4), 163–4
Armilustrium on 19 Oct., 231–2
armistice, 183–4
armor and tactics, 216
Arpinum, 73, 135
Arretini, 72 n.
arsfertur, 48–56, 67
Arulenses, Sodales, 134 n.
Arval Brothers, *see* Fratres Arvales
Arx, 86, 87, 89, 91, 108 n., 126 n., 236, 309
Ascanius, 9, 290
[Asconius]
    Stangl (212–13), 68–70, 125, 258; (227), 7 n.; (238), 217
assembly, 3, 70, also see *comitia*
    called, 68, 83, 95, 191–5
    centuriate, 2, 3, 69, 80, 184, 190, 193–5, 212, 214, 218–19, 223–5, 247–8, 252, 254, 256–7, 272; defined, 70; order of voting in, 256–7; its rosters, 251–2
    curiate, 2, 3, 69, 100–2, 146, 184, 187, 189 ff., 209–10, 212 n., 213 ff., 245–6, 254, 271–4, 284–6 and *passim*; defined, 70; elects priests, 80–2, 95, 130 n., 269 n.; elects tribunes of plebs, 187, 219–22, 224–5, 294; its meeting-places, 78, 83, 221; procedure in, 202–13; votes exile, 250, 286, also see *lex curiata*

kumnakle of Iguvium, 49–53
    tribal, 2, 3, 203, 212 n., 219, 221 n., 223–5, 239, 241, 254, 270–2, 274; defined, 70
Atellus, *see* Mamilius
Aternius, A. (cos. 454), 243
Athens, 14–15, 34
Atiedian Brotherhood, 41–57, 93, 113, 129, 150, 170, 208
Atiliae Serranae, 237
Atratinus, *see* Sempronius
atrium, 97–8, 120; *atria, septem*, 130–1; *atrium Titium*, 120, 146
Atticus, *see* Pomponius
Attidium (Attigio), 55 n.
Attus, *see* Navius
auctor, 198–9, 208, 269, also see *patrum auctoritas* and *uhtur*
auctoritas, see *patres*
augur, 86, 90–5, 121, 126 n., 128–9, 138–9, 144–50, 153 n., 177, 181, 198, 200, 203, 208, 251–3, 269, 272–3, 285, 293, 295–6; curial, 92–5, 202–4, 209–10, 269 n.; number of, 91–2, 94, 152–3; plebeian, 147
auguraculum, 85–6, 92, 207, 308–9
auguratorium, 89
augurium salutis populi, 90–2, 129–31; *verniserum*, 92
augury, 88–9, 141, 144–5, 210; at Iguvium, 56, 86, 93, 129, 149 n.
Augustales, 60, 93, 136
Augustine, 17, 22
    Civ. Dei (6.3), 23–4; (6.6), 24; (19.1), 23
Augustus, 61, 104, 114, 222, 232–3, 265
Aulius, Q. (cos. 323), 292
Aurelii, 259, 292
Aurelius, emperor Marcus, 237
Aurelius Symmachus, Q.
    Ep. (10.15) = *Rel.* (15.1), 92 n., 100–1
[Aurelius Victor]
    Vir. Ill. (33. 10), 78
auspication, 87–8, 149–50
auspices, 87–8, 126 n., 130, 200, 202–4, 222, 248; of censors, 149 n., 158–9, 210, 212, 222–4; at Iguvium, 56; of magistrates, 185, 198, 200, 202–3, 206–9, 211 n.; of new year assembly, 100–2; renewal of, 202–3, 227; of tribune consul, 228 n., 232–3
Aventinum, 108 n., 132, 221, 285, 308–9
Avillius, 77 n., 292

bay, 100–2
Bellona, 105, 109 n.
Beloch, K. J., 139

Palatua, 102 n., 128
Palatuar, 123, 128
Pales, 182
Pallottino, M., 176–9
Panda Cela, 116
Papirii, 165, 166, 244, 249–50, 258–9, 265
Papirius, C. (pont. max. 509), 274 n.
Papirius, M. (rex sacr. 509), 274
Papirius, M. (pont. max. 449), 221 n., 269 n.
Papirius Crassus, L. (cos. 336), 244 n., 258
Papirius Crassus, M'. (cos. 441), 221 n.
Papirius Cursor, L. (cos. 326), 165, 202–3
Papirius Cursor, L. (cos. 293), 165
Papirius Mugillanus, L. (tr. cos. 427), 227 n., 233, 244 n.
Papirius Praetextatus (cens. 272), 165
Papus, see Aemilius
parentatio, 107, 120, 141
Parilia on 21 April, Rome's birthday, 21, 182–4
Parma, 73
pater Curritis, 63 n.
pater Falacer, 102 n., 105–6
pater patratus, 186, 187 n.
patres 'Fathers', 31, 273–4; powers of, 197–202; auctoritas of, 198, 200, 208, 223 n., 246, 252, 256–7, 269–72; in senate, 206–9
patricii 'patricians', 70, 133 n., 187, 192 n., 196 ff., 243–53, 273–4, 290–302; definition of, 290; powers of, 197–202; priesthoods of, 199, 200, 207, 274–6, 296; and plebs, 196; also see gens and magistratus
patronus, 273–4
Paulus Diaconus, see Pompeius Festus
pedarius, 257–8, 266
pellets, inscribed, 155–6
Penates, temple of, 85, 87, 308–9
Peter, H., 30
Petronia Amnis, 308–9
Pexus, see Veturius
phetrium, 60
phiditia, 14–15, 80–1
Philippus, see Marcius
Philo, see Publilius and Veturius
Philus, see Furius
phratriarch, 32
phratry, 14–16, 37–8, 68, 112, 155–6; rendition of curia, 2–3, 32, 81–2
phylē, 14–16, 31–2, 37–8, 68, 155–6; as military unit, 216; Etruscan, 155, 216
Pictor, see Fabius
picus, 103 n.; at Iguvium, 45–7, 170; Martius, 150, 170

Pisaurum, 73
Piso, see Calpurnius
Plato, 14–15, 65
Plautius Proculus, C. (cos. 358), 268
Plautius Venox, C. (cens. 312), 257–8
Plautus, see Maccius
plebiscite, 70, 198, 204; validity of, 252 n., 255, 270–2
plebs, 126 n., 187, 197 ff., 222, 243–53; priesthoods of, 146–7; powers of, 197–202; see also secession and tribunus
Plinius Secundus, C.
  Nat. Hist. 3. (52–3), 138–9; (68–70), 10–13, 77, 104, 119, 132, 136 n., 176–9; (116), 5 n.; 7. (119), 147; 16. (37), 119, 126 n., 271; 18. (6–8), 28 n., 110; (8), 28 n., 33, 93 n., 98–100, 120–1; 22. (5), 100–2; 25. (105), 100–2; 34. (25), 110; (29), 87
Plutarch
  Cam. (22. 4), 163–4; (36), 151
  Numa (10), 153
  Rom. (4–5), 109–10, 113–14; (9), 22; (11–12), 20–1, 182–4; (14), 30; (20), 7, 124; (21–2), 115–16; (22. 2–3), 17, 18 n.
  Qu. Rom. (35), 109–10, 113–14; (56), 115–16; (69), 129
Poetelii, 146, 151, 250–1
Politorium, 11–13, 108 n., 132, 177
Pollux, see Castor
Polybius
  1. (16. 2), 8; 6. (20), 8–9; (25–6), 8–9; 12. (5, 16), 65
pomerium, 26, 70, 114 n., 182–4, 203
Pometia, see Suessa
Pomona, 105
Pomonal, 51, 131, 144, 151, 307
Pomonus Poplicus, 43, 51, 105 n., 113
Pompeius Festus, Sextus
  4, Lindsay 'Albiona', 105, 106; 6 'adlecti', 262–8; 18 'adsidelae', 102; 36 'conscripti', 263–8; 42 'curia', 2 n., 71 n., 83; 42 'curionium aes', 146; 43 'curia Tifata', 78, 94 n., 132; 43 'curis', 168 n.; 43 'Curitim', 168 n.; 47 ('centumviralia iudicia'), 58; 54 'curionia sacra', 71 n.; 56 'Corniscarum divarum', 106; 56 'curiales mensae', 102, 168; 59 'dici', 158; 63 'demoe', 67–8; 66 'depontani', 90; 71 'equirine', 167; 82 'flaminius camillus', 98–9; 82 'Fornacalia', 98 n.; 106–7 'Lucereses', 'Lucomedi', 7; 117 'Mancina tifata', 78; 117 'Marti-

Tarquinius Superbus, 170, 190, 262–3, 275

Tarquitii, 76, 268

Tarquitius Flaccus, L. (mag. eq. 458), 268

Tarracina, 143

Tarutius, 20–1, 182

Tatius, king Titus, 6, 31, 77, 81, 93 n., 100, 108 n., 136, 144, 154 n., 167, 181, 236 n., 292; house of, 87

Taurus, *see* Statilius

Taylor, L. R., 73, 74, 134 n., 138–9, 152 n., 165

tekvias, 44–7, 53–4

Tellenae, 11–13, 108 n., 132, 307

Tellus, 121, 181, 183

Ten Men, see *decemviri*

Terentius Varro, M., encyclopedist, 16–24, 61, 70–1, 93 n., 95, 97–8, 127 n., 150, 154, 168, 182, 258–9, 290–2; his influence on Dionysius, 3 n., 16–19, 28–32, 80–2, 99 n., 124; his influence on Ovid, 30–2; his works and method, 19–24; on augurs, 90–2; on meaning of *curia*, 68, 82; on names of curias, 29–30, 71, 75–6, 118, 124–5; on variety in curial religion, 81–2, 118; on military terms, 5–7; on Plautus, 68, 125; on Roma Quadrata, 22, 26–34; on Sabines, etc., 17, 29–31, 102 n., 168, 171–2, 259, 291–2

Antiquitates Romanae, 3 n., 16–24, 26–34, 61, 63 n., 68, 75–6, 93 n., 97 n., 115–16, 124, 136 n., 182–3, 186 n., 258–9, 269 n.

Atticus de numeris, 20

De familiis Troianis, 136, 290–1

De gente populi Romani, 19

Hebdomades, 20, 23

De lingua Latina 5. (32), 139 n.; (33), 138–9; (34–5), 26; (41), 128–9; (45–54), 84–97; (46), 125–6; (49), 119, 151; (54), 117–18; (55), 6–9, 154–5; (81), 6–9, 32, 215 n., 219–20; (85), 93, 112; (89), 6–9; (91), 6–9, 31, 215 n.; (143–4), 26; (154), 94; (155), 68, 83; (164), 108

6. (13), 97, 98 n.; (18), 185 n., 230–2; (19), 103; (22), 112; (23), 115; (23–4), 106–10; (24), 122–4, 128; (33–4), 29 n., 30–4; (46), 68, 71; (86), 149, 158–9, 256, 259

7. (7–9), 88, 92 n.; (34), 99 n.; (43), 95–6, 102; (45), 102–5

Liber de philosophia, 23

De principiis numerorum, 19–20

De re rustica 1. (2. 10), 26; (10), 27–8, 48 n.

Saturae Menippeae, 22, 134 n., 258

Liber tribuum, 125

Tubero de origine humana, 21

De vita populi Romani, 68, 87, 97 n., 125, 186

fr. in Aug. *CD* (18. 10), 124 n.; in Frontinus *De limitibus*, 26–7; in Macr. *Sat.* (1. 16. 18), 183–4; in Seneca *NQ* (5. 16. 4), 103 n.

Terminalia on 23 Feb., 99–100, 111–12, 120–1, 170 n., 183

termini, 93 n., 99–100, 111–12, 121, 152

territory, curial, 93–4, 99–100, 121, 138–52

Tertullianus, *see* Septimius

tesca, 88–9

testamentum in procinctu, 69–70, 87–8, 193–4

Thessalonica, 285–6

Tiberinus, 90, 103

Tiberius, emperor, 136

Tibur, 13, 61–3, 79, 157 n., 168, 174, 179, 307

tie-votes, 209–10

Tifata, 13, 77–8, 132

tigillum sororium on 1 Oct., 137

T⟨i⟩tienses, 177–8

Tities, 144

Tolerienses, 11–13, 134

Tolerinus, *see* Tullius

Tolumnius, Lars, 232–3, 236

totas, 41–3

transitio ad plebem, 133 n., 249, 293

transvectio equitum on 15 Quinctilis, 217, 232, 260

treaty, 138, 159–60, 166–70, 180–4, 214

Trebatius, 126 n.

tremnu, 86

trial by curias, 250, 284–5

triarii, 261–2

tribune, see *tribunus*

tribunus, 6, 32, 219–20

celerum, 102 n., 152–3, 190, 215, 236 n., 260 n., 267–8, 286; number of, 215

consul, 222–43, 263–5; 286; abolished, 224, 235–6; auspices of, 228 n.; number of, 215 n., 224–6, 239–40

militum, 145, 151–3, 156 n., 212, 215, 217, 219–20, 224–6, 251–2, 294; number of, 224–6

militum consulari potestate, see *tribunus consul*

plebis, 70, 135, 166, 187, 198, 212 n., 219–21, 225, 226 n., 228–9, 243–53, 266, 274–5, 285–6, 299; elected by curias, 187, 219–22, 224–5, 294; number of, 219–20

tribus, 5–6, 29–33, 38–9, 43; Greek and Etruscan, see *phylē*

327

Vesta, 120, 164; shrine of, wreathed and given new fire, 99–102
Vestal virgin, 84, 95–8, 110, 121, 141–3, 153, 161–4; chief, 121
Veturii, 244–5, 249, 250 n., 294–5
Veturius, L., equest., 295
Veturius Calvinus, T. (cos. 334), 294
Veturius Cicurinus, C. (cos. 455), 244, 246, 269 n.
Veturius Gracchus Sempronianus, Ti. (aug.), 295–6
Veturius Pom. Pexus, Q. (lup. Fab.), 135
Veturius Philo, L. (cos. 220), 294
Veturius Philo, L. (cos. 206), 294–5
Veturius Philo, Ti. (fl. Mart.), 295
Vibenna, see Caele
Victor, see Aurelius
vicus, 40, 81 n., 85, 104, 115, 117, 126 n., 129–30, 190; *septem vici*, 129; German, 58
Vimitellani, 13, 178
Virae Querquetulanae, 118–19
Virbius, 114–15
virites, 167–70
vitium, 251

Vitruvius
  (2. 1. 5), 86 n.
vitulatio, 230–1, 260 n.
Volcanalia on 23 Aug., 169
Volesus, see Valesius
Volnius, 6, 154 n.
Volturnalia on 27 Aug., 102–3
Volturnum, 103
Volturnus, 102–3
Volumnius Flamma, L. (cos. 307), 269–70, 296
Volupia, 107–9
vote by assembly units, 202–3
vulture, 20, 22, 103

War, Latin, 64, 125, 187
War, Second Punic, 145, 150 n., 186, 292–3
War, Social, 139, 155
Werner, R., 191 n.
wills and inheritance, 69, 193–5

year, beginning of magisterial, 229–32, 260; beginning of religious, 30, 99–102

Zaleukos, 65

Date Due